# The Cross of Reality

# The Cross of Reality

## Luther's *Theologia Crucis* and Bonhoeffer's Christology

H. Gaylon Barker

Fortress Press
*Minneapolis*

THE CROSS OF REALITY
Luther's Theologia Crucis and Bonhoeffer's Christology



Cover image: The Sermon (Luther is Preaching), Lucas Cranach the Elder (1472-1553 German), Church of St. Marien in Wittenberg, German, SuperStock / SuperStock
Cover design: Tory Herman

Library of Congress Cataloging-in-Publication Data
Print ISBN: 978-1-4514-8880-7
eBook ISBN: 978-1-5064-0049-5

The paper used in this publication meets the minimum requirements of American National Standard for Information Sciences — Permanence of Paper for Printed Library Materials, ANSI Z329.48-1984.

Manufactured in the U.S.A.

This book was produced using PressBooks.com, and PDF rendering was done by PrinceXML.

*To Carla*

*Wife, Colleague, Friend*

# Contents

# Preface

This book, which is a revision of my doctoral dissertation, has a long history. The seed was first planted in seminary while serving as student assistant to James Burtness, who at that time was working on Lutheran themes in Bonhoeffer's thought. Over the years, the ideas presented here were nurtured through presentations at churches and conferences, and most especially in conversations with James Burtness, Larry Rasmussen, Eberhard Bethge, Wolfgang Huber, Ernst Feil, John Godsey, Michael Ryan, and Gerhard Ebeling, among others, who both encouraged and helped to formulate the ideas that lie at the heart of this work.

Therefore, while any limitations in this work remain the responsibility of the author, since no work is done in complete independence, acknowledgments and thanks are an appropriate way to begin. In addition to those mentioned above, friends and colleagues from the various International Bonhoeffer Societies, which continue to provide inspiration and resources to continually reflect on Bonhoeffer's legacy, remain constant conversation partners. Additional thanks are owed to the library staffs of Luther Theological Seminary, Drew University, Union Theological Seminary, the University of Heidelberg, and Molloy College. Thanks go to the editorial staff at Fortress Press as well. Through the thoughtful work of Will Bergkamp, Michael Gibson, Lisa Gruenisen, and Travis Ables, along with the others at Fortress Press, the process of bringing this work to publication has been a reward in itself. Finally, the greatest and most sincere thanks goes to my wife, Carla, who has provided assistance and inspiration all along the way. Without her, this project would never have reached completion; therefore, it is to her that this work is dedicated.

Gaylon Barker

Ridgefield, CT

April 9, 2015

Seventieth anniversary of Dietrich Bonhoeffer's death

# Abbreviations

| | |
|---|---|
| AC | Augsburg Confession, in *The Book of Concord* |
| *BC* | *The Book of Concord: The Confessions of the Evangelical Lutheran Church.* Edited by Robert Kolb and Timothy J. Wengert. Minneapolis: Fortress Press, 2000. |
| FC | Formula of Concord, in *The Book of Concord* |
| *DB-ER* | *Dietrich Bonhoeffer: A Biography.* Revised edition by Eberhard Bethge. Minneapolis: Fortress Press, 2000. |
| DBW | Dietrich Bonhoeffer Werke, German edition |
| DBWE | Dietrich Bonhoeffer Works, English edition |
| *SC* | *Sanctorum Communio.* Vol. 1 of DBWE |
| *AB* | *Act and Being.* Vol. 2 of DBWE |
| *LT* | *Life Together.* Volume 5, part 1 of DBWE |
| *LPP* | *Letters and Papers from Prison.* Vol. 8 of DBWE |
| *GS* | *Gesammelte Schriften.* 6 vols. Munich: Kaiser Verlag, 1958–74. |
| *LW* | American Edition of *Luther's Works.* St. Louis: Concordia Publishing House; Philadelphia: Fortress Press, 1955–86. |

*TDB* Ernst Feil. *Theology of Dietrich Bonhoeffer*. Translated by Martin Rumscheidt. Philadelphia: Fortress Press, 1985.

*TF* *A Testament to Freedom: The Essential Writings of Dietrich Bonhoeffer*. Revised edition. Edited by Geffrey B. Kelly and F. Burton Nelson. New York: HarperCollins, 1995.

*WA* *D. Martin Luthers Werke*. Kritische Gesamtausgabe. Weimar: Böhlaus, 1883–1957.

# Introduction

Toward the end of his life, in a letter written on April 30, 1944, Dietrich Bonhoeffer posed the question that may well serve as a summary of his life and his theology: "What keeps gnawing at me is the question, what is Christianity, or who is Christ actually for us today?"[1] From beginning to end, Christology was the driving force that gave shape to Bonhoeffer's theology,[2] marked by an intense

1. This is from the April 30, 1944 letter to Eberhard Bethge, in which Bonhoeffer begins reflecting on "non-religious interpretation of Christianity," and is included in his final *Letters and Papers from Prison* (DBWE 8:362). While this has long been recognized as a decisive statement for understanding Bonhoeffer's prison reflections, it must be emphasized that it does not represent a new departure in his thinking; rather, it is the culmination all of his thinking up to this point, bringing to clear expression the driving center of his entire theological enterprise. An example of this can be seen in that long before this question was posed, he raised a similar question in 1928 at the beginning of his career: "What does the cross say to us today?" (Dietrich Bonhoeffer, *Barcelona, Berlin, New York, 1928–1931* (DBWE 10:358).
2. From John Godsey's earliest interpretive reflections to Ralf Wüstenberg's more recent comments, the key to understanding Bonhoeffer's theology and witness is Christology. According to Godsey, *The Theology of Dietrich Bonhoeffer* (Philadelphia: Westminster, 1960), 264, "The unifying element in Bonhoeffer's theology is his Christology, and it is precisely the Christology that impelled his theological development." In fact, "for Bonhoeffer theology was essentially Christology" (ibid.). "It is his Christological concentration, that is, his meditation upon and understanding of the person and work of the living Christ, which accounts for his drive toward concretion. In fact, the Christocentric focus and the demand that revelation be concrete are characteristics of Bonhoeffer's theology from the beginning, but it is his understanding of the revelation of God in Jesus Christ which develops and thus provides the real clue to the development within his theology itself" (265). Developing that same line of thought, Wüstenberg, after noting the misinterpretations of the 1960s, says they failed "to take into account how profoundly his theology was informed by his Christology. . . . Ignoring the christological center in Bonhoeffer's theology inevitably means misconstruing him altogether."

concentration on the person Jesus and the cross. In both his life and his theology, Bonhoeffer was concerned to give expression to the presence of the living Christ in the world.

Bonhoeffer's question is our question. Each generation of Christian believers, indeed every believer, must answer that question for themselves, which is what the church has been doing for nearly two thousand years. Reflecting on the biblical witness, the early church spent centuries sorting out the various answers to that question.

The answer Bonhoeffer arrives at is a particular Christology, shaped by the tradition with which he identified. It was on based solidly on Luther's *theologia crucis* (theology of the cross), with the *communicatio idiomatum* (communication of attributes) at its center.[3] When seen from this perspective, his Christology became the definition of all reality in his *Ethics* and came to full expression as *etsi deus non daretur* (as if there were no God)[4] in the theological letters from Tegel prison, where he was imprisoned after his arrest in 1943.

While finding his answer in Luther's *theologia crucis*, at the same time Bonhoeffer recognized the difference between Luther's time and his own. In the same letter, he acknowledges that the time of religion is past. "We are approaching a completely religionless age; people as they are now simply cannot be religious anymore. Even those who honestly describe themselves as 'religious' aren't really practicing that at all; they presumably mean something quite different by 'religious.'" In fact, "the foundations are being pulled out from

("'Religionless Christianity:' Dietrich Bonhoeffer's Tegel Theology," in *Bonhoeffer for a New Day: Theology in a Time of Transition*, ed. John de Gruchy (Grand Rapids: Eerdmans, 1997), 58.

3. For an analysis of this point in Luther's theology, see Johann Anselm Steiger, "The *Communicatio Idiomatum* as the Axle and Motor of Luther's Theology," *Lutheran Quarterly* 19 (2000): 125–58; Dennis Ngien, "Chalcedonian Christology and Beyond: Luther's Understanding of the *Communicatio Idiomatum*," *Heythrop Journal* 45 (2004): 54–68; and Neal J. Anthony, *Cross Narratives: Martin Luther's Christology and the Location of Redemption* (Eugene, OR: Pickwick, 2010), esp. ch. 3.

4. DBWE 8:476.

under all that 'Christianity' has previously been for us, and the only people among whom we might end up in terms of 'religion' are 'the last of the knights' or a few intellectually dishonest people."[5] This means that Bonhoeffer's goal was not simply to replicate Luther's theology; however, what he finds in Luther is the key to unlocking the church's witness for this new time.

Seen in this light, the challenging and, to some, disturbing thoughts at the end of his life, rather than marking a decisive break from his earlier theological formulations, were the culmination of his theological orientation. Because God in Christ is never absent or detached from the world but is intimately involved with the world, Bonhoeffer's theology was always contextual. He never dealt with the traditions of the church simply as doctrines to be handed down from one generation to the next as if they were entities separated from the lives of people and of daily living; Christian doctrine, if it was to be true to Christ, was to be placed in the service of Christian living. This, in turn, necessitated giving attention to matters like reality and the world, which for Bonhoeffer were simply opposite sides of the same coin.

As a result, the contours of his thought appeared to change and take on different accents from one period to the next. However, when his writings are viewed from the perspective of the core of his thinking,[6] his life and thought are marked by continuity. The continuity is provided by his christological question, which in one form or another stands in the center of his theology. When this christological orientation is examined at its core, one key element

5. Ibid., 363–64.

6. Hans Pfeifer, "The Forms of Justification: On the Question of Structure in Dietrich Bonhoeffer's Theology," in *A Bonhoeffer Legacy: Essays in Understanding*, ed. A. J. Klassen (Grand Rapids: Eerdmans, 1981), 14ff, for example, states "that certain characteristics of Bonhoeffer's theology can only be understood if one pays attention to the core of his thinking," which is centered on Luther's doctrine of justification by faith.

emerges. Bonhoeffer's portrayal of Jesus is carried out in a consistent manner: Jesus is always the crucified Christ. In other words, the cross looms on the horizon, casting its shadow over Bonhoeffer's entire theological enterprise.

## Defining the Problem

Dietrich Bonhoeffer's theology invariably has been labeled a *theologia crucis*. The reason for this designation becomes even more apparent when the christological core of his theology is examined. That Bonhoeffer's christological orientation shares many common elements with Luther's becomes obvious when Bonhoeffer is compared to other theologians with whom he was in dialogue; when there are disagreements, for example, it is usually in the area of Christology that he levels his harshest judgments.[7]

Therefore, in order to understand Bonhoeffer's Christology, both in terms of its foundations and developments, the role of Luther and Luther's theological heritage are essential elements. This is not to say, however, that there were not other influences at work in the background shaping Bonhoeffer's emerging theology.[8] Nevertheless,

7. Gerhard Ebeling, "The 'Non-Religious Interpretation of Biblical Concepts,'" in *Word and Faith*, trans. James W. Leitch (Philadelphia: Fortress Press, 1963), 106, makes the point that in areas where Barth and Bonhoeffer were the closest, it is there that they have the greatest disagreement. This is especially true in the area of Christology, in which such difference emerges most clearly. It is on the basis of Christology that Bonhoeffer states his strongest criticism of nineteenth-century liberalism, as well as of Barth's dialectical theology. Among others making this point, see James Woelfel, *Bonhoeffer's Theology: Classical and Revolutionary* (Nashville: Abingdon, 1970), who stresses the Lutheran character of Bonhoeffer's Christology as dominant. See also Martin Rumscheidt, "The Formation of Bonhoeffer's Theology," in *The Cambridge Companion to Dietrich Bonhoeffer*, ed. John W. de Gruchy (Cambridge: Cambridge University Press, 1999), 50–70; Hans-Jürgen Abromeit, *Das Geheimnis Christi: Dietrich Bonhoeffers erfahrungsbezogene Christologie* (Neukirchen-Vluyn: Neukirchener, 1991); Andreas Pangritz, *Karl Barth in the Theology of Dietrich Bonhoeffer*, trans. Barbara and Martin Rumscheidt (Grand Rapids: Eerdmans, 2000), 18ff; and Joachim von Soosten, "Editor's Afterword to the German Edition," in *Sanctorum Communio*, by Dietrich Bonhoeffer, ed. Clifford J. Green, trans. Reinhard Krauss and Nancy Lukens, Dietrich Bonhoeffer Works, vol. 1 (Minneapolis: Fortress Press, 1998), 290–306.

it is Luther and his theology that were the predominant influences; it was in Luther that Bonhoeffer found a common ally and readily turned to him as his line of defense, even in the case of disagreement with Karl Barth,[9] with whom he shared much in common.

In spite of the importance of Luther's thought for understanding the developing trajectory of Bonhoeffer's theology, this is not a subject that has been emphasized enough—this, in spite of Bonhoeffer's own claims to be consciously Lutheran. The major trends in Bonhoeffer research have focused on other areas—either using Bonhoeffer to break new ground in theology, as was the case of the secular theology or "Death of God" Movements in the 1960s, or, when examining Bonhoeffer's theology itself, analyzing its development from within its context.

An example of the latter tendency can be seen in John Godsey's work, *The Theology of Dietrich Bonhoeffer.*[10] As the first full-length treatment of Bonhoeffer's theology, it set the tone for a great deal of the research that followed. As a comprehensive examination of Bonhoeffer's theology, it described the contours of Bonhoeffer's theology and its interplay with its context, but it did not examine the

8. For example, see Peter Frick, ed. *Bonhoeffer's Intellectual Formation: Theology and Philosophy in His Thought* (Tübingen: Mohr Siebeck, 2008). This volume examines several major theological and philosophical influences on Bonhoeffer, including that of Martin Luther (Wolf Krötke, "Dietrich Bonhoeffer and Martin Luther," 53–82). See also Martin Rumscheidt, "Formation of Bonhoeffer's Thought"; and Michael DeJonge, *Bonhoeffer's Theological Formation: Berlin, Barth, and Protestant Theology* (Oxford: Oxford University Press, 2012), among others.

9. Even though Bonhoeffer found much in Barth's theology with which to identify, nevertheless he kept his distance and did not want to be labeled a Barthian, nor did he refrain from critiquing Barth's theological position when there was disagreement, as he did in *LPP*, when he accused Barth of ending "up with a positivism of revelation" (DBWE 8:364; cf. DBWE 8:373). See below, chapter 2, nn82 and 92 for more on Bonhoeffer's relationship to Barth and his theology.

10. John Godsey, *Theology of Dietrich Bonhoeffer*. Among other works that can be noted in this category are those by Woelfel, *Bonhoeffer's Theology* and Ernst Feil, *The Theology of Dietrich Bonhoeffer*, trans. Martin Rumscheidt (Philadelphia: Fortress Press, 1985; hereafter *TDB*). Even Feil's work, one of the most thorough works on Bonhoeffer's theology, does not give adequate attention to the sources and background of Bonhoeffer's thought. We are now sufficiently distanced from the immediate context of Bonhoeffer's theology, thereby giving us a new opportunity to examine Bonhoeffer's theological development.

nature of its development from within the long-standing traditions of the church, nor was that its purpose. Ultimately, however, this is important, since Bonhoeffer saw himself within both the larger doctrinal tradition of the church more generally, and the Lutheran tradition more specifically, and attempted to find ways for that tradition to address the modern world.

Likewise, by concentrating on the immediate context of Bonhoeffer's theology, scholars were led to make comparisons to and conclusions about the role of Barth's theology in influencing Bonhoeffer's stance;[11] this, in turn, led to the belief that Bonhoeffer and Barth shared the same theological outlook, thereby lending credence to the belief that Barth's theology was the dominant influence in shaping Bonhoeffer's thought and in turning him away from his Berlin teachers. What such a stance has failed to do, however, is to point out the differences between them and the sources for that disagreement. The emphasis on the continuities between Bonhoeffer and Barth, to cite one example of the many comparisons made, has clouded the distinct differences between the two—differences that are fundamental for a fuller understanding of Bonhoeffer's theological development.

Now, some seventy years after Bonhoeffer's death, we are entering a new period in Bonhoeffer research;[12] being removed from the immediate context of Bonhoeffer's theology, we are able to examine

11. See Stephen R. Haynes, *The Bonhoeffer Phenomenon: Portraits of a Protestant Saint* (Minneapolis: Fortress Press, 2004), 14.

12. See, for example, Eberhard Bethge, "The Response to Bonhoeffer," author's introduction to *Bonhoeffer: Exile and Martyr*, ed. John W. de Gruchy (New York: Seabury, 1975), 11–25, for a survey and analysis of the history of Bonhoeffer interpretation and the problems posed at each stage. One of the problems from the early stages was that Bonhoeffer's distinctive voice was muted and "had little chance of being heard" in its own right, caught up as it was in the theological debates of the time, in which case each side championed Bonhoeffer as a partner or inspiration in their efforts. The result has been that many pertinent questions about Bonhoeffer's contribution to the ongoing theological conversation have not been adequately addressed.

these relationships and influences with new eyes.[13] Godsey admits that his earlier conclusions are subject to reexamination for that very reason. Writing nearly thirty years after completing his dissertation, he notes the difficulty he had in adequately examining the Bonhoeffer/Barth relationship. His later conclusions, by implication, stress the need to reexamine Bonhoeffer's theology in light of his Lutheran tradition. Commenting on his earlier work, Godsey writes, "Barth was my *Doktorvater* and Bonhoeffer's theology the subject of my doctoral dissertation, and yet during all the subsequent years of studying and wrestling with their thought, I have never felt that I had adequately comprehended their theological differences." Although differences existed from the beginning to the end, "I have never found it easy to get to the heart of the matter. . . . Bonhoeffer and Barth held so much in common that, in a sense, it is easier to depict where they walked together than where they parted company."[14] But differences there were, differences that are attributable to their backgrounds.[15]

13. When *LPP* (now DBWE 8) appeared in Germany in the 1950s, for example, Bonhoeffer's emphasis could not be understood. According to Bethge, "The time was not favorable for Bonhoeffer's fragments to speak in their own right. They had their greatest effect wherever there was experimentation in small groups, wherever new parish structures and forms of political solidarity were being tried out. . . . Here Bonhoeffer has proven to be someone who encourages people to sail quickly out of harbors that have silted up" (Eberhard Bethge, *Dietrich Bonhoeffer: A Biography,* revised and ed. by Victoria J. Barnett [Minneapolis: Fortress Press, 2000], 891 [Hereafter *DB-ER*]).
14. John D. Godsey, "Barth and Bonhoeffer: The Basic Difference," *Quarterly Review* (1987): 9 and 17; see also Eberhard Bethge, "The Challenge of Dietrich Bonhoeffer's Life and Theology," *The Chicago Theological Seminary Register* 51, no. 2 (February, 1961): 8–9; Charles Marsh, *Reclaiming Dietrich Bonhoeffer: The Promise of His Theology* (New York: Oxford University Press, 1994); Jonathan D. Sorum, "The Eschatological Boundary in Dietrich Bonhoeffer's 'Nachfolge,'" ThD diss., Luther Northwestern Theological Seminary, 1994; and James Burtness, "As Though God Were Not Given: Barth, Bonhoeffer and the *Finitum Capax Infiniti*," *Dialog* 19 (Fall 1980): 249–55. Pangritz, *Karl Barth in the Theology of Dietrich Bonhoeffer*, while stressing the enduring influence Barth had on Bonhoeffer beginning in 1925–1926 and extending through the prison letters, admits that there was a reserve in Bonhoeffer's acceptance of Barth that was marked by the differences between Bonhoeffer's Lutheranism and Barth's Calvinistic position. See, for example, his discussion of *Act and Being*: "There is no doubt: this is a Lutheran protesting against the Calvinian '*non capax*'" (27).

Godsey analyzed these differences by focusing on the differences in the methodology by which each approached the theological task.[16] This methodological orientation has significant theological and christological implications. According to Godsey, "Barth tended to emphasize the divinity of Jesus; Jesus Christ is the 'Royal Man' whose power is the decisive thing. . . . Bonhoeffer, on the other hand, stressed the hiddenness of divinity in the humiliated One; for him Jesus Christ is the man for others, the one whose power is shown forth in weakness."[17] As a result, "Barth's theology tends toward a *theologia gloriae* [theology of glory] in order to ensure the *graciousness* of God's action in Jesus Christ . . . [whereas] Bonhoeffer's theology quite evidently is a *theologia crucis* in order to ensure the *costliness* of God's grace in Christ."[18]

15. For a discussion of the differences between Barth and Bonhoeffer on Christology, see Michael DeJonge, "The Presence of Christ in Karl Barth, Franz Hildebrandt and Dietrich Bonhoeffer," *Dietrich Bonhoeffer Jahrbuch 4 2009/2010,* ed. Kristen Busch Nielson, Hans Pfeifer, Christiane Tietz, and Clifford Green (Gütersloh: Gütersloher, 2010), 96ff. DeJonge points to the differences between Bonhoeffer's Lutheran theology, shaped by Luther's *est*, and the Reformed rejection of that position.
16. See also Bethge, "Challenge of Dietrich Bonhoeffer's Life and Theology," 10, where he points out that their differences led Bonhoeffer and Barth to different starting points in their theological methods. Heinrich Ott, *Reality and Faith: The Theological Legacy of Dietrich Bonhoeffer*, trans. Alex A. Morrison (Philadelphia: Fortress Press, 1972), 120ff, is also one who sees the differences between Barth and Bonhoeffer as one of method. In addition, he notes the importance of Christology in Bonhoeffer's thought. Cf. Feil, *TDB*, who makes a similar point: "From the outset, Bonhoeffer wanted to overcome the constrictions of Barth's dialectics which appeared to him to be marked by a strongly logical character. He set out, therefore, to find other ways of expressing God's reality. . . . Bonhoeffer attempted to begin with God's reality in history, from Jesus Christ" (48).
17. Godsey, "Barth and Bonhoeffer," 26.
18. Ibid, 26–27. This description of the differences between Barth and Bonhoeffer matches the similar conclusions Bethge draws with regard to Bonhoeffer's *Act and Being*: "To Bonhoeffer, the old *extra calvinisticum* was in error if it ultimately denied the complete entry of God's majesty into this world. Bonhoeffer suspected it at work when he saw Barth establishing the majesty of God by the methods of Kantian transcendentalism. To greatly oversimplify: while the early Barth, desiring to proclaim God's majesty, began by removing him to a remote distance, Bonhoeffer's starting point, inspired by the same desire to proclaim his majesty, brought him into close proximity" (*DB-ER*, 134). See also Douglas John Hall, *Lighten Our Darkness* (Philadelphia, Westminster, 1976), 139, in which he offers a similar evaluation of the relationship between Barth and Bonhoeffer: "Barth moved more and more away from the theology of the cross and toward something that must be called a theology of glory, even if

The differences to which Godsey points become obvious when statements from Barth and Bonhoeffer are compared. In one section of *Church Dogmatics,* Barth makes the following descriptive statement: "We not only have a *theologia crucis*, but a *theologia resurrectionis* [theology of the resurrection] and therefore a *theologia gloriae,* i.e., a theology of the glory of the new man actualized and introduced in the crucified Jesus Christ who triumphs as the Crucified."[19] In a later place he states that we have to "do with the Crucified only as the Resurrected. . . .There is no going back behind Easter morning. To the extent that they may contain or express such a going back, all theologies or pieties or exercises or aesthetics which centre on the cross—however grimly in earnest they may be—must be repudiated at once."[20] By contrast, Bonhoeffer presents a very different picture: "We can have the Exalted One only as the Crucified One. The resurrection of Christ does not get us around the stumbling block. Even the Risen One remains the stumbling block for us. If it were not so, he would not be for us."[21] When compared to one another, these two statements point to two different approaches to Christology; unlike Barth, Bonhoeffer would always insist that we know the resurrected Christ only as the crucified one. As a result, the

it is not identical with the *theologia gloriae* that Luther attacked. It is this movement which Bonhoeffer deplores when in the *Letters and Papers from Prison* he refers to Barth's 'positivism.'"

19. Godsey, "Barth and Bonhoeffer," 26; Karl Barth, *Church Dogmatics* II/2 (Edinburgh: T. & T. Clark, 1957), 355.
20. Karl Barth, *Church Dogmatics* IV/1 (Edinburgh: T. & T. Clark, 1956), 344.
21. Godsey, "Barth and Bonhoeffer," 27; Dietrich Bonhoeffer, "Lectures on Christology," DBWE 12:180. On this point, see also Hall, *Lighten Our Darkness*, 139. Interestingly enough, Hall places Bonhoeffer among the "exemplars of a thin tradition" (as one who reflects Luther's *theologia crucis*), and it is out of this tradition that Hall sees Bonhoeffer's questioning of Barth in *LPP*. Bethge drew a similar conclusion about the Bonhoeffer/Barth relationship in 1961 when he stated, "While Barth, in order to save God's majesty, started by pushing God away, Bonhoeffer starts by drawing him in—in order to save the same majesty of God" ("Challenge of Dietrich Bonhoeffer's Life and Theology," 10). See also James H. Burtness, *Shaping the Future: the Ethics of Dietrich Bonhoeffer* (Philadelphia: Fortress Press, 1985), 26, and John A. Phillips, *Christ for Us in the Theology of Dietrich Bonhoeffer* (New York: Harper & Row, 1967), 69.

differences in their christological orientation remain, and this basic difference leads to further divergences in the development of their theological stances.

In addition to the above observations, it should be noted that in spite of Bonhoeffer's attraction to Barth, Bonhoeffer resisted being labeled a Barthian.[22] While he was quick to recognize the strength of Barth's position over against that of the liberal theologians,[23] he did not hesitate to criticize Barth at those points where he detected Barth's weaknesses. But at the same time, in his attempt to map out his own theological position, Bonhoeffer distanced himself from his Berlin teachers, citing several weaknesses in liberal theology, as well as spelling out his differences with them.

Eberhard Bethge, Bonhoeffer's friend and biographer, has summarized this tension in Bonhoeffer's theology for us. On the one hand, he says that Bonhoeffer gained a lifelong appreciation for Luther's doctrine of justification from Holl; and yet, due to the weakness he perceived in Holl's position, he became highly critical of his teacher at an early age because he found it too weakly anchored in Luther's Christology.[24] On the other hand, while he became a dedicated student of the new dialectical theology, he never abandoned his criticism of it. He criticized Barth's inaccessible God for threatening "the due emphasis on man's concrete, earthly plight." Instead of God being free from the world, God "entered into the

22. For Bonhoeffer's self-description of not wanting to be labeled a Barthian, see his comments upon being passed over to contribute an essay for a Festschrift honoring Barth on his fiftieth birthday. He admitted that it was not so bad after all, because "I do not want to be branded as a Barthian, for I'm not one" (quoted in Wolf-Dieter Zimmermann and Ronald Gregor Smith, eds., *I Knew Dietrich Bonhoeffer* [New York Harper & Row, 1973], 66).

23. Geffrey B. Kelly and F. Burton Nelson, eds., *A Testament to Freedom: The Essential Writings of Dietrich Bonhoeffer*, rev. ed. (San Francisco: Harper Collins, 1995; hereafter *TF*), 6–7.

24. Cf. Krötke, "Dietrich Bonhoeffer and Martin Luther," 54, indicates that while Bonhoeffer was introduced to Luther by the leading voices of the Luther renaissance, such as Holl and Seeberg, he came to disagree with their interpretation, based on "his own reading of Luther." In fact, "'to return to the real Luther' was his objective in studying the Reformer and guided his lifelong theological orientation towards him."

world, since the freedom of God had committed itself to the human community. . . . It was his grounding in Luther gained from Holl and Seeberg that allowed him to remain independent from the onslaught of Barth's theology."[25]

In the preface to the 1983 volume *Bonhoeffer und Luther,* German Bonhoeffer scholar Christian Gremmels called for this kind of examination, and also pointed out a major weakness in Bonhoeffer scholarship when he expressed dismay over the lack of attention that has been given to the relationship between Luther and Bonhoeffer. While all kinds of comparisons have been made and influences have been examined, he maintains that attention to the most obvious one is lacking. In fact, by even raising the question about Bonhoeffer and Luther, one still creates "the impression of coming upon uncharted territory in Bonhoeffer research."[26] This situation is astonishing, he insists, since the influence of Luther cannot be seriously contested. An examination of Bonhoeffer's theological development reveals the

25. *DB-ER*, 68, 75, 70. It is with this background in mind that Robin Lovin, "Biographical Context," in *New Studies in Bonhoeffer's* Ethics, ed. William J. Peck, Toronto Studies in Theology, vol. 30, Bonhoeffer Series, no. 3 (Lewiston, NY: Edwin Mellen Press, 1987), 71, concludes, "So Bonhoeffer was a theologian of the new generation, but he was never simply a Barthian." This states in summary fashion Bonhoeffer's position in early-twentieth-century theology; it must also be noted that the *but* is important for discerning the nature of Bonhoeffer's theology and his relation to dialectical theology, and thus important for understanding Bonhoeffer's unique contribution and in determining the influences that gave shape to his thought. Others, like Abromeit, *Geheimnis Christi*, 199ff, and Ralf K. Wüstenberg, *A Theology of Life: Dietrich Bonhoeffer's Religionless Christianity,* trans. Doug Stott (Grand Rapids: Eerdmans, 1998), 39, also make the point that this distancing on Bonhoeffer's part begins quite early while he was still a student; in spite of his criticism, however, Bonhoeffer never completely broke ties with Barth. For additional observations on the relationship and tensions between Bonhoeffer and Barth, see von Soosten's afterword to *Sanctorum Communio,* DBWE 1:292ff, and Pangritz, *Karl Barth in the Theology of Dietrich Bonhoeffer*, esp. 22ff. For a different analysis of their relationship and a framework for understanding Bonhoeffer's theology, see Marsh, *Reclaiming Dietrich Bonhoeffer*, ch. 1.

26. Christian Gremmels, ed. *Bonhoeffer und Luther. Zur Sozialgestalt des Luthertums in der Moderne.* Internationales Bonhoeffer-Forum, No. 6 (Munich: Chr. Kaiser Verlag, 1983), 9. One attempt to address the concerns raised by Gremmels was a conference sponsored by the Vereinigten Evangelisch-Lutherischen Kirche Deutschland in 2006 in celebration of the hundredth anniversary of Bonhoeffer's birth. See Klaus Grünwaldt, Christiane Tietz, and Udo Hahn, ed. *Bonhoeffer und Luther: Zentrale Themen ihrer Theologie.* (Hanover: VELKD, 2007).

ever-present concern with Luther. Gremmels summarizes the Lutheran orientation of Bonhoeffer's theology as follows:

> The student, who in the zenith of the Luther renaissance with Karl Holl, wrote two seminar papers about Luther, and of whom it would be later recalled, he had interjected a Luther saying, "the curses of the godless rang much better in God's ears than the Hallelujahs of the pious," into a seminar with Karl Barth, whereupon the delighted Barth asked: "Who has contributed that here?" (*DB,* 216 [*DB-ER*,176]); the lecturer at the University of Berlin, who together with Franz Hildebrandt published the "Attempt at a Lutheran Catechism" with the intent "to formulate what the Lutheran faith is saying today" (GS III, 248-257; 248. See also GSIII, 335-367 [DBWE 11:258–59]); the prisoner in Tegel, who reported of himself that he had "quite spontaneously experienced Luther's instruction to 'bless oneself with the cross' at morning and evening prayer as a help." (WEN, 154 [DBWE 8:189]); finally, the author, who in his writings cited no one more frequently than Luther and in whose library (next to the work of Adolf Schlatter) was handled more completely (DB, 81 [*DB-ER*, 54])—already these few examples are enough to perceive that we have before us in Bonhoeffer's life-long discussion with Luther, through all the transformations, "an enduring fundamental impulse" (Ebeling, MW II, 17) of his theological development.[27]

As Gremmels's outline shows, when Bonhoeffer's theology is examined from the perspective of its development, the one constant is the prevailing influence of Luther's theology. The focus of this work will be to shed light on this relationship by examining Bonhoeffer's

27. Gremmels, *Bonhoeffer und Luther*, 9–10. Cf. John de Gruchy, "Editor's Introduction to the English Edition," DBWE 8:25–26, who insists that even at the end of his life while formulating his new understanding of the church and its message, "Bonhoeffer did not see his task as popular 'apologetic' in the sense of adapting the gospel to the modern mind, that is, a 'secular gospel.' Unfortunately, this was too often how his 'new theology' was understood, especially in the Anglo-Saxon world. Bonhoeffer countenanced not a reduction of the gospel but a recovery of its meaning in a new historical context. Whereas during the Church Struggle his emphasis was on Christ as Lord confronting Nazi ideology and calling the church to faithful obedience to Christ as the 'One Word of God,' now Bonhoeffer's emphasis was far more on Christ crucified (following Luther's *theologia crucis*) for the sake of a world in which humanity had become responsible 'before God' yet 'without God.'"

theology at its center—Christology—by using a central characteristic of Luther's theology—*theologia crucis*—as a tool for evaluation. His Christology, when viewed through the lens of Luther's *theologia crucis*, forms a "cross of reality."[28]

By way of introduction, the term *theologia crucis*, or "theology of the cross," should be presented in its historical context. The term has had a long but narrow history of use in the history of theology,[29] having been first used by Martin Luther in 1518 in his *Heidelberg Disputation*[30] to make a distinction between his theological method and that of the *theologia gloriae* or "theology of glory," a theological model built on speculation. Luther made a distinct differentiation between theological methods that concentrated on the invisible nature of God, making that the basis for theological reflection, and methods that took their orientation from God's revelation in Jesus Christ. According to Luther, the one who "deserves to be called a theologian [is the one] who comprehends the visible and manifest things of God seen through suffering and the cross. A theologian of glory calls evil good and good evil. A theologian of the cross calls the thing what it actually is."[31]

What we have in these words is a methodological statement with a strong christological orientation. It is a way of doing theology that has at its focus the revelation of God in Jesus Christ crucified. But

28. Jürgen Moltmann, *The Crucified God: The Cross of Christ as the Foundation and Criticism of Christian Theology*, trans. R. A. Wilson and John Bowden (New York: Harper & Row, 1974), 4, refers to a theology that has the crucified Christ as its criterion as a "cross of reality."
29. See Douglas John Hall, *Thinking the Faith: Christian Theology in a North American Context* (Minneapolis: Augsburg Fortress, 1989) and Alister McGrath, *Luther's Theology of the Cross: Martin Luther's Theological Breakthrough* (Oxford: Basil Blackwell, 1985) for further discussion of this point.
30. Martin Luther, "Heidelberg Disputation," in *Luther's Works*, ed. Jaroslav Pelikan and Helmut T. Lehmann (Philadelphia: Fortress Press, 1957), vol. 31:40; see also 52–53, for Luther's own commentary on his position.
31. Ibid, 40: theses 20 and 21.

even more so, as a theological stance, it says something about God and the world.

Martin Brecht offers the following explanation about what Luther was attempting to do in the *Heidelberg Disputation*:

> Looking at God's power, wisdom, righteousness, and goodness does not make one worthy and wise. What is visible in God is his humanness, weakness, and foolishness. Since people have abused the recognition of God in his works, he wishes to be known in suffering,. . . God allows himself to be seen only in the humility and shame of the cross; recognizing his glory and majesty is of no avail. In the crucified Christ the true theology and recognition of God is to be found. . . . The theologian of glory does not know the principle of God's action hidden under the cross. He prefers works instead of suffering, glory instead of cross, strength instead of weakness, wisdom instead of folly. These theologians are enemies of the cross of Christ. They believe that the good of the cross is an evil. But God allows himself to be found only in the cross and suffering.[32]

Hence, the phrase *the cross alone is our theology*[33] became Luther's motto. Such thinking is dominated by a preference for Christology, for it is through Christ alone that we understand God and God's presence in the world for us.

For Luther the *theologia crucis*, rather than simply being one aspect of theology, is the method for doing all true theology.[34] It is not

32. Martin Brecht, *Martin Luther: His Road to Reformation, 1483–1521*, trans. James L. Schaaf (Philadelphia: Fortress Press, 1985), 233.

33. "Psalmus V. Operationes in Psalmos," *WA* 5:176, 32–33.

34. Paul Althaus states it as follows: "Luther's theology is a way of thinking." (Paul Althaus, *The Theology of Martin Luther,* trans. Robert C. Schultz [Philadelphia: Fortress Press, 1966], iv). See Walther von Loewenich, *Luther's Theology of the Cross* (Minneapolis: Augsburg, 1976), 17–24. The following is especially descriptive of this orientation: "The theology of the cross is not a chapter in theology but a specific kind of theology. The cross of Christ is significant here not only for the question concerning redemption and the certainty of salvation, but it is the center that provides perspective for all theological statements. Hence it belongs to the doctrine of God in the same way as it belongs to the doctrine of the work of Christ.
"There is no dogmatic topic conceivable for which the cross is not a point of reference. In this sense Luther's theology desires to be a theology of the cross. And now it must be said: While the Lutheran church has clung faithfully to the 'for the sake of Christ' (*propter Christum*)

limited to the retelling of the passion narrative; on the contrary, it provides the orientation for all theological discourse. Its intention is to make clear that God comes to us as a hidden God (*deus absconditus*); that God comes to us in lowliness and suffering (*sub contraro*), in the person of Jesus Christ, thereby meeting us in our weakness, in our guilt, and in our suffering.

By Luther's own definition, this theological stance is a theology of reality[35] for it takes its orientation, in Douglas John Hall's words, from "the intersection between gospel and world" and is realistic about the world; therefore, one can be truthful about the ways things are. According to Hall, this realism means that one never has "to lie about what 'actually is.'. . . In fact, Christian faith should make [one] *more honest* about the world as [one] finds it, not less." This is possible

it surrendered Luther's theology of the cross all too quickly. The theology of glory that Luther opposed has made a triumphal entry also into his church." (von Loewenich, 18) As was true of Luther's theology, wherein no topic was conceivable where the cross was not the reference point, so too with Bonhoeffer: Christology is the reference point and that Christology is characterized by the cross. Also cf. von Loewenich, *Luther's Theology of the Cross*, 27, where he stresses that the theology of the cross forces us to remain creatures and to take the world seriously. Likewise, Bonhoeffer's theology takes the world seriously. The theme of the world in Bonhoeffer's theology has been thoroughly examined by several authors. Note especially Feil, *TDB*, and Wüstenberg, *Theology of Life*. In both instances, the stress is on the value of the world because of Christ. Finally, note the comments of John Dillenberger, *God Hidden and Revealed: The Interpretation of Luther's* Deus Absconditus *and Its Significance for Religious Thought* (Philadelphia: Muhlenberg Press, 1953), 148ff., on the necessity for understanding the whole of Luther's theology as a *theologia crucis*. It is the key to the unity and continuity of Luther's thought. Cf. Gerhard Forde, *On Being a Theologian of the Cross* (Grand Rapids: Eerdmans, 1997), who also makes the point that Luther's *theologia crucis* is more a question of method or orientation than it is of content. Luther's *theologia crucis* and the *theologia gloriae* represent "two different ways of being a theologian"; it is not a matter of two "competing set[s] of doctrines," but "different way[s] of operating" (4). See also his discussion of theses 19–21, 70ff. See also Dennis Ngien, *The Suffering God according to Martin Luther's* "Theologia Crucis," (Eugene, OR: Wipf and Stock, 2001), ch. 2.

35. Althaus, *Theology of Martin Luther*, 32–33: "The theology of the cross results in a new understanding of what we call 'reality.' True reality is not what the world and reason think it is. The true reality of God and of his salvation is 'paradoxical' and hidden under its opposite. Reason is able neither to understand nor to experience it. Judged by the standards of reason and experience, that is, by the standards of the world, true reality is unreal and its exact opposite is real. Only faith can comprehend that true and paradoxical reality. As a result, throughout Luther's theology of the cross the viewpoint of reason, the senses, experience, and the 'world' appears in opposition to the viewpoint of faith."

because Christians do not have to create a earthbound optimism, but rely instead on God: "God who is able to bring something out of nothing, righteousness out of unrighteousness and human wrath, life out of death. The Christian is free to be honest about the world–to call the thing what it really is."[36]

Similarly, Gerhard Forde understands Luther's theological orientation to be that of an "exodus from virtue to grace," in which

> justification can be understood only as a complete break with all attempts to view it as a movement according to a given standard of "Law," either natural or revealed. Righteousness is imputed by God and such imputation means a complete shattering of all our schemes. The justification which results comes neither at the beginning or end of a movement. It establishes–creates–an entirely new situation.

Justification, therefore, is "a creative act of God which ends all previous schemes and begins something absolutely new." [37] There is a new reality created by God, but one lived out in this world.

Eric Gritsch draws a similar conclusion when he describes Luther's *theologia crucis* as a practical theology, a theology that "is related to the reality of life—with its struggles, sufferings, joys, frustrations—for, realistically seen, life is overshadowed by one's continual desire to be in charge, to dominate, 'to be like God.'"[38] This is but a reflection of Luther's own position: "True theology is practical, and its foundation is Christ, whose death is appropriated to us through faith."[39]

36. Douglas John Hall, "Luther's Theology of the Cross," *Consensus* 15, no. 2 (1989): 8 and 10. See also Forde, *On Being a Theologian of the Cross*, 9–10, 70ff, and Robert Kolb, "Luther's Theology of the Cross Fifteen Years after Heidelberg: Lectures on the Psalms of Ascent," *Journal of Ecclesiastical History* 61, no. 1 (January 2010): 70–71.

37. Gerhard Forde, "The Exodus from Virtue to Grace: Justification by Faith Today," *Interpretation* 34, no. 1 (January 1980): 36–38.

38. Eric Gritsch, *Martin—God's Court Jester: Luther in Retrospect* (Philadelphia: Fortress Press, 1983), 164–65. Gerhard Ebeling also calls Luther's theology "practical" because of its link to reality: "The aim of the *theologia crucis* is in a pre-eminent sense 'practical,' for its aim is a right use of reality" (*Luther: An Introduction to his Thought* [Philadelphia: Fortress Press, 1970], 228).

39. *LW* 54:22.

The *theologia crucis*, therefore, is a lens through which to view all theology.[40] When it is used as a hermeneutical tool to evaluate the foundations and developments within Bonhoeffer's theology, it will bring into focus the major theological orientation, perspective, and themes in Bonhoeffer's Christology, the organizing center of his theology. The cross always marks his Christology; Jesus is always the crucified one, the humble one. It must be stated, however, that inasmuch as Bonhoeffer saw himself within the Lutheran camp, *theologia crucis* was not a term he himself used to describe his theological stance.[41]

As a point of entry into our subject, observations by two individuals who knew Bonhoeffer well, and whose theological orientations were influenced by him, might be considered indicative of the Luther/Bonhoeffer relationship, both in terms of the developments within Bonhoeffer's own theology and his position over against other Lutherans.[42] The first is from Eberhard Bethge,

40. Another way of saying this would be to say that it is a "perceptual foundation"–"a window through which to observe and relate the great variety of things that we see, hear, feel, sense, experience, or know. Without such a perspective, we are at the mercy of the world's apparent randomness." (Douglas John Hall, *Professing the Faith* [Minneapolis: Fortress Press, 1993], 364).
41. Its absence from the Bonhoeffer corpus should not prevent it from being applied to Bonhoeffer's theology, however. Research indicates that this description of Luther's theology is a relatively new phenomenon, growing out of the twentieth-century Luther renaissance. Also, it is not known whether Bonhoeffer was familiar with von Loewenich's work, which dates back to 1926; while its publication corresponds with Bonhoeffer's time at the university, it was not a part of his surviving library; see below, chapter 2, n11.
42. These comments grew out of conversations with Eberhard Bethge and Gerhard Ebeling that took place in their homes on October 6, 1991, and November 11, 1991, respectively. It should be noted that Ebeling believes that in his theological work he is very near to Bonhoeffer, because Bonhoeffer was very near to Luther. For him, this is an important connection. Wolfgang Huber, in response to questions following his address on "Bonhoeffer's Critical Theology of Modernity," presented August 17, 1992, at the 6th International Bonhoeffer Conference, Union Theological Seminary, New York City, also stressed that the Luther/Bonhoeffer relationship was the key to understanding Bonhoeffer's *theologia crucis*. The proceedings of the conference were published as *Theology and the Practice of Responsibility: Essays on Dietrich Bonhoeffer*, ed. Wayne Whitson Floyd Jr. and Charles Marsh (Valley Forge, PA: Trinity Press International, 1994). It should also be noted at this point that there was a struggle within theological circles over how to appropriate Luther's theological heritage in the church of that day. Hence, Bonhoeffer's concern, together with many other theologians and

both a student and close friend of Bonhoeffer who, when discussing the role of Luther's theology in the development of Bonhoeffer's own position, said, "Bonhoeffer had to find his own Luther." And indeed, Bonhoeffer did find his own Luther, which was a Luther different from the one presented by his teachers as well as many of his contemporaries.[43] The other comment that lends itself to a concentrated focus on this relationship was made by Gerhard Ebeling, one of Bonhoeffer's students at Finkenwalde in 1935, who went on to become a noted Luther scholar. Commenting on Bonhoeffer's Lutheran orientation, he said, "In my heart, I believe Bonhoeffer and Luther are one."[44] In fact, Ebeling believed it was Bonhoeffer's intention to "re-win" Luther over against the

church leaders, was not solely academic but had implications for the church's witness in the world. This became one of the decisive issues that divided German Protestantism in the 1930s as the church attempted to respond to the challenges of Nazi ideology. See Wolfgang Huber, *Konflict und Konsensus: Studien zur Ethik der Verantwortung* (Munich: Chr. Kaiser Verlag, 1990), 79–98; Uwe Siemon-Netto, *The Fabricated Luther: The Rise and Fall of the Shirer Myth* (St. Louis: Concordia, 1995); and William Lazareth, *Christians in Society: Luther, the Bible, and Social Ethics* (Minneapolis: Fortress Press, 2001), ch. 1, for an overview of the divergent views in which Luther was held.

43. See James M Strayer, *Martin Luther: German Saviour* (Montreal, ON: McGill-Queen's Unversity Press, 2000) and Christine Helmer, "The American Luther," *Dialog* 47, no. 2 (Summer 2008): 114–24, for background and how Luther is interpreted and perceived in different contexts, which leads to the conclusion that there is not just one answer to the question, "Who is Luther?" Helmer's essay reviews Luther scholarship, particularly in North America, and shows how the picture of Luther(s) has developed in recent decades. As this essay reveals, the question of the "real" or "authentic" Luther is an open-ended one. As she notes, the leading German Protestant theologians of the early twentieth century "contributed in significant ways to our understanding of Luther. . . . German Protestantism's development is intertwined with Luther" (118). While Bonhoeffer did not enter into the conversation of the 1930s–1940s as a Luther scholar, he certainly relied on Luther for his theological foundation, carving a path between the "confessional Lutherans" and the "Barthians." See also Doris L. Bergen, *Twisted Cross: The German Christian Movement in the Third Reich* (Chapel Hill, NC: The University of North Carolina Press, 1996) for a description of how the German Christians used Luther to recapture the true character of German Christianity, a "manly Christianity"; and Guy Carter, "Martin Luther in the Third Reich: Recent Research on Luther as Iconic Force in Hitler's Germany," *Seminary Ridge Review* 12, no. 1 (Autumn 2009): 42–62 for a reevaluation of the Nazi's use of Luther.

44. His reaction to the appearance of *LPP* in the 1950s sounds similar: "I should like to state explicitly that I am especially interested in the theological perspectives. Not, indeed because I find them strange, but because they are a surprisingly major confirmation to me that I am a pupil of Bonhoeffer, precisely in those matters in which I have developed beyond the

interpretations of the nineteenth century and of his time to come to the original Luther.[45]

Significantly, for Bonhoeffer, as for Luther, Christology is not just one element of theology, but that which provides the content and distinctiveness of all theology. In such a manner, Bonhoeffer's Christology can be described as a *theologica crucis*,[46] for it parallels Luther's conception of a *theologia crucis* as being a specific type of

theological level of the Finkenwalde period and which have guided me toward a path which I only now know was his also" (letter, 9.30.1951, in *DB-ER*, 889).

45. It should also be pointed out that Bethge has stated clearly that Luther is the most widely quoted theologian in Bonhoeffer's works and, at the same time, holds the most widespread influence on his thought. See *DB-ER*, 79, 133. Krötke, "Dietrich Bonhoeffer and Martin Luther," 53, draws the same conclusion, saying that Luther appears in Bonhoeffer's works more than any other theologian.

46. Eberhard Bethge has described Bonhoeffer's theology consistently in these terms, beginning as early as his 1961 Chicago lecture. See Bethge, "Challenge of Dietrich Bonhoeffer's Life and Theology," 34; see also, Bethge, "Bonhoeffer's Christology and His 'Religionless Christianity,'" in *Bonhoeffer in a World Come of Age*, ed. Peter Vorkink (Philadelphia: Fortress Press, 1968), 47; Bethge, *DB-ER*, passim. Several other scholars use the same designation. Included among them are John Godsey, "The Legacy of Dietrich Bonhoeffer," in Klassen, *Bonhoeffer Legacy*, 162; Larry Rasmussen, "An Ethic of the Cross," in *Dietrich Bonhoeffer—His Significance for North Americans* (Minneapolis: Fortress Press, 1990), 149–60; Rasmussen, *Dietrich Bonhoeffer: Reality and Resistance* (Nashville: Abingdon, 1972), 15ff; Geff Kelly, "Revelation in Christ: A Study of Bonhoeffer's Theology of Revelation," *Ephemerides Theologicae Lovanienses* 50, no. 1 (May 1974): 60–65; Clifford Green, *Bonhoeffer: A Theology of Sociality*, rev. ed. (Grand Rapids: Eerdamns, 1999), passim (Green stresses the continuity in Bonhoeffer's theological development by claiming that Bonhoeffer's theology of the cross emerges in his early writings and comes to fruition in *Letters and papers from Prison*); John de Gruchy, ed., *Dietrich Bonhoeffer: Witness to Jesus Christ*, The Making of Modern Theology Series (San Francisco: Collins, 1988), 9, 17; Rainer Mayer, *Christuswirchlichkeit: Grundlagen, Entwicklung und Konsequenzen der Theologie Dietrich Bonhoeffers* (Stuttgart: Calwer Verlag, 1969), 257ff; Ebeling, "Non-Religious Interpretation of Biblical Concepts," 158; Regin Prenter, "Bonhoeffer and the Young Luther," in *World Come of Age*, ed. Ronald Gregor Smith (Philadelphia: Fortress Press, 1970), passim; Tiemo Rainer Peters, *Die Präsenz des Politischen in der Theologie Dietrich Bonhoeffers* (Munich: Chr. Kaiser; Matthais-Grünewald, 1976), 113ff; Michael Plathow, "Die Mannigfaltigkeit der Wege Gottes: zu Dietrich Bonhoeffers kreuztheologischer Versehungslehre," *Kerygma und Dogma*, 26, no. 2 (April/June 1980): 109–27; Feil, *TDB*, 92–93 [see also 187, where, in referring to Bonhoeffer's theology of the cross, he insists that this perspective that is prominent in *LPP* pervades all of Bonhoeffer's theology]; Phillips, *Christ for Us*, 193; Benkt-Erik Benktson, *Christus und Religion. Der Religionsbegriff bei Barth, Bonhoeffer und Tillich* (Stuttgart: Calwer, 1967), 122ff; and Abromeit, *Geheimnis Christi*, 227ff. Others, including Douglas John Hall and Wolfgang Huber, have used this designation as a hermeneutic for understanding Bonhoeffer's focus on the world and responsibility in the modern era; see Floyd and Marsh, *Theology and the Practice of Responsibility*. Such a representation indicates that there is a growing consensus

theology that concentrates on the revelation of God in Christ's death on the cross.[47]

Finally, why the title, *Cross of Reality*? Implicit in this title is the recognition that Bonhoeffer, in his relationship to Luther, reworks or reappropriates Luther's "theology of the cross." Bonhoeffer's theology is not simply a rigid interpretation of Luther's theology, but rather it is an appropriation of that theological tradition designed to address the modern world.

Bonhoeffer believed himself to be a part of the modern world and that point of view was a strong determiner in shaping his theological orientation. It is this sense of belonging to the modern age that accounts for some of the differences between Bonhoeffer's "cross of reality" and Luther's *theologia crucis*. Bonhoeffer himself, for example, admitted that in many cases, Luther would say the opposite today of what he had said in the sixteenth century.[48] In light of this comment alone, one cannot insist that Bonhoeffer blindly followed Luther;[49]

as to the Lutheran nature of Bonhoeffer's theology as well as to a major impulse in shaping its character.

47. This points out the rationale for a study such as this. Early research on Bonhoeffer's theology, especially the studies that began to emerge in the 1960s and '70s, revealed a diverse landscape with little or no consensus on the major themes or influences on his thought. Rather than reaching any agreement, these early studies have identified several issues that were to become the foundation for subsequent research. Clifford Green has summarized several of these issues, two of which are relevant for this current study, because they get to the heart of Bonhoeffer's theology and are ones that still need to be addressed: 1) "Granted that Christology is central to Bonhoeffer's theology, are there tensions and changes within it, or is it essentially unchanging? What role does the *theologia crucis* play in the Christology? Does Christology per se render intelligible Bonhoeffer's theological development—whether an expanding Christology, a Christology of many tensions, or a Christology which remains essentially the same?" 2) "Given Bonhoeffer's frequent references to Luther, the acknowledgment by all interpreters of Luther's significance for him, and the attempt of Lutheran interpreters to understand Bonhoeffer in traditional Lutheran categories, what does a comparison of the two theologians reveal about their similarities and differences?" Green, *Bonhoeffer: A Theology of Sociality*, 12–13. Christian Gremmels's work also highlights the extent of the research and introduces us to the nature and history of the research on this subject. See Gremmels, *Bonhoeffer und Luther*, 9.
48. See DBWE 8:173 .
49. Bonhoeffer's own comments are indicative of this stance. See his *Ethics* (DBWE 6:150), for example, where he insists that we cannot return to either Luther or St. Paul.

rather, what we see is that he reshaped Luther's theology[50] in a fashion appropriate for the modern world.

The *cross of reality* serves as a way of getting at the character of Bonhoeffer's theology, by emphasizing the nature of his Christology. It can be seen as an answer to Bonhoeffer's question: Who is Christ actually for us today? As he develops his answer to that question, one sees Bonhoeffer's *theologia crucis* showing through. In the end, his is a cross of reality, because he wanted a theology that tied him and all to the world, rather than separating them from it. And the world he wanted all to see was not an idealized version of the world, but the world as it really is: exposed, judged, and redeemed by God in Christ.[51]

The cross of reality also points to the inherent continuity that shapes Bonhoeffer's thought, for if Christology is the controlling theme that shapes Bonhoeffer's theology, an examination of his Christology will shed light on the development of his whole theological perspective. In that case, it can be stated that *Letters and Papers from Prison* is the logical conclusion to the theological principles laid down in the earlier works.[52]

Yet it must be recognized that any relationship that Bonhoeffer had with Luther's legacy was a complex one. Bonhoeffer was not

50. In a recent work, Klemens von Klemperer states that while Bonhoeffer's theology is grounded in and takes its orientation from Luther's theology, his involvement in the resistance indicates that he eventually moved "beyond" Luther. See his "Beyond Luther? Dietrich Bonhoeffer and Resistance against National Socialism," *Pro Ecclesia* 4, no. 2 (Spring 1997): 184–98.

51. Cf. Douglas John Hall's analysis of Luther's theology (*Lighten Our Darkness*, 122–23).

52. Feil, *TDB*, 59; de Gruchy, *Dietrich Bonhoeffer: Witness to Jesus Christ*, 18–19; Ebeling, "Non-Religious Interpretation of Biblical Concepts," 107; Woelfel, *Bonhoeffer's Theology*, 134; Bethge, *DB-ER*, 118. Commenting on Bonhoeffer's "new theology" in *LPP*, Bethge concludes that when people finally began to read Bonhoeffer's early works, after having discovered him through *LPP*, they discovered "with astonishment that there was a broad continuity between the Berlin beginnings and the Tegel period. Formulations and theological suggestions in *Letters and Papers from Prison* that people found shocking proved to be not as new as had been thought; they could be found, even in the same wording, in *Sanctorum Communio* or *Act and Being*, as well as in various other writings" (*DB-ER*, 889).

a historical theologian who concentrated on understanding the particular historical context of Luther's theology. Instead, according to Gerhard Ebeling, he was a systematic thinker, quoting from Luther those things that supported what he wanted to say.[53] Because Bonhoeffer took his own context seriously, his concern was interpreting his tradition and applying it in ways to address a "new" situation.

The analysis of this complex relationship will be structured along the following lines: Part 1 (chapters 1 and 2) will serve as a background to our discussion by introducing the parameters that structure Bonhoeffer's theology. Luther's role in the development of Bonhoeffer's theology will be seen, first of all, through the influence of Karl Holl. This, in turn, will be followed by a presentation of Luther's *theologia crucis.* Finally, it will provide a perspective on the place of Christology in Bonhoeffer's theological scheme.

Part 2 (chapters 3–5) will turn to Bonhoeffer's writings themselves, particularly the period 1925–1933. During this time Bonhoeffer lived in the academic world, first as a student and then as a professor. It was during this time that the foundations of Bonhoeffer's thought were laid and reached their fullest systematic presentation in his university lectures. Our examination will begin with a review of Bonhoeffer's student papers written for Karl Holl and conclude with his Christology lectures, which were delivered in the summer of 1933. These lectures were the highpoint of his academic career as well as the occasion that marked its end.

Part 3 (chapters 6–10) will continue with an analysis of Bonhoeffer's writings that were written under different circumstances and take on a different character from the earlier academic ones. They are no longer the systematic presentations

53. Conversation of November 11, 1991.

stemming from a university setting, but are occasional pieces written to address specific issues arising out of the German Church Struggle. During this period, 1933–45, Bonhoeffer's academic interests fall into the background as his theology is placed in the service of the church. Moving from his academic concerns, these writings lead us through the twists and turns that led to Bonhoeffer's imprisonment and death. Bonhoeffer's "cross of reality" will emerge as the thread that holds his life and theology together.

Part 4 (chapter 11) will present conclusions and expound the significance of Bonhoeffer's cross of reality. Based on the overview of Bonhoeffer's writings, it will show that the *theologia crucis* provides the continuity to Bonhoeffer's thought, weaving all his concerns together.

Such a study can also situate us to point beyond Bonhoeffer to our current context. By using his theological legacy as a model, we can see how the *theologia crucis* can serve as an important resource for the church's witness in a changing world. Finally, in addition, it may provide a preliminary answer to the question if Bonhoeffer's cross of reality represents a "creative moment in Lutheran theology"[54] and, if so, what its continuing significance is.

## Significance

Seventy years after his death in 1945, Bonhoeffer remains an enduring witness of Christian discipleship. At the same time, the nature of his life and witness, together with his theological reflections, have launched a revolution that changed the nature of theological thought in the last half of the twentieth century and will continue to influence theological thinking in the twenty-first century. It is an influence that continues to be felt around the world.

54. Larry Rasmussen, in a conversation with the author, August 14, 1989, Union Theological Seminary, New York City.

The extent of this influence has been summarized by Wolfgang Huber:

> When we remember Paul Tillich and Karl Barth, the thought would hardly occur to us that they could still be alive, that they could represent the present. How different is the case of Dietrich Bonhoeffer. . . . The image of Bonhoeffer continues unmistakably to have an intense effect in ecumenical Christianity. When Christians, on grounds of conscience, see themselves forced to protest the violation of basic human rights, they too derive encouraging strength from his example. And for many who seek new breakthroughs in theology, Bonhoeffer is one of the most important sources of inspiration. The Lutheran Church in East Germany has been influenced by the Bonhoeffer heritage, but so has the theology of the people of South Korea. The resistance in South Africa leans on him, as does the Latin American Liberation Theology.[55]

In order to properly understand the power of Bonhoeffer's witness and theology, his christological orientation cannot be ignored. In spite of all the attempts to make Bonhoeffer a secular or radical theologian, as one who turned away from God and the church and toward the world,[56] it is impossible to make sense of his life and witness without Jesus Christ.[57] As a result, we must say that the secular theologians and the "Death of God" movements of the 1960s

55. Wolfgang Huber, "Wer ist Christus für uns? Bonhoeffers Bedeutung für die Zukunft der Christenheit" *Evangelische Kommentare* (April 1986): 191; translation from Joseph Robinson, Union Theological Seminary's "Heroes of Conscience" concert program, April 5, 1992. See also Haynes, *Bonhoeffer Phenomenon*, introduction. It must also be stated that Bonhoeffer's influence extends far beyond the boundaries of Christian theology; his writings have had an impact on Jewish thought and political philosophy, among other academic disciplines.

56. See, for example, John A. T. Robinson's *Honest to God* (London: SCM, 1963), Hanfried Müller's *Von der Kirche zur Welt: Ein Beitrag zu der Beziehung des Wortes Gottes auf die Societas in Dietrich Bonhoeffers theologischer Entwicklung* (Hamburg-Bergstedt: Herbert Reich Evangelisch, 1961), or the works by Thomas Altizer and William Hamilton for this tendency.

57. In quite simple terms the commemorative plaque on the wall of Flossenberg's village church says it all: "Witness for Jesus Christ." Bonhoeffer sought to live his life responsibly as a disciple of Jesus Christ. This commitment not only gave meaning to his life, it was the governing center of this theological reflections as well—reflections based not on a personal piety, but that sought to give witness to Jesus Christ as Lord of the earth, the one who stands at the center of all creation and all history. Bonhoeffer claimed in his *Ethics* that Jesus Christ determines and shapes all reality; so too with his theology, Jesus Christ stands at the center.

falsely portrayed Bonhoeffer as a radical theologian—one who threw off the vestiges of the past and turned toward a non-eligious faith that left the church behind. In claiming that Bonhoeffer's concept of "the world come of age" was an affirmation of the optimistic view of progress dominant in liberal thinking, for example, they forgot to take his theological heritage into account; they failed to see that Bonhoeffer was "the heir of the Reformation who never forgot [Luther's] *cor corvum in se.*"[58]

Certainly, Bonhoeffer's thought was radical and revolutionary,[59] but it was so precisely because of its adherence to the classical traditions of the church, especially Luther's *theologia crucis.* When his theology is understood in light of this tradition, his "non-religious interpretation of biblical concepts," which he set out to describe in his theological letters from Tegel prison, is not a radical departure from his earlier theology, but is the mature expression of his theology of the cross. His Lutheran roots would not allow him to turn his back on the problems and tragedies of the world. In fact, because God had turned toward the world, had entered into the world and identified with suffering individuals, the only proper sphere for theological reflection was this world. Theology properly conceived, therefore, is very this-worldly.[60] It is this worldly character that gives it its power to speak.

By investigating the connections between Bonhoeffer's theology and the tradition out of which it arose, we can be led to a better understanding of his theology. When his theology is viewed through the lens of the *theologia crucis*, it is possible to make some evaluations

58. Bethge, *Bonhoeffer: Exile and Martyr*, 144.
59. Woelfel's study, *Bonhoeffer's Theology*, attempts to address the relationship between classical theological formulations and the modern world; this dialogue is what gives it its revolutionary character.
60. Ernst Feil claims that Bonhoeffer's *theologia crucis* does not renounce the world but rather embraces it (*TDB*, 187).

regarding Bonhoeffer's place in modern theology. It is also possible to correct some errors in earlier Bonhoeffer scholarship—or at least to note why such differences in interpretations exist.

This topic is of concern because of Bonhoeffer's theological position itself. At the end of his life, Bonhoeffer left us a legacy that points us not to the past but to the future. This can be seen in his "Outline for a Book," notes scribbled in his prison cell, and later included in *Letters and Papers from Prison*.[61] If Bonhoeffer's future vision of the church is to be taken seriously, then his thought still holds the power to influence the church's witness in the coming decades. If Bonhoeffer's theological position can still be declared as valuable, and if one can locate the key to his theology in a classic Christian position such as the theology of the cross, then this position becomes an important means of translating the traditions of the church into contemporary thought forms. If, as Larry Rasmussen claims, Bonhoeffer's thoughts at the end of his life were a "creative moment" in Lutheran theology, the question remains, are they in continuity with the Lutheran tradition or are they a departure from that tradition?

But Bonhoeffer's theology remains an enduring witness for reasons other than its connections to a particular tradition. Bonhoeffer, by turning his attention to the future, has provided us with a posture that still characterizes the relationship between the church and the world. Because of the ambiguities that now mark the societies in the Christian West, it is even more urgent that we reexamine the traditions of the church in an effort to make them speak clearly to an ever-changing world.

We must continue to wrestle with the identity of the church and its place in society. For that reason, the task is a hermeneutical one

61. DBWE 8:499–504.

and, in this situation, Bonhoeffer's theology speaks clearly. Taking this into consideration, an analysis of Bonhoeffer's theological stance and its implications, which were aimed at a nonreligious world, is most valuable. Even though our context might not be considered to be nonreligious, at least in the way Bonhoeffer imagined it,[62] it bears many similarities with the nonreligious situation Bonhoeffer was describing. Our context is marked by a plurality of religions, as well as a growing sector of religiously "nonaffiliated" for whom the language of faith lacks significance,[63] both of which present an equally challenging environment in which the church must bear witness.[64]

Therefore, Bonhoeffer's task, which he began to lay out in his final writings, is not done. We are facing changes like never before—the disintegration of culture and a unitary worldview[65]—changes that

62. But it also needs to be emphasized that this change does not affect the appropriateness of Bonhoeffer's theology for today, for his concern was for a credible witness to Jesus Christ in the modern world. At the same time, however, his reflections on the nonreligious world still apply. Today in large cities, there is no room for religion in the public square. Churches blend into the urban landscape as architectural designs from the past and go unnoticed, except as dispensers of cheap social services to be delivered in emergencies. For a discussion of the changed context, see H. Gaylon Barker, "Without God, We Live with God: Listening to Bonhoeffer's Witness in Today's Public Square," in *Dietrich Bonhoeffers Theologie heute: Ein Weg zwischen Fundamentalismus und Säkularismus ?/Dietrich Bonhhoeffer's Theology Today: A Way between Fundamentalism and Secularism?*, ed. John de Gruchy, Christiane Tietz, and Stephen Plant (Gütersloh: Gütersloher, 2009).

63. For a description of this phenomena, see the Pew Research Center's October 9, 2012 report, "'Nones' on the Rise: One in Five Adults Have No Religious Affiliation." http://www.pewforum.org/2012/10/09/nones-on-the-rise.

64. If we take Bethge's analysis of Bonhoeffer's "non-religious interpretation" seriously, then we must recognize that "non-religious interpretation" was not Bonhoeffer's primary concern. Rather it was the hermeneutical tool used to clear the way for a more effective proclamation of the Christian message in the modern world. If Bethge is correct, then it is possible to look behind Bonhoeffer's terminology to locate his real concern. In this regard, in spite of the contextual changes that separate us from Bonhoeffer, the challenge his theology presented remains valid for our situation. See Eberhard Bethge, "Bonhoeffer's Assertion of Religionless Christianity—Was He Mistaken?" in Klassen, *Bonhoeffer Legacy*, 3–13.

65. Douglas John Hall's work is an example of one who takes such claims seriously; this is a subtheme of his entire three-volume work on theology for a North American context: *Thinking the Faith*, *Professing the Faith*, and *Confessing the Faith*. See also his "The Changing North American Context of the Church's Ministry," "A Theological Proposal for the Church's

are likely to alter the nature of society and our approach to life. These are changes for which we are not adequately prepared to draw conclusions, but living in the midst of such flux provides the context to which we are called to faithfully proclaim the gospel. Bonhoeffer's theology can help us do that.

We begin with what's important to Bonhoeffer—and to us.

## Conclusion

In the summer months of 1939, when the war was heating up in Europe, one of its future victims came to America for refuge. Under the sponsorship of Reinhold Niebuhr and Paul Lehmann, Bonhoeffer was able to get out of the troubling atmosphere of Hitler's Germany. As had been done for Paul Tillich in 1933, Niebuhr had hoped to bring yet another German theologian to this country. It almost worked. However, in the now famous letter Bonhoeffer wrote to Niebuhr, he told him that he could not stay in this country. He wrote,

> Sitting here in Dr. Coffin's garden I have had the time to think and to pray about my situation and that of my nation and to have God's will for me clarified. I have come to the conclusion that I have made a mistake in coming to America. I must live through this difficult period of our national history with the Christian people of Germany. I will have no right to participate in the reconstruction of Christian life in Germany after the war if I do not share the trials of this time with my people. . . . Christians in Germany will face the terrible alternative of either willing the defeat of their nation in order that Christian civilization may survive, or willing the victory of their nation and thereby destroying

Response to Its Context," and "The Church and Its Ministry: Responding to the Changing Context in Worship, Preaching, Education, Outreach," all published in *Currents in Theology and Mission* 22 (December 1995): 405–433; and *The Cross in Our Context: Jesus and the Suffering World* (Minneapolis: Fortress Press, 2003). The Pew Research Center (www.pewforum.org) and the Barna Group (www.barna.org), among others, are both examining the changing nature of religion and religious practices as well as developing resources to address such changes.

> our civilization. I know which of these alternatives I must choose; but I cannot make that choice in security.[66]

But while he was here, he gathered some perceptions of America that are perhaps still helpful, especially for those who seek to avoid the Scylla of enculturation and the Charybdis of repristinating the traditions of the church. Written in August 1939, and published as an article entitled "Protestantism without Reformation," Bonhoeffer observed,

> The failure in Christology is characteristic of all current American theology (with the exception of fundamentalism). . . . God did not grant a Reformation to American Christendom. He gave strong revivalist preachers, men of the church, and theologians, but no reformation of the church of Jesus Christ from the word of God. Those churches of the Reformation that came to America either stand in deliberate seclusion and distance from general church life or have fallen victim to Protestantism without Reformation. . . . Christendom in American theology is essentially still religion and ethics. Hence, the person and work of Jesus Christ recedes into the background for theology and remains ultimately not understood, because the sole foundation for God's radical judgment and radical grace is at this point not recognized. The decisive task today is the conversation between the Protestantism without Reformation and the churches of the Reformation.[67]

Drawing on Bonhoeffer's observations from an earlier time, Rasmussen comes to a similar conclusion: "There are religion and ethics in North American culture but no *theologia crucis*."[68]

If Bonhoeffer was correct, it is fair to say that religion in America could very easily fall into the category of his "cheap grace." The problem with a religion without a theology of the cross is that there is no recognition of the failings, weakness, or evil in life that touches and shapes humanity. Everything is marked by optimism.[69]

66. DBWE 15:210.
67. DBWE 15:460–462.
68. Rasmussen, "Ethic of the Cross," 147.

As a result, Christianity in America is religion "without Luther's *simul iustis et peccator*," it is Christian liberalism without the judgment of God's grace.[70] It was against such a mind-set, characteristic of nineteenth-century liberal theology, that Bonhoeffer reacted. It was that character of his theology that the secular theologians missed. It is that same characteristic of his theology that has caused it to be an enduring witness.

Christology is necessary for the work of the church.[71] It lies at the center of the church's identity and mission. How it answers the question, "Who is Christ actually for us today?" will determine how the church sees its mission in the world, or better perhaps, who it believes Jesus to be will shape who it sees itself to be as God's people. The picture of Christ that it holds will radically influence the image it has of itself and the world. A Christology shaped by a cross of reality enables the church to approach its context realistically and responsibly. It is to that theological stance, in the hands of Dietrich Bonhoeffer, that we now turn.

69. See Douglas John Hall's treatment of this aspect of American life in *Lighten Our Darkness.*
70. Ibid, 147–48.
71. See Carl Braaten, *No Other Gospel! Christianity among the World's Religions* (Minneapolis: Fortress Press, 1992) for a discussion of how the major issues of theology are focused on Christology.

PART II

# The Background and Context of Bonhoeffer's Christology

# 1

# Bonhoeffer and Karl Holl

If we seek to locate Bonhoeffer's position on the map of the twentieth-century theological landscape, invariably many comparisons will be made, many relationships examined, and nuances in his thought emphasized; a survey of the Bonhoeffer literature indicates the extent to which this has already been done. Such a study is done to help us better understand his context, but it also brings clarity to his theological position.

Bonhoeffer's theological background was that of liberal theology, which was the dominant voice in Berlin. But he was also a part of the twentieth century in that he was influenced by the two strong reform movements in early-twentieth-century German theology: the Luther renaissance (represented by Karl Holl) and dialectical theology (Karl Barth and others). Even though he was influenced by both movements, he maintained a critical distance from them. This is indicative of Bonhoeffer's theological orientation. He remained fiercely independent in his thinking, consistently claiming Luther as his only real ally. So while he learned from Holl and found inspiration from Barth, he finds an alternative to both of them in Luther.[1] It is this influence of Luther that separates Bonhoeffer from Barth as well as from his teachers. The integration of these influences by Bonhoeffer gives his theology its own independent voice.[2]

## Bonhoeffer's Independent Theological Stance

One of the first persons to critically evaluate Bonhoeffer's theology was his dissertation advisor, Reinhold Seeberg. In his written evaluation of *Sanctorum Communio*, Bonhoeffer's doctoral dissertation, Seeberg's comments show the extent to which

1. Seeing the deficiencies in twentieth century theology, Bonhoeffer concludes his analysis with what might be seen as a programmatic statement for his own theology: "Luther was able to write *On the Bonadage of the Will* and his piece on usury at the same time. Why can't we do that anymore? *Who will show us Luther?*" (DBWE 11:24). The extent of Luther's influence on Bonhoeffer's theological project has been pointed out by Wayne Floyd, "Editor's Introduction to the English Edition," *Act and Being*, DBWE 2:7, for example, where he concludes that the heart of Bonhoeffer's argument in *Act and Being* was "deeply indebted to theological insights from Martin Luther, especially his *Lectures on Galatians.*"
2. After submitting Barth's theology to examination in his lectures on systematic theology in the twentieth century along the same lines as begun in *Act and Being*, Bonhoeffer makes the following statement that, in essence, is descriptive of his theological task: "Lutherans of today should be ashamed that they don't know how to define the Lutheran understanding of revelation by differentiating it both from Catholic substance thinking and from Reformed actualism" (DBWE 11:243n331; this is an alternative rendering of Bonhoeffer's lecture, as recorded by Otto Dudzus). Commenting on this work, Jonathan Sorum, "The Eschatological Boundary in Bonhoeffer's 'Nachfolge,'" (ThD diss., Luther Northwestern Theological Seminary, 1994), 29, draws the following conclusion: "Luther could do both dogmatics and ethics at the same time. For him, everything was of a piece; dogmatics, ethics, God, human beings, and world were all one reality, but precisely God's being God is what made everything else real. Bonhoeffer seeks to follow Luther. Any understanding of the theology of Dietrich Bonhoeffer must begin with an understanding of his understanding of the theology of Martin Luther, for Bonhoeffer's task was nothing else that to 'show us Luther.'" See also Joachim von Soosten, "Editor's Afterword to the German Edition," *Sanctorum Communio*, DBWE 1, where he describes the nature of Bonhoeffer's disagreement with Barth growing out of his Lutheran commitments (292, 305). It is the nature of such tensions between Barth and Bonhoeffer that leads Cliff Green to conclude that in spite of what Bonhoeffer learned from Barth and his siding with Barth over against his teachers, "nevertheless, in his alignment with Barth, Bonhoeffer remained typically independent ("Editor's Introduction to the English Edition," *Sanctorum Communion*, DBWE 1:3). For a further description of the relation/influences of Holl/Barth, see Hans Pfeifer,"Editor's Afterword to the German Edition," *The Young Bonhoeffer 1918–1927*, DBWE 9:571ff.

Bonhoeffer as a young scholar garnered the respect of one of the leading theologians of the day:

> The author is not only well oriented in the theological field but also thoroughly acquainted with sociology. He is decidedly gifted in systematic thinking, as demonstrated by the dialectic in the structure of his work both in general and in particular. He seeks to discover his way on his own. He is always prepared for intelligent discussion of other opinions. Even if one does not share his opinions, one will readily acknowledge the scientific interest and the energy of the argumentation. . . . They are only the converse of the many good qualities of the work: Its enthusiasm for Christianity, the precise systematics in the method of the entire study, the inner concentration of his task, the ingenious particularity of his view, and his critical ability to cope with over views. On the whole, the work can be characterized as a very satisfactory model of serious academic erudition.[3]

In addition to praising Bonhoeffer's intellectual skills, Seeberg notes Bonhoeffer's *independence*, seeking "to discover his way on his own." He recognized that Bonhoeffer did not simply repeat the language and thought patterns of his teachers; both in the way he approached his subject and his overall orientation indicated an independence that could not be easily categorized.[4]

Independence was a characteristic of Bonhoeffer's long before this point in his academic career, however; it was a characteristic of Bonhoeffer's person as well as his thought. He was never subject to hero worship and was always able to approach a subject or person with an independent spirit (only his family members exerted such an influence on him that even to the end of his life their basic orientation and philosophy of life would shape the decisions he would make).

3. DBWE 9:176–77.
4. Bonhoeffer's text indicates independence of another sort as well. What he proposed was a "systematic" rather than a "historical" study. This methodological independence sets him apart from his teachers and the mainstream liberal theology of the nineteenth century. See Cliff Green, *Bonhoeffer: A Theology of Sociality* (Grand Rapids: Eerdmans, 1999), 25.

Even his choice to become a theologian is one that is marked by his independence. In spite of the overwhelming influence of his family, Bonhoeffer chose a profession that would enable him to make a contribution in ways that others in his family would not. According to Bethge,

> At the root of his choice [to become a theologian] was a basic drive toward independence. This did not exclude his insatiable appetite for all kinds of different knowledge, but the driving force in his life was the need for unchallenged self-realization. The presence of theologians among his forebears made his choice of career not that unusual; while this no doubt played a part, it was hardly a decisive factor. His isolation among his brothers and sisters was probably of far greater importance; it may have nourished his urge to surpass them all.[5]

This independence was noted by fellow students as well. Perhaps while it is not an expert judgment, it nevertheless sheds light on Bonhoeffer's theological make-up, which was exhibited quite early. One fellow student from Adolf von Harnack's 1925–26 seminar on Augustine, Helmut Goes, for example, observed,

> I had already noticed Dietrich Bonhoeffer at the very first sessions. Not just because he surpassed almost all of us in theological knowledge and ability; that was for me the most impressive thing. But what really drew me to Bonhoeffer was that here was someone who did not merely study and absorb the words and writings of some master, but who thought for himself and already knew what he wanted and also wanted what he knew. I actually had the experience (and to me it was rather alarming and a tremendous novelty) of seeing the young blond student contradict the revered polyhistorian His Excellency von Harnack politely, but on objective theological grounds. Harnack replied, but the student contradicted him again and again. I no longer know the topic of discussion—Karl Barth was mentioned—but I still recall the secret enthusiasm that I felt for this free, critical and independent theological thought.[6]

5. *DB-ER*, 37.

While such an observation may not carry the same weight as that of Bonhoeffer's professors, it nevertheless sheds light on Bonhoeffer's theological make-up, which, as these observations point out, was exhibited early.

Because of that independent spirit, differences with his teachers emerged at an early date as well; by his own admission Bonhoeffer said that he felt out of place in Berlin. In a December 25, 1931 letter to his friend Erwin Sutz, for example, he shared this observation: "My theological origin is gradually becoming suspect here, and they seem to have somewhat the feeling that they have been nurturing a viper in their bosom."[7]

The same conclusion can be drawn with regard to his relationship to Karl Barth. At the same time as he was distancing himself from his Berlin teachers, Bonhoeffer found Barth to be a positive source for theological reflection, while maintaining a critical distance.[8] He did not refrain from challenging Barth, especially when it "conflicted with the more deeply ingrained convictions animating his own understanding of how theology was related to both faith and experience."[9] According to Bonhoeffer, Barth's emphasis on God's majesty threatened the concreteness of God's revelation. Therefore, inasmuch as he praised Barth for restoring God as theology's proper subject, he never failed to point out dangers in Barth's thought. Though he found Barth to be a worthy conversation partner, when

6. Quoted in ibid., 67. Another student in Harnack's seminar recalled Bonhoeffer's frustration with Harnack, pointing out what Bonhoeffer perceived as his weakness: "Harnack never goes beyond the *Epistle of Clement*. If only he would hold a seminar on the Reformation" (ibid). This statement, while identifying Bonhoeffer's independence, also points to Bonhoeffer's own interests.

7. DBWE 11:76.

8. Kelly and Nelson summarize the relationship in the following manner: "The young Bonhoeffer had, indeed, been won over to Barth's dialectical theology, but not without critical reservations and that flair for maintaining his independence from any system regardless of the insights he might absorb from Barth or any other source of inspiration." Kelly and Nelson, "Editors' Introduction," *TF*, 6.

9. Ibid., 7.

it came to Christology he had long-lasting reservations;[10] for that reason he retained his independence.[11]

This independent strain in Bonhoeffer's thought has been picked up and emphasized by Bonhoeffer scholars as well. Michael DeJonge acknowledges that Bonhoeffer's reading of Barth placed his "student theology in tension with the theological climate in Berlin." At the same time, he never completely rejected the Berlin tradition, but "was apparently content to live at least a little while longer among the corpses." As a result, Bonhoeffer concluded that theology had arrived at an "impasse, oriented *either* to the world *or* to the Word. A central task of Bonhoeffer's early theology, from 1927 to 1933, is the negotiation of this impasse."[12]

Similarly, Jonathan Sorum describes Bonhoeffer's independence as growing out of this same tension, which leads to a "third way:" "While gratefully borrowing from both the liberal tradition of his Berlin teachers and Karl Barth's revolt against that tradition, Bonhoeffer went his own way, a way that he believed encompassed the main concern of both and at the same time avoided their serious deficiencies. Bonhoeffer conceived of this third way as an attempt to recover Luther."[13]

10. See *DB-ER*, 178.

11. See ibid., 75, where, after describing Bonhoeffer's early embrace of Barth's theology, Bethge concludes, "Thus, despite his gratitude for the essence of this theology, Bonhoeffer retained his right to think critically and independently." See also Green, "Editor's Introduction," DBWE 1:3.

12. Michael DeJonge, *Bonhoeffer's Theological Formation: Berlin, Barth, and Protestant Theology* (Oxford: Oxford University Press, 2012), 3–5.

13. Sorum, "Eschatological Boundary," 24. He goes to explain that from liberal theology Bonhoeffer learned "loyalty to the world and respect for what exists. . . . He, like them, did not wish to make claims about God that would somehow devalue the reality of the empirical." With Barth, on the other hand, he knew that all theology must begin with God. "But his teachers could only affirm the world by, in effect, denying God" and Barth could only affirm God by denying the world. As a result, "the liberals have only ethics (the world) and cannot make dogmatics (God) intelligible and Barth has only dogmatics (God) and cannot make ethics (the world) intelligible." To overcome this deficiency, Bonhoeffer turned to Luther, who "was not caught in such a bind. For Luther, God is not free *from* the world but free *for* the world. The Word and Sacraments set Christians in a 'Christmas world,' a world in

As a result, Hans Pfeifer, commenting on Bonhoeffer's student years, concludes, Bonhoeffer "cannot be assigned to a particular school. K. Holl, R. Seeberg, and K. Barth all influenced him; from all three he inherited crucial elements, and over against all three he maintained his independence in theological questioning and searching."[14] Eberhard Bethge concurs, when in his attempt to locate Bonhoeffer on the twentieth-century map, he asks, "On what stool does Bonhoeffer belong?"[15] Finally, Renate Wind makes a similar point in the introduction to her biography of Bonhoeffer; she begins with a statement that cannot fail to draw the reader into imaging the independent person Bonhoeffer really was:

> The prisoner in cell 92 of Tegel Military Prison in Berlin is a special case. Dietrich Bonhoeffer, aged thirty-seven, a lecturer in theology and a pastor banned from teaching, most recently acting as a courier for the Abwehr, arrested on suspicion of conspiracy against the Fuhrer and the Reich, is the star prisoner. He comes from those better-class circles which so far have not been associated with conspiracy against the state. For years his father has been head of the Berlin clinic, the Charite,

which God is truly present, present in the church itself. 'Die Gemeinde ist der gegenwärtige Christus selbst.' The church's life in the world is God's life in the world. So dogmatics and ethics are one. . . . Luther could do both dogmatics and ethics at the same time. For him, everything was of a piece; dogmatics, ethics, God, human beings, and world were all one reality, and not only was God really God within this one reality, but precisely God's being God is what made everything else real. Bonhoeffer seeks to follow Luther" (25–29). Cf. Jonathan Sorum, "Bonhoeffer's Early Interpretation of Luther as the Source of His Basic Theological Paradigm," *Fides et Historia* 29, no. 2 (Summer 1997): 39, where he states this same conclusion more pointedly: "Bonhoeffer seeks to follow Luther. Bonhoeffer's way between his teachers and Barth is not some compromise between the two, but a third way, the way of Martin Luther. Any understanding of the theology of Dietrich Bonhoeffer must begin with an understanding of his understanding of the theology of Martin Luther, for Bonhoeffer's task was nothing else than to 'show us Luther.'" Finally, von Soosten, "Editor's Afterword," DBWE 1:305, makes the following conclusion concerning their relationship: "The debate with Karl Barth also is continued in these letters [from prison]. And again and again it is Martin Luther—as already in *Sanctorum Communio*—who in this tension was consulted, who posed questions, and who precisely as such was the mediating theologian."

14. Hans Pfeifer, "Vorwort der Herausgeber," *Jugend und Studium, 1918–1927*, DBW 9:2. See also Pfeifer, "Dietrich Bonhoeffer's Studienfreundschaft mit Walter Dreß: Briefe aus den Jahren 1920–1927," *Zeitschrift für Neure Theologiegeschichte* 4 (1997): 266–67.
15. Bethge, conversation with author, October 6, 1991.

> and his uncle is City Commandment of Berlin. In 1943 a man with such connections is still a rare phenomenon in the prisons of Hitler's Germany. So the prison staff is not sure how to treat him. The warders in Tegel prison have clear images of those who are their enemies. Anyone sent here is either a "Bolshevik agent," a "destroyer of morale," a "cowardly deserter," or simply a "Communist swine." So anyone in this prison may with impunity be abused as a "hooligan" and be victimized as an "enemy of the state." However, one cannot take that tone with the new occupant of cell 92. Nor does he fit into any of the usual categories. He is not where he belongs.[16]

This independence is one factor that must be considered when examining the character of Bonhoeffer's theological development. But at the core of this independence from all theological "schools" is the one constant—the influence of and commitment to the theology of Martin Luther. It is that constant that gives him a unique voice. By and large, Luther is the only theologian of whom Bonhoeffer is not critical; Luther is always quoted in a favorable light. By means of his reading of Luther, Bonhoeffer is able to steer a middle path between his teachers and Barth.

While Bonhoeffer draws on Luther to establish his theological independence from his teachers, his interpretation of Luther is also marked by that same independent spirit. As both Bethge and Ebeling, among others, point out, his orientation taken from Luther forms the basis for the new direction of his theology. Jörg Rades picks up on this notion when he states that Bonhoeffer moved toward "new

16. Renate Wind, *Dietrich Bonhoeffer: A Spoke in the Wheel,* trans. John Bowden (Grand Rapids: Eerdmans, 1991), ix. In addition to being a description of Bonhoeffer's personality, such a statement also points to what was perhaps the most important factor in Bonhoeffer's leaving the safety of America behind and returning to Germany and what awaited him there—his faith in Jesus Christ. It would be a mistake to focus only on Bonhoeffer's independence in thought, for it was his having been "conformed to Christ" that shaped his response to Hitler and the political events within Germany and the church. For Bonhoeffer Jesus was always more than a subject for theology, Jesus was a living person—the subject of his faith. It was for that reason that Christology could not be reduced to an abstract principle but was always an expression of faith. See James Burtness, *Shaping the Future: The Ethics of Dietrich Bonhoeffer* (Philadelphia: Fortress Press, 1985), 31.

Lutheran horizons" and "his own Luther interpretation."[17] Pfeifer draws a similar conclusion: "Bonhoeffer elaborated this interpretation of Luther independently; it went far beyond anything that Holl and Seeberg saw in Luther. In fact, Bonhoeffer explicitly distinguished between Holl's interpretation of Luther and his own, and he agreed with Gogarten when he criticized Holl for underestimating the importance Luther attached to Christ."[18]

Bonhoeffer's independence, even when it comes to Luther, was due in part to the fact that it was not his intention or desire to duplicate Luther's thought.[19] In his *Ethics* he clearly pointed out that the goal of theology was not to "return to Luther or Paul," but to be faithful to God's word in this time and place:

> From the beginning, the qualitatively ultimate word of God forbids us from looking at the way of Paul or the way of Luther as if we had to go that way again. . . . Strictly speaking, we should not repeat Luther's way any more than the way of the woman caught in adultery, the thief on the cross, Peter's denial, or Paul's zealous persecution of Christ. The qualitatively ultimate word excludes every method once and for all. It is the word of forgiveness, and only in forgiving does it justify.[20]

17. Jörg Rades, "The Intellectual Background of Dietrich Bonhoeffer" (University of Saint Andrews, unedited manuscript), 4.
18. Hans Pfeifer, "The Forms of Justification," in *A Bonhoeffer Legacy: Essays in Understanding,* ed. A. J. Klassen (Grand Rapids: Eerdmans, 1981), 20.
19. Bonhoeffer's position also reflects the changed context of the twentieth century. He was quite conscientious in his reading the "signs of the times," insisting that theology always be done from within the midst of the world. Theology was not an abstraction apart from reality but was embedded in reality. Because Bonhoeffer's theology bore this characteristic, scholars such as Klemens von Klemperer, "Beyond Luther? Dietrich Bonhoeffer and Resistance against National Socialism." *Pro Ecclesia* 6, no. 2 (Spring 1997): 192, and William Kuhns, *In Pursuit of Dietrich Bonhoeffer* (New York: Doubleday, 1969), 88, say that Bonhoeffer moves "beyond Luther" or "diverts from" Luther, and Green can conclude that since Bonhoeffer doesn't think in "sixteenth-century conceptuality," he "unwittingly assimilates Luther into the modern era, thereby translating him with one stroke through four centuries of history" (*Bonhoeffer: A Theology of Sociality,* 289), while Burtness characterizes Bonhoeffer's theological agenda as one that "reformulates" or "recasts" Luther and the Lutheran tradition (*Shaping the Future,* 70ff).
20. *Ethics,* DBWE 6:150. Bonhoeffer provides additional insights into his understanding of Luther later in the *Ethics* manuscript; in describing "Luther's return from the monastery into the

God's word prevents any such replication.

However, in all cases, Luther is the one theologian that Bonhoeffer sides with, as is seen in his disagreement with church leaders in Germany. In fighting for "genuine Lutheranism" in the twentieth century, Bonhoeffer insisted that if Luther were alive at this time in history, he would say the opposite of what was being said. He was not seeking to change Luther; instead, he was using Luther against the Lutherans in 1930s Germany. What he meant was that Luther would say the opposite,[21] not of what Luther himself said in the sixteenth century, but of what the Lutherans were saying Luther said. Bonhoeffer observed what had become of the church in his day and wrote about the "loss of the Reformation calling and of Reformation responsibilities in society."[22] In responding to what he perceived to be an acculturated church, which by its very nature was in danger of losing the gospel, he used Luther against what had become a "pseudo-Lutheranism" that had given up its role as a protest movement: "It is certainly in line with Luther that the response to the call of Jesus Christ might in a concrete case consist in leaving a particular earthly vocation in which it is no longer possible to live responsibly. It is only pseudo-Lutheranism, with its faith in the sanctity of vocational obligations and earthly orders as such, that cannot conceive this thought."[23]

To say that Bonhoeffer possessed an independent voice does not imply that he ignored or turned his back on the traditions of the church. Instead, he uses those traditions and, in so doing, transforms them. Seeing the weaknesses of the contemporary voices of his day,

world," he insists that Luther correctly understood the New Testament understanding of vocation. In this same discussion, he contrasts Luther with "pseudo-Lutheranism" (291).

21. See James Woelfel, *Bonhoeffer's Theology: Classical and Revolutionary* (Nashville: Abingdon, 1970), 313n39.

22. Larry Rasmussen, "A Community of the Cross" *Dialog* 30, no. 2 (Spring 1991): 158.

23. *Ethics*, DBWE 6:291.

he drew upon the classical formulations of the faith to speak with a renewed voice. When he did not agree with his teachers, he was quick to point out places of disagreement; when he believed the church of 1930s Germany had compromised its witness, again he drew upon the rich traditions of the past to correct it. In every case, Luther was his conversation partner. But at the same time, his interest was not in merely repeating the words of Luther. What he found in Luther was an authentic voice that spoke the truth of the gospel as clearly in the twentieth century as it had in the sixteenth.[24] As a result, Bonhoeffer was able to remain free of any and all influences that did not take the picture of Christ as portrayed in Scripture at its center. His independence is demonstrated in his relationships with his teachers, foremost Karl Holl, from whom he was introduced to Luther.

## Influences on Bonhoeffer's Theological Orientation

Eberhard Bethge's detailed biography of Dietrich Bonhoeffer reminds us of the importance of the connection between Bonhoeffer's life and his theology.[25] His is a contextually-based

24. Bonhoeffer's intent should be discerned. Gerhard Ebeling (November 11, 1991 interview) says Bonhoeffer is best described as "a systematic, not historical" theologian. He was not a Luther scholar nor was he interested in doing historical research into Luther's theology. He never taught a course on Luther. He wanted, however, to proclaim the gospel and for that he found Luther's witness the best. As such, what he sought to do was to bring the tradition of the church into dialogue with the modern world. As a creative thinker, he used Luther to address issues facing the his world. Cf. Wolf Krötke, "Dietrich Bonhoeffer and Martin Luther," in *Bonhoeffer's Intellectual Formation: Theology and Philosophy in His Thought*, ed. Peter Frick. (Tübingen: Mohr Siebeck, 2008), 57; Bonhoeffer was not interested in creating a "picture of Luther": "For him, Luther—who himself rejected such a picture—represented an unparalleled theological, intellectual, and spiritual impulse and source for his own experiences of faith and reality."
25. A couple of examples illustrate this. Bethge quotes from a 1933 radio address given by Bonhoeffer, in which Bonhoeffer recognizes that his social/historical location has had an effect on him and his understanding of the world: "There is an invisible but impenetrable line dividing those who were in the war from those, only slightly younger, who grew up and became mature at the time of the collapse" (*DB-ER*, 21). Another early example comes from Bethge's description of Berlin's influence: "Dietrich Bonhoeffer was neither born in

theology, the contours of which were shaped by the prevailing issues confronting the church of his day. Therefore, in order to properly understand the shifts and developments in his theology, one must consider the context out of which it arises and to which it responds.

This is especially important when attempting to understand the context for Bonhoeffer's intellectual development, for which Bethge and others give ample information. Particularly important for his emerging theological position is the academic milieu of liberal Berlin in the 1920s.[26] The University of Berlin had become the center of liberal Protestant theology in the late nineteenth and early twentieth centuries. By the time Bonhoeffer had become a student there in the 1920s, however, reform movements were changing the theological landscape of Germany. As a theological student in Berlin at this time, Bonhoeffer was a part of this changing context.

Berlin nor did he die there, but it was the scene of all the important turning points in his thought and actions. From the beginning to the end of his career, the ideas that drew recognition and conflict developed here. In Berlin he enjoyed all the privileges of his sphere of life, and it was there that he eventually risked life and limb for their sake" (*DB-ER*, 23). For further examples of this emphasis, see Renate Bethge, "Bonhoeffer's Family and Its Significance for His Theology," in Larry Rasmussen, *Dietrich Bonhoeffer—His Significance for North Americans* (Minneapolis: Fortress Press, 1990), 1–30; Ferdinand Schlingensiepen, *Dietrich Bonhoeffer 1906–1945: Martyr, Thinker, Man of Resistance*, trans. Isabel Best (New York: T & T Clark, 2010); Renate Wind, *Dietrich Bonhoeffer: A Spoke in the Wheel,* trans. John Bowden (Grand Rapids: Eerdmans, 1991); Peter Frick, ed, *Bonhoeffer's Intellectual Formation: Theology and Philosophy in His Thought* (Tübingen: Mohr Siebeck, 2008); John A. Moses, *The Reluctant Revolutionary: Dietrich Bonhoeffer's Collision with Prusso-German History.* (New York: Berghahn Books, 2009); John W. de Gruchy, ed., *The Cambridge Companion to Dietrich Bonhoeffer* (New York: Cambridge University Press, 1999); Thomas Day, *Dietrich Bonhoeffer on Christian Community and Common Sense*, Toronto Studies in Theology, vol. 11, Bonhoeffer Series, no. 2 (New York: The Edwin Mellen Press, 1982); Christian Gremmels and Hans Pfeifer, *Theologie und Biographie. Zum Beispiel Dietrich Bonhoeffer* (Munich: Chr. Kaiser, 1983); Joachim von Soosten, *Die Sozialität der Kirche: Theologie und Theorie der Kirche in Dietrich Bonhoeffers* "Sanctorum Communio" (Munich: Chr. Kaiser, 1992), 196ff; Hans-Jürgen Abromeit, *Das Geheimnis Christi: Dietrich Bonhoeffers erfahrungsbezogene Christologie* (Neukirchen-Vluyn: Neukirchener, 1991); and Robin Lovin, "Biographical Context," in *New Studies in Bonhoeffer's Ethics*, ed. William J. Peck (Lewiston, NY: Edwin Mellon, 1987), 67–101.

26. See DeJonge, *Bonhoeffer's Theological Formation*, among others.

Two renewal movements had the profound effect of redrawing the theological boundaries: the Luther renaissance, represented primarily by Karl Holl,[27] and dialectical theology, with Karl Barth, among others, as its proponents. In the aftermath of World War I, the intellectual world of Germany was in ferment. In the field of theology, this was exhibited by a radical questioning of, and loss of faith in, the theological orientation of liberal theology, the dominant theological voice in late-nineteenth–early-twentieth-century German Protestantism, as expressed by Albrecht Ritschl and others. Whatever weaknesses this theological school exhibited came to be strongly questioned following the experiences of the war. Against this backdrop the theologies of both Holl and Barth emerged, and they offered their criticisms against it. It is with these two movements that Bonhoeffer identifies himself and, indeed, it might be part of the enduring quality of his theological reflections that he was able to integrate these influences into his own developing theology.[28]

One of the lasting results brought by these theological movements was the redirection of theology to the rediscovered sources of the Reformation, anchoring it once again in some of the Reformation's central categories. This was the intent as well as an important contribution made by both Holl and Barth. Holl, for example, developed his Luther interpretation in response to Ernst Troeltsch's claim that Luther was a medieval man with nothing to say to the modern world. In contrast to Troeltsch, Holl claimed that Luther was relevant for the modern world; in fact, "he based his study

27. See Gregory A. Walter, "Historical Introduction," in Hans Iwand, *The Righteousness of Faith according to Luther,* ed. Virgil F. Thompson, trans. Randi H. Lundell (Eugene: OR: Wipf & Stock, 2008), 4: "This movement consisted of theologians and historians who aimed to renew German church and political life by drawing from the theology of the early Luther. It brought together students of Karl Holl such as Emanuel Hirsch and 'positive theologians' such as Carl Stange, Rudolf Hermann, and Paul Althaus."

28. Bonhoeffer studied under Holl at the University of Berlin, but only later did he discover Barth's theology in the years 1924–1925. See *DB-ER*, 68ff.

upon exacting historical and philological examination of sources, relating Luther to the whole spiritual development of the West."[29] Taking Luther's understanding of justification as the central point for theology, Holl wrote several essays relating the issues of modern theology to it. The title of one such essay illuminates this orientation: "Was hat die Rechtfertigungslehre dem modernen Menschen zu sagen? (What does the doctrine of justification say to modern humankind?)"[30]

Although it did not do so in the same manner as Holl and the Luther renaissance, dialectical theology likewise captured the spirit of the Reformation with its emphasis on the primacy of the revelation of God's word, thereby giving theology a new starting point. In this regard, Karl Barth made a sharp break from nineteenth-century liberal theology by making God's revelation and not human experience the starting point for all theology.

Early in his career, these diverse influences began to shape the direction and character of Bonhoeffer's theology. Each was influential in its own way, but neither of them decisively. By Bonhoeffer's own admission, he was captivated by the new dialectical theology, while at the same time refusing the label *Barthian* for himself. He always maintained a careful distance from Barth's position, at times leveling harsh criticism against it. For example, in Bonhoeffer's *habilitationschrift*, defended at the end of his student days in December 1927, he stated his fear that dialectical theology

29. See John Dillenberger, *God Hidden and Revealed: the Interpretation of Luther's* Deus Absconditus *and Its Significance for Religious Thought* (Philadelphia: Muhlenberg Press, 1953), 39. Dillenberger's study defines the context for the change in Luther interpretation from that of Holl's generation; hence, it also provides insights into the context for Bonhoeffer's Luther interpretation. Bonhoeffer followed Holl's lead in this regard, to the point of insisting in *LPP* that Luther's reform movement was the beginning of the modern era; it was on this basis that he called for a nonreligious Christianity.

30. Karl Holl, *Gesammelte Aufsätze zur Kirchengeschichte*, vol. 3, *Der Westen,* (Darmstadt: Wissenschaftliche Buchgesellschaft, 1965), 558–67.

"is in danger of neglecting the historicity of Jesus."[31] That was a fear that would only grow in coming years. And while he leveled severe criticism against liberal theology, he could never escape what he believed to be its open and honest dealings with the world.[32] But while all these influences converged to shape Bonhoeffer's theology, it is the figure of Martin Luther who stands out as the strongest influence. Bonhoeffer's introduction to Luther can be traced back to Karl Holl, who was Bonhoeffer's professor at the University of Berlin. It is the influence of Luther that turns Bonhoeffer away from both the liberal school and dialectical theology.[33] As will be demonstrated in what follows, the figure of Luther is the dominant influence shaping Bonhoeffer's theology. According to Bethge, it is Karl Holl and his studies of Luther that had the deepest impact on the young theological student.[34]

31. DBWE 9:441. See also the notes from his reading of Karl Barth's *Christliche Dogmatik*, ibid, 473ff; in his argument with Barth, Bonhoeffer makes use of Luther's doctrine of justification to clarify his point. Cf. Bonhoeffer's comments in his curriculum vitae, DBWE 10:235.
32. Regarding the lasting affect of liberal theology on Bonhoeffer's theology, please note Bonhoeffer's comments on the occasion of Harnack's death (see n42, below), speaking of his admiration for liberal theology's honest approach to the world, while at the same time identifying its weakness by allowing the world to set the agenda; mixed with this are his comments in *LPP* about being a "modern theologian" who owes much to the nineteenth-century liberal theology; DBWE 8:498–99.
33. See Joachim von Soosten, "Editor's Afterword," DBWE 1:290ff. He describes the intellectual context that shapes the development of Bonhoeffer's theology in the following manner. Referring to Bonhoeffer's own description of his *Sanctorum Communio* as "half-historical, half-systematic," he maintains that Bonhoeffer placed himself in the middle of the twentieth century rather than being a part of the nineteenth century. Not content to reducing the Christian witness to historical investigation, Bonhoeffer joined the new dialectical theology in reintroducing the systematic (dogmatic) question into theological dialogue. "Theology is unable and unwilling to remain on a historical level, especially if the historical approach itself is fraught with theological implications that require clarification; theology presses toward doctrinal theology, since the past witness of faith needs to be justified critically before one's own present" (291). But, as becomes evident in *SC*, from the very beginning Bonhoeffer "seeks to correct the fundamental theological decisions of Barth, though out of basic sympathy for those decisions. It can be safely assumed, moreover, that Bonhoeffer consciously intends this controversy with Barth" (292). Consciously intended, because Bonhoeffer's position comes directly from that of Luther, as taught by Karl Holl. But in addition, he "now draws on Luther's own writings, in which [the] link between the christological basis and the social structure of the church-community is developed intensively" (293).
34. See below, pg. 52.

It was in Holl's seminars that Bonhoeffer was introduced to and came to love Luther. So highly influenced by Holl was Bonhoeffer that in student papers he relied almost completely on Luther quotes used by Holl, taking the same position as that of his teacher.[35] But only a cursory reading of Bonhoeffer's writings is necessary to see that differences between teacher and student developed early. Not much time elapsed before Holl's conclusions were challenged and eventually replaced by new research. Bonhoeffer, like others of his generation, saw flaws in Holl's interpretation and, based on new readings of Luther's works, made needed changes.[36] With regard to Bonhoeffer's relationship to Holl, these challenges and changes came primarily in the area of Christology and allowed Bonhoeffer to move beyond Karl Holl, while at the same time remain independent from Karl Barth.

## Holl and Luther: Bonhoeffer's Introduction to Luther

Dietrich Bonhoeffer began his university studies in 1923 at the age of seventeen. Having already declared his intention of becoming a theologian as a boy,[37] he enrolled at the University of Tübingen,

35. Bonhoeffer's papers written for Holl will be examined in chapter 3.
36. It should be noted, however, that Bonhoeffer did not enter the debate as a Luther scholar; see Christian Gremmels, "Rechtfertigung und Nachfolge: Martin Luther in Dietrich Bonhoeffer's Buch 'Nachfolge,'" in *Dietrich Bonhoeffer Heute: Die Aktualität seines Lebens und Werkes*, ed. Rainer Mayer and Peter Zimmerling (Giessen and Basel: Brunnen Verlag, 1992), 82, where he indicates that in Bonhoeffer we are not dealing with Luther research for its own sake nor do we have a Luther apologetic at any price. Cf. Krötke, "Dietrich Bonhoeffer and Martin Luther," 54, who indicates that Bonhoeffer was not convinced of the interpretations of either Holl or Seeberg, so "to return to the real Luther" became the objective of his study.
37. See *DB-ER*, 34–37. This declaration was very surprising to the members of his family who were not churchgoing; rather, at least from his father's and brothers' perspective, the church was a "poor, feeble, boring, petty and bourgeois institution." Nevertheless, when he met with opposition from his family he replied, "In that case I shall reform it." Along these lines, Bethge has also pointed out a significant difference between Bonhoeffer and Paul Tillich. While the latter moved from the church to the world, Bonhoeffer moved from the world to the church. This difference in orientation accounts for some of the differences in theological method between the two. See also Schlingensiepen, *Dietrich Bonhoeffer 1906–1945*, 16–17.

according to family tradition, and began his theological studies under Adolf Schlatter,[38] a leading New Testament scholar, who, according to Bethge, was the only teacher at Tübingen "who had any lasting influence on him" and the only theologian, apart from Luther, who "was so fully represented in Bonhoeffer's library in later years, or so frequently consulted."[39] Even in later life, after Bonhoeffer and Schlatter had disagreed over National Socialism, Bonhoeffer held him in high regard. "Bonhoeffer always acknowledged that Schlatter drew attention to *loci classici* usually left to the Catholics. He hoped to go beyond Schlatter and free these passages from earlier interpretations, and make them binding again for Protestants by linking them to Christology."[40]

It was while he was at Tübingen that Bonhoeffer was also introduced to liberal theology, as represented by Schleiermacher and Ritschl; in addition, he spent time studying the history of religion and philosophy, including a seminar on Kant's *Critique of Pure Reason.* Of Bonhoeffer's time at Tübingen, Bethge says it was a year "characterized by his wide range of interest, without a firm commitment to any particular area, and by a persistent exploration of the epistemological field."[41] Nevertheless, as these brief remarks indicate, Bonhoeffer's early training provided the foundations for his study of theology.

38. See Mark R. Correll, *Shepherds of the Empire: Germany's Conservative Protestant Leadership—1888–1919* (Minneapolis: Fortress Press, 2014), esp. chapter 4, for a discussion of Schlatter's life and theology.

39. *DB-ER*, 53–54.

40. Ibid., 54.

41. Ibid., 56. Another significant influence on Bonhoeffer during these years, one that extended beyond the short time in Tübingen, was the friendship that he developed with Walter Dress, who would later become Bonhoeffer's brother-in-law. The significance of Dress's relationship to Bonhoeffer is displayed in a series of letters written between 1925 and 1927. These letters make clear the extent to which these young theologians were influenced by Luther's theology. See Hans Pfeifer, "Dietrich Bonhoeffers Studienfreundschaft mit Walter Dreß." The letters have been translated and are included in DBWE 9. See chapter 3 for an examination of the letters.

After his initial year of study in Tübingen, Bonhoeffer returned to Berlin where he studied under Adolf von Harnack,[42] the church historian; Reinhold Seeberg,[43] the systematic theologian and historian of dogma; and Karl Holl,[44] the leader of the "Luther renaissance."[45]

42. The influence that Harnack wielded can be seen in Bonhoeffer's praise of him. When Bonhoeffer had finished his studies in Berlin, he wrote a note of thanks to Harnack, in which he stated, "What I have learned and come to understand in your seminar is too closely associated with my whole personality for me to be able ever to forget it" (DBWE 9:439). Later, in 1930, on the occasion of Harnack's death, Bonhoeffer, speaking on behalf of Harnack's pupils, said, "It became clear to us through him that truth is born only of freedom. We saw in him the champion of the free expression of a truth once recognized, who formed his free judgment each and every time, and expressed it clearly whatever the anxious inhibitions of the crowd. This made him . . . the friend of all young people who spoke their opinions freely, as he asked of them. . . . Because we knew that with him we were in good and solicitous hands, we saw him as the bulwark against all trivialization and stagnation, against all the fossilization of intellectual life" (DBWE 10:380). Harnack's influence can still be seen in *LPP*; see Bethge, "The Challenge of Dietrich Bonhoeffer's Life and Theology," *The Chicago Theological Seminary Review* 51, no. 2 (February 1961), 5: "We might remember Bonhoeffer's strong plea for intellectual honesty in the prison letters!"
43. See *DB-ER*, 69–81; Bethge identifies what is a complex relationship with Seeberg. While Bonhoeffer "learned about Augustine, Thomas Aquinas, the scholastics, Melanchthon and Luther" under Seeberg's tutelage, their obvious fundamental differences emerged quite early while Bonhoeffer was still a student, preventing Seeberg from having a lasting influence. In 1925, Bonhoeffer wrote his first student essay for Seeberg and its "result was near-failure" (79) (cf. DBWE 9:299n101). Seeberg's impression was that it was simply "a disturbing exercise in Barthianism." According to Bethge, while Bonhoeffer learned much from Seeberg, he quickly became critical of "Seeberg's attempt to harmonize the Bible and the modern spirit, Luther and idealism, theology and philosophy" (70–71). Bonhoeffer's marginal notes on Seeberg's interpretation of Luther show the differences between the two. "In the volume on Luther in Seeberg's history of dogmatics, Seeberg stated: 'This enables one to understand the remarkable circumstance that Luther uses religious *experience* as well as the Scriptures as the witness and canon of truth. But in this it is experience that establishes the certainty of the truth of the contents of Scripture.' Here Bonhoeffer wrote a few words in the margin that underscore his basic and theological difference with Seeberg: 'No! Scripture is the Lord's and is conveyed via the church: preach!" (71). John A. Phillips provides a brief commentary on Bonhoeffer's relationship and response to Seeberg's theological position, which was marked by tension and disagreement over fundamental theological categories. As result, he concludes, "There was little theological *rapport* between Bonhoeffer and his teacher once his dissertation was completed. One suspects that Seeberg never had the personal influence over Bonhoeffer that Harnack and Barth enjoyed. In a letter to a friend in 1930 Bonhoeffer wrote of one of Seeberg's sermons which he had recently heard as 'shameful . . . a religious chat.' Both Seeberg and Bonhoeffer were teaching at the university for the next several years, but after 1931, Bonhoeffer never mentioned his teacher in his writings again" (*Christ for Us in the Theology of Dietrich Bonhoeffer* [New York: Harper & Row, 1967], 41–44).
44. Bethge, "Challenge of Dietrich Bonhoeffer's Life and Thought," 4: "When Bonhoeffer took up theology in Berlin . . . Troeltsch had just died. Karl Holl was still lecturing. In his Luther

While the relationship with Harnack is too complex to analyze solely along the lines of theology,[46] Seeberg's influence was quite marginal and transitory, this in spite of Seeberg having been Bonhoeffer's faculty advisor; it was Karl Holl and his interpretation of Luther that made their impact on Bonhoeffer.[47]

seminar Bonhoeffer got a magnificent introduction and came to love Luther above anyone else, though he soon criticized Holl's interpretation."

45. Although this term is regularly applied to Karl Holl, as Johannes Wallmann has suggested, it is probably more appropriate to distinguish between various approaches to Luther's theology, thereby limiting the role of Holl and his followers, so designated as the "Holl School." See Walter F. Bense, editor's introduction, in Karl Holl, *The Reconstruction of Morality*, ed. James Luther Adams and Walter F. Bense (Minneapolis: Augsburg, 1979), 9. See also Walter, "Historical Introduction." Martin Rumscheidt, "The Formation of Bonhoeffer's Theology," in de Gruchy, *Cambridge Companion to Dietrich Bonhoeffer*, 59–60, provides a perspective on what was at stake: "The critical question about how the legacy associated with Luther's name was to be properly received was very much in the air, especially with regard to the widely held perception of Luther as the 'essential German' who helped 'the metaphysical essence of the Germans attain to self awareness.'. . . One of the liabilities of focusing on the theology of Luther rather than on its objectification in the changing historical forms of church-practice and polity and their results in civil life was that it became connected with other systems of thought and their epistemologies. Consequently, Luther's theology came into the hands of left-wing and right-wing epigones: the orthodox scholastics and the humanists, both of whom developed the anthropocentrism which led to what modernity came to call 'religion.' Whether we look at Pietism, the Enlightenment or Idealism, the system of thought prevailed over legacy. Through the study of the early Luther and his theology, the 'Luther Renaissance' sought to overcome a *Luther Orthodoxy* that was becoming vacuous, and a *Luther Pietism* that turned faith into a matter of pious, individual conscience."
46. Yet even in terms of theology, there is a complexity that cannot easily be defined, other than to say that while Bonhoeffer held Harnack in high esteem and praised his contributions, they differed on the basic understanding of theology. This is clearly the case with regard to Christology. On that point, they held opposite views. Carl-Jürgen Kaltenborn, "Adolf von Harnack and Bonhoeffer," in Klassen, *Bonhoeffer Legacy*, 49–52, for example, notes the marked difference on this question, labeling Harnack's a "Jesuology"in which no mention is made of God and man, while Bonhoeffer, who focuses on the humanity of Jesus, "demonstrates a Christology in the full sense of the word."
47. According to Bethge, the essays Bonhoeffer wrote at this time "reveal which ideas Bonhoeffer was exposed to and which ones remained foreign to him. At the university in Berlin he was confronted with the historical-critical method, early Christianity, Luther and Lutheranism, and the nineteenth century. In comparison, he had little interest in or exposure to the Old Testament, Calvin and his world (which he almost completely ignored), and the great medieval theologians. Yet he discovered the new world of dialectical theology on his own" (*DB-ER*, 88). See also Rumscheidt, "Formation of Bonhoeffer's Theology," 51–59, for a summary of Bonhoeffer's teachers and their influence on him.

Bethge summarizes both the orientation and the lasting appreciation that Bonhoeffer gained from Holl in the following manner:

> Bonhoeffer appreciated Holl's epochal move into the center of Luther's doctrine of justification, as a contrast to a vague cultural Protestantism, although he felt it to be too weakly anchored in Luther's Christology. But Holl had a lasting impact on him. In 1943, in Tegel prison, Bonhoeffer had the three volumes of Holl's collected essays on church history sent to him. As a student, Bonhoeffer had seriously considered studying under Holl; Holl's early death ended such considerations.[48]

In particular, it was Holl's doctrine of justification that had a lasting impact. Holl "irrevocably reinforced in him the doctrine of 'by grace alone' as the one article by which the church stands and falls."[49] Thereafter, Luther's *cor curvum in se* became a keyword for Bonhoeffer, who used it in his fight against the optimism of idealism and the localization of God in the individual's mind. Yet, while the insights of Luther's doctrine of justification remained central for Bonhoeffer's theology, at an early age he became critical of Holl's particular interpretation, because it threatened the *extra me* character of faith. It therefore becomes important to remember Bethge's caveat, which is crucial to understanding Bonhoeffer's theology: while he liked Holl's concentration on Luther's doctrine of justification, he found that it was too weakly anchored in Luther's Christology.[50]

48. *DB-ER*, 69.
49. Ibid., 68; see also Sorum, "Eschatological Boundary," chapter 1.
50. *DB-ER*, 68. This point will be brought out later in the section examining Bonhoeffer's response to Holl. It must be noted, however, that justification, which he reframed in terms of Christology to more accurately reflect Luther's position, remained central to Bonhoeffer's thought. Christian Gremmels's study on the role of justification in Bonhoeffer's *Nachfolge* indicates the extent to which this doctrine remained a central premise for understanding God's working in the world. See Gremmels, "Rechtfertigung und Nachfolge," 82–99. The central importance of the doctrine of justification for Bonhoeffer's argument in *Nachfolge* has also been favorably evaluated by Jonathan Sorum, "Cheap Grace, Costly Grace, and Just Plain Grace," *Lutheran Forum* 27, no. 3 (August 1993): 20–23. See also his "Eschatological Boundary," chapter 1.

Holl's popularity had soared as a result of the publication in 1921 of his volume of essays on Luther's theology,[51] leading the likes of Harnack to call him "the renewer of Lutheranism."[52] Reflecting on the significance of Holl's work on Luther, Hans Lietzmann, Harnack's successor at the University of Berlin, said,

> In 1921, when Holl's "Luther" appeared, the book seemed like a sudden and tremendous revelation. It was a victorious symbol of unity for our evangelical church, broken up by so many kinds of conflicts. Holl succeeded in overcoming many old hatreds and awakening again in many hearts the awareness of the integrated foundation of all our religious and churchly life in the Gospel, recovered and interpreted by the genius of Martin Luther. Here Luther's spirit was called upon in a time of inner turmoil and reeling misconceptions to rescue our severely sick people.[53]

As a result of his newfound insights into Luther's theology, Holl became an influential teacher at the university in Berlin and beyond. He was viewed positively by liberals and Barthians alike, as he was seen as a bridge between the two.[54]

While this indeed may have been a factor in Bonhoeffer's response to him, it must be noted that it is unlikely that it was Holl's reputation alone that made him an attractive teacher to the young Bonhoeffer. It may be more the case that Holl's theological stance addressed some of Bonhoeffer's own personal needs.[55]

As a student of this great teacher Bonhoeffer wrote two seminar papers on Luther.[56] These papers show the widespread influence Holl had on Bonhoeffer's theological development. This same influence is

51. Karl Holl, *Gesammelte Aufsätze zur Kirchengeschichte*, vol. 1, *Luther* (Tübingen: J. C. B. Mohr [Paul Siebeck], 1921).
52. See E. Gordon Rupp, *The Righteousness of God: Luther Studies* (London: Hodder and Stoughton, 1953), 30.
53. Hans Lietzmann, "Ansprache bei der Beerdigung am 26 Mai 1926," in *Karl Holl: Zwei Gedächtnisreden von Adolf von Harnack und Hans Lietzmann* AKG 7, (Bonn, 1926), 4.
54. See Rupp, *Righteousness of God*, 30.
55. See von Soosten's discussion of the popularity of Holl's theology, *Sozialität der Kirche*, 130ff.

displayed in a paper written during the winter semester 1926–1927 on the problem of suffering in the book of Job, where Bonhoeffer once again simply relied on Holl's interpretation of Luther for his analysis.[57] In fact, Bonhoeffer's reliance on Holl was so strong that in many places he "simply follows the quotations given by Karl Holl."[58]

## Holl's Luther Interpretation[59]

While Holl's understanding of Luther grew out of the scholarship that preceded him, his interpretation of Luther surpassed the previous work and set new standards for Luther research.[60] Building on the work of such late-nineteenth-century scholars as Albrecht Ritschl

56. See Bonhoeffer, DBWE 9:257–84, 324–70. In addition, Bonhoeffer wrote another paper as a student that is indicative of his Lutheran orientation; see ibid., 285–300. For further reference to these papers, see chapter 3 below.
57. Ibid., 420ff.
58. Wolfgang Huber, in a letter to the author, May 27, 1992.
59. For background on Holl's Luther interpretation, see Gregory Walter, "Karl Holl (1866–1926) and the Recovery of Promise in Luther," *Lutheran Quarterly* 25 (2011): 398–413. A full-length study is provided by Walter Bodenstein, *Die Theologie Karl Holls im Spiegel des Antiken und Reformatorischen Christentums* (Berlin: Walter De Gruyter, 1968). Additional references to Holl's role in the Luther Renaissance and modern Luther research can be found in von Soosten, *Sozialität der Kirche*, 130ff; Rupp, *Righteousness of God*; Dillenberger, *God Hidden and Revealed*; Gerhard Forde, *The Law-Gospel Debate: An Interpretation of Its Historical Development* (Minneapolis: Augsburg, 1969), 120ff; David W. Lotz, *Ritschl and Luther: A Fresh Perspective on Albrecht Ritschl's Theology in the Light of His Luther Study* (Nashville: Abingdon, 1974), 153ff; and Walter F. Bense's introductions, in Karl Holl, *What Did Luther Understand by Religion?*, ed. James Luther Adams and Walter F. Bense; trans. Fred W. Meuser and Walter R. Wietze (Philadelphia: Fortress Press, 1977) and Holl, *Reconstruction of Morality*.
60. Bense provides the historical context: "Holl's essay must be understood as directed squarely against Ritschl's understanding of Luther at this point. While Ritschl (following J. C. K. von Hofmann) had sought to distinguish Luther's thought from that of Melanchthon and Lutheran Orthodoxy, Holl was able to show that Ritschl had not gone far enough in this endeavor. Holl points out elsewhere that it was Melanchthon who assumed, and taught a whole generation of Lutheran clergymen (if not all of Lutheranism) to assume, that religion necessarily aims at blessedness. But according to Holl, this assumption would give up one of Luther's greatest accomplishments; namely, the consistent elaboration of a religion that teaches one to assume full responsibility for oneself, simultaneously to recognize that all one is and has is God's free gift, and, above all, to participate (in a kind of active passivity or passive activity) in God's transformation of oneself, of others, and of the world itself. It is this basic conception that prompted Holl to look upon Calvin, in Hans Lietzmann's words, as Luther's 'only truly congenial disciple'" ("Editor's Introduction," *What Did Luther Understand By Religion?*, 3).

and Theodosius Harnack, Holl was able to overcome the impasse at which they seemed to have arrived.[61] Suffice it for our purposes to note the following achievements.

First, as a result of his training in the historical method, Holl believed that all studies of Luther must be based on a thorough examination of sources.[62]

Second, this, in turn, led him to differentiate between Luther and Lutheranism.[63] This insight enabled Holl to step into a direct relationship with the reformer that was free of all confessional narrowness.[64]

Third, his experiences of World War I led him to believe that Luther's theology was relevant for the modern context.[65] It was out

61. See Lotz, *Ritschl and Luther*, 154; Dillenberger, *God Hidden and Revealed*, Forde, *Law-Gospel Debate*, and Bodenstein, *Theologie Karl Holls* for further discussion about the developments in Luther research leading up to Karl Holl.

62. Rupp, *Righteousness of God*, 30, summarizes Holl's achievement: "But it was the great work of Karl Holl to show that Luther research [Lutherforschung] and Luther interpretation [Lutherdeutung] belong inseparably together. Holl was a great Church historian at home in many fields of ecclesiastical history, and his knowledge of Luther was profound and detailed. Lietzmann described the publication of his essays on Luther as 'like a sudden and mighty revelation,' while Harnack called him 'the renewer of Lutheranism.' Ernst Wolf has summarized his achievements in three directions. First, he made it plain that the basis of all Luther study must be the exact, historical and philological examination of the sources. Next, from his own wide knowledge of Church history, he was able to relate Luther to the whole spiritual development of the West, and to show the relevance of Luther to many important modern problems, because in fact it had been the historical work of Luther to raise them, and to point forward to their solution. Third, he showed the religion of Luther to be the theology of conscience, and that this was no relapse into subjectivism, but part of a genuinely theocentric religion based on personal relations between man and God."

These remarks parallel those of Bense, "Editor's Introduction," *What Did Luther Understand by Religion?*, 2, who describes three marks of Holl's Luther renaissance, "all of them characteristic of the historical-critical method": 1) new resources for studying Luther's theology; 2) emphasis on Luther's views as opposed to Lutheranism; 3) limited treatment of specific themes in Luther's theology and not comprehensive study of the whole.

63. See von Soosten, *Sozialität der Kirche*, 130; Bense, "Editor's Introduction," *What Did Luther Understand by Religion?* 2, 4; Lotz, *Ritschl and Luther*, 154. Bense, in his introduction to Holl, *Reconstruction of Morality*, 10, remarks that Holl's approach to interpreting Luther's theology follows that of Ritschl and von Hofmann, by focusing "on Luther as distinct from Lutheranism and on the gospel (the expression of God's love) as the perfection of religion and the source of true morality."

64. See von Soosten, *Sozialität der Kirche,* 131; Lotz, *Ritschl and Luther*, 156.

of this conviction that justification became the key to his theological interpretation of Luther. As opposed to Troeltsch, who viewed Luther as a medieval man with little to contribute to the modern discussion, Holl sought to show that Luther was a modern man and, therefore, relevant for the twentieth century.[66]

Since a full-scale investigation of Holl's theology lies beyond the scope of this this work, the focus will be limited to Holl's understanding of the doctrine of justification. This is justifiable for two reasons. Interpreters of Holl's theology have stated that justification lies at the heart of Holl's Luther interpretation. Second, according to Bethge, it was Holl's understanding of justification that had a significant impact on the young Bonhoeffer. Therefore, for the sake of understanding the changing nature of the relationship between Bonhoeffer and Holl, the doctrine of justification leads us to the heart of the matter. A place to examine this theme in Holl's theology is the essay, "What Did Luther Understand by Religion?"[67]

According to Holl, Luther's Reformation discovery of justification stemmed from his experience of being justified:[68] "Luther's

65. "[Johannes] Wallmann makes a persuasive case that Holl's *Luther* was a product of the war of 1914–1918 and its immediate aftermath." See Bense, "Editor's Introduction," *Reconstruction of Morality*, 11ff; von Soosten, *Sozialität der Kirche,* 131, makes a similar point. Cf. Pfeifer, "Dietrich Bonhoeffers Studienfreundschaft mit Walter Dreß," 266, for a description of Bonhoeffer's motivation for studying theology; the effects of WWI were decisive.

66. Holl describes Troeltsch's weakness as lying in his failure to see Luther apart from Melanchthon. Troeltsch's unwillingness to see Luther as a proponent of progress, thereby rendering him a medieval man, prevented him from seeing Luther's greatness. See *What Did Luther Understand By Religion?*, 106n74.

67. Holl, *What Did Luther Understand by Religion?*. References to this work in what follows are presented in parentheses.

68. Von Soosten, *Sozialität der Kirche*, 131, identifies experience as the key to Holl's understanding of justification. In fact, it was this conception that gave Holl's studies their united and unifying character. He writes, "According to Holl's view, the experience of justification is simply the crucial event that brings about the turn in Luther's theology. The breakthrough to the reformation insight is not so much the result of the complete formation of the doctrine of justification, but rather the consequence of the experience of justification by Luther. This, in concise words, is the meaning that Holl presents in his essay, 'What Did Luther Understand by Religion?'" He insists, however, that Holl's focus on Luther's inner psychological development was problematic.

beginnings were marked by an ingenuous devotion to the piety of the church. When he became concerned about his soul's salvation, he chose the way provided by the church for the serious-minded—he entered the monastery" ("What Did Luther Understand by Religion?," 32) where one could turn one's feelings of "unworthiness before God into the strongest possible conviction" (33). "Moreover, the monk was in a position to fulfill the Christian's supreme obligation—wholehearted love to God—more freely and therefore more perfectly than the person living in the world, and thereby was able to enhance his position before God." The monastic discipline was to provide a certain balance between the two extremes, contrition and inner satisfaction, that, while not providing absolute certainty with regard to one's own personal relationship to God, made "one's condition bearable" (34).

This piety, which had served the church for centuries, could not satisfy Luther for long. "The experience that led him into the monastery had provided an impulse that prevented his becoming really content with himself.[69] The fear of death, in which he had made his vow, affected him so deeply because it was associated with fear of the divine judgment" (34). This deep-seated fear is the *key* to understanding Luther's "inner development," for it arose out of Luther's fear of a personal "accounting to God" (35). "The prospect of rendering his account by himself" bothered Luther most of all, because he realized that at the last judgment "he would be totally on his own" (35). According to Holl's Luther, judgment was so closely tied to a sense of personal accountability that, in turn, he was driven to take it more seriously than did his contemporaries. From the outset he was forced "to go his own way in opposition to a church that

69. Cf. Bonhoeffer's understanding of Luther's going to and emerging from the monastery, *Discipleship*, DBWE 4:48–49.

favored the evasion of responsibility and emphasized the uncertainty of God's verdict" (35).

When Luther came to view this not simply as an ideal to strive after, but as God's "divine commandment," the problem became even more urgent for him. No longer was love of God a goal for life that one could seek to attain through monastic discipline; it was the expression of the "inflexible will" of God, who demanded "nothing short of perfection," the result of which was that it became "unconditional duty" (36). His perception of God led Luther to believe that "nothing short of perfection satisfied him." With that, Luther encountered an insurmountable problem. Not only was it a "difficult" task, it was "impossible" (37). As a result, he was driven to despair, so that not even the remedies of the church could bring any comfort. But such a discovery would lead Luther to only more despair: "He knew that he should seek God in love, and he desired this as earnestly as anyone. But as soon as he exerted himself he discovered that at the very outset the exertion itself invalidated the act. This was the noose in which he was caught and which threatened to strangle him" (38).

It was this experience, created by inner turmoil and upheaval, that was the breakthrough to Luther's Reformation insight. So while "Catholicism started with human ability in its effort to determine what might be attained; Luther started with God, whose honor required absolute insistence upon his will" (36).

Since fulfilling God's will was an impossibility, "the only possible solution for him was the discovery of a new side of God, particularly with respect to his attitude toward sin" (41).[70] It was the apostle Paul who "opened Luther's eyes to the fact that all his striving was a mistake." Paul helped Luther see that acceptance by God was not the prize for human struggle, because "we can never produce

70. Sin is defined as imperfection, "the very opposite of what God desires" (36).

anything perfect enough to force God's hand. However, what cannot be extorted from him, God freely gives. We do not first seek God; God seeks us. God wants us in spite of our sin. He himself builds a bridge for us by his forgiveness. His pardon is as complete as his demand" (42).

This new direction to Luther's theology could only come about, according to Holl, because Luther had been "inwardly prepared for this decisive change." It was not Luther's discovery of Paul alone that led him to this new insight, it was something he had learned "by personal experience" (42).[71] "There must have been a moment in which the presentiment flashed through the midst of his inner anguish that God, through this very torment, was seeking and drawing him to himself. This thought led to his deliverance" (42).

The "awesome experience of the presence of God" (45) becomes the foundation upon which Holl arrives at his definition of Luther's religion as a "religion of conscience," (48) based as it is on the "conscientious experience" of the conflict between responsibility and demand. It is in this sense of obligation, in which the divine demand and the natural will come into conflict, that "divinity reveals itself most clearly" (49). "Over against his own 'rational' striving, Luther perceives the emergence in himself of another, unconditional will, which he is bound to distinguish from his own and yet cannot avoid recognizing as right. Thus the concept of God, and specifically of a personal God, is for Luther directly connected with the sense of obligation." Or more precisely stated: "Luther's conception of God faithfully reflected what he had experienced" (51).

71. This can be compared to the position of Reinhold Seeberg; see n43 above. By contrast, Bonhoeffer would not accept another authority, in addition to the Bible. In this Bonhoeffer followed the dialectical theologians, whose rediscovery of Luther's *sola scriptura* was important in marking their break from nineteenth-century liberal theology, which Holl and Seeberg are accused of following at this point.

This conscious experience, however, demanded a deeper, more complete, understanding of God. The experience of God's love is one thing, but prior to that experience comes the experience of God's demand, which cannot be satisfied. Because God will not settle for less than perfection, God in his judgment "must be angry"(53).[72] How are these two sides to God's nature to be resolved? If one carried the notion of "God's wrath" too far, one would come "to the point where God could only condemn and destroy" (54). But that contradicted an understanding of God's love. Yet, at the same time, to be true to the nature of God, the concept of God's wrath could not be weakened. There has to be some kind of unity that transcends the apparent antitheses. Holl believed that Luther was able to resolve this problem after reading Isa. 28:21,

> [which] speaks of wrath as an "alien" or "strange" work of God. From this Luther concluded that wrath and love in God are not on the same level. Love is his "proper" work, wrath is not. Wrath is the mask behind which God hides himself.[73] It belongs to God's nature that he reveals himself even in his antithesis. He does this, however, not out of caprice but according to a definite plan. God uses wrath to accomplish his goal, to dispose of the hindrances that stand in the way of the complete achievement of his highest purpose. For in comparison with the ultimate, the totally perfect, even the partially perfect is a barrier, a stop along the way (54).

While Holl acknowledges that there are different types of wrath in God, it is the "wrath of mercy" (54) that is a part of the process of justification; it is the wrath "that purges and liberates." Such wrath

72. See the discussions in Dillenberger, *God Hidden and Revealed*; Lotz, *Ritschl and Luther*; and Forde, *Law-Gospel Debate*. Scholars have identified Holl's attempts to come to grips with the opposing notions of wrath and love in Luther's doctrine of God as one of his achievements in overcoming the impasse at which an earlier generation of scholars had arrived.

73. See Dillenberger's comments, *God Hidden and Revealed*, 20ff, regarding the limitation of the role of the *deus absconditus* in Holl's thought. This, in turn, limits the role that Christ plays in his interpretation, leading Holl to misinterpret Luther at this point. By recapturing the proper christological emphasis in Luther, Bonhoeffer corrects that weakness in Holl.

is an act of God whereby "a person is shattered by God, but only in order to be transformed and recreated. God must shatter again and again those to be drawn up to himself, who are to share his own nature with him. In this way, in and through wrath, a love is revealed which desires the ultimate for people and which works tirelessly to this end" (54–55). In this way, by combining love and wrath in God, Luther deepens his concept of love. "Love is now understood as a power that does not hesitate to inflict hurt in order to liberate its object from itself and to raise it above itself." It is this love that is the "innermost, the deepest reality in God" (55).

With such an understanding of God and one's relationship to God, Holl reaches his highest expression of religion's purpose. In contrast to a natural desire for happiness, which would tend to make God into a servant "whom we summon for our purposes" (65), religion, for Holl's Luther, is "service to God, and the fulfillment of a duty to him." Therefore, rather than basing religion "on the desire for benefits or on any will originating in us," Luther based his understanding of religion "on the impress that is given by God, which lays hold of us and shatters us in our of feeling of selfhood. . . . It is the sensation of the majesty of God, of the 'Holy'" (66).[74] "This sensation always means that we become aware of a higher reality that tears us loose from our ordinary existence and world-view. The Holy obtrudes upon us as something far above common experience, something that seeks to draw us up to itself and yet at once sets up limits if we rashly approach too closely." As a result, we are, at the same time, "under obligation" and bear "an unbearable judgment"(67), which "renders our whole personal existence uncertain" (68). It is this "fear of God" that is the "first step toward religion; note well, *toward* religion, for

74. It was this understanding of religion that enabled Holl to distinguish Luther's faith from that of Melanchthon, thereby making the distinction between Luther and Lutheranism. See above, n63.

fear in itself is not yet religion. Real religion for Luther begins only when a person is united with God" (68).

Such is the argument that encompasses Holl's understanding of justification in Luther. However, as Holl emphasizes, one only moves *toward* this state in "continual shifts," as one undergoes an "inner progress" or transformation until one is united with God. "Justification, if a person takes it seriously, means a going back to one's innermost being in the sight of God; the whole person emerges renewed; the selfless ego that is entirely devoted to God is born ever anew, and from the deepened relationship to God it derives the power to conquer the natural, selfish ego." (95)

Holl's argument rests on Luther's experience of judgment and justification. According to Holl, it was Luther's experience of feeling impotent and helpless in the face of God's demands that led him to question the medieval church's system of penance. What had been designed to soothe a troubled spirit served only to create a sense of despair and hopelessness. Unable to find relief, Luther was driven to a new understanding of God, one centered on an understanding of justification.

For all that Holl's studies on Luther did to restore the emphasis on the centrality of justification in Luther's thinking, they were not met without criticism. In the first place, Holl's explicit emphasis on Luther's experience colored his understanding of justification. Labeled an analytic understanding of justification, it has been met with severe criticism.[75] Such an understanding of justification contrasts with a synthetic concept of justification. The latter places the emphasis on God's declaration of one as righteous, in spite of one's sinful state. An analytic justification, on the other hand, which

75. See Rupp, for example, who documents the reactions to Holl's understanding of justification; *Righteousness of God*, 182ff. Also, Regin Prenter, *Spiritus Creator: Luther's Concept of the Holy Spirit*, trans. John M. Jensen (Philadelphia: Muhlenberg Press, 1953), 96ff; Walter, "Historical Introduction," 3ff.

stems from Holl's emphasis on an "inner progress" that leads to transformation, stresses the gradual renewal that comes about as a result of inner change. In this scheme, justification is but one step in the process and, at the same time, because of its emphasis on inner change, has the tendency to lapse into issues of morality, thereby losing the objective character of God's act. Such divergent interpretations of justification have led to a weakening of its normative function in Lutheran theology to the point where there is no longer a consensus on either its understanding or its function.[76]

Holl's position has been also criticized for not having escaped the influence of nineteenth-century liberalism's idealistic framework. Dillenberger, for example, claims that Holl's Luther interpretation, which placed Luther's *deus absconditus* at the center of his investigation, represented progress in Luther interpretation. Nevertheless, in identifying the lingering influence of Ritschl, he locates a weakness in Holl's interpretation. Even more than Ritschl, he insists, Holl emphasized the ethical "as the determinative factor in relation to salvation. It is as if the elliptical character of Ritschl's thought had been transformed into a circle, of which the center is a single point in which grace is determined by morality."[77] These were problems that Holl's presentation of Luther's understanding of justification could not overcome.[78]

76. See Carl Braaten, *Justification: The Doctrine by which the Church Stands or Falls* (Minneapolis: Fortress Press, 1990), chap. 1.
77. Dillenberger, *God Hidden and Revealed*, 25.
78. Cf. Woelfel, *Bonhoeffer's Theology*, 74, who points to statements by Luther that serve to invalidate Holl's interpretation, which he judges as inadequate because it was "dominated by a theological method based on the religious consciousness and not on the biblical revelation which is the source and prior correlative of the religious consciousness." In opposition to Holl, Luther gives the biblical witness, which places Christ and not consciousness at the center, priority: "The substance, or the object, or (as some say) the subject of the gospel is Jesus Christ, the Son of God."

### The Place of Christology in Holl's Luther Interpretation

While Holl's interpretation of Luther was on a level different from those that preceded him, there were obvious weaknesses in his understanding of Luther that new research uncovered. One area of such explicit weakness was that Holl developed his entire argument about Luther's understanding of justification without reference to Luther's Christology.[79] For that reason, Lohse gives Holl's contribution to Luther research a mixed evaluation. He begins by saying,

> Among all the Luther scholars at the beginning of the twentieth century, Karl Holl's studies are on a higher level than those of anyone else. The reason was that Holl was very learned in all facets of church history and was better able than anyone else to place Luther in the context of the history of theology. . . . Holl was the first to combine historical and systematic perspectives in his study of Luther. . . . Holl focused his interpretation of Luther around the question of our position in relationship to God. As human beings, we know that we are confronted by an absolute demand that we cannot meet. We experience both this absolute demand and our own inadequacy in our conscience. This is the place where we meet God. This experience of God's ethical demand and our own failure to meet that demand is the basis on which we experience the judging and the gracious God. It is this experience which is the specifically religious experience.[80]

At the same time, he tempers his comments by pointing out Holl's obvious limitations, stating that Holl committed a serious

> error when he asserted that "Luther's piety was not Christ-centered in the sense that his whole faith was based totally and solely in Christ." This thesis about "the forgetting of Christ" has since been properly

79. This is the point at which the next generation of scholars, including Gogarten, Althaus, Iwand and Prenter, focused their criticisms against Holl. As their research has shown, in contradiction to Holl, Luther's theology was highly christocentric.

80. Bernhard Lohse, *Martin Luther: An Introduction to His Life and Work* (Philadelphia: Fortress Press, 1986), 224–25.

> abandoned by Luther scholars of all persuasions. At this point, it is necessary to disagree explicitly with Holl and to assert that Luther's theology is focused on Jesus Christ as the crucified and risen Lord.[81]

Another interpreter of Luther's legacy, John Dillenberger, likewise, after having studied the developments in Luther research in early part of the twentieth century, concluded,

> The emphasis which Holl puts upon the miracle of God's grace might have served as a framework for understanding the hiddenness of God. But its development was prematurely arrested by moral considerations which finally won the ascendance in man's relation to God. This had its effect also upon his study of Luther, in which conscience and forgiveness are equated and in which forgiveness is often spoken of without a Christological reference.[82]

Perhaps the harshest criticism, however, comes from Holl's own student, Wilhelm Pauck, who stated that Holl "interpreted Luther's religion in terms of Kantian and Ritschlian moralism, . . . that he . . . 'modernized' Luther by his failure to recognize the impact of the traditional dogmas, especially the Christological one, upon Luther's mind."[83] This is an assessment maintained by other, more recent scholars as well. Marc Lienhard, for example, in his study on Luther's Christology, insists that "Luther always appealed to tradition," particularly in terms of his Christology.[84]

The christological weakness in Holl's interpretation has been located in his understanding of God, which poses problems for the incarnation. According to Dillenberger,

81. Ibid., 225–26.

82. Dillenberger, *God Hidden and Revealed*, 25.

83. Wilhelm Pauck, "The Historiography of the German Reformation during the Past Twenty Years," in *Church History*, December 1940, p. 311, cited in Dillenberger, *God Hidden and Revealed*, 25.

84. Marc Lienhard, *Luther: Witness to Jesus Christ* (Minneapolis: Augsburg, 1982), 307.

> It can be safely said of Holl, that in his own thought and in his interpretation of Luther, the *deus absconditus* could not be equated with the *deus in carne* (God incarnate) because the latter is not sufficiently crucial. The grace of God is real for Holl, but there is no identification of grace with the incarnation except as it points to grace. In his own thought, the hidden God has no real place. In his interpretation of Luther, hiddenness is applied to God's wrath, in the service of that grace which is the basis of the new morality. Thus Holl's advance over Ritschl consists in sympathetically exploring hiddenness in Luther's thought in respect to predestination and wrath, under the criterion of love. The concepts, however, do not yet come into decisive theological focus.[85]

It has already been noted that Holl was able to discuss Luther's understanding of justification without reference to Christology. In fact, in the essay, "What Did Luther Understand By Religion?" Holl's most detailed discussion of Luther's Christology takes place in footnotes;[86] when reference is made to Jesus Christ, it is made in a way that limits the role of Christology in Luther's theology.[87] In moments of *Anfechtung*, for example, Holl's Luther often believed it to be God himself, albeit God in his wrath, testing him. In such times, says Holl, Luther gained a new appreciation for Christ. "Now he saw Christ not merely as the one who, in the past, had once for all placated God's wrath, but as the one who even now was interceding effectually in his behalf. He perceived how a power flowed into him from Christ's death and resurrection which gave him both the assurance of pardon and the confidence to defeat the power of the sin the still clung to him" (76). In this instance, Christ is linked to the wrathful expression of God, but nowhere does Holl link Christ to God's love.

85. Dillenger, *God Hidden and Revealed*, 25.
86. See Holl, *What Did Luther Understand by Religion?*, 76–78.
87. Cf. Sorum, "Bonhoeffer's Early Interpretation of Luther as the Source of His Basic Theological Paradigm," *Fides et Historia* 29, 2 (Summer 1997): 40–41.

In addition, it must be noted that there were also times when Christ simply vanished, leaving Luther alone in his *Anfechtung*. These moments when Christ receded were for Holl the confirmation that

> contrary to common opinion, Luther's piety was not Christ-centered in the sense that his whole faith was based totally and solely on Christ. Moreover, we must recall that Luther never regarded this "forgetting of Christ" as sin or as unfaithfulness to him but as a trial imposed by God himself. Thus there really were times when he felt himself to be facing God directly and alone. Only at this level does his most profound piety emerge, and only here do we see clearly how he was able to advance from fear of God to union with him.[88]

It is at this point that elements most closely linking Holl to the Ritschlian concept of morality enter. He continues:

> What sustained Luther in such moments of extreme crisis was something surprisingly simple, the First Commandment. In his mortal need he always clung to its opening words, "I am the Lord thy God." Nowhere is it so obvious as here that the feeling of obligation forms the basis of his whole piety and that obligation to God is the most basic of all duties. His final resort was to a commandment—the very one that was judging him. For the First Commandment sums up all duty to God, the duty of which he had been neglectful—for all his sin was self-seeking, and therefore ultimately unbelief and ingratitude. He laid hold of this commandment in order earnestly to affirm both the commandment and its judgment upon himself. . . . The more earnestly Luther determined to do this, the more clearly he heard the word of comfort contained in the same commandment. Just as his sense of unworthiness had driven him to the verge of despair and he felt ready to sink into the ground before God, the continuing obligation of the commandment came into clear focus in his mind. We must always obey God, always[89]

While, in this instance, there was little need for Jesus Christ in Holl's thought, it is not to say that Holl had no place for Jesus

88. Holl, *What Did Luther Understand by Religion?*, 79.
89. Ibid.

elsewhere; however, Jesus, when given a place, has limited role. In another work, *Distinctive Elements of Christianity*,[90] we see a fuller expression of Holl's understanding of Jesus; but even here, it falls short of Luther's christocentric preoccupation.

In this essay, Holl develops his argument by stressing the common denominator that Christianity shares with the other religions and even ancient philosophy. He goes so far as to state that within the Roman Empire of that time a religious movement centered on a coming salvation was beginning to develop. The one clarification he makes, however, is that in the case of the movement developing within the Roman Empire such a salvation "was understood in a purely this-worldly sense," with its focus on emperor worship (3).

The oriental religions, among which Christianity is numbered, however, emphasized a salvation of a different sort, offering a "hope that went out beyond life" (4). Nevertheless, as becomes clear, these religions, as do all religions, have their basis in human longing and thinking. Salvation and redemption are the philosophical concepts (or myths) that arose out of these cultures themselves. As is the case with his discussion of these early developments, these myths correspond to the needs of the "inner man," who, living in a hostile world, seeks some kind of wholeness (5).

Recounting the research of others, which found such elements of salvation already present in various religions, Holl's comparative analysis of Christianity's beginnings reflects the same orientation, including an commonality of the themes of the death and resurrection of the god and the necessity of the virgin birth (7). Another element shared by these religions was the believer's appropriation "to carry over to himself what had happened to the God" (7). From this line of thinking arose the necessary connection

90. Karl Holl, *Distinctive Elements in Christianity*, trans. by Norman V. Hope (Edinburgh: T. &. T. Clark, 1937); references to this work in what follows are presented in parentheses.

between belief and morality, as well as the idea of the sacraments depicting the presence of God.

While Holl admits to not being able to share all the conclusions about the interrelationship of these religious ideas, he nevertheless concludes that Christianity is a "syncretistic religion" from its beginnings. "To put it crudely, only the names have changed, the reality remains the same" (12). As a result, only one essential question remains for him: How did Christianity win out over the other religions? (ibid.). The answer, according to Holl, must lie in Christianity's uniqueness—in other words, not in what it shares with other religions, but in what sets it apart.

Holl finds his answer in the uniqueness of Jesus' "conception of God." Unlike his contemporaries, Jesus identifies with tax collectors and sinners, seeing them as worthy in God's eyes. "Jesus preaches a God who wants to have dealings with sinful men, a God to whom he who has sunk deep stands, in circumstances, especially near" (15). God is not an aloof judge seeking to hand out justice at the last day, but is one who comes seeking out humanity with his grace.

The distinct character of Christianity shows itself here precisely as a redemption religion, in contrast to all the other religions, where "liberation is founded on the conviction of the ineradicable nobility of mankind, on a metaphysical likeness of the soul with God" (16). Jesus' conception of God, however, is different; instead of building on the likeness shared by God and humanity, the emphasis is placed on the "deep gulf between God and man " (17). Nevertheless, salvation occurs because "God of His free grace comes down to meet man." This is the revolutionary core of Christianity that contradicts all other religious conceptualities. To Jews and all others alike, "the idea that a pathway to God was available to the impure, to the sinful, could appear only as a reversal of all religious and moral conceptions, as an outrage on the most fundamental feeling for the dignity and sublimity of the Godhead" (21).

But on the contrary, according to Holl, Jesus' conception of God did not destroy morality; instead, it built up the "most exacting ethic conceivable . . . for it demands the whole life, and a life not only of renunciation, but of devotion and service" (21–22).

For Holl, Jesus, or least one like Jesus, was necessary, because it is impossible to conceive of the possibility that such a conception of God, which is contrary to all human thinking, could arise from nowhere. A single individual, albeit an "extraordinary" one, was necessary—

> one who knew how to walk with sure tread along the dizzy path where divine and satanic are divided sharply from each other! For on such a height, where faintness overcomes the ordinary earnest man, is not every gracious trait in the character of God only a seductive illusion? Is not this contempt for what is righteous, dangerous in the highest degree? Jesus' teaching about God revolves round such a notion. (23)

What must be concluded is that Jesus is seen as an extraordinary individual and the founder of a religion, but that does not necessarily identify him with God. In fact, Holl makes this distinction clearly, claiming that Christ was only an instrument of God (35) or was "God's messenger" (36). It is this conception of Christology that led to scholarly criticisms of Holl's interpretation of Luther. It is in this light that we must view Bonhoeffer's changing relationship to Holl.

### Bonhoeffer's Reception of Holl

Inasmuch as Holl was able to raise Luther research to a new level, we have seen that it was not long before his approach was questioned and eventually overturned. A whole cadre of younger scholars began to see the weakness of Holl's approach and sought to overcome it.[91] Building on the foundations that Holl so convincingly built, they corrected his insights and by so doing moved beyond him. Bonhoeffer was only one of many who found himself in that position.[92]

In this light, while Bonhoeffer had gained many insights from Holl, it was not very long before he placed himself in a critical stance vis-à-vis Holl because of Holl's lack of attention given to the importance of Christology.[93] These differences begin to appear as early as 1928, while Bonhoeffer was still a student.[94] The criticism becomes even more clearly defined only a couple of years later. In his inaugural address as a lecturer at the University of Berlin, he

91. The important new interpreters included Hirsch, E. Seeberg, Althaus, Elert, and Heim, all of whom were contemporaries of Bonhoeffer and with whose work Bonhoeffer most likely was familiar. It should be noted, as well, that the work of Walter von Loewenich *Luther's Theology of the Cross,* 5th ed. and trans. H. J. A. Bouman (Minneapolis: Augsburg, 1976), fits into this period. It is he, among others, who brought out the theme of the *theologia crucis* in Luther and emphasized a christocentric approach to his theology.

92. According to Walter, "Karl Holl (1866–1926) and the Recovery of Promise in Luther," 398, "The paths he created in the study of Luther's thought led in various directions: his students Emannuel Hirsch and Erich Vogelsang both attempted to solve his religion of conscience by interpreting Luther's thinking about Christ, while Dietrich Bonhoeffer, Rudolf Hermann, and Hans-Joachim Iwand would seek other paths. Beyond these theologians, who tried to carry out Holl's program of promise in some fashion, many others such as Paul Althaus or Karl Barth criticized his work from their own perspectives."

93. See, for example, Rumscheidt, "Formation of Bonhoeffer's Theology, 57: "A number of scholars, including Dietrich Bonhoeffer, challenged Holl's position. Indeed, Luther's Christology and his claim that the assurance of faith rest solely on God's gracious act *extra nos sed pro nobis* (independently of but for us) gave Bonnoeffer a basis for repudiating the notion 'religion of conscience.' To Bonhoeffer, Holl appeared to derive the assurance of faith from some aspect of conscience itself."

94. See, for example, his examination paper from that year, in which Bonhoeffer raised questions about Holl's presentation of Luther's doctrine of justification, by saying, "In this way Luther constantly returns to the idea of the gracious God. One could paraphrase Luther's certainty of his salvation with the words (in spite of Holl) *'having found a gracious God'*" (DBWE 9:442). In this same essay, the christological orientation of Bonhoeffer's theology emerges. In commenting on the contrasting understandings of the church between Luther and Roman Catholicism, for example, he makes the point that God and the crucified Christ are one and the same; see ibid., 444. This becomes a central tenet of his theology, which he takes over from Luther. (For Luther, the identification between God and Christ crucified is so strong that Luther can refer to God as the "crucified God" ["Explanations of the Ninety-Five Theses," *LW* 31:225]). See also Bonhoeffer's "Note on Luther's Lectures on the Letter to the Romans," (DBWE 9:300), in which he questions Holl's psychological interpretation of Luther.

stated his position over against Holl quite clearly, criticizing Holl's failure to base his interpretation on Luther's Christology. This lecture came only four years after Holl's death and at a place where Holl's theological position was still highly respected. Nevertheless, the young lecturer said,

> We mention the name of Karl Holl here merely as one particularly impressive representative of the overwhelming majority of contemporary theologians. [Holl characterized Luther's religion as "religion of conscience." For now I will merely point out that this position included a peculiarly meager estimation of Christology in Luther. The human being finds God within himself in some fashion; he has God in self-reflection. Because the human being is able to hear and have God within his conscience, he is able to understand himself from within his conscience as his most authentic possibility of being human.][95]

Such a criticism stems from Bonhoeffer's own understanding of God. He differs from Holl by insisting that God can never be identified with the human conscience. God is an external reality and comes to humanity from the outside. In this criticism, Bonhoeffer sides with the other movement in theology bringing about renewal, the dialectical theologians. If there is any question about Bonhoeffer's break from his teachers, it can be seen at this point.

> The question in which the human being reflects on himself always remains a question; he cannot find answers from within himself since there is no point within him at which God might gain space. Indeed, the essence of human being is to be *incapax infiniti*, that is, it is impossible

95. DBWE 10:400–1. In a letter to his friend, Erwin Sutz, Bonhoeffer gives expression to this diverging viewpoint that is beginning to separate him from his faculty colleagues: "My theological origin is gradually becoming suspect here, and they seem to have somewhat the feeling that they have been nurturing a viper in their bosom" (DBWE 11:76; see n2, in which the editors indicate that Bonhoeffer's theologial position "attracted negative attention" because of his "orientation toward Karl Barth"). Examining this letter, Bethge says, "Not only did he dare to question their theological assumptions; he also appeared to be striving toward a different nature. It soon struck his students that something about him intrinsically distinguished him from the behavior and ideals of a professor" (*DB-ER*, 211).

> for the finite human essence to unite directly with the infinite, and this precludes the possibility that the human being might absolutize himself at even a single point within his essence. He remains totally unsecured because he remains completely within himself.[96]

It was against such a position, based as it was on a false premise of God, according to Bonhoeffer, that he would argue all of his life.

It was only a short time later, in his lectures on "The History of Twentieth-Century Systematic Theology," given during the winter semester of 1931–1932, that he went even further in clarifying his differences with Holl, while at the same time outlined his own emerging Christology. He characterized Holl's understanding of Jesus in the following manner: "Jesus is the one who proclaims this new religion, but Holl leaves the cross and the resurrection to the history-of-religion. Thus he comes through empirical observation to perceive something new in Christianity, even though he doesn't find his way out of the liberal view of Jesus."[97] After further analyzing the developments in modern theology during the modern period, Bonhoeffer noted that a significant, but negative, change had taken place.[98]

96. DBWE 10:401. See also Phillips, *Christ for Us*, 63, where following this line of argument, he notes that in *Act and Being* Bonhoeffer uses "Luther to telling advantage against Holl, sharpening his attack on conscience as man's 'final grasp at himself': 'The conscience and remorse of man in Adam are his final grasp at himself, the final confirmation and justification of his self-lordly, self-masterly attitude. Man makes himself the defendant and exhorts himself upward to his better self. But the cry of conscience serves only to dissemble the mute loneliness of his desolate isolation, it sounds without echo into the world that is governed and construed by the self. Man in Adam reaches the confines of his solitude but, misreading his situation, continues to 'seek himself in himself:' he hopes by remorse still to preserve his sinful existence. . . . Therefore this conscience is of the devil, who leaves man to himself in untruth, so this conscience must be mortified when Christ comes to man."
97. DBWE 11:208–9
98. On this point see Bethge (*DB–ER*, 219): Describing Bonhoeffer's Christology lectures from 1933, which he calls "the highpoint" of Bonhoeffer's academic career, Bethge says, "Christology, which he had once regarded as having been so remarkably neglected in Holl's seminars on Luther, ultimately lay behind the 'turning point' he had acknowledged in his 1931 lecture. It was magnetic or even the explosive center of 'The Nature of the Church' in 1931; and it was to be the basis for ethics and the refutation of the misuse of the concept of 'orders of creation' concept."

Siding with Luther over against Holl and other modern theologians, Bonhoeffer insisted that the central theological question was that of justification, which, out of necessity, is tied to Christology, for salvation comes through Christ alone.[99] It was Holl's

99. "For Luther, Christ [is] *exemplum* or *donum*. In the first case [*exemplum*] Jesus is a divine teacher whom we are to imitate; if he is the ulmate lawgiver, then the understanding of justification becomes impossible. . . . For a teacher of morality, there can no longer be mercy, except perhaps leniency, *benignitas,* 'letting up.' . . . The God of liberal theology [is] a sentimental God. To Troeltsch's question, 'How can I find my soul?' the Bible gives no answer. The Reformation knew it was answering only the question, How can I have a merciful God?" (DBWE 11:213). This conclusion corresponds to the argument Luther put forth in his lectures on Hebrews, where he insisted the medieval theologians got it wrong when they gave priority to *Christus exemplum* over *Christus sacramentum:* "Therefore he who wants to imitate Christ insofar as he is an example must first believe with a firm faith that Christ suffered and died for him as this was a sacrament. Consequently, those who continue to blot out sin first by means of works and labors of penance err greatly, since they begin with the example, when they should begin with the sacrament" ("Lectures on Hebrews." *LW* 29:124). See Dennis Ngien, *The Suffering of God according to Martin Luther's* "Theologia Crucis" (Eugene, OR: Wipf & Stock), 36, for a discussion of Luther's position. For further evidence on how Bonhoeffer reads his theology in relationship to that of the nineteenth-century liberal position, see DBWE 11: 214–15; Bonhoeffer examines a contrasting understanding of the cross as it appears in the work of Cremer and Kähler. It is the latter who attempted to respond to the challenge of nineteenth-century liberal theology with a mediating position, which became influential in shaping the theologies of Barth and Tillich, both of whom had ties to the nineteenth century but who made significant contributions in the twentieth century due to their critique and reformulation of the theology of their teachers. The core of Kähler's theology was shaped by Luther's doctrine of justification by faith, which contributed significantly toward giving Kähler his unique voice over against his contemporaries. For a discussion of the background of Kähler's theology and his role in modern theology, see Carl Braaten's "Introduction: Revelation, History, and Faith in Martin Kähler," in Martin Kähler, *The So-Called Historical Jesus and the Historic Biblical Christ*, ed. and trans. Carl E. Braaten (Philadelphia: Fortress Press, 1964) and Correll, *Shepherds of the Empire*, chapter 3. Paul Tillich also paid tribute to the significant role that Kähler played his theological development; see Paul Tillich, *The Protestant Era*, trans. James Luther Adams, abridged ed. (Chicago: The University of Chicago Press, 1957), x–xi. One further comment on Kähler's theology that adds a perspective on this discussion is the following from Ernst Käsemann in his discussion on the death of Jesus in St. Paul: "The catchword 'theology of the cross' means more than this ['the saving significance of Jesus' death for Paul'], and we must not turn it into something mildly edifying. For it belongs from the very outset to the controversial theology which Protestant fervour inaugurated through the *particula exclusiva*—the 'through Christ alone, through faith alone.' This means: *crux sola est nostra theologia*. In his excellent essay, 'Das Kreuz: Grund und Mass für die Christologie,' ('The Cross: the Basis and Test of Christology') Martin Kähler interpreted this in precise terms: 'Without the cross no Christology, and in Christology no single feature which cannot find its justification in the cross.' In a way, this statement introduces and anticipates the subject of demythologizing, which is of such concern today. Kähler therefore went on to say, 'At the same time, however, from this starting point and under this aspect, Christology is transferred from metaphysics with

mistake to base his understanding of justification on the first commandment rather than Christology.[100] If we read Bonhoeffer's theology as a response to this development in modern theology, we can see the reason for the radical concentration on Jesus Christ; his understanding of justification demands it.

This brief survey has shown that Bonhoeffer's theological development took place in and was influenced by the ongoing developments in the study of Luther's theology. Even though he did not enter into the debate as a Luther scholar, these developments are critical to his theological evolution, both positively and negatively. He was introduced to Luther by Holl and his generation of scholars, but then parted from them and entered into a battle for genuine Lutheranism against his contemporaries in the 1930s. Believing Bonhoeffer to be well-read, one who would have kept abreast of the developments and debates within theological circles, especially as it affected such an important issue as Luther, it is reasonable to assume that he would have followed the arguments of other theologians, such as Althaus, Elert, and Erich Seeberg, who were also engaged in this work.

As this generation of scholars built upon and moved beyond the interpretation of Holl, the *theologia crucis* moved to the forefront for understanding the contours of Luther's theology. Therefore, it must be assumed that this had an impact on his thought. As our examination of Bonhoeffer's work will reveal, the cross becomes the key to his understanding of Christology and the foundation for

its sterile logical necessity, into history and thus into the kingdom of our own reality.'" (Ernst Käseman, "The Saving Significance of the Death of Jesus in Paul," in *Perspectives on Paul,* trans. Margaret Kohl [Philadelphia: Fortress Press, 1971], 34). Both Kähler and Käsemann insist that Christology and the cross are bound together.

100. DBWE 11:218. This is a criticism shared by others as well. See Rupp, *Righteousness of God*, 30–31, for a sample of these responses. Walter F. Bense, "Editor's Introduction," *What Did Luther Understand by Religion*, 10ff, provides details of Gogarten's critique and the ensuing controversy between Holl and Gogarten.

all theology. It is out of the context of his Luther study that this understanding emerged.

# 2

# Bonhoeffer and Luther

Even though Karl Holl did much to reclaim Luther and his theology for the twentieth century and beyond, it was to be the next generation of scholars that corrected the preliminary insights Holl gained from his reading of Luther and rediscovered the core of Luther's thought.[1] It was in this wave of research in the 1920s and '30s that Luther's *theologia crucis* was identified as the foundation and core of Luther's thought;[2] it was a discovery that changed the picture of Luther that emerged.[3] Signaled by the work of Walther

1. See Gregory Walter, "Karl Holl (1866–1926) and the Recovery of Promise in Luther," *Lutheran Quarterly* 25 (2011): 398.
2. For example, Walter von Loewenich, *Luther's Theology of the Cross* (Minneapolis: Augsburg, 1976), 13 and 219, insists that the *theologia crucis* is a principle of theological knowledge in Luther's theology, while Paul Althaus, "Die Bedeutung des Kreuzes in Denken Luthers," 51-62, *Evangelium und Leben* (Gütersloh: C. Bertelsmann, 1927), says that the *theologia crucis* belongs "to what is most profound in Luther's theology" (52; English as cited von Loewenich, 20). Cf. Althaus, *Theology of Martin Luther* (Philadelphia: Fortress Press, 1966), 30. Similarly, Gerhard Ebeling sees the theology of the cross as an accurate description for Luther's understanding of theology, being the sole "criterion and subject of all true theology" (*Luther: An Introduction to His Thought* [Philadelphia: Fortress Press, 1970], 226).
3. See John Dillenberger, *God Hidden and Revealed: The Interpretation of Luther's* Deus Absconditus *and Its Significance for Reilgious Thought* (Philadelphia: Muhlenberg Press, 1953), especially

von Loewenich and E. Vogelsang,[4] as well as that of Paul Althaus, Friedrich Gogarten, Werner Elert, Emmanuel Hirsch, and Eric Seeberg, this new theological orientation was to give a new dynamic to Luther studies.[5]

This orientation, which had been stated first by Luther in the *Heidelberg Disputation* and remained central throughout his life,[6] was

chapter 2, for a survey of the developments in Luther interpretation in the early twentieth century.

4. See Walter von Loewenich, *Luther's Theology of the Cross*, and Erich Vogelsang, *Der Angefochtene Christus* (Berlin: Walter de Gruyter, 1932). Both Anna M. Madsen, *The Theology of the Cross in Historical Perspective*, Distinguished Dissertations in Christian Theology Series (Eugene, OR: Pickwick, 2007) and Philip Ruge-Jones, *Cross in Tensions: Luther's Theology of the Cross as Theologico-Social Critique,* Princeton Theological Monograph Series (Eugene, OR: Pickwick, 2008) provide a review of von Loewenich's work. In addition, Madsen provides a brief biography of von Loewenich, indicating that he entered the university in 1922, which makes him a contemporary of Bonhoeffer; however, there is no indication in Bonhoeffer's work or surviving library that he was familiar with von Loewenich's Luther interpretation.
5. It should be pointed out, however, that these scholars were not all of one mind; rather, the opposite is true. According to Dillenberger, *God Hidden and Revealed*, "The unity which exists is primarily one of opposition to previous interpretations" (37). Later he goes on to describe their differences. For example, when it comes to Luther's *theologia crucis,* Dillenberger says it was Althaus who developed this most clearly, using Luther's dichotomy of the *theologia gloriae* and *theologia crucis* as stated in the *Heidelberg Disputation.* "The general similarity between Seeberg, Althaus, and Elert in respect to the basis of Luther's theology is unmistakable. The *theologia crucis* is the emphasis upon the cross as the one crucial point in the broader context of revelation described by Seeberg." (55). Elert, however, limited the *deus absconditus* to be the "knowledge of God which men have through natural theology." Therefore, Elert understands the *deus absconditus* and the *deus revelatus* as antithetical; Seeberg, on the other hand, sees their identification (56). Of Hirsch, he states that his interpretation remained essentially theocentric (51). On the other hand, "most current interpretation points to the primacy of the *theologia crucis*" among those who, like E. Seeberg and Althaus, had a christocentric approach.
6. See, for example, Marc Lienhard, *Luther: Witness to Jesus Christ*, trans. Edwin H. Robertson (Minneapolis: Augsburg Publishing House, 1982), 257, who argues that "the principle of the theology of the cross not only dominates the works of the young Luther, but that it is found to the end in his works." Even though Luther did not continue to use this language, the thought that informed his theology and gave shape to it "was the object of his constant concern, the fundamental orientation of theological thought" (Ebeling, *Luther: An Introduction*, 227). This judgment is also shared by scholars such as von Loewenich, Prenter, and Dillenberger, as well as more recent writers, such as Pierre Buhler, *Kreuz und Eschatologie* (Tübingen: J. C. B. Mohr [Paul Siebeck], 1981) and Alister E. McGrath, *Luther's Theology of the Cross: Martin Luther's Theological Breakthrough* (Oxford: Basil Blackwell, 1985). Even though the phrase *theologia crucis* disappears from Luther's terminology, the same principle remains at work. At the core, *theologia crucis* has to do with the proper knowledge of God, who in spite of his revelation remains hidden in the cross of Jesus Christ. Robert Kolb, "Luther's Theology of the Cross 15 Years after Heidelberg: Lectures on the Psalms of Ascent," *Journal of Ecclesiastical History*, 61, no.

identified by those who picked up on the work of Karl Holl. It was precisely because of the nature of such statements made by Luther in his *Heidelberg Disputation* and elsewhere that these scholars found it difficult to agree with Holl's conclusion that Luther's theology was theocentric rather than christocentric.[7] Such changes in perspective opened up "new vistas of interpretation,"[8] which produced new insights into the nature of Luther's theology.

This can be seen, for example, in the work of Eric Seeberg in his concentration on linking the hidden and revealed God to Christology, which was an emphasis that had been ignored by Holl. In addition, Seeberg was led to have a different perspective on Luther's theology because this christological center was seen as being a *theologia crucis*. In such a revelation God remains both hidden and paradoxical; nevertheless, this is the true nature of God. According to Dillenberger, linking the *deus absconditus* with the *deus revelatus* was the dynamic of Seeberg's theology; he characterizes this in the

1 (January 2010): 70, likewise argues that Luther's theology continued to be shaped by his theology of the cross, remaining "vital to the structure of his thinking." However, the same cannot be said of Luther's followers. Again Kolb, "Luther on the Theology of the Cross," *Lutheran Quarterly* 16 (2002): 444: Unfortunately, Luther's followers "did not find Luther's theology of the cross particularly helpful" and did not maintain his orientation and, as a result, the cross came to represent something different entirely. In Melanchthon's use, for example, the "'cross' treated human suffering, not God's suffering on the cross," with the result that "the cross served a very different, and less all-encompassing, purpose than providing the point of view from which to assess God's revelation of himself, humanity—defining trust in that revelation, the atonement accomplished through Christ's death and resurrection, or the Christian life. In subsequent Lutheran dogmatic textbooks, this topic consistently treated only one aspect of the Christian life, persecution and afflictions of other kinds." Gerhard Forde takes a similar stand by saying that the Heidelberg Disputation is "almost a kind of outline for the Luther's subsequent theological program" (*On Being a Theologian of the Cross: Reflections on Luther's Heidelberg Disputation* [Grand Rapids: Eerdmans, 1997], 21).

7. This christocentric interpretation replaced Holl's and has remained the dominant perspective. See Bernhard Lohse, *Martin Luther: An Introduction to His Life and Work* (Philadephia: Fortress Press, 1986), and Dillenberger, *God Hidden and Revealed*, for an analysis of this change as well as a survey of the positions represented. See also Marc Lienhard, *Luther: Witness to Jesus Christ*: "Certainly, according to Holl and the researchers who follow him, Christ played only a secondary role in Luther's thought. But that is a thesis which our work wishes to invalidate."
8. Dillenberger, *God Hidden and Revealed*, 37.

following manner: "It signifies that true wisdom is hidden in the world, since God works in opposition, and particularly in opposition to reason. He works life in the midst of death, contrary to ordinary sight and knowledge. This is God's spirituality and involves the kind of positive hiddenness which faith alone can see."[9]

While Bonhoeffer did not enter the debate as a Luther scholar, the same emphasis can be seen emerging in his own theological perspective.[10] In this respect, even though it is impossible to establish direct historical links between these scholars and Bonhoeffer on issues concerning the interpretation of Luther's theology, what can be seen is a shared perspective.[11]

9. Ibid, 51.

10. Wolf Krötke, "Dietrich Bonhoeffer and Martin Luther," in *Bonhoeffer's Intellectual Formation: Theology and Philosophy in His Thought*, ed. Peter Frick (Tübingen: Mohr Siebeck, 2008) 55, maintains that while Bonhoeffer was introduced to Luther by the leading voices of the Luther Renaissance, his own reading of Luther led him to disagree with their interpretation; as a result, the search for the "real Luther" guided Bonhoeffer's "lifelong theological orientation."

11. While Bethge and others agree that Bonhoeffer was an avid reader who was familiar with the theological developments and movements of his day, what remains of Bonhoeffer's library gives no indication that he had these books, nor does his theological legacy deal with these concerns directly. (See Dietrich Meyer, *Nachlaß Dietrich Bonhoeffer: Ein Verzeichnis; Archiv–Sammlung–Bibliothek* [Munich: Chr. Kaiser Verlag, 1987], 176–240, for a detailed listing of the books that remained in Bonhoeffer's library following the war). At the same time, according to both Ebeling and Bethge, Bonhoeffer was involved in the fight for "genuine Lutheranism" in 1930s Germany, so it is unlikely that these developments could not have gone unnoticed by Bonhoeffer. In fact, it can be seen that Bonhoeffer entered into this debate in his own way with his discussion of the definition of "conscience" in *Act and Being* (DBWE 2), which indirectly questioned Holl's interpretation of Luther; see 140–41, esp. the footnotes.

In the same way, the developments within Bonhoeffer's own theology can be seen as reflecting the changes in his understanding of Luther's theology. His interpretation and appropriation of Luther began with the work of Karl Holl, but eventually expressed a critical perspective on that very same theology as Christology became the core of his thinking. In this way, Bonhoeffer's theology reflects the changes and developments in the understanding of Luther that emerged in the early part of the twentieth century.

## Luther's *Theologia Crucis*

Even before Luther became a reformer,[12] his thoughts were focused on and he took his cues for his understanding of God from the cross of Christ. In a brief fragment of a sermon prepared for November 11, 1515, everything was reduced to one point—the cross. "Preach one thing: the wisdom of the cross."[13] By the time references to the cross emerged again in the *Heidelberg Disputation*,[14] the cross had become the centerpiece of Luther's emerging theological position.[15] Stated

12. See Bernhard Lohse, *Martin Luther's Theology: Its Historical and Systematic Development*, ed. and trans. Roy A. Harrisville (Minneapolis: Fortress Press, 1999), 36–37, for a "prehistory" of Luther's position. See also the work of Alister McGrath for a summary of the positions and issues. According to Paul Althaus, who was a contemporary of Bonhoeffer and with whose work Bonhoeffer was familiar, "The theology of the cross permeates all of Luther's theological thinking. . . . This means that the cross of Christ is the standard by which all genuine theological knowledge is measured, whether of the reality of God, of his grace, of his salvation, of the Christian life, or of the church" (Althaus, *Theology of Martin Luther*, 30). See also Dillenberger, *God Hidden and Revealed*, 146ff., and Regin Prenter, *Luther's Theology of the Cross* (Philadelphia: Fortress Press, 1971), 3, among others.
13. "Early Sermons," *LW* 51:15. Note the editor's comments regarding the series of sermons on the Ten Commandments that Luther preached between June, 1516 and February, 1517 in Wittenberg; these "pre-reformation sermons" breathe "the spirit of Luther's 'theology of the cross,' which he summed up in a statement occurring in a fragment of a sermon on St. Martin's Day, Nov. 11, 1515: *Unum praedica: sapientiam crucis!*–'Preach one thing: the wisdom of the cross!'" Another sermon given a few months later displays this same emphasis (see ibid., 17ff.), as does *Crux sola est nostra theologia* (The cross alone is our theology), as cited in Forde, *On Being a Theologian of the Cross*, 3.
14. Pierre Bühler, *Kreuz und Eschatologie. Eine Auseinandersetzung mit der politischen Theologie, im Anschluß an Luthers theologia crucis* (Tübingen: J. C. B. Mohr [Paul Siebeck], 1981), 64ff, insists that the *Heidelberg Disputation* is without a doubt one of the most important documents for understanding Luther's *theologia crucis*. E. Gordon Rupp, "Luther's Ninety-Five Theses and the Theology of the Cross," in *Luther for an Ecumenical Age*, ed. Carl Meyer (St. Louis: Concordia Publishing House, 1967) identifies the *Heidelberg Disputation* as the first real "theological manifesto of the Protestant Reformation" (69). Gerhard Forde, *On Being a Theologian of the Cross*, draws a similar conclusion when he says the *Heidelberg Disputation* is critical for understanding Luther; in fact, it is "almost a kind of outline for Luther's subsequent theological program" (21).
15. According to Rupp, Luther had a breakthrough over his understanding of the gospel in 1516 that formed the basis for what came later. "It is a theology we can detect in the first course of lectures that Luther gave on the Psalms, where we find such phrases as 'the cross of Christ runs right through the Scriptures.'" This theological orientation guides Luther for the rest of his life: "It is a theology which Luther never needed to unlearn. It is powerfully expounded in a sermon he preached in the Castle Coburg in 1530 on Christ's sufferings in relation to the cross of Christians, and in fact it underlies the very last sermon he preached in 1546" (Rupp,

in terms of a *theologia crucis*, it was identified as being a theological orientation or method that Luther characterized as the only authentic theology.[16] By contrasting his *theologia crucis* with a *theologia gloriae*, the term he used to describe the theological method of scholastic theology, Luther changed the nature or definition of theology.[17] Drawing a distinction between these two orientations' approaches to understanding or knowing God, Luther states the contrasts in theses 19 and 20 of the *Heidelberg Disputation*:

> 19. That person does not deserve to be called a theologian who looks upon the invisible things of God as though they were clearly perceptible in those things which have actually happened [Rom. 1:20].
> 20. He deserves to be called a theologian, however, who comprehends the visible and manifest things of God seen through suffering and the cross.[18]

"Luther's Ninety-Five Theses," 68–69). Likewise, Roland Bainton, in his biography of Luther, insists that Luther's understanding of Christ and God as expressed in the *theologia crucis* were already evident in 1516 in his first lectures on the Psalms (Roland Bainton, *Here I Stand: A Biography of Martin Luther* [Nashville: Abingdon Press, 1950], 62ff).

16. Von Loewenich explains Luther's thinking in this way: "For Luther the cross is not only the subject of theology; it is the distinctive mark of all theology. It has its place not only in the doctrine of the vicarious atonement, but it constitutes an integrating element for all Christian knowledge. The theology of the cross is not a chapter in theology but a specific kind of theology. The cross of Christ is significant here not only for the question concerning redemption and the certainty of salvation, but it is the center that provides perspective for all theological statements. Hence it belongs to the doctrine of God in the same way as it belongs to the doctrine of the work of Christ. There is no dogmatic topic conceivable for which the cross is not the point of reference." (*Luther's Theology of the Cross*, 17–18.) Likewise, Ebeling states that for Luther the theology of the cross was not a special kind of theology or one of theology's many themes, "but the criterion and subject of all true theology: 'True theology and knowledge of God lies in the crucified Christ'" (*Luther: An Introduction*, 226). Because this is so, Ebeling can insist that even though the language disappears from Luther's writings, the central impulse remains constant and central throughout Luther's career. Cf. also Dillenberger, *God Hidden and Revealed*, 146ff, and Robert Kolb, "Luther's Theology of the Cross 15 Years after Heidelberg."
17. Kolb, "Luther on the Theology of the Cross," 443–44, concludes that such ideas created a "paradigm shift within Western Christian thought." In his *Heidelberg Disputation*, Luther was not offering a new "treatment of a specific biblical teaching or two;" rather he "called for a different way of thinking about—and practicing—the proclamation of the gospel of Jesus Christ." In fact, his "theology of the cross" provided "a framework that is designed to embrace all of biblical teaching and guide the use of all its parts. It employs the cross of Christ as the focal point and fulcrum for understanding and presenting a wide range of specific topics within the biblical message."

Whereas the *theologia crucis* is defined as embracing God's suffering on the cross, its contrast, the *theologia gloriae*, is seen as being blind to the "crucified and hidden God."[19] For Luther this distinction is all-important, because the proper knowledge of God comes only by focusing on Christ who suffers and dies on the cross.

As an example of how Luther's theology of the cross turns theology upside down, Berndt Hamm, in tracing Luther's transition from medieval theologian to reformer, says that Luther did not write for spiritual mountain climbers or virtuosi. For that reason, he was averse to the traditional image of a heavenly ladder upon which the soul climbs on its mystical upward journey to union with God. For him there was no special virtue or deed, experience, or knowledge, through which a pious person could climb to God. When he spoke of grace, he never meant it as a special endowment graciously given to a

18. "Heidelberg Disputation," *LW* 31:40. McGrath questions the accuracy of the translation of thesis 20, indicating that it obscures Luther's intent: "Not only is the important allusion to Exodus 33:23 overlooked: on the basis of this translation, it is impossible to speak of the *hiddenness* of God's revelation–yet it is clear that this is precisely what Luther intended to convey by the phrase." Instead, he proposes the following: "The man who perceives the *visible rearward parts of God* as seen in suffering and the cross does, however, deserve to be called a theologian" (emphasis added). Such a translation lends clarity to Luther's thinking: "For Luther, the sole authentic *locus* of man's knowledge of God is the cross of Christ, in which God is to be found revealed, and yet paradoxically hidden in that revelation. Luther's reference to the *posteriora Dei* serves to emphasize that, like Moses, we can only see God from the rear; we are denied a direct knowledge of God, or a vision of his face (cf. Exodus 33:23: *videbis posteriora mea, faciem autem meam videre non poteris*). The cross does indeed reveal God—but that revelation is of the *posteriora Dei*. In that it is the *posteriora Dei* which are made visible, this revelation of God must be regarded as an indirect revelation—but a genuine revelation nonetheless" (McGrath, *Luther's Theology of the Cross*, 148–49.) Eric Gritsch provides another alternate translation of art. 19: "That person does not deserve to be called a theologian who perceives and understands the invisible nature of God through God's own works (Rom 1:20);" and art. 20: "But he deserves to be called an theologian who comprehends what is *visible* and *world-oriented* in God through suffering and the cross." (Gritsch, "The Origins of the Lutheran Teaching on Justification," in *Justification by Faith: Lutherans and Catholics in Dialogue VII*, ed. H. George Anderson, T. Austin Murphy, and Joseph A. Burgess [Minneapolis: Augsburg, 1985], 162–71).
19. The "hidden God" is an underlying assumption of Luther's *theologia crucis*. Only in suffering is God's power shown forth. God works through opposites; therefore, God remains hidden. As a result, God is only known and recognized through faith. It is not something the world at large knows or understands. It can come only from without and is dependent upon revelation.

mystical elite, who went beyond the normal plane of Christian life in order to take part in extraordinary experiences of salvific and blessed nearness to God. No, for him grace in all its divine fullness and peer was a movement that embraced all believing Christians.[20]

This comes out even more clearly in his *Explanations of the Ninety-Five Theses*, which Luther completed in early 1518 before leaving for Heidelberg. In thesis 58 he contrasts the *theologia gloriae*—"the deceiving theology"—with the *theologia crucis*, the true theology. It is only in the wake of scholastic theology's ascendance that "the theology of the cross has been abrogated, and everything has been completely turned up-side-down." Tracing the *theologia crucis* back to the New Testament, especially to the apostle Paul, Luther identifies his theology of the cross as the true theology, while scholastic theology's *theologia gloriae* has created falsehood and led people astray.

> Yet in the meantime they [scholastic theologians] have opened the floodgates of heaven and flooded the treasury of indulgences and the merits of Christ so that by this deluge almost the whole Christian world is ruined, unless my faith deceives me. A theologian of glory does not recognize, along with the Apostle, *the crucified and hidden God alone* [1 Cor. 2:2]. He sees and speaks of God's glorious manifestation among the heathen, how his *invisible* nature can be known from the things which are *visible* [cf. Rom. 1:20] and how he is present and powerful in all things everywhere. This theologian of glory, however, learns from Aristotle that the object of the will is the good and the good is worthy to be loved, while the evil, on the other hand, is worthy of hate. He learns that God is the highest good and exceedingly lovable. Disagreeing with the theologian of the cross, he defines the treasury of Christ as the removing and remitting of punishments, things which are most evil and worthy of hate. In opposition to this the theologian of the cross defines the treasury of Christ as impositions and obligations of punishments, things which are best and most worthy of love. Yet the theologian of

20. Berndt Hamm, *The Early Luther: Stages in a Reformation Reorientation,* trans. Martin J. Lohrmann, Lutheran Quarterly Books (Grand Rapids: Eerdmans, 2014), 197–98. Compare Luther's own words from his lectures on Galatians, see below, pg. 95 n49.

> glory still receives money for his treasury, while the theologian of the cross, on the other hand, offers the merits of Christ freely. Yet people do not consider the theologian of the cross worthy of consideration, but finally even persecute him.[21]

In the proofs that accompanied the *Heidelberg Disputation* Luther clearly defined his position vis-à-vis scholastic theology. Elaborating on thesis 20, Luther draws the following conclusions: First, he places the "visible things of God" in opposition to the "invisible," saying that because humankind misused its God-given wisdom,[22] God has chosen to be known in visible things, namely in God's "human nature, weakness, foolishness," in order that "those who did not honor God as manifested in his works should honor him as he is hidden in his suffering." As a result of this action on God's part, "it is not sufficient for anyone, and it does him no good to recognize God in his glory and majesty, unless he recognizes him in the humility and shame of the cross."[23] It is for this reason that "true theology and recognition of God are in the crucified Christ."[24] This, however, is the opposite of what "speculative" theology teaches, for it reasons about "God and his properties," elaborating on its own "ideas of God, sometimes on the basis of his works in creation, sometimes from

21. "Explanations of the Ninety-five Theses," *LW* 31225, 227 (emphasis added).
22. "Of course, Luther did not deny that natural human beings have some knowledge of God based on the works and the law of God. . . . In fact, this knowledge, as the apostle Paul shows, has not led to the adoration of God, but to idolatry. That is why God chose another way to reveal himself to human beings in order to save them. He presents himself to them, hiding his glory under the weakness of the cross. Basing himself on Exod. 33:18–23, Luther says that it is necessary for us to see the *back of God, that is to say, in his weakness, and not to see his face* directly, that is to say his glory" (Lienhard, *Luther: Witness to Jesus Christ*, 256). On this, see also von Loewenich, *Luther's Theology of the Cross*, 18ff, McGrath, *Luther's Theology of the Cross,* 149–52, and Ebeling, *Luther: An Introduction*, 227ff.
23. Again Lienhard: "Instead then of recognizing God on the basis of his works, a possibility which has not led human beings to true worship and which is now in fact lost to us, and instead of serving him by works, it is necessary hereforth to find him in the suffering of Christ and to serve him by accepting the sufferings of the Christian life itself. Thus the theology of the cross is found to be opposed to the theology of glory" (*Luther: Witness to Jesus Christ*, 256).
24. "Heidelberg Disputation," *LW* 31:53.

reason itself which postulates a supreme being and thereby attributes a certain number of properties to him."[25]

This led Luther to only one conclusion, which he states clearly and distinctly in his comments on thesis 21: "God can be found only in suffering and the cross."[26] For Luther it had been the scholastic theologians' failure in recognizing this that led them to focus on works, glory, strength, wisdom, and goodness instead of suffering, the cross, weakness, folly, and evil;[27] yet this is what true theology demands. Because humanity has distorted what knowledge of God it has, leading to idolatry, God chose to be known by visible things and wished to be recognized in suffering, and to condemn wisdom concerning invisible things by means of wisdom concerning visible things, so that those who did not honor God as manifested in his works should honor him as he is hidden in his suffering.[28]

Instead of focusing on this visible act of God, however, the theologian of glory looks to the invisible nature of God, which means that theologians must speculate and use analogy to describe and understand God's true nature.[29] Rather than enlightening theologians about God, however, this only served to lead them astray.

Theology as defined by Luther takes a different approach. By limiting itself to the visible things of God, it gives its attention and takes its orientation from the places where God has chosen to be found. Rather than looking behind the events of Scripture to uncover secret symbols and meanings, it places its trust in the events themselves. This theology of the cross, according to Gerhard Ebeling, is opposed to attempts to "perceive the invisible nature of God from

25. Lienhard, *Luther: Witness to Jesus Christ*, 256.
26. "Heidelberg Disputation," *LW* 31:53.
27. Ibid.
28. Ibid, 52.
29. See McGrath's discussion of Luther's rejection of analogy as a means of knowing God, *Luther's Theology of the Cross*, 158–59.

the works of creation, through reason." The direction seeks not to locate the invisible glorious God, but discerns "God shamefully crucified, who came forth in visible form, into the flesh, into history and into suffering." It locates God in the reality of this world and not in an otherworldly transcendence. Whereas a theology of glory establishes "a harmony between God and the world, . . . establishing a correspondence between them," the knowledge of God that comes via the theology of the cross is that of contradiction. "In spite of this, or in fact because of this, it is only the latter which does justice to reality. Alluding to Isa. 5:20, Luther says that 'the theology of glory calls evil good and good evil: the theologian of the cross says what is true'; that is, he gives a true account of reality." It's for that reason that the "aim of the theology of the cross is in a pre-eminent sense 'practical', for its aim is a right use of reality."[30]

According to James Nestingen, what emerges in these early writings of Luther is the unfolding of "his developing insight into a way of thinking in which the cross and resurrection of Jesus of Nazareth function not merely cognitively but paradigmatically, shaping both theology and theologian." By all accounts, what Luther sets out to do in the Heidelberg Disputation is "cruciform" in organization and design, an organization "in which Good Friday and Easter together shape the very form of Luther's thinking."[31]

30. Ebeling, *Luther: An Introduction*, 227–28. Cf. Kolb's description of Luther's theology: "Of all the places to search for God, the last place most people would think to look is the gallows. Martin Luther confessed that there, in the shadows cast by death, God does indeed meet his straying, rebellious human creatures. There God reveals who he is; there he reveals who they are. Not in flight beyond the clouds, but in the dust of the grave God has come to tell it like it is about himself and about humanity" ("Luther on the Theology of the Cross," 443).

31. James Nestingen, "Luther's Heidelberg Disputation: An Analysis of the Argument," *Word and World* Supplement No. 1 (1992): 147, 151–52. It should be noted that in Luther's usage the *theologia crucis* always refers to the whole Christ event, incorporating incarnation, crucifixion, resurrection, and ascension. Together these form the cross event. Note also Eric Gritsch's description of Luther's theological orientation: "Good biblical theology, Luther contended, will always have to insist on the centrality of 'Christ crucified.' In that sense, theology is cruciform because it must be shaped by the event that intersected the history of the world, God's

Reflecting the same point of view, Gerhard Forde describes the manner in which the cross becomes the organizing principle of Luther's theology this way:

> The word "cross". . . is, of course, shorthand for the entire narrative of the crucified and risen Jesus. As such it includes the OT preparation (many of the foundational passages for the theology of the cross come from the OT!), the crucifixion and resurrection of Jesus, and his exaltation. It is important to include resurrection and exaltation because there is considerable confusion abroad about their place in a theology of the cross. It is often claimed, for instance, that a theology of glory is a theology of resurrection while a theology of the cross is "only" concerned with crucifixion. Nothing could be further from the truth. As a matter of fact, a theology of the cross is impossible without resurrection. It is impossible to plumb the depths of crucifixion without the resurrection.[32]

In this regard, with Paul's theology as a background, it is understood that Luther clearly carried into the *Heidelberg Disputation* Paul's use of the cross and the resurrection as paradigm for the life of the believer—"If we live, we live to the Lord, and if we die, we die to the Lord" (Rom. 14:8). Or as Luther put it, "God does all this because it is his nature first to destroy and to bring to nothing whatever is in us before he gives us of his own, as it is written, 'The Lord makes poor and makes rich; he brings down to hell and brings back again' (I Sam 2:7,6)."[33]

incarnation in Jesus of Israel. Law and gospel, faith and love are the four extensions of a cross which is the incarnation" (*Martin: God's Court Jester; Luther in Retrospect* [Philadelphia: Fortress Press, 1983], 168). Cf. also Lienhard, *Luther: Witness to Jesus Christ*, 19.

32. Forde, *On Being a Theologian of the Cross*, 1. He goes on to explain further: "It is vital to realize that a proper theology of the cross does not isolate attention just on the cross event. To speak of the 'cross story' is a shorthand way of intending the entire story culminating in cross and resurrection. The cross is the key to unlocking the entire story" (8–9). See also Deanna Thompson, *Crossing the Divide: Luther, Feminism, and the Cross* (Minneapolis: Fortress Press, 2004), 26: Luther's cross theology does not stop with Good Friday, for in order for the crucifixion to become good news, "it must be viewed from the other side of the resurrection." In fact, "the life of faith is defined by constant movement from cross to resurrection and back again, from condemnation to justification and back."

Luther concentrated on the visible act of God on the cross because it is there that we see the true God; it is from there that we gain a proper knowledge of God.[34] Commenting on Luther's understanding of the knowledge of God, Ebeling says,

> The knowledge of God which is given in Jesus Christ does not therefore constitute a particular item of doctrine which supplements a general knowledge of God, but it the beginning of all true knowledge of God and man. It is the complete opposite of speculation concerning God in his nakedness, god in his majesty, and points us towards God who came in the flesh and was therefore clothed in promises, who came close to us, imparted himself to us, and was thereby revealed; not towards the God who is wordless, and therefore renders us speechless in temptations, but towards the word of God, God proclaimed, God who bestows faith and gives assurance.[35]

There is no doubt in Luther's mind that the proper knowledge of God comes only through Jesus and the cross. This, however, is not a denial of other ways of knowing God; in fact, he recognizes a general knowledge of God and admits that even pagans have some knowledge of God.[36] The problem, as Luther sees it, however, is not

33. Nestingen, "Luther's Heidelberg Disputation," 152.

34. See Paul Hinlickly, *Luther and Beloved Community* (Grand Rapids: Eerdmans, 2010), 33ff, for a discussion of the role of apocalyptic in Luther, which he insists is the true import of Luther's *theologia crucis*.

For Paul, the cross brings about an epistemological crisis, creating a watershed, inaugurating a "new creation," "God's coming reality," something that has been "hidden from the ages but which is now coming to pass. Apocalypse reveals . . . because it is first of all this assertion of God's reign, the invasive new creation, the event in time and space of incorporation of those dead in their sins to new life in the Beloved Community."

For Luther, a pupil of Paul, this epistemological crisis rendered by the apocalyptic, "is triggered by the real presence of the crucified and risen Lord to bestow Himself with His gifts in evoking human faith in the corporate assembly of those called out to the new creation. This real presence of Christ the subject both for us and in us accordingly constitutes for Luther the exclusive point of departure for theological knowledge."

35. Ebeling, *Luther: An Introduction*, 234.

36. See, for example, the discussion by Ernest L. Simmons Jr. ("Creation in Luther's Theology of the Cross," *Dialog* 30, no. 1 [Winter 1991]: 50ff) in which he stresses Luther's distinction between a "general knowledge" of God and the "proper knowledge" of God that comes through Christ. "The general knowledge of God is discernable by reason and is capable of affirming *that* God is, creates, is righteous, and judges. . . but this can never be used to discern

knowledge per se, but the "proper knowledge" of God. Reflecting on St. Paul, what humankind usually does with its knowledge of God is to create idols. Idolatry, or false knowledge, therefore is the real problem that must be countered. According to Lienhard,

> Commenting on Rom. 1:23ff, Luther admitted a certain knowledge of God among the pagans. But he had equally shown that the natural knowledge of God had turned to perversion, in the sense that human beings had not been content to adore the mysterious God, certain of whose properties appeared to them through the works of creation. Following the apostle, Luther called that idolatry into which the pagans fell. One of the particular forms of idolatry stressed by the reformer is justification by works. Therefore, the true revelation of God in Jesus Christ is not only a revelation which complements that which people know already from nature on the subject of God, but it is opposed to this knowledge. In fact, in Jesus Christ God must first of all destroy a certain number of false ideas about God and salvation that human beings had formed. That is where the theology of the cross is rooted.[37]

Therefore Luther is led to say that while humankind has knowledge of God, that knowledge is confused and unreliable. Natural human resources, that is, reason, only leads humanity to idolatry. While it may indeed lead to a god, it will not be to the God who saves. It is for the sake of knowing the true God, according to Luther, that God comes to humankind. In order for true knowledge of God to come about, all the false conceptions must be destroyed.[38] So the cross

God in God's self, only God in creation." For this reason, because it is "in the order of creation," general knowledge of God is limited and "the gospel is hidden from it." On the other hand, a proper knowledge of God, which is "inside knowledge of God particularly in God's attitude toward the sinner. This is the Gospel. . . . The proper knowledge is not contrary to reason but rather beyond it because it can only be embraced through faith. . . . The proper knowledge then is knowledge of God in Christ, the special revelation of God in human flesh" (51–52).

37. Lienhard, *Luther: Witness to Jesus Christ*, 265.

38. Cf. Gerhard Forde's comments, which make the same point: "That is the point of a theology of the cross. God cannot come directly to people bound to their own illusions. God can only die at the hands of such piety. God can only be rejected. So it must be if God is to unmask the bondage for what it is. Hence Luther maintained that in Christ, God comes 'under the form of opposites,' under the opposite of what an aspiring free will wants or expects. God comes not as the great and glorious ruler but as the humble, suffering, despised, and rejected outcast

destroys all approaches to God, in order to allow God to properly make himself known.[39]

The proper knowledge of God is important because of what we learn about God in this revelation. As opposed to the general knowledge of God that enables us to acknowledge the reality of God, the proper knowledge of God reveals God's intention for us.[40] What we see displayed on the cross is a God of love, a God who desires the salvation of humankind. It is a knowledge based on relationship, in which God comes to us and identifies with us. On the cross, we see God at work for us.

But this knowledge of God is a hidden knowledge discernible only by faith.[41] The concealment of God, which stands in contrast to

who is beaten, spit on, and executed, as one quite superfluous to the way we must run things. 'He came to his own home, and his own people received him not' (John 1:11). So it had to be. There is no way to get through to the bound, disaffected will directly. Hence life comes only through death. To put it most bluntly, our so-called freedom cannot stop until it has done away with God altogether. Only when that happens, only when the blood is actually spilled, is there a chance that we might be saved. Only if God comes–*actually* will there be any help" ("The Work of Christ," *Christian Dogmatics*, vol. 2, ed. Carl Braaten and Robert Jenson [Philadelphia: Fortress Press, 1984], 67–68). Bonhoeffer's statement in *LPP* that "only a suffering God can help" reflects this same orientation (DBWE 8:479). See chapter 10 for a further discussion of Bonhoeffer's thinking on this point.

39. See Ebeling, *Luther: An Introduction*, 228ff.

40. Reason can only aver that God exists, but it cannot determine anything about the nature of God. In the truest sense, there is a limit to reason. According to Ebeling, "The rational knowledge of God is a challenge to seek God in the darkness. [Quoting Luther, he continues:] '. . . Reason can not rightly accord him his deity nor attribute it to him as his own, though it rightly belongs to him alone. It knows that God exists. But who or what person it may be who is properly called God, it does not know. . . . Thus reason plays blindman's-buff with God and makes vain errors and always misses the mark, calling God what is not God, and not calling god what is God, which it would not do if it did not know that God existed, or if it did know what thing was God, or what God was. Thus it rushes in and accords the name of and the divine honour, and the title, God, to what it thinks God is, and so never hits on the true God, but always finds the Devil or its own darkness, which the Devil rules. Thus there is a great difference between knowing that a god exists, and knowing what or who God is. The first is known to nature, and is written in every heart. The second is taught only by the Holy Spirit'" (ibid., 229–30).

41. "A theology of the cross turns to God in suffering and on the cross through faith precisely because it is only faith, and not reason, that can discern the activity of God in this hiddenness particularly in the resurrection. This hiddenness of God is the 'the form of the opposite' and for Luther is there precisely to allow for faith. It is faith alone which is capable of discerning the activity of God in such destruction. The God of sovereignty and law disclosed through

human reason, is necessary because it "becomes for the believer the abrogation of all his own wisdom and righteousness, so that God can do his work." In the truest sense, it is a "theology of faith," because rather than relying on one's own wisdom or works, "it is a theology of the work and word of God, a theology which is 'practised' [*sic*] in temptation, and in this way and for this reason alone it is a theology of certainty."[42] Because of the contradiction between human wisdom and the way in which God desires to be known, only faith can understand the hidden God, the *deus absconditus*. "The revelation of God in the cross lies *abscondita sub contrario*, so that God's strength is revealed under apparent weakness, and his wisdom under apparent folly."[43] The revealed God remains the hidden God and is discerned only in faith. Nevertheless, through these events, it is the true God working to save humankind. While the eyes of reason might see only God's wrath, the eyes of faith see God's mercy. "In the one unitary event of revelation in the cross, God's wrath and mercy are revealed simultaneously—but only faith is able to recognize the *opus proprium* as it lies hidden under the *opus alienum*; only faith discerns the merciful intention which underlies the revealed wrath; only faith perceives the real situation which underlies the apparent situation."[44]

The cross is God's chosen way to reveal himself to a world that is blinded by its own wisdom and understanding. Because of this blindness, instead of God having been revealed through the visible works of creation, God has been concealed. "Yet God wants to be known, his being seeks revelation. How, then, shall God reveal himself so that his revelation might really become a revelation for

the works of creation by reason now is encountered through the mediation of suffering and the cross in weakness and humility. At the cross there is no room for pride and this avoids the danger of idolatry found in a theology derived from reason alone" (Simmons, "Creation in Luther's Theology of the Cross," 52–53).

42. Ebeling, *Luther: An Introduction*, 228.

43. McGrath, *Luther's Theology of the Cross*, 65.

44. Ibid., 165.

man?" When the world is blinded and cannot perceive what should naturally reveal God, God chooses a different way to reveal himself. That way is the cross.[45]

The question that remains, however, is what do we see there? According to the eyes of wisdom, everything there stands contrary to God. But for Luther that is the point of the *theologia crucis*. There is "nothing else to be seen than disgrace, poverty, death, and everything that is shown us in the suffering Christ."[46] As von Loewenich points out,

> These are all things that in our opinion have nothing divine in them but rather point to man's trouble, misery, and weakness. There especially no one would of himself look for God's revelation. Into such a concealment God enters in order to reveal himself. If there is to be revelation of God, the visible God must become the hidden God. God becomes "hidden in suffering." As God hides himself, the "visible things of God" become manifest: "His human nature, weakness, foolishness" (Explanation of Theses 20, Heidelberg Disputation).[47]

In terms of what we really know about God, Luther's definition limits that knowledge to "the crucified and hidden God."[48] We know a suffering God who is at the same time a hidden God, and knowledge of this God comes *sub contrario*, under the sign of the opposite. This aspect of Luther's thought keeps him tied to both the human Jesus and the cross.

That this is central to Luther's conception of theology can be seen in his commentary on Galatians. Guided by his own conviction

45. Von Loewenich, *Luther's Theology of the Cross*, 28.

46. *WA* 5, 108, 1ff; quoted in von Loewenich, *Luther's Theology of the Cross*, 28.

47. Von Loewenich, *Luther's Theology of the Cross*, 28–29.

48. This phrase is from his "Explanations of the Ninety-Five Theses" (*LW* 31:225). This language is significant and becomes one of the primary expressions of his *theologia crucis* and therefore one of the ways Luther understands God. This has implications for Christology, because for Luther it is not just the human Jesus that dies on the cross, but God is crucified. This he can say because his christological orientation is shaped by the *communication idiomatum*. This emphasis is what Bonhoeffer picks up in his own Christology.

that Scripture, which is the rule and norm for Christian thinking, warns against speculation about the majesty of God, but rather directs our attention to Christ and to him alone as a means of knowing God, Luther gives the following explanation for the centrality of Jesus for Christian theology. Reflecting on St. Paul's salutation to the Galatians, he clearly indicates why Christian theology finds its center in the person of Jesus.

> But true Christian theology, as I often warn you, does not present God to us in His majesty, as Moses' other teachings do, but Christ born of the Virgin as our Mediator and High Priest. Therefore when we are embattled against the Law, sin, and death in the presence of God, nothing is more dangerous than to stray into heaven with our idle speculations, there to investigate God in His incomprehensible power, wisdom, and majesty, to ask how He created the world and how He governs it. If you attempt to comprehend God this way and want to make atonement to Him apart from Christ the mediator, making your works, fasts, cowl, and tonsure the mediation between Him and yourself, you will inevitably fall, as Lucifer did (Is. 14:14), and in horrible despair lose God and everything. For as in His own nature God is immense, incomprehensible, and infinite, so to man's nature He is intolerable. Therefore if you want to be safe and out of danger to your conscience and your salvation, put a check on this speculative spirit. Take hold of God as Scripture instructs you (1 Cor. 1:21,24): "Since, in wisdom, the works did not know God through wisdom, it pleased God through the folly of what we preach to save those who believe. We preach Christ crucified, a stumbling block to Jews and folly to Gentiles, but to those who are called, both Jews and Greeks, Christ the power of God and the wisdom of God." Therefore begin where Christ began—the Virgin's womb, in the manger, and at His mother's breasts. For this purpose He came down, was born, lived among men, suffered, was crucified, and died, so that in every possible way He might present Himself to our sight. He wanted us to fix the gaze of our hearts upon Himself and thus to prevent us from clambering into heaven and speculating about the Divine Majesty. . . . Therefore whenever you consider the doctrine of justification and wonder how or where or in what condition to find a God who justifies or accepts sinners, then you must know that there is no other God than this Man Jesus Christ. Take

> hold of Him; cling to Him with all your heart, and spurn all speculations about the Divine Majesty: for whoever investigates the majesty of God will be consumed by His glory.[49]

In his argument with Erasmus in *Bondage of the Will*,[50] Luther makes it clear why this concentration on what God has revealed in Christ is important.

> We have to argue in one way about God or the will of God as preached, revealed, offered, and worshiped, and in another way about God as he is not preached, not revealed, not offered, not worshiped. To the extent, therefore, that God hides himself and wills to be unknown to us, it is no business of ours. . . . God must therefore be left to himself in his own majesty, for in this regard we have nothing to do with him, nor has he willed that we should have anything to do with him. But we have something to do with him insofar as he is clothed and set forth in his Word, through which he offers himself to us.[51]

Luther is quick to admit that there is more to God than we know, as the paradoxical mysteries of the universe exhibit; but what is important and necessary for us to know comes through his word.

> God does many things that he does not disclose to us in his word; he also wills many things which he does not disclose himself as willing in his word. Thus he does not will the death of a sinner, according to his word; but he wills it according to that inscrutable will of his. It is our business, however, to pay attention to the word and leave that inscrutable will alone, for we must be guided by word and not by that inscrutable will.[52]

49. "Lectures on Galatians," *LW* 26:28–29. For an overview of Luther's argument, see Gerhard Forde, *The Captivation of the Will: Luther vs. Erasmus on Freedom and Bondage* (Grand Rapids: Eerdmans, 2005).
50. These comments, as well as those from Luther's Galatians commentary quoted above, indicate the continuing influence of the *theologia crucis* on Luther's thought, even though the term itself is absent. Reference can also be made to his commentary on Isaiah 53, which gives ample indication that *theologia crucis* is present even at the end of Luther's life. See Lienhard, *Luther's Theology of the Cross*, 36–37. For an analysis of Luther's *theologia crucis*, together with a rationale for its centrality in understanding Luther's theology and bringing continuity to Luther's thought, see Dillenberger, *God Hidden and Revealed*, 146ff.
51. "The Bondage of the Will," *LW* 33:139.
52. Ibid., 140.

In this way, the *theologia crucis* is not limited to concerns about the doctrine of atonement, but rather is an overall orientation that provides the center from which Luther is able to view all theology. But because of this orientation, his theology is characterized by its christological focus. Nevertheless, an indelible link between justification and Christology is maintained. This is because Luther's thought is always focused on the soteriological aspects of the Christian faith. Luther's concern was not for God in and of God's own self, but with God for us. Therefore Christ is always linked to soteriology, the person of Christ with the work of Christ—which is justification.[53]

The issue that brought about Luther's reformation was that of salvation, which Luther came to define in terms of justification by faith as opposed to salvation by works. *Justification by faith* became Luther's shorthand phrase to describe the work of Christ and his benefits for believers. In other words, for Luther the justification by faith formula was the encapsulation of the gospel; hence, its central place in determining Christian thinking. It is justification that affirms that humanity, in spite of its sinful nature, might enter into a gracious relationship with God through the death and resurrection of Jesus Christ. For Luther, according to McGrath, "Jesus Christ is the righteousness of God, revealing at one and the same time God's condemnation of sin and remedy for it."[54] This is what stands at the heart of Luther's *theologia crucis*.

53. Cf. Lienhard, *Luther: Witness to Jesus Christ*, 371–75. The importance of this connection for Luther was stated quite explicitly by Wilhelm Maurer, "Die Anfänge von Luthers Theologie," *Theologische Literaturzeitung* 77 (1952), 4: "The doctrine of justification by faith is not the root, but the fruit, not the fundamental principle, but the ultimate consequence of the young Martin Luther's theology. It has grown out of a new understanding of the great early church doctrines of the Trinity and Christology. It is a result of a return to the roots, which the young Martin Luther has undertaken, getting beneath the surface of Scholasticism, down to the theology of the Fathers of the church" [quoted in Lienhard, *Luther: Witness to Jesus Christ,* 77n3].

54. McGrath, *Luther's Theology of the Cross*, 21.

For Christians justification or forgiveness of sins is tied explicitly to the man Jesus.

> Therefore whenever you consider the doctrine of justification and wonder how or where or in what condition to find a God who justifies or accepts sinners, then you must know that there is no other God than this Man Jesus Christ. Take hold of Him; cling to Him with all your heart, and spurn all speculation about the Divine Majesty; for whoever investigates the majesty of God will be consumed by His glory. . . . Take note, therefore, in the doctrine of justification or grace that when we all must struggle with the Law, sin, death, and the devil, we must look at no other God than this incarnate and human God. . . .
>
> This is why Paul makes such a frequent practice of linking Jesus Christ with God the Father, to teach us what is the true Christian religion. It does not begin at the top, as all other religions do; it begins at the bottom. It bids us climb up by Jacob's ladder; God Himself leans on it, and its feet touch the earth, right by Jacob's head (Gen. 28:12). Therefore whenever you are concerned to think and act about your salvation, you must put away all speculations about the Majesty, all thought of works, traditions, and philosophy—indeed, of the Law of God itself. And you must run directly to the manger and the mother's womb, embrace this Infant and Virgin's Child in your arms, and look at Him—born, being nursed, growing up, going about in human society, teaching, dying, rising again, ascending about all the heavens, and having authority over all things. In this way you can shake off all terrors and errors, as the sun dispels the clouds. This vision will keep you on the proper way, so that you may follow where Christ has gone.[55]

Rightly understood, justification and Christology are opposite sides of the same coin for Luther. The former speaks of the benefits of Christ's work, while the latter focuses on God working through Christ; the former is the reason we are interested in God, the latter provides the assurance that it is indeed God that we are dealing with. So what we see in Luther's *theologia crucis* is an orientation that unites both justification and Christology into an inextricable whole, so that

55. "Lectures on Galatians," *LW* 26:29–30.

it is not possible to think of God without the world, or of forgiveness of sins without Christ. As a result, Luther's concern for not separating Christology from its soteriological intent is maintained.

Therefore, while the *theologia crucis* is certainly a christological term, it is much more. It encompasses the whole of theology, orienting us to an understanding of God, both as hidden and revealed, and of God in relationship with the world. For Luther, the cross is the one element that is both the necessary and distinctive mark of Christian theology. In that way the *theologia crucis* does not stand in opposition to or in competition with justification or Christology as being central themes in Luther's thinking, but rather properly unites them and ties Christology to soteriology, and God to the life of the believer.[56]

In this light, rightly understood, Luther's concern for the proper knowledge of God is important because it is connected to the proper work of God, namely salvation of the sinner. Distinguishing between the proper and alien works of God, Luther demonstrates his understanding of how salvation comes to the individual. The proper work of God through Christ is to create "grace, righteousness, truth, patience in the spirit of a man who has been predestined. For the righteousness of Christ and his merit justifies and remits sins. . . . The merits of Christ perform an alien work," on the other hand, "in that they effect the cross, labor, all kinds of punishment, finally death and hell in the flesh, to the end that the body of sin is destroyed, our members which are upon earth are mortified, and sinners are turned into hell."[57]

56. It should be stated that for Luther the *theologia crucis*, while it places the emphasis on the cross of Christ, is not limited to that; it is not just the crucifixion, but rather the whole Christ event. With the soteriological motif always in the forefront of Luther's thinking, we can see a natural relationship of all these elements in Luther's theology. See above, notes 16, 31 and 32.

57. "Explanations of the Ninety-five Theses," LW 31: 224–25.

In the early Luther, where the *theologia crucis* is prominently displayed, these concerns are voiced not only in the heat of academic debate, but occur also as themes in his preaching; of particular importance are the sermons from 1519, which are significant for this work not only because they display Luther's vision, but because they were also important influences on Bonhoeffer's theological development. Von Soosten, for example, has demonstrated that Bonhoeffer had a preference for the early writings of Luther, noting that Luther's 1519 sermons played an important role in Bonhoeffer's dissertations. In *Sanctorum Communio*, for example, Bonhoeffer drew on Luther's sermon on Holy Communion of that year to shape his understanding of the church,[58] while the argument of *Act and Being* was developed using insights from this same work and "A Sermon on Preparing to Die."[59] This latter sermon, in particular, is marked by christological concerns that were been shaped by Luther's *theologia crucis*.

In "A Sermon on Preparing to Die," Luther focused his thoughts on the human Christ who dies on the cross. This is where one finds God's grace; by concentrating solely on "the death of Christ" one finds life. It is with Christ's death on the cross that the punishment due humanity is taken away, having been borne by Jesus himself. "He takes your death upon himself," said Luther, "and strangles it so that it may not harm you."[60] What emerges clearly in these reflections are

58. Luther, "The Blessed Sacrament of the Holy and True Body of Christ, and the Brotherhoods," *LW* 35:49–73. See Joachim von Soosten, *Die Sozialität der Kirche: Theologie und Theorie der Kirche in Dietrich Bonhoeffers "Sanctorum Communio"* (Munich: Chr. Kaiser, 1992) 148–72, where he provides an extended discussion on the nature of this document and its influence on Bonhoeffer's thinking. According to Lienhard, these sermons were a part of a series Luther prepared that year, "instruments deliberately chosen for the purpose of making known his views on the subject of the gospel to a vast audience." In each the cross of Christ was "accorded special importance" and would remain "at the center of his reflections for the whole of his life." (*Luther: Witness to Jesus Christ,* 100–1).

59. "A Sermon on Preparing to Die," *LW* 42:95–15.

60. Ibid., 104–5.

the themes of the *theologia crucis*: in the human Jesus we encounter God, seeking God outside of Jesus is the work of the devil, Christ's suffering is both an example to follow and a consolation in time of trouble.[61]

These very themes continue to be of importance in Luther's thought throughout his life. Consider, for instance, the following statement from *Bondage of the Will*, which, by contrasting the invisible and visible things of God and a proper and improper knowledge of God, provides a summary of Luther's theological position:

> The secret will of the Divine Majesty is not a matter for debate, and the human temerity which with continual perversity is always neglecting necessary things in its eagerness to probe this one, must be called off and restrained from busying itself with the investigation of these secrets of God's majesty, which is impossible to penetrate because he dwells in light inaccessible. . . . Let it occupy itself instead with God incarnate, or as Paul puts it, with Jesus crucified, in whom are all the treasure of wisdom and knowledge, though in a hidden manner; for through him it is furnished abundantly with what it ought to know and ought not to know. It is God incarnate, moreover, who is speaking here: "I would . . . you would not"—God incarnate, I say, who has been sent into the world for the very purpose of willing, speaking, doing, suffering and offering to all men everything necessary for salvation.[62]

As persons of faith contemplate the appalling spectacle of Christ dying on the cross (the sheer foolishness and its scandalous nature, according to St. Paul [1 Cor. 1:18ff]), they are forced to concede that God does not appear to be revealed there at all. This orientation is fundamental to a correct appreciation of the significance of Luther's *theologia crucis*. The God who is crucified is the God who is hidden in his revelation. Any attempt to seek God in a place other than in

61. See Lienhard, *Luther: Witness to Jesus Christ,* 107–9, for a fuller discussion of these themes.
62. "Bondage of the Will," *LW* 33:145–46.

the cross of Christ is to be rejected out of hand as idle speculation: the theologian is forced, perhaps against his or her will, to come to terms with the riddle of the crucified and hidden God. As Luther liked to quote, "Truly you are a God who hides himself" (Isa. 45:15 NRSV).

Perhaps Luther himself provides the best summary of this theological orientation: *Crux probat Omnia*.[63] In this way, we see how the cross is more than a reference to a singular event but becomes "the paradigm of God's working"[64] providing "humankind its best view of the nature of God, for it reveals his *modus operandi*."[65] But even more, the cross reveals the true nature of God ("love and mercy")[66] and human beings (sinners clothed in the righteousness of God); seen together in this relationship at the foot of the cross, humanity finds life and is given hope, because human beings receive what is rightfully God's in exchange for its own sin.

Hans Iwand explains it this way:

> The Cross is not only an historical event, but it is a sign for us that uncovers all that we are in terms of power and worth, feelings and perceptions, and that renders us naked before God. The Cross tests our faith as it tests whether or not we actually intend to know only God and have only him in mind. In all of the sufferings that come our way, the Cross puts us to the test. "*Crux probat omnia*," the Cross is the test of everything.[67]

While more could be said about Luther's theology, for our purposes let the following points serve as a summary.[68]

63. "Psalmus V. Operationes in Psalmos," *WA* 5:179,31.
64. Joseph E. Vercruysse, "Luther's Theology of the Cross at the Time of the Heidelberg Disptutation," *Gregorianum* 57 (1976), cited in Neal J. Anthony, *Cross Narratives: Martin Luther's Christology and the Location of Redemption* (Eugene, OR: Pickwick, 2010), 53.
65. Kolb, "Luther on the Theology of the Cross," 451.
66. Ibid.
67. Hans J. Iwand, *The Righteousness of Faith according to Luther*, ed. Virgil F. Thompson, trans. Randi H. Lundell (Eugene, OR: Wipf & Stock, 2008), 36.
68. Cf. von Loewenich, *Luther's Theology of the Cross*, 19–22, McGrath, *Luther's Theology of the Cross*, 149–51, and Kurt K. Hendel, "Theology of the Cross," *Currents in Theology and Mission*

First, the *theologia crucis* is a theology of revelation. Rather than concentrating on the invisible unknowable aspects of God, the *theologia crucis* contents itself with the visible revelation of God. It is the theologian's task "to concern himself with God as he has chosen to reveal himself, instead of constructing preconceived notions of God which ultimately must be destroyed."[69] It is forced to deal with God where God is present.[70]

Second, the *theologia crucis* is a theology of faith. By the nature of the definition of God's revelation, it remains an indirect revelation—God remains hidden in his revelation. "In that it is God who is made known in the passion and cross of Christ, it is *revelation*; in that this revelation can only be discerned by the eye of faith, it is *concealed*." We are denied access to God's being in himself; we don't see God as he is in his essence; God is only revealed through masks; it is never a total revelation, but always partial. "Although it is indeed God who is revealed in the passion and the cross of Christ, he is not immediately recognisable *as God*."[71] In faith, however, God

39, no. 5 (October, 2012): 223–31. Cf. Ulrich Luz's study of the New Testament ("*Theologia crucis* als Mitte der Theologie im Neuen Testament," *Evangelische Theologie* 34 [1974]: 116–41); he sees a true *theologia crucis* as having three essential characteristics; summarized by Charles Cousar, they are the following: "(1) It understands the cross as the exclusive ground of salvation, with the result that all other saving events (such as the resurrection and the parousia) are considered in relation to it and all current understandings are critiqued by it. (2) It understands the cross as the starting point of theology, in the sense that it is not merely an isolated component of theology, but theology itself pure and simple, in the light of which all issues are at stake. (3) It understands the cross as the hub of theology, in the sense that from it statements of anthropology, views of history, ecclesiology, ethics, etc., radiate." (Charles B. Cousar, *A Theology of the Cross: The Death of Jesus in the Pauline Letters* [Minneapolis: Fortress Press, 1990], 8.)

69. McGrath, *Luther's Theology of the Cross*, 149.

70. The *theologia crucis* explains the way God is present. Cf. Leinhard, *Luther: Witness to Jesus Christ*, 65: "God is present in weakness; he makes alive by death; he judges in order to be gracious. At the center of this *theologia crucis* is the suffering humanity of Jesus Christ. God hides himself there is order to reveal himself there."

71. Ibid. Cf. 22: "Luther discovered in the incarnation the dialectic of God hidden and revealed. God does not hide himself by remaining far from human beings, he hides himself *in* the humanity of Christ. But he hides himself there in order to be revealed to faith. If he were not there, there would be no assurance; if he were not hidden there, there would be no faith."

is seen hidden under the weakness of human flesh. It is God who is present in the man who is humiliated and crucified. For Luther, if it is not God who is present in Jesus Christ to save us, then we are without hope.[72] Because God is truly present in Jesus, Luther can claim that it is God who suffers and dies on the cross. It was Luther's understanding of the *communicatio idiomatum* that enabled him to see God as participating in the life of the world.[73]

Third, this means it is a theology of limitation. Rather than claiming to know everything about God, it concentrates on discerning God where God has revealed himself. This means the place where God is to be found is not in the glorious works of creation, but in suffering and the cross. God has rejected the invisible for the visible, and the visible presence of God is in the crucified Christ. "The cross shatters human illusions concerning the capacity of human reason to discern God in this manner."[74]

Fourth, by definition the *theologia crucis* is a christological theology. Because God's revelation is hidden in suffering and the cross, it is perceived only in faith and knowledge of God cannot be known apart from Christ. God is never known outside of this world, but always within it.[75] But even more than that, because God and

72. See ibid., 52, 133, and 227–28.

73. See ibid., 136ff and 364ff. Lienhard, 338, quoting from Luther, summarizes how Luther understood the unity of the two natures of Christ: "What pertains individually to one nature must be attributed to the whole person." He then continues: "It is in this sense that we must understand Luther's parable: when a dog bites a child in the leg, one says quite rightly that it is the child who has been bitten, even though the bite was only on the leg. 'Because God and a man are one person, one Christ, one Jesus, one Son of God and Mary, and not two persons, not two Christs, not two Jesuses, not two Sons, the result is that the properties of the two natures in Christ must all be, and in the same manner, attributed to the person'" (*WA* 45, 301, 21–25 [not translated].

74. Ibid, 150.

75. In the classic debate between Lutherans and Calvinists, whereas the Calvinists always held out the possibility that God's revelation was present both in the humanity of Jesus and apart from him, known as the *extra calvinisticum*, Lutherans insisted that God's revelation in Christ contains the whole truth about God and no longer occurs outside of God's activity in Christ, the *infra Lutheranum*. See Lienhard, *Luther: Witness to Jesus Christ*, 341ff and 375, among others, for a

humanity are so strongly united in Christ, Luther could claim that God is found nowhere else than in the man Jesus.[76] There is a christological orientation that shapes all theological statements. Therefore, even though it takes its cues from the passion of Christ, the implications are far greater. It governs the nature of the entire theological enterprise. To seek God apart from Christ, therefore, is "the work of the devil." Because God remains hidden in his revelation in Christ, it addresses itself to faith.

Fifth, in that regard, it follows that a *theologia crucis* is incarnational. It is God up close and personal, God not distant or removed from the world but intimately involved with the world. The incarnation displays the extent to which God is willing to go, the risks God is willing to bear to become like us, not for the mere fact of identification, but in order to save us. That is the scandal—the stumbling block—of Christianity, but at the same time, is its distinguishing mark.

Sixth, it is also a theology of hope. Suffering, rather than being something that is to be avoided, becomes something to be treasured. God is at work through Christ's suffering to bring about justification. Explained in terms of Luther's distinction between the proper work of God and the alien work of God, God works through the suffering of Christ first to humble the sinner and thereafter to justify the sinner. Therefore, rather than viewing suffering as a "nonsensical intrusion into the world," it is a precious treasure, "for revealed and yet hidden in precisely such sufferings is none other than the living God, working out the salvation for those whom he loves."[77] The

more detailed discussion on these issues. On the related *finitum capax infiniti/finitum non capax infiniti* debate, see James Burtness, "As Though God Were Not Given: Barth, Bonhoeffer and the *Finitum Capax Infiniti*," *Dialog* 19 (Fall 1980): 249–55.

76. At the center of Luther's Christology is the *communicatio idiomatum*, which means that any discussion of Christ cannot be separated from God. It is not just the man Jesus who suffers on the cross, it is God who suffers and dies. From within this framework Luther has no problem talking about a suffering God. See Lienhard, *Luther: Witness to Jesus Christ*, 341ff.

"crucified and hidden God" is not merely present in human suffering, but is a God who works through it to create life.

Seventh, in addition, it is a critical theology. According to Larry Rasmussen, Luther's phrase *crux probat omnia* ("the cross tests all things") "means, among other things, that the community of the cross is the source of unrelenting critique, a questioner of ideology, a destroyer of idols."[78] That means the *theologia crucis* stands over and against all human ways—including the church and it religious practices,

> passing judgment on the church where she has become proud and triumphant, or secure and smug, and calls her to the foot of the cross, there to remind her of the mysterious and hidden way in which God is at work in the world. The scene of total dereliction, of apparent weakness and folly, at Calvary is the theologian's paradigm for understanding the hidden presence and activity of God in the world and in the church.[79]

Ultimately, that means the *theologia crucis* can never be fit into our human schemes, allowing us to justify ourselves before God and the world. It will always remain "offensive" and "polemical."[80]

Because of its very nature, the *theologia crucis* must be critical. By revealing a God different from the God that human endeavors might disclose and forcing us to rely on faith if we are to know the true God, it becomes a "critical theory of God." Because the God on the cross can never fit into human constructs of God, "thus because of its subject, the theology of the cross, right down to its method and practice, can only be polemical, dialectical, antithetical, and critical

77. Ibid., 151.
78. Larry Rasmussen, "A Community of the Cross," *Dialog* 30, no. 20 (Spring 1991): 158.
79. McGrath, *Luther's Theology of the Cross*, 181. See also Udo Kern, "*Theologia crucis* als Fundamentalkritik," *Theologische Zeitschrift* 50 (1994): 63–70, and Bühler, *Kreuz und Eschatologie*, esp.73ff.
80. Forde, *On Being a Theologian of the Cross*, 2–4.

theory. . . . It is also crucifying theology, and is thereby liberating theology."[81]

Eighth, finally, it is an earthbound, this-worldly theology. Central to Luther's theological perspective is the *finitum capax infiniti.* The transcendent is never located outside (*extra*) of the physical world but always in (*infra*) it. That means Luther wanted to avoid the danger of separating God from humanity. Instead Luther's christological thought tied God to the world and the world to God.[82] Rather than providing the Christian an escape from the problems of living in the world, the *theologia crucis* places the Christian firmly in this world at the foot of the cross, there to see the world and be in it in the same manner as God. God's hidden presence on the cross will not allow the Christian to flee this world in search of a better one elsewhere. "It is a great thing to be a Christian and to have one's life hidden, not in some place, as in the case of hermits, or in one's own heart, which is exceedingly deep, but in the invisible God himself, namely, to live amid the things of the world and to be nourished by what appears

81. Jürgen Moltmann, *The Crucified God: The Cross of Christ as the Foundation and Criticism of Christian Theology*, trans. R. A. Wilson and John Bowden (New York: Harper & Row, 1974), 69.

82. See Carl Braaten, "The Person of Jesus Christ," in *Christian Dogmatics*, vol. 1, ed. Carl Braaten and Robert Jenson (Philadelphia: Fortress Press, 1984), 506–10, where he discusses the differences between the Reformed and Lutheran positions, perspectives that are reflected in the differences between Barth and Bonhoeffer. In particular, he points out the differences in the two positions being centered on their understanding of Christ captured in the phrases *finitum non capax infiniti* and *finitum capax infiniti.* The Reformed position sought to make clear distinctions between the divine and human natures of Christ. "The Calvinist zeal for the distinction of the natures was backed by the old-fashioned Nestorian logic. If the Logos is divine, then it could not limit itself to the flesh of Jesus. Accordingly, the Calvinists taught that the Logos, being infinite, must exist *extra carnem* (outside the flesh) and not be limited by its union with the flesh. The Heidelberg Catechism states: 'Because the divinity is everywhere present, it must follow that it is indeed outside its adopted humanity and yet none the less also in the same and remaineth in personal union with it.' Among Lutherans this doctrine was dubbed the *extra-Calvinisticum.* It implied a very loose linkage between the Logos and the man Jesus of Nazareth and led to a theology of glory, opening the door to exalted language about the Logos apart from its enfleshment. The Lutherans countered with a theology of the cross, holding that the Logos can be known only in the flesh. So they coined the phrase '*totus intra coarnem and numquam extra carnem*' (wholly in the flesh and never outside the flesh)" (508–9).

nowhere except by means of ordinary verbal indication and hearing alone."[83] Because this is God's way of being in the world, it also serves as a model of how Christians are to live in the world.

The *theologia crucis* is a critique of the world, while at the same time is a source of hope for the world. The cross of Jesus is both God's judgment on all sin and God's grace for all sinners. In faith, each believer experiences this anew. This is the basis for life in this world, for judging and knowing what is life and what is death. The cross passes judgment on that which thwarts God's plans, so that God's plans can make all things new.[84] The cross event both kills and makes new; it is both law and gospel. While it passes judgment on us, it kills the old so that the new creation might emerge.[85]

It is Christ crucified who defines God and God's mission in the world. The marks of God that become evident in Jesus Christ are not self-serving love, but a self-giving, other-directed love; not indifference and distance, but involvement and intimacy, compassion and love; not dominating arrogance, but humble servanthood; not power and invincibility, but vulnerability. It is a costly love and the marks are there to prove it—nail-pierced hands and a wounded side

83. "Lectures on Hebrews," *LW* 29:216.

84. See Isa. 66:10–14, for example, where the prophet draws on the most primal image to describe such a God: God is a mother offering her child milk at the breast, bouncing her child up and down on her knees, offering her child comfort. Such a God can and does make all things new.

85. In this connection it should be briefly stated that an important aspect of Luther's *theologia crucis* is the related concept of Christ's cross also being the Christian's cross. "'Cross' and 'suffering' refer, in the first place, to Christ's suffering and cross. But Luther is thinking at the same time about the cross of the Christian. For Luther the cross of Christ and the cross of the Christian belong together. For him the cross of Christ is not an isolated historical fact to which the life of the Christian stands only in a causal relationship (cf. WA I, 219, 30), but in the cross of Christ the relationship between God and man has become evident. The essence of the ultimate character of reality has become clear at this point. . . . That is to say, the cross of the Christian corresponds to the cross of Christ. To know God 'through suffering and cross' means that the knowledge of God comes into being at the cross of Christ, the significance of which becomes evident only to one who himself stands in cross and suffering" (von Loewenich, *Luther's Theology of the Cross*, 20). See also Walter Altmann, *Luther and Liberation: A Latin American Perspective* (Minneapolis: Fortress Press, 1992), 21, in which he discusses Luther's "conformitas Christi."

are the marks of God's enduring love. In contrast to the expectations of how and where God should be found among us, the gospel of Jesus Christ is cruciform in shape. From Luther's perspective, this was the best insight into who God is for us.

For Luther, this reflects the message of the New Testament, indeed all of Scripture.[86] In contrast to scholastic theology, in which the categories and terms for thought were shaped by philosophical categories, Luther's *theologia crucis* responds to the biblical witness. What Luther found in the New Testament at its center was the cross—that in the suffering and resurrection of Jesus God's love for us was duly displayed.

Having made these distinctions between the *theologia crucis* that characterizes his approach to theology and the *theologia gloriae*, Luther arrived at a definition of theology that differed from his contemporaries:

> A theologian of the cross (that is, one who speaks of the crucified and hidden God), teaches that punishments, crosses, and death are the most precious treasury of all and the most sacred relics which the Lord of this theology himself has consecrated and blessed, not alone by the touch of his most holy flesh but also by the embrace of his exceedingly holy and divine will, and he has left these relics here to be kissed, sought after, and embraced.[87]

As was discussed above, this *theologia crucis* has come to be viewed as being the key to understanding the dynamic of Luther's theology. McGrath puts it this way:

86. As Forde notes with regard to Luther's distinction between a *theologia gloriae* and a *theologia crucis*, "The cross story becomes our story. It presses itself upon us so that it becomes inescapable. It fights to displace the glory story. The cross thereby becomes the key to the biblical story and opens up new possibilities for appropriating–or better, being appropriated by–the entire story" (*On Being a Theologian of the Cross*, 8).

87. "Explanations of the Ninety-five Theses," *LW* 31:225.

> *Crux probat omnia*. For Luther, Christian thinking about God comes to an abrupt halt at the foot of the cross. The Christian is forced, by the very existence of the crucified Christ, to make a momentous decision. Either he will seek God elsewhere, or he will make the cross itself the foundation and criterion of his thought about God. The "crucified God"—to use Luther's daring phrase—is not merely the foundation of the Christian faith, but is also the key to a proper understanding of the nature of God. The Christian can only speak about the glory, the wisdom, the righteousness and the strength of God as they are revealed in the crucified Christ. For Luther, the cross presents us with a riddle—a riddle whose solution defines the distinctively Christian understanding of both man and God. If God *is* present in the cross, then he is a God whose presence is hidden from us. As Luther observed, citing Isaiah 45:15, "Truly you are a hidden God!" And yet the unfolding of that hidden presence of God in the scene of dereliction upon the cross holds the key to Luther's protracted search for a gracious God. No one would dream of seeking God in the "disgrace, poverty, death and everything else that is shown to us in the suffering Christ"—nevertheless, God is there, hidden and yet revealed, for those who care to seek him.[88]

Thus, for Luther the *theologia crucis* was a method for doing theology that leads us to the proper understanding of God. While Christology provides the framework for such thinking to take place, it involves more than the simple retelling of the passion narrative. It provides the whole orientation for theological discourse. But even more, the *theologia crucis* reflects the reality of the gospel and, as such, reflects God and God's ways in the world. In addition, the cross that is laid upon Christ is laid upon the Christian. As a result, the *theologia crucis* demands responsibility, and is practical, political, and worldly. In each of these ways the *theologia crucis* reflects the reality of God in our world as well as shapes the nature of the Christian life. According to Ebeling,

88. McGrath, *Luther's Theology of the Cross*, 1–2.

> The most astonishing feature of Luther's theological thought is that the distinction between the God of majesty and the crucified God, between the naked God and the incarnate God, between God himself, who remains withdrawn from us, and the word of God, to which we have to cling, did not mislead him into turning to one without being aware of the other, or into seizing hold of the one without knowing that he was seized by the other. Luther does not retreat into the kind of piety which venerates God in is own small corner, making him a personal and household idol and not daring to acknowledge him as Lord of the world. It would have been easy to have allowed the theology of the cross to become a quiet hold-and-corner piety such as this, venerating Jesus and living in his spirit, but not associating him with the God who is completely withdrawn from us, completely incomprehensible, who through his omnipotence does all things in his foreknowledge, and, since his is pure will, predetermines everything.[89]

Ultimately, what emerges in Luther's orientation is a new concept of God that has radical implications for how one does theology. Who is this God who deals thus with humankind? Luther's answer to this question, as it developed over the years 1513–1519, can be summarized in one of his most daring phrases: the God who deals with sinful humanity in this astonishing way is none other than the "crucified and hidden God" (*Deus crucifxus et absconditus*)—the God of the *theologia crucis.*[90]

Unfortunately this theological orientation, which was so important to Luther, was lost in the years following his death. In the debates that went on after Luther's death the interest lay elsewhere. During the period of orthodoxy the focus was on building a complete system of doctrine—thus leading Protestantism to fall back into the same situation out of which Luther and the reformers tried to break free.[91]

89. Ebeling, *Luther: An Introduction*, 239–40.
90. McGrath, *Luther's Theology of the Cross*, 147.
91. Cf. Altmann, *Luther and Liberation*, ix, in which he questions the loss of the dynamic of Luther's *theologia crucis*: "Why and how did it happen that so many of Luther's truly revolutionary insights were later domesticated, losing so much of their impact and power, when they were not actually turned into their opposites? How could a radical and uncompromising theology,

It was to this extreme concentration on correct doctrine that both the pietistic movements and the Enlightenment responded. It was only after World War I and the tragedies that came with the failure of progress and civility that Luther's theology of the cross was rediscovered. According to McGrath, this was no accident:

> What, then, is the significance of this theology of the cross? For the theologians of the liberal Protestant era, it had little, if any significance, being seen as little more than an ascetical or ethical principle, a relic of a bygone age. The shattering of liberal Protestant values and aspirations through the devastation and dereliction of the First World War, however, gave a new urgency and relevance to Luther's insights. It is no accident that the first serious studies of Luther's *theologia crucis* date from the period immediately after this war. Those who still considered Luther's *theologia crucis* to be of ephemeral significance found themselves stultified when the unthinkable happened, and the horrors of a second World War were unleashed upon Europe. Luther's theology of the cross assumed its new significance because it was the theology which addressed the question which could not be ignored: is God *really* there, amidst the devastation and dereliction of civilisation? Luther's proclamation of the hidden presence of God in the dereliction of Calvary, and of the Christ who was forsaken on the cross, struck a deep chord of sympathy in those who felt themselves abandoned by God, and unable to discern his presence anywhere.[92]

With this background in mind, we now turn our attention to Bonhoeffer's theology. For it is Christology shaped by Luther's

developed in the midst of life-threatening situations, come in so many instances–as in Nazi Germany, for example–to be abused as a theology of the preservation of the status quo and of full obedience to the state, to arbitrary and atrocious authorities?"

92. McGrath, *Luther's Theology of the Cross*, 179. These comments fit with Bonhoeffer's own search for identity, especially in light of his brother Walter's death during World War I. Rasmussen, *Earth Community, Earth Ethics*, (Maryknoll, NY: Orbis Books, 1996), 272, draws a similar conclusion about the devastating affects of World War I, which called for a new starting point for theology. His analysis points to a divergence in approach: Barth emphasizes the majesty of God as remote from the earth (*finitun non capax infiniti*); Bonhoeffer, following Luther, sees the majesty and power of God in his close proximity to the earth (*finitum capax infiniti*). For Barth's own understanding of Luther's theology, see his introductory essay in Ludwig Feuerbach, *Essence of Religion* (New York: Harper & Row, 1957), x–xxxii.

*theologia crucis* that comes to dominate his thinking, giving it its distinct character as well as shaping the nature of his witness.

## Christ the Center

Having examined the background of Bonhoeffer's independent theological stance, we now turn to his Christology, which provides both the focus and the driving force of his thought and his actions in the world.[93] From the earliest interpreters to the present, Christology has been identified as the core of Bonhoeffer's theology, both giving it its character and separating him from his teachers.[94] It will be the influence of Luther's *theologia crucis* and its effect on Bonhoeffer's Christology that will be the focus of this work; for "there was one fundamental and most crucial aspect in which Bonhoeffer was always in agreement with Luther: taking seriously the solus Christus."[95]

James Burtness, in his examination of Bonhoeffer's ethical theology, frames his discussion of Bonhoeffer's theology by identifying the key to Bonhoeffer's life: "There can be no question but that he was a witness for Jesus Christ throughout his life. That witness meant concrete confession in specific times and specific places."[96] It is because of his faith in Jesus Christ that Bonhoeffer constantly sought concrete answers about the meaning of Christian discipleship in the real world. Therefore, even though "much was not clear to him, . . . in the midst of massive uncertainties, he was able

93. See, for example, Craig Nessan and Renate Wind, forward to Dietrich Bonhoeffer, *Who Is Christ for Us?*, ed. and intro. Craig L. Nessan and Renate Wind (Minneapolis: Fortress Press, 2002), 2: "The insistence on Christ as the center of history, which runs from the beginning to the end of Bonhoeffer's theological legacy, means that his political commitments are informed by his Christology while his Christology is only realized in political engagement."
94. See above, pages 45–47.
95. Krötke, "Dietrich Bonhoeffer and Martin Luther," 56.
96. Burtness, *Shaping the Future: The Ethics of Dietrich Bonhoeffer* (Philadelphia: Fortress Press, 1985), xvi.

to live calmly and in good humor, delighting in simple pleasures and making effective use of each day." On the other hand,

> What he was supremely clear about was the name of the incarnate, crucified, and risen Christ, who was located *not* in the private conscience or the immortal soul or the spiritual experience or the religious yearnings of the individual, but rather in the center of history and therefore in the center of this world. The earth for Bonhoeffer was always the place "in which the cross of Jesus Christ is planted," and the church was always "a piece of the world for which Christ died."[97]

Consistently Bonhoeffer has been described as one who took the world seriously, sought the concreteness of revelation, and focused on reality. In everything we read from Bonhoeffer's hand, those themes emerge and weave their way through all he thinks and does. If those are his questions and concerns, the foundation for an answer comes in the person of Jesus Christ. To say that Christology is the center of Bonhoeffer's theology is to acknowledge that Bonhoeffer was convinced that what one believed about Jesus Christ affected everything else in one's theology.

Therefore, even when Bonhoeffer focuses on issues other than Christology, he does not do so without a christocentric focus and orientation. Ecclesiology, for example, becomes christocentric inasmuch as one cannot understand the church without understanding the inherent relationship it has to the core confession of Christianity. Likewise, in ethics, if one is to talk about Christian ethics at all, it must be done in light of the meaning of Jesus for life in the here and now. Accordingly, the image of Christ that one holds will shape all the contours of one's theology. Bonhoeffer was convinced that what one believes matters.

To place the emphasis on Christology, however, does not mean that a particular idea or doctrine about Christ is at the center of

97. Ibid.

Bonhoeffer's focus; rather, it is the person of Jesus Christ. Burtness clarifies this distinction:

> To say that Jesus Christ is the center of Bonhoeffer's life and work is different from saying that Christology is its center. In his 1933 Christology lectures, Bonhoeffer says that the real question is not how, but who. The how question must be asked. The church must continue to reflect on how Jesus of Nazareth comes to be the Christ of the church. Christology is done by Bonhoeffer not only in his 1933 university lectures but periodically throughout his life. Yet it is always the person Jesus Christ, rather than reflections or speculations about him, that is the radical center of Bonhoeffer's life and of his efforts toward the formulation of an ethical theology. Seen from this perspective, the continuity is overwhelming. . . . "[It] is the person of Christ, not Christ as idea or doctrine or symbol or experience, that controls Bonhoeffer's work toward an ethical theology.[98]

Hans-Jürgen Abromeit, in his detailed study of Bonhoeffer's theology, focuses in particular on Bonhoeffer's understanding of Christ. There is no theological theme to which Bonhoeffer gives more attention than to the person Jesus Christ. From *Sanctorum Communio* through *Letters and Papers from Prison*, Bonhoeffer's theology is "christologically oriented throughout." In turn, this christocentric orientation is marked by "the living crucified Christ," on the one hand, and the "real concrete situation of humankind," on the other. As a result, Bonhoeffer's attention is not limited to abstract discussions of Christology, but rather always attempts to relate the crucified Christ to the life of faith in the here and now.[99]

98. Ibid., 30–31, 32. See also Hans-Jürgen Abromeit, "Die Einzigartigkeit Jesu Christi: Die Frage nach dem Absolutheitsanspruch des Christentums bei Dietrich Bonhoeffer," *Pastoraltheologie* 80 (1991): 590.

99. Note, for example, Bonhoeffer's discussion of discipleship in *Discipleship* where he says that such a notion stands in contradiction to faith: "Discipleship is commitment to Christ. Because Christ exists, he must be followed. An idea about Christ, a doctrinal system, a general religious recognition of grace or forgiveness of sins does not require discipleship. In truth, it even excludes discipleship; it is inimical to it. One enters into a relationship with an idea by way of knowledge, enthusiasm, perhaps even by carrying it out, but never by personal obedient

Following Luther, Bonhoeffer acknowledges that God is present throughout creation, albeit in hidden form; it is only through God's own revelation in Christ on the cross that we know God *pro nobis*. This christocentric emphasis comes from Luther's understanding of God as *deus absconditus* and *deus revelatus*.[100]

In the same way that this theological orientation in Luther is called a *theologia crucis*, it is therefore possible to characterize Bonhoeffer's Christology as a *theologia crucis* as well. Following Luther, rather than speculating on the traditional christological questions, such as the *how* question, as he terms it in his Christology lectures, Bonhoeffer makes the person of Jesus, the God-man, the man for others, the driving force that gives structure and movement to his theology. In those same lectures, Bonhoeffer reveals his core conviction, which is one he shares with Luther. He insists that if one wants to speak of God, it is necessary to point to the man Jesus. Likewise, Bonhoeffer insists with Luther that "the child in the manger is God."[101] Or as he continues, "If we speak of the human being Jesus Christ as we speak of God, we should not speak of him as representing an idea of God, that is, in his attributes as all-knowing and all-powerful, but rather speak of his weakness and manger."[102]

It is because he is clear about Jesus Christ, the incarnate, crucified, and risen one, through whom God is present in and for the world, that Bonhoeffer was free to shed the safe confines of the academic and churchly worlds to venture into the dangerous world of political

discipleship. Christianity without the living Jesus Christ remains necessarily a Christianity without discipleship; and a Christianity without discipleship is always a Christianity without Jesus Christ. It is an idea, a myth" (DBWE 4:59). Bonhoeffer is drawing on the thought of Soren Kierkegaard for this concept.

100. See Abromeit, *Die Geheimnis Christi: Dietrich Bonhoeffers erfahrungsbezognene Christologie* (Neukirchen-Vluyn: Neukirchener, 1991), 16–17, 20, 54–55, and 124ff.

101. DBWE 12:354. See n167, where it indicates that Bonhoeffer draws on Luther's Christmas hymn, "All Praise to You, Eternal Lord," for this imagery.

102. Ibid. See Steiger, "The *Communicatio Idiomatum* as the Axle and Motor of Luther's Theology," *Lutheran Quarterly* 14 (2000): 127–28 for other examples in Luther.

resistance "without inner turmoil. He was able to make bold moves, as he did with amazing frequency, because he trusted not in the rightness of his own actions but in the right-making activity of the living God who takes even our inadequate deeds and misguided judgments and uses them for good."[103] Not mere speculation on the nature of Christology, but confession of Jesus as the Christ was that clarity Bonhoeffer possessed. And it was such clarity on the central claim of Christian faith that "gave Bonhoeffer freedom for responsible action that moralists—on the left as well as on the right of the political spectrum—seldom begin to understand." It is for that reason that "Dietrich Bonhoeffer reminds us to focus clearly on the incarnate, crucified, and risen Jesus Christ who leads his church into free and responsible action for the sake of the future of God's world."[104] To show how this theme or orientation is worked out in the various theological discussions and contexts that made up the world in which Bonhoeffer lived and worked is important as the church attempts to venture out into the new world facing it in the twenty-first century. While our world is not the same as the one Bonhoeffer inhabited, Bonhoeffer's approach to theology and his understanding of Christ are still valuable resources for us.

There are no shortage of references that point to the centrality of Jesus Christ for Bonhoeffer's theology. Christology serves both as the organizing principle of his theology and providing its continuity. What follows is a representative summary.

In his 1961 Alden-Tuthill lectures at Chicago Theological Seminary, Eberhard Bethge lays claim to the central role that Christology plays from the beginning of Bonhoeffer's writing. "Revelation, even in Bonhoeffer's first writing, is opposed to any philosophical idea of transcendence or metaphysics called God. In

103. Burtness, *Shaping the Future*, xvi–xvii.

104. Ibid., xvii.

Christ the human 'Thou' is where God meets us."[105] This christocentric understanding of God's revelation holds the key to all of Bonhoeffer's theology, pushing Bonhoeffer to seek "concrete" expressions of God's presence in the world. Bethge, therefore, concludes,

> Incarnation is thus at the heart of Bonhoeffer's theology. There cannot be any speculation about a God before or outside this concreteness. The incarnated God is the only one we know. We cannot even think of concreteness as an addition God put on later to his being. All we know, and this is breath-taking, is that the incarnated concreteness is *the* attribute as far as we can think.[106]

In one of the earliest commentaries on Bonhoeffer's theology, Martin Marty is equally clear in identifying both the motive for and content of Bonhoeffer's theological exploration:

> In a world of displacement, Bonhoeffer rejected angelism, pure transcendence, revelatory illusion from the first. October 1931: "This invisibility smashes us indeed. . . . This madness of being thrown back again and again on the invisible God himself—who can stand that anymore?" [*GS* I, 61] It led him to pursue the concrete nature of revelation and to focus on Christology: "Indeed, what *is* Christ for us today?"[107]

In another early work that sought to provide a complete picture of Bonhoeffer's theology, James Woelfel concludes, "The one word which best sums up Bonhoeffer's entire theological development is *christology.* It is the golden thread which ties together his works from first to last. . . . Jesus Christ as the object of all theology is the

105. Bethge, "The Challenge of Dietrich Bonhoeffer's Life and Theology," *The Chicago Theological Seminary Review* 51, no. 2 (February 1961): 8.

106. Ibid. In this manner of thinking, which remains consistent throughout his life, "are dormant all the explosives which will catch fire again and again in Bonhoeffer's life."

107. Martin E. Marty, "Introduction," in *The Place of Bonhoeffer*, ed. by Martin E. Marty (New York: Association Press, 1962), 15.

key to the 'Christianity without religion' of the prison writings no less than to Bonhoeffer's earlier writings."[108] Christology is the key to understanding the development of his thought. More precisely, according to Woelfel, it is the Lutheran quality of his Christology, namely the *finitum capax infiniti*, that is the distinguishing mark:

> The importance of Bonhoeffer's Lutheran understanding of the Incarnation, in contrast to the Reformed interpretation of the early Barth, cannot be overstressed. *Finitum capax infiniti* could well be the theological motto of Bonhoeffer's whole theological development. His writings show him pushing this "material" doctrine of the Incarnation in an ever more concrete direction with creative passion and rigor. Here is the key to Bonhoeffer's whole theological method, including the final "non-religious interpretation of biblical concepts": God is God become man, the man Jesus Christ, and that is all we can concern ourselves with as men. The only majesty, sovereignty, glory, and freedom of God which we know are what he has revealed in Jesus Christ. God is God-turned-toward-man in the Incarnation.[109]

Sounding a similar note, Ernst Feil has also concluded that Christology is the central key to understanding Bonhoeffer's understanding of reality, which was a critical concept for him. Feil says Christology is the "cardinal point of Bonhoeffer's whole theology."

> In his dissertation, in his initial lectures, and in the seminary, he seemed to want to begin with ecclesiology, but it always led him back to Christology as the foundation for ecclesiology and of every other theological undertaking. Christology may therefore be regarded as the constant, the *cantus firmus,* with the understanding of the world as the most important of those "contrapunctal themes which have their full *independence,* but are still based on the *cantus firmus.*" Christology is the constant for Bonhoeffer's own theology too, beginning with the Christology lecture in Barcelona, continued in *Act and Being* (in contrast

108. James Woelfel, *Bonhoeffer's Theology: Classical and Revolutionary* (Nashville: Abingdon, 1970), 134.
109. Ibid., 141.

> to *The Communion of Saints*[110]), carried on during his lectureship in Berlin (especially in connection with the question of the concretion of the commandment), emphatically set forth in *The Cost of Discipleship* (where discipleship, as the discipleship of Jesus Christ, has a particularly Christological character), and finally climaxed in *Ethics* and *Letters and Papers from Prison*.[111]

Reflecting the position of Feil, Andreas Pangritz finds that Bonhoeffer's christological question "forms the *cantus firmus* of Bonhoeffer's theological development from the beginning to the end." Originally "latent" in *Sanctorum Communio*, it became "explicit" in the Christology lectures in 1933 and formed the "starting point of Bonhoeffer's new theological reflections" in 1944. "The centrality of Christ serves as the decisive motive for opening the horizons of the church towards the world in its concrete reality. . . . The

110. This caveat is important in marking Feil's position off from that of many other Bonhoeffer interpreters. Feil insists that Christology does not emerge as a theme for Bonhoeffer until after *Sanctorum Communio*. For examples of those who question Feil's conclusion, see von Soosten, *Sozialität der Kirche*, 24, 64–75; von Soosten, "Editor's Afterword to the German Edition," *Sanctorum Communio* (DBWE 1:293–95), Abromeit, *Geheimnis Christi*, 16ff; Huber, "Wahrheit und Existenzform: Anregungen zu einer Theorie der Kirche bei Dietrich Bonhoeffer," in *Konsequenzen: Dietrich Bonhoeffers Kirchenverständnis heute*, ed. Ernst Feil and Ilse Tödt, IBF 3 (Munich: Chr. Kaiser Verlag, 1980), 93–94; and Jonathan Sorum, "The Eschatological Boundary in Dietrich Bonhoeffer's 'Nachfolge,'" (ThD diss., Luther Northwestern Theological Seminary), 48nn50–51. Because Bonhoeffer's theology is christocentric from beginning to end, in contrast to Feil, it will be the position of this work to show that ecclesiology, the subject proper of *Sanctorum Communio*, is conceivable only when understood from a christocentric perspective. Bonhoeffer cannot talk about the church without talking about Jesus. The church, apart from Christ, is not the church. Only as an expression of God in Jesus Christ and only so long as it proclaims that message is the church the church. It is for this reason that Bonhoeffer refers to the church as "Christ existing as community" (see *Sanctorum Communio*, DBWE 1:189). The very phrase denotes a christological foundation for any understanding of the church. It can be argued that Bonhoeffer was quite intentional in this regard in that he reworks Hegel's "God existing as community." See von Soosten, "Editor's Afterword," 293ff, for Bonhoeffer's use of Luther in grounding his ecclesiology in Luther's thought. If Bonhoeffer is following Luther, Christology is a necessity for discussion of any Christian doctrine. It is in and through Christ that we know God. He is God's revelation.
111. Ernst Feil, "Dietrich Bonhoeffer's Understanding of the World," in *A Bonhoeffer Legacy: Essays in Understanding*, ed. A. J. Klassen (Grand Rapids: Eerdmans, 1981), 241–42. See also Feil's *TDB*, part 2, for a more detailed discussion of Christology's role in Bonhoeffer's theology.

Christological *cantus firmus* is continuously accompanied by 'worldly' counterpoints."[112] This is what forms the dynamic of his thought.

Similarly, Kelly and Nelson state that Bonhoeffer's question, "Who is Christ actually for us today?," rather than being asked for the first time in 1944, "expresses his lifelong concern to seek out the incarnate presence of Christ, not only in the people who would enter his life or who would evoke his compassion, but also in the historical events that had led to his imprisonment as a willing conspirator against a morally corrupt government."[113] It is Bonhoeffer's understanding of and relationship to Jesus Christ that shapes his response to the world.

Renate Wind draws a similar conclusion when she notes that Bonhoeffer's central theme, answering the question, "Who are you, Christ?," was sounded already in *Sanctorum Communio*. "In pursuit of a sustainable community and a practicable way of life for himself, driven also by the necessity both of finding a credible identity as a theologian and scholar, he fused together ecclesiology and Christology in the formula, 'Christ existing as community.'"[114]

In his 1968 essay, "Bonhoeffer's Christology and his 'Religionless Christianity,'" Bethge provides us with the following statement that

112. Andreas Pangritz, "Who Is Jesus Christ, for Us, Today?" in *The Cambridge Companion to Dietrich Bonhoeffer*, ed. John W. de Gruchy (New York: Cambridge University Press, 1999), 134–35.

113. Geffrey B. Kelly and F. Burton Nelson, *The Cost of Moral Leadership: The Spirituality of Dietrich Bonhoeffer* (Grand Rapids: Eerdmans, 2003), 37. Cf. Geffrey B. Kelly and F. Burton Nelson, *TF*, in which they stress the importance of Christology for Bonhoeffer's theology. Kelly, in an earlier essay, makes the point that the christocentric emphasis running throughout Bonhoeffer's writings is the unifying theme. Throughout Bonhoeffer attempted to find concrete expressions of God in the world; this he finds in Jesus Christ. See Kelly, "Revelation in Christ: A Study of Bonhoeffer's Theology of Revelation," *Ephemerides Theologicae Lovanienses* 50, no. 1 (May, 1974): 40ff. In addition, this christological orientation is informed by Luther's *theologia crucis*, which serves "as the basis for Bonhoeffer's proposed reform of theological discourse and for an explanation of how God chooses to affirm the world and exert his salvific power in that world. Luther understood the deepest significance of the world reality in Christological categories but always–and here there are strong parallels with Bonhoeffer's prison theology–in a hidden manner" (ibid., 64n75).

114. Renate Wind, "Church Struggle and Contemplation: A Rediscovery of Bonhoeffer's Political Christology," in Bonhoeffer, *Who Is Christ for Us?*, 6.

may well serve as a summary of Bonhoeffer's christological orientation:

> There is indeed no difficulty in demonstrating explicitly Bonhoeffer's essential Christocentrism which, to be sure, remained trinitarian, as the main trend in his writings. In 1927, in *Sanctorum Communio,* the quest for Christ's presence is developed under the formula "Christ existing as church." . . . In 1935, we find the same quest for Christ's presence in Bonhoeffer's emphasis on actual, visible discipleship, without any eschatological reservations. . . . In 1942 we find, against a static Lutheran separation of the two realms, the quest for Christ's presence in ethical responsibilitiy for the concrete, guilt-covered world. Finally, in 1944, the presence of Christ is found in the conformation of man with Christ's messianic suffering, risking a "church" which allows itself to be drawn anonymously into the world. . . . In Bonhoeffer's 1933 lectures on Christology . . . our theme assumes the distinct form of a constant question, "Who are You?" and this question shapes the peculiar architecture of the lectures.[115]

If Christology is central to Bonhoeffer's thinking, the remaining question is, "What is this Christology like?" Assuming that Christology was the driving force at work in all of Bonhoeffer's theology, Bethge says we can "detect four features which characterize Bonhoeffer's Christology."[116]

> First, he wanted to get away from *speculative* descriptions of the natures of Christ; second, he interpreted the traditional christological formulas *relationally;* third, he claimed that all reality was *universally* Christ-centered; and fourth, Christology is fundamentally an *open* and ever unfinished task, living in new responses to the challenge of the encounter with Christ and the world.[117]

115. Bethge, "Bonhoeffer's Christology and his 'Religionless Christianity,'" in *Bonhoeffer in a World Come of Age,* ed. Peter Vorkink (Philadelphia: Fortress Press, 1968), 48–49.
116. Ibid., 61.
117. Ibid., 61–62.

This christological focus drives Bonhoeffer not to abandon his faith commitments while in prison, as the secular theologians of the 1960s attempted to claim, but drove him more intensely and deeply into the heart of his faith. "Jesus, the man for others," the phrase that emerges in *Letters and Papers from Prison*, while a new formula for him at that time, "is nothing less than an answer to his over-arching question." Bethge, therefore, can conclude that with "Jesus, the man for others," Bonhoeffer's Christology is marked by a continuity, that is at the same time "theological, "existential," and filled with "ethical implications."[118]

As we turn to Bonhoeffer's writings themselves, with this background in mind, Jesus emerges as the incarnate, crucified, and risen one. In what follows, by examining Bonhoeffer's own texts we will see how Luther's *theologia crucis* shapes the structure of, gives continuity to, and provides the content of Bonhoeffer's own Christology.

118. Ibid., 69.

PART III

# Theological and Christological Foundations: 1925–1933

# 3

# University Studies

"In *Fiction from Tegel Prison* Dietrich Bonhoeffer himself had put into words his legacy from childhood."[1] Rephrased, we might say that Bonhoeffer's life in the resistance and now famous theological formulations in *Letters and Papers from Prison* were his actions and reflections on the theological heritage that marked his life from beginning to end. What we find in Bonhoeffer's final words, in other words, is not a radical reorientation of his thought that leaves the Christian tradition behind, but rather the latest version of ideas formulated early in his life that now find "radical" articulation because this tradition is placed in the service of a radically changed world.[2] Continuity, not discontinuity, is what marks Bonhoeffer's theology.

1. Hans Pfeifer, "Editor's Afterword to the German Edition," *The Young Bonhoeffer: 1918–1927*, DBWE 9:563.
2. As Bonhoeffer's own writings would seem to indicate, his theological reflections from prison were not meant to be a theological "last will and testament," but were the nascent thoughts that were seeds for future development should he survive his imprisonment. As such they were expressions of his faith and hope in the face of death. His "Outline for a Book," included in one of his final letters, gives evidence of this (see *LPP*, DBWE 8:499–504).

As we turn to his early writings, we see the intellectual foundations on which he builds the rest of his life; these foundations provide both the continuity and the dynamic that shaped his actions and thought. Through an examination of his writings from 1925 to 1933, one can see the emergence of determining forces that are operative from this point onward. Here the importance of Luther for Bonhoeffer's theology is first formulated, his early understanding and appropriation of Luther begins to be expressed, and his christocentric focus, shaped by Luther's *theologia crucis*, emerges.

Since attention has already been paid to the context of Bonhoeffer's young adult life, especially as it relates to his university studies, that will not be repeated here. Instead, with that background in mind, we turn to an examination of Bonhoeffer's thinking at the time. However, before turning to Bonhoeffer's works, the important role that his family plays should be noted. In addition to the theological impulses that gave shape to his thought, family influences were the one other constant in his life. Renate Bethge, Bonhoeffer's niece and later wife of Eberhard Bethge, has indicated the extent to which Bonhoeffer's theological formulations reflected the influences of his family. "Whenever I read or hear anything about Bonhoeffer, I am struck by the close relationship of his thoughts with the attitudes, reactions, thinking, and interests of his family. Indeed, I sometimes recognize sentences that were spoken in a similar way during family conversations."[3] While he gained new theological insights from his university studies, his family and its values were critically important influences on his thinking, and as the opposition to Hitler grew his family continued to contribute to his thought as it developed.

3. Renate Bethge, "Bonhoeffer's Family and Its Significance for His Theology," in *Dietrich Bonhoeffer—His Significance for North Americans*, ed. Larry Rasmussen (Minneapolois: Fortress Press, 1990), 1. See also Fritz de Lange, *Waiting for the Word: Dietrich Bonoeffer on Speaking about God* (Grand Rapids: Eerdmans, 2000), chapter 3, and Pfeifer, "Editor's Afterword to the German Edition," DBWE 9:564ff.

What Renate Bethge sees emerging in Bonhoeffer's later theology is nothing other an intensification of these influences. "He reflected on courses of action, values, and estimations of worth in his family tradition, discovered their Christian roots, and consciously and unconsciously incorporated much of this into his theology." In fact, she argues that some of the central theological categories that Bonhoeffer formulated conformed to his family's views; these views were ones "that diverge from the viewpoint in vogue in the church during that period."[4] Included in this list are the familiar formulations "correspondence with reality," "telling the truth," "costly and cheap grace," "non-religious interpretation," "Jesus, the Man for Others," and "Who is Christ for us today?"[5] In every instance, these formulations express Bonhoeffer's concern for living a life of faith in Jesus Christ in this world. Not only do they give expression to his belief that one's faith ties a person to the concerns of this world, they provide a theological interpretation and foundation to his family's values.

These early works become important because they provided the foundations for all that follows. In his early writings, we "discover strands of thought and influence that continue into Dietrich Bonhoeffer's subsequent life as a pastor and theologian." In addition, these formative writings display the abilities of an original thinker who demonstrated "significant scholarly skill" and a "willingness to go beyond the perspectives of his teachers and develop insights of his own."[6] In order to properly understand these impulses, we must begin with his student writings from his time at Berlin. It was both what he learned from his professors, as well as what he questioned, that we gain insights into his developing theological position.

4. Bethge, "Bonhoeffer's Family and Its Significance for His Theology," 15.

5. Ibid., 15–16.

6. Paul Matheny, "Editor's Introduction to the English Ediition," *The Young Bonhoeffer: 1918–1927*, DBWE 9:11.

Martin Rumscheidt provides an example of this. He notes that while Bonhoeffer studied Luther's doctrine of justification by faith in Seeberg's seminars, and was convinced

> that even the most devout cannot find God, Bonhoeffer recognised that seeking to establish one's identity on one's own inevitably leads to an exaggeration of the self and to a concomitant prison-like solitude. This led Bonhoeffer to Christology. Luther's emphasis on the crucially important dimension of the *extra nos et pro nobis* meant that reconciliation is for us, but also outside or beyond us, in the person and work of Christ. Reconciliation, Bonhoeffer claimed, frees us from the solipsistic solitude of the exaggerated self that results from the attempt to derive identity through focusing on the consciousness of self. With Luther, Bonhoeffer spoke here of the *cor curvum in se*, discovered in Seeberg's seminars. The *extra nos et pro nobis* came to be integrated into the concept of sociality within a dialectic of "the other."[7]

Along with his own questions of identity, Bonhoeffer discovered in the work of Luther the key to his theological development. This discovery of Luther was so strong that Rumscheidt concludes, "Clearly Bonhoeffer's theological development was decisively shaped by the Luther he encountered during his Berlin years. This lasted right through to the end of his life."[8] An analysis of the materials that follow will be an explication of this observation; there we will see the foundations and future direction of Bonhoeffer's theology being set.

We now turn our attention to Bonhoeffer's writings themselves, focusing on the period 1925–1933. During this time Bonhoeffer lived in the academic world, first as a student and then as a professor. It was during this time that the foundations of Bonhoeffer's thought were laid and reached their fullest systematic presentation in his university lectures. We begin with a review of Bonhoeffer's student papers

7. Martin Rumscheidt, "The Formation of Bonhoeffer's Theology,"in *The Cambridge Companion to Dietrich Bonhoeffer*, ed. John de Gruchy (Cambridge: Cambridge University Press, 1999), 59.
8. Ibid.

written for Karl Holl and conclude with his Christology lectures, which were delivered in the summer of 1933. Between these two poles, Bonhoeffer traveled to Rome, wrote two dissertations, spent a year as a vicar in Barcelona, and an additional year in New York, attending Union Theological Seminary as an exchange student. The 1933 Christology lectures were both the highpoint of his academic career and, at the same time, marked it's end.

As we begin an analysis of his student writings, particularly the early ones, one caveat is worth bearing in mind. According to Gerhard Ebeling,[9] we should be cautious about drawing definitive conclusions from Bonhoeffer's student papers. Not everything Bonhoeffer wrote will be helpful in terms of conclusions to be drawn. These were papers written for particular professors, in many cases dealing with themes that either were not of Bonhoeffer's own choosing or were not of particular interest to him. In some cases, when his comments are helpful in providing insights into his own thinking, it is usually because they deviate from the assignment or reflect positions that challenge or otherwise do not reflect the position of the professor for whom the paper was written. Therefore, while they provide insights into the future direction of Bonhoeffer, the writings in the following section should be interpreted as being of limited value in terms of their contribution to Bonhoeffer's overall development.

In the writings we have from this time, we see the awakening and development of a theologian who exhibited an early fascination with Luther. While it is premature to determine how he understood Luther, the significance of this attention should be marked.

Two references are made to Luther in the extant letters to his family and friends. In a letter written to his grandmother, Julie

9. These comments were made during an November 11, 1991 conversation.

Bonhoeffer, shortly after his confirmation (March 15, 1921), in the course of telling her what he had been doing while on break from school as well as about a couple of the gifts he has received for confirmation, he concludes the letter with the line, "On April 18 we are having a party commemorating Luther's public appearance at Worms."[10] While this doesn't tell us anything about the young Bonhoeffer's understanding of Luther, the event his family would soon be celebrating was significant enough to warrant sharing with his grandmother.

In another letter written while a student at Tübingen, this time to his great aunt Helene Yorck von Wartenburg, a sister of his maternal grandmother, who after her death in 1903 took on the role of grandmother for the Bonhoeffer children, Bonhoeffer writes to thank her for the gift of books she had given him. He is particularly thankful to receive Julius Köstlin's *Life of Luther.* He tells her that he "had longed for Köstlin's book for a long time so that I could complete my library on Luther. I believe I now have all the major works that were written about him. The absence of Köstlin's book was the only regrettable gap. I am therefore particularly pleased that you have given it to me."[11]

These remarks indicate that he was familiar with and more than a little intrigued by Luther before he arrived at the University of Berlin and began his studies with Karl Holl. Once he was a student in Berlin,[12] however, Bonhoeffer's comments in letters, particularly to his cousin Walter Dress, begin to give us more details about his

10. Handwritten letter dated April 7, 1921, in DBWE 9:41.

11. Handwritten letter dated November 3, 1923, in DBWE 9:67.

12. Bonhoeffer started his university studies in Tübingen, as was the family custom. See chapter 1 for a description of Bonhoeffer's time there, as well as for the importance of Adolf Schlatter. See also Eberhard Bethge, *DB-ER*, 47ff, and Ferdinand Schlingensiepen, *Dietrich Bonhoeffer 1906–1945* (New York: T & T Clark, 2010), 18–20, for accounts of Bonhoeffer's time in Tübingen. After spending two semesters there (1923–1924), he returned to Berlin, where he took up his studies with some of the leading voices in Protestant theology. None of his student papers from Tübingen survive.

understanding and appreciation of Luther and his theology. While he was a student in Berlin, Bonhoeffer carried on a regular correspondence with Dress, another theology student, who later became a member of the Bonhoeffer family through marriage. According to Hans Pfeifer, several characteristics of Bonhoeffer and his theological development are revealed in these letters. Primary among these developments is the conversation that develops around Luther. After studying the correspondence, Pfeifer concludes that these letters make it "unmistakably clear, that the two young theologians Dietrich Bonhoeffer and Walter Dress became deeply influenced by an understanding of Luther's Reformation theology, which was rediscovered and interpreted by Karl Holl. And even though Bonhoeffer later became a fervent student of Barth's theology, his 'Barthianism' was inseparably linked to his 'Lutheranism.'" In addition to a particular connection with Luther's theology, these letters also "allow us to glimpse his dealings with the academic world, which often appeared uninteresting and a little shallow. . . . But we also find in these letters the reflections of a very devoted young man, deeply occupied with his academic work, who reveals his troubled self-esteem and the search for answers that would hold against all tribulations of modern times."[13]

## Seminar Paper on 1 Clement[14]

Bonhoeffer wrote several papers during the course of his student career, many of which are included in his collected works.[15] Since it was Karl Holl who is credited with introducing Bonhoeffer to Luther's theology, the papers written for Holl are of particular

13. Pfeifer, "Dietrich Bonhoeffer's Studienfreundschaft mit Walter Dreß: Briefe aus den Jahren 1920–1927," *Zeitschrift für Neure Theologiegeschichte* 4 (1997): 280.
14. DBWE 9:216ff. This was a paper written for Adolf von Harnack during the winter semester 1924–1925.
15. DWBE 9 contains material from 1918–1927.

importance. In addition to these, however, are other papers that shed light on his thinking; two such papers are included in this discussion.

In the earliest surviving paper written by Bonhoeffer while a student at Berlin, he wrote an essay on 1 Clement. What is noteworthy for this study is the one problem area identified by Bonhoeffer has to do with Clement's Christology. According to his reading of the text, Clement deviated from Pauline Christology and, as a result, ended up turning Jesus into a religious hero rather than a savior. "It can only be understood psychologically that, for Clement, Christ's greatest act of love was that he allowed himself to be nailed to the cross."[16] He noted that while Clement retained some of the Pauline language, "he fills it with a completely different content, because he believes that Christ's death is merely the perfection of his life's work. Even though Christ's death is the goal of everything that preceded it, Christ's deeds are seen as belonging to the same typology as those of the pious people of the Old Testament and the pious pagans."[17] As he approached his final evaluation of Clement's letter, he had one significant question that has to do with the "remarkable transformation of the concept of Christology along with the concept of justification that is connected with it. How did it happen," he asks, "that the person of Christ was forced from the centrally significant role in religious and salvation history to become the object of religious contemplation? How is it that Christ was reduced from the position he occupied in Paul, which was the intersection of the divine and human planes, to a religious-heroic model?"[18] In place of the Pauline Christology, where the emphasis was on the sacrificial death of Jesus, in Clement "everything that was connected with the meaning of the sacrificial death 'for all people,' and with it to the

16. Ibid., 250.
17. Ibid., 250–51.
18. Ibid., 253.

person of Jesus Christ as the center of salvation history, must be relegated to the margins in favor of the ideas of election through Christ and the Christian ethical way of life that was founded upon it."[19]

These words from the young theological student reveal some insights into the theological motivations and orientations that will shape his theology. Far from being of tangential interest, the problem with Christology identified here becomes central to his theological position.

### Seminar Paper on Luther's Feelings about His Work[20]

In his first paper written for Karl Holl in 1925,"Luther's Feelings about His Work as Expressed in the Final Years of His Life Based on His Correspondence of 1540–1546," Bonhoeffer "summarized and expanded on Holl's article, 'Luther's Judgement of Himself.'" While his writing demonstrates that he is content to simply cite Holl's references to Luther, which shows the extent of Holl's influence on him, he begins to emphasize another side of Luther that separates him "from all optimistic theology of progress, which was represented in Berlin in different ways."[21] What Bonhoeffer emphasized as an important aspect of Luther's theology was the belief that salvation was not a matter of conscience, shaped by an internal struggle, as was the case for Holl. Rather, "the entire history of the world is to be seen under the aspect of this battle between gospel and devil. This was especially true in this final crisis that had emerged as the gospel was proclaimed anew, i.e., in Luther's work."[22]

19. Ibid., 255.
20. Ibid., 257ff. Written for Holl during the summer semester 1925.
21. Pfeifer, "Afterword to the German Edition," DBWE 9:573.
22. DBWE 9:263; see also 320.

When reading Holl's essay on Luther, one sees that his interpretation of Luther's theology fits clearly with his understanding of Luther as a man. According to Holl's account, which seeks to delve into Luther's "inmost life," Luther was a man marred by inner struggle, filled with self-doubt, and lacking self-esteem; he was a man who would have liked nothing better than to fade into the woodwork. Accordingly, Holl sees Luther's understanding of justification as being based completely on his own feelings of lacking self-worth. Even at the height of the Reformation, he was filled with self-doubt and perceived himself as unworthy. If it weren't for the cause of the Reformation, for which he even had doubts about his abilities to lead, Luther would probably have given up in despair.

Nowhere in Holl do we read anything about faith and the role it played in Luther's life. Even justification is interpreted in terms of Luther's inner feelings, situated entirely in an anthropological sphere of the individual's experience of conscience. Holl's final evaluation of Luther was that he was able to arrive at a "new form of self-perception." By binding "together self-negation and self-affirmation, Luther transcended the inner contradiction which dominated contemporary feelings of personality." Neither giving into the "absolute self-rejection of the monk or the equally absolute self-affirmation of the strong man of the Renaissance," Luther was able to bridge the gap in the extremes of human understanding of the time to create a new perception of himself. Unlike his contemporaries who fell into one camp or the other, "Luther was able to unite the truth of both because his faith in God encompasses them both. For his certainty of forgiveness came a self-confidence of the highest sort; but it was only a gift of which he could not feel worthy."[23]

23. Karl Holl, "Martin Luther on Luther," in *Interpreters of Luther: Essays in Honor of Wilhelm Pauck*, ed. Jaroslav Pelikan (Philadelphia: Fortress Press, 1968), 30. This essay is a translation of Holl's "Luthers Urteile über sich selbst," which was included in his *Gesammelte Aufsätze zur Kirchengeschichte*, vol. 1, *Luther,* published in 1921, and used by Bonhoeffer in his essay.

It is this essay and Holl's overall approach to interpreting Luther that Bonhoeffer followed when writing his first paper for Holl. His task, according to the opening section of his paper, was to understand the "psychology of the older Luther."[24] Rather than being content with what he had accomplished or being overjoyed by his triumphs, Luther could not escape the constant doubt that marked his life: "How can he, the *peccator pessimus*, proclaim God's word? All of Luther's comments intersect at this point when he confronts his divine task head-on." This calling or responsibility, which was not his choosing, brought out feelings of inadequacy while at the same time making Luther aware of the absolute nature of God. Not being worthy, but at the same time being a necessary instrument in proclaiming God's word, left Luther with serious questions and doubts that accompanied him throughout life, forcing him to second guess much of what he had done.[25]

At the same time, this duality enabled Luther to be consciously aware of the difference between his person and his work, which, in turn, enabled him to recognize that what good is accomplished through the Reformation struggles were not due to his goodness, but rested solely on God alone, whose work the Reformation truly was. Because it was God's work, "this means that it is a divine task that he must fulfill."[26] Therefore, in spite of whatever doubts he might have had about his own person and the perceived weaknesses of his own acts, Luther took his calling seriously, seeing it as a responsibility for which he could be confident. After all, "the Holy Spirit really did not need us for the accomplishment of its plans. If, however, by grace the Holy Spirit once desired us, then it would not call in vain. Instead, the Holy Spirit would command loyal service to the gospel."[27]

24. DBWE 9:257.
25. Ibid., 260.
26. Ibid., 267.
27. Ibid., 268.

In contrast to Holl, in Bonhoeffer's presentation, Luther's certainty of faith prevents him from giving in to despair. Even when the reforms put in place as a result of his teaching did not produce the hoped-for changes in people, Bonhoeffer said that "Luther knows well that this should not provoke him to lay his hands in his lap." Quoting from Luther himself, he makes the point that we are to "do what is commanded according to your calling and leave the rest to God." Such an attitude, given expression in letters, shows that Luther never doubted his work; instead, what Luther himself demonstrated is that even though "his belief in this world is completely lost, his belief in God's guidance is unshakable."[28] That is not to say, however, that Luther didn't have fits of depression; he did. They were due, however, to external circumstances, rather than any lack of confidence in God, and therefore are of little consequence when viewed as a whole.

What marks Bonhoeffer's discussion of Luther's psychology is the attention he paid to Luther's confidence. Unlike Holl, Bonhoeffer went on to spell out a more christological basis for this confidence that Luther exhibits. Quoting from one of the two final letters Luther writes to Katie, in which Luther wishes to convey comfort to her, Bonhoeffer made this point: "Leave me in peace with your worrying. I have someone who is better able to worry about me than you and all the angels. He lies in a manger and hangs on a virgin's breasts. But at the same time he sits at the right hand of the all powerful Father."[29] That Bonhoeffer selected these words from Luther is significant in light of how Bonhoeffer's theology develops. Coming as it does at the end of Luther's life, it captures the heart of Luther's understanding of Jesus, shaped as it was by a radical interpretation of the *commicatio idiomatum*, but it also comes to be a central affirmation of

28. Ibid., 279.
29. Ibid., 281.

Bonhoeffer's as well. Even though such a christological emphasis does not come clearly to the fore at this early stage in Bonhoeffer's writings, for his language is not yet fully christological but is characterized by a more general use of the word *God*, it points us to a significant insight that will continue to find expression in Bonhoeffer's theology. In a variety of ways and in a number of different settings, Bonhoeffer will return to the image of the baby in the crib to express the presence of God. Such a presence becomes for him, too, as it had been for Luther, a source of confidence, especially when expressed during the struggles of those on the margins. Such language is used by Bonhoeffer when he struggles with his understanding of the church and tries to find a source of hope for the expatriate community he served in Barcelona, for example, and again when he writes to his former seminarians who are struggling with the issues of war.

Even as Bonhoeffer followed the same line of reasoning as Holl, picking up on the same themes and emphases, including an emphasis on Luther's experience, a difference between the two emerged. Rather than presenting an objective description of Luther's person as Holl approached the subject, Bonhoeffer developed a more personal connection with Luther. He identified Luther's struggles as his own, making Luther's struggles a self-affirming confirmation of his own.[30] Using Holl's structure, Bonhoeffer's essay focuses not so much on Luther's self-doubts but on his faith as a source of confidence. So, although any differences between the two may be subtle, the way Bonhoeffer appropriated Luther created a different response to him.[31]

30. See ibid., 572.

31. According to von Soosten, *Die Sozialität der Kirche: Theologie und Theorie der Kirche in Dietrich Bonhoeffers "Sanctorum Communio"* (Munich: Chr. Kaiser, 1992), 159, this work can be read from the perspective of Bonhoeffer's own self-discovery, in which Bonhoeffer identifies with the person and theology of Luther.

### Paper on the Historical and Pneumatological Interpretation of Scripture[32]

In the essay, "Can One Distinguish between a Historical and a Pneumatological Interpretation of Scripture, and How Does Dogmatics Relate to This Question?" written for Seeberg's seminar on systematic theology during the summer semester 1925, some factors that point toward future developments in his theology emerge. First, Bonhoeffer pointed out the limitations of the historical-critical method for understanding Scripture, contrasting it with a pneumatological approach.[33] By so doing, he challenged the assumptions of many of his teachers. As the notes Seeberg included in his critique of Bonhoeffer's paper indicate, one begins to see that Bonhoeffer's position is founded on a different basis from that of Seeberg and his colleagues.[34] Second, several references are made to Karl Barth, whose theology insisted on the historical reality of God's revelation; these show the extent of Barth's influence on Bonhoeffer's thinking at the time.[35] Certainly Bonhoeffer's interpretation reflects Barth's position on Scripture vis-a-vis his Berlin teachers; at the same

32. DBWE 9:285ff. This paper was written for Seeberg's seminar on systematic theology. Seeberg, in his evaluation, gave Bonhoeffer a satisfactory grade, "the lowest grade Bonhoeffer received for his work in systematic theology" (DBWE 9:285n1).

33. Bonhoeffer believed "the texts are not just historical sources, but agents of revelation, not just specimans of writing, but sacred canon. . . . Revelation is contained in Scripture because God speaks in it; that is undemonstrable—not a conclusion but a premise. Divine revelation enables people to recognize divine revelation, that is, the Holy Spirit" (*DB-ER*, 79–80).

34. As several of Seeberg's comments throughout the paper indicate, he was questioning Bonhoeffer's theological assumptions, most of which had come from his reading of Karl Barth. See *DB-ER*, 79. According to Schlingensiepen, "The fact that Barth was being attacked by most of his colleagues in Germany made him that much more interesting to young people." But while many students, were going to Göttingen to hear Barth, Bonhoeffer showed no such inclination. "Barth's discoveries fired him with enthusiasm, but he remained centered on his parent's home. He wasn't looking for a master, but rather seeking his own way. He wanted to acquire as much knowledge as possible as quickly as possible, and to show what he could do; for this, his own insights would serve" (*Dietrich Bonhoeffer 1906–1945*, 26–27).

35. As the editors indicate in the editorial notes, in addition to Barth, Bonhoeffer also relies heavily on Eduard Thurneysen, who, like Barth, was an early exponent of dialectical theology (DBWE 9:286ff).

time, Bonhoeffer has reservations about where Barth's approach to theology could lead.[36] Third, his authority was Luther. Quoting from both Holl and Barth, in some cases utilizing Luther quotes that they had cited,[37] Bonhoeffer found in Luther's understanding of Scripture and interpretation the source for his own understanding of Scripture and its meaning.

At the center of Bonhoeffer's presentation is the proper understanding of Jesus. In the first sentence of the essay he lays out what for him was a basic principle, not only for this essay, but for theology as a whole: "Christian religion stands or falls with the belief in a historical and perceptibly real divine revelation."[38] There can be little doubt that for Bonhoeffer this is a christological statement. For him the center of the Scripture's revelation is Jesus; in fact, Jesus is the revelation. It is historical criticism's handling of Jesus that raises questions in his mind about its limitations.

> Its [historical criticism's] general principles are based on a scientific-mechanistic worldview. Its epistemological methods are, for that reason, those of the natural sciences. Every dogmatic connection is eliminated. . . . The content of the Bible is leveled and made to match contemporary history. Parallels to the miracle stories are found. Yes, even the person of Jesus is stripped not only of the divine but also of

36. According to Pfeifer, "A certain distance from Karl Barth's theology is nonetheless evident. Bonhoeffer tried to avoid a paradoxical situation to which the dialectical theology of the twenties could lead. If Barth wanted to hold fast to the sovereignty of the word of God in every case over against all historical reality as well as over against the written word in the Bible, he had to address the question of how to avoid the danger of completely removing revelation from historical reality, because in this case revelation could only be demonstrated dialectically. Did not the danger exist, as Bonhoeffer formulated in his outline of the paper on Luther, that the existence of a theologian would be divided into an earthly being and a 'heavenly double'? 'From its very beginning, Bonhoeffer's theology is informed by the conviction that the truth which is believed must a have concrete locus within the reality of the world.' That the theologians in Berlin wanted to hold fast to the concrete demonstration of divine truth in history impressed him; that in doing so they lost credibility because of their historical-theological or ethical optimism led Bonhoeffer to agree with Barth's critique" ("Editor's Afterword to the German Edition," DBWE 9:573).
37. See, for example, ibid., 288n23, and 289n32, where specific citations are identified.
38. DBWE 9:285. See the discussion by Bethge, *DB-ER*, 65ff.

> human majesty. He disappears unrecognizably among various rabbis, teachers of wisdom, and religious visionaries."[39]

At the same time, however, it should be noted that Bonhoeffer, with such statements, is not a fundamentalist who wants to avoid the use of the historical-critical method altogether. He goes so far as to say that the scriptural witness could be fallible, "so that we can recognize the miracle that we really do hear God's words in human words."[40] Nor is he advocating a return to a precritical approach to the Bible. In fact, he says we cannot return to a pre-modern worldview. What he advocates, rather, is the use of both the historical-critical and pneumatological methods.[41]

The christological core of his thinking comes to the fore when, from a pneumatological perspective, Scripture is properly interpreted as revelation. Scripture is nothing other than God's own self-revelation that can be understood only from the perspective of faith. Standing "before a circle,"[42] Scripture qua Scripture is believed to be God's revelation only because God has revealed it to be so. Those who wrote the scriptural witness were those to whom God's revelation had already been revealed. Scripture

> was written by those to whom the Spirit had disclosed that revelation could be found precisely in this historical person, Jesus—fully human, appearing completely in the framework of ordinary events. . . . Each of these written words of the Spirit, which mediate the understanding of the facts, is an incarnate image of the person of Jesus Christ himself. These are contained in a fully historical, insignificant, and unimposing husk, but behind that there is the other, what "inculcates Christ," where Christ is truly alive and present.[43]

39. DBWE 9:286–87.
40. Ibid., 297.
41. Ibid., 294.
42. Cf. Jonathan Sorum, "Bonhoeffer's Early Interpretation of Luther as a Source of His Basic Theological Paradigm," *Fides et Historia* 29, no. 3 (August 1993): 39ff, for a discussion of the "Holy Circle" in Bonhoeffer's writing.
43. Ibid., 293–94.

Jesus is both the content and the revealer of God, both subject and object of our faith. Scripture, when read from the perspective of faith, is christological at its core.

## Seminar Paper on Luther's Understanding of the Holy Spirit[44]

Bonhoeffer wrote a second paper, "Luther's Views of the Holy Spirit according to the *Disputationen* of 1535–1545 edited by Drews," for Holl's seminar, Luther and the Holy Spirit, held in the winter semester 1925–1926. Like the previous paper written for Holl, here Bonhoeffer once again demonstrated the extent of Holl's influence on his thinking. As he did previously, he again relies heavily on Holl's writings[45] for both the content as well as the structure of his essay; at the same, however, there is evidence that Bonhoeffer is moving beyond Holl's interpretation. His discussion of conscience, which will be examined below, is a case in point.

While the title given to this work would indicate that Bonhoeffer wanted to limit his attention to Luther's understanding of the Holy Spirit, his concerns far exceed that. The Holy Spirit is a way of talking about the presence of God in the world and the manner in which God works to make God's grace a reality in the life of the believer. Bonhoeffer's talk of the Holy Spirit, following Luther, was one way of insuring that talk about justification remains the work of God and not that of human beings, and is something human beings receive as a gift from God. Therefore, Bonhoeffer's paper provides insights

44. DBWE 9:325ff. This work is based on a reading of seven disputations presented by Luther at Wittenberg during the years 1535–1545; in them Luther deals with themes and issues that remained important to him; primary among them was the discussion of justification. See 325, editorial n1.

45. Bonhoeffer used two of Holl's essays, *What Did Luther Understand by Religion?* (Philadelphia: Fortress Press, 1977) and *The Reconstruction of Morality* (Minneapolis: Augsburg, 1979), as primary sources for this essay.

into his understanding of the total workings of God, justification, Christology, faith, and the Christian life.

Bonhoeffer began his discussion by explaining that for Luther the primary category for understanding the Holy Spirit is that of experience. To that end, it is Bonhoeffer's conclusion that for Luther, whose starting point is a Pauline view of the Holy Spirit, the "experience-of-conscience and faith are understood by him as belonging together in essence."[46] Human beings first experience the work of the Spirit that comes through the law, as an act of judgment, which leads them to "despair with themselves and God." As a consequence, they are terrified and "begin to hate God, to slander, to curse, to doubt not only themselves, but also God; and so they sin against the first commandment."[47]

The terror that human beings experience as a result, however, is not to be understood in purely psychological terms. For Luther, it is not an "inner surging of emotion of a humble heart. Instead, he saw the true confrontation between God and the human being."[48] While it was true for some that the human will was involved in and through this whole process of judgment and justification, for Luther no such connection could be made. Luther's experience was of a different sort.

> He experienced it as something that ran totally counter to one's will, as something that wanted to destroy even his innermost being, as something against resistance could not help. The condition into which human beings would be brought could not be claimed to have any worth before God in itself. Its essence lay in the fact that the person would be overcome by God and, indeed, *morally* overcome through the word in the conscience.[49]

46. DBWE 9:326.
47. Ibid.
48. Ibid., 328.
49. Ibid., 329.

Luther's experience of God's judgment that came through the law is the work of the Holy Spirit, the author of both natural and the Mosaic law. Even though "in every person there lives a conscience," which has been formed by the law, it is weak, making the "giving of the law by Moses to recall what had been forgotten and to show us 'what we were and what we are.'"[50] The Holy Spirit works through the law to make

> its requirements clear and plain to the conscience. . . . Only in the conscience awakened by the Spirit does humanity feel the Holy Spirit, i.e., only when the person feels judged and destroyed by conscience is the Holy Spirit active and present. Thus the conscience becomes the place where the Holy Spirit is truly *experienced* by humanity. Therefore, not every conscience is the voice of the Holy Spirit, but the voice of the Holy Spirit is *felt* only in the conscience.[51]

The workings of the Holy Spirit in this manner are none other than God himself, albeit a God hidden in majesty, working to convict human beings of their sin. However, what is noticeable in Bonhoeffer's analysis is that the conscience no longer is an adequate means by which to talk about this experience. Even though the Holy Spirit works through the law to shape the conscience, the human conscience "is too weak to be able to understand the whole intention of the law by itself." In addition, one cannot equate the conscience with God. "Thus conscience is especially not something like God's voice in humanity as though, if conscience were silent, then God had nothing to say."[52] All of which is to say that conscience, as a psychological construct, is not adequate to understand the workings of God; likewise acts of contrition or penance cannot be judged adequate theologically for understanding justification, as if it is a

50. Ibid., 332.
51. Ibid., 333.
52. Ibid.

process in which the human will, left intact, can participate. Justification, as experienced and understood by Luther, was an act of God's grace that human beings cannot fully understand or appreciate.

It is at this point that Christology becomes necessary and critical to Bonhoeffer's appropriation of Luther's theology. He clearly differentiates between the objective working of God and any subjective experience of human beings, and places the work of justification solely in the hands of God; through faith, believers receive it as a gift. It is through faith that the work of Christ becomes real. In a statement that could well serve as a summary of his argument, he said,

> God desires the sinner. How can the human being grasp this? The human being can hear and understand it intellectually, because it is certainly said in words. However, the human being can grasp it and relate to it only through a means that is analogous to the divine will. Like can only be known by like. This would be an instrument that the human being could never acquire independently, precisely because humanity is unacquainted with it. It must therefore be personally created by God; and it is created through the Holy Spirit, which is given to us as a gift (donum) "in" faith. In faith God, who through the Spirit as maiestas destroys us through the law, gives us the Spirit as gift. Luther often says that the Holy Spirit gives us faith; in this way he can equate fides and Spiritus Sanctus. The object of faith, however, is God, not God's absolute being, because this cannot be conceived (if the Holy Spirit is donum!), but gift and ability, and that means Christ. Thus Luther says once, "Christ is ours through faith." This means Christ has been brought to us as a gift of the Holy Spirit. In faith, which is the action of the Holy Spirit, we grasp the pro nobis of his death and his resurrection. We not only see the historical events objectively, we recognize that he died for our sins and was raised for our justification. In that we grasp this, we possess Christ as gift. Christ is in us through the fact that the Holy Spirit is in us. Because, however, Christ has earned this Spirit for us, we can say that in faith, that is, in the Spirit who is acting in us, Christ being always attendant, Christ is in us in the same way as our faith is in us, that he is in us, lives, is raised, etc. So, faith from the Spirit, Christ in faith, Spirit from Christ, and therefore in faith Christ

> gives the Spirit. This is the essential interrelationship. If I begin with the perspective of faith, then faith grasps Christ and God and receives the Holy Spirit therefrom.[53]

From this, we can say that Bonhoeffer, in agreement with Luther, insisted that we can know God only as he is revealed in Christ. While it indeed limits our understanding of God, it is one that can be grasped in faith, giving the believer the assurance of God's grace *pro nobis.* In fact, "Wherever God speaks in divine *unveiled* majesty the only thing God can do is destroy."[54] It is through faith that the believer experiences the transforming power of God at work. Apart from faith, which is created in the believer by the Holy Spirit, human beings can grasp the facts of God through reason but they cannot know the newness of life that God does.

"The gift of the Spirit is only there where there is revelation; and the Holy Spirit in the human person leads only to the place where revelation is, to Christ." And where Christ is, there the believer experiences God. Reflecting the concerns of Luther's *theologia crucis,* Bonhoeffer dismisses any attempts to find God outside of faith in Christ: "Also those who believe that they can ferret out God's mysteries miss their goal. What God has not revealed to us we should not attempt to grasp.[55]

Several themes emerge in this paper. The first has to do with theological method. While not quoting Luther, but iterating a position that reflects Luther's theology of the cross, Bonhoeffer's brief discussion about theology points us to an understanding of his theological method. The truth of theological statements cannot be based on the reason or wisdom of the theologian, but rather find their foundation in God's Spirit, which is the only way "to present

53. Ibid., 337–39.
54. Ibid., 340.
55. Ibid., 340-41.

an exegesis that is not the theologian's own. . . . Thus theology must be cautious about what it says; it should reject those things that exceed reason and should repeat the formulations that the Holy Spirit has given and through which the Holy Spirit supports theology."[56] Related to this is Bonhoeffer's insistence that the Holy Spirit speaks through human words, works through "concrete persons."[57] Because it is not the Spirit's purpose to appeal to human emotions but rather to facilitate "a clear knowledge of God, it enters into this word." But in so doing, the Spirit remains hidden and veiled. "The Spirit accommodates itself to *our* ability to grasp, and thus remains the Holy Spirit. The Spirit must hide in earthly forms in order to be revealed to earthly beings."[58]

Tied to this, second, is his understanding of Scripture. Scripture is the word of God as both law and gospel. It is through Scripture that the believer receives Christ, but at the same time, "Christ is the meaning and the criterion of Scripture, the whole of Scripture."[59] Third, is justification. Regarding his understanding of justification, we can begin to note that Bonhoeffer moves away from Holl's position. When it comes to one's certainty of justification, "here the conscience also fails." Even a "'good' conscience in Christians" is an "ambiguous phenomenon" that cannot "'feel' faith." Rather than understanding justification as something that takes place within the heart or conscience of the individual, it is an act of God initiated from outside. Bonhoeffer notes that the certainty of justification does not depend upon one's conscience. Justification is not an internal experience; rather, "something had approached from outside, had overpowered and morally broken the person."[60]

56. Ibid., 363–64.
57. Ibid., 360.
58. Ibid., 357.
59. Ibid., 359.
60. Ibid., 354.

These early papers, which offer a limited view of Bonhoeffer's developing theology, nevertheless show us the extent to which Luther occupied Bonhoeffer's thinking while a student. This influence emerged early, and while his writings show a dependence on Holl, it is possible to see how, at the same time, Bonhoeffer begins to distance himself from his teacher. More evidence for this can be found in the "Note on Luther's Lectures on the Letter to the Romans,"[61] which comes from this same time; here we have an indication that Bonhoeffer rejects the psychologism of Troeltsch and Holl. Coming as it does from Bonhoeffer's reading of Luther, the clear distinction between Bonhoeffer and his teachers is seen. According to him, theology is not about psychology and neither are sin and revelation concepts that can be fit into our understanding of human consciousness; rather, theology "speaks of them as realities of revelation: acknowledgment of what is spoken in revelation and by the authorities."[62]

This same orientation is presumed by Bonhoeffer when writing his graduation theses in 1927. He stated his eighth thesis as follows: "Logically considered, faith is based not on psychological experiences but on itself."[63] For Bonhoeffer, as for Luther, the salvation event

61. DBWE 9:300. This is one of three handwritten notes that had been inserted into Bonhoeffer's copy of *Luthers Vorlesung über dem Römerbrief*, 1908, edited by Johannes Ficker. Both from the placement and the nature of the comments, it appears to be a reflection on Luther's commentary on Rom. 3:4. In providing background to this text, Hans Pfeifer remarks on its significance: "This is the longer text, which clarifies Bonhoeffer's reception of Luther" (DBWE 9:300n1). The note itself was undated but fits with other student notes from this time.

62. Sorum, "Bonhoeffer's Early Interpretation of Luther," 42, seeing the direct influence of Luther on Bonhoeffer's thought, concludes, "For Bonhoeffer, the conscience could not possibly be the bridge to the transcendent, much less its guarantor. In that case, the human religious impulse would be entirely in control. But it is this very impulse . . . that must come to an end with the actual coming of God."

63. DBWE 9:440. Bonhoeffer's personal copy had handwritten notes. At this point he punctuates his statement with the comment: "Sola fide! The whole act. Intellect *and* will," after which he quotes from Luther's *Lectures on Romans*. As an aside, but important nevertheless, after quoting Luther at length, his ninth thesis clearly identifies the weakness of dialectical theology: "The dialectic of the so-called dialectical theology bears logical, not real character and is in danger of neglecting the historicity of Jesus" (441). Cf. Bonhoeffer's "The Religious Experience of Grace

begins and ends with God. Because of sin, human beings are not able to save themselves.

At this stage, it is again worth noting Bonhoeffer's relationship to his teachers, which helps explain the direction Bonhoeffer's theology began to take. First, as was previously noted, Bonhoeffer had been introduced to Barth's theology during this time. His introduction came through his cousin, Hans-Christoph von Hase, who had been studying at Göttingen at the time. Yet, despite his cousin's urgings, he refused to go to Göttingen to study with Barth, because he wanted to retain his independence. Therefore, even though Bonhoeffer cites Barth's theology, it could be argued that Bonhoeffer follows Barth where (or to the extent that) Barth follows the basic Reformation teachings over which there was no essential conflict between the Lutheran and Reformed positions. For example, Luther as well as Barth emphasized "the Word of God." In such cases, there was no conflict between their positions. In the area of Christology, however, there were differences and it is at that point that Bonhoeffer departed from Barth.[64]

At the same time, when it came to selecting a doctoral advisor, both Harnack and Holl would have appeared to be more natural choices than Seeberg, yet he chose Seeberg. Inasmuch as the importance of Harnack in Bonhoeffer's life extended far beyond

and the Ethical Life," DBWE 10:449 "'Grace' here cannot be defined by the experience of Grace; on the contrary, the psychological category of experience must be criticised, modified and interpreted anew by the theological category of grace. It is essential for grace not to unite with human beeing (sic), to be conceivable only in the any happy experience of union with God; but grace is in its essence directly opposed to every human beeing (sic), to human experience of value and of God. It condemns all human effort to reach God as the attempt of man to be like God, as justification by works, by ethics, by religion" (written while at Union Theological Seminary in 1930–1931, the English here is Bonhoeffer's).

64. In the second paper written for Holl, in discussing the work of sanctification, Bonhoeffer refers to Barth's position in which the working of the Holy Spirit creates a "heavenly double," a replacement who stands before God without sin. Bonhoeffer dismisses such a notion, insisting instead that the new person created through the Holy Spirit's work is the real person, but now seen from God's perspective (see DBWE 9:343). In this case, Bonhoeffer sides with Luther over against Barth.

the university,[65] Bonhoeffer "considered Harnack's foundation of theology in the 'holy spirit of Christianity' too optimistic and incompatible with Luther's theology of history." By the same token, even though Bonhoeffer was indebted to Holl, he, "in complete agreement with Barth, could not accept [Holl's] moral optimism. The church needed a more fundamental theological basis." When it comes to Bonhoeffer's own interests at this time, his papers show that the third article's attention on the Holy Spirit, the church, and eschatology had become the "central theme" of his work. Therefore, "he found the best point of departure for a work on the church in Seeberg's dogmatics, even though he did not agree with him that the church would, in the course of history, develop into the kingdom of God."[66] What he did find in Seeberg, however, was not only an historical grounding for human reality but a social understanding as well. "With this he was able finally to bridge the gap between the theology of revelation and tangible concrete reality."[67]

In these works both the fascination that Luther held for Bonhoeffer and the extent of Holl's influence on his thinking can be seen. Bonhoeffer followed Holl in interpreting Luther and justification in terms of Luther's internal struggle. At the same time, however, other themes begin to enter into Bonhoeffer's analysis. These changes are due to his reading of Barth and texts of Luther independent of Holl. These themes and influences will come to the fore in the next stage of Bonhoeffer's theological development. By the time he writes his dissertations, Holl's theological orientation is left behind, with the result that Bonhoeffer modifies his categories for understanding and

65. He lived in the same Berlin neighborhood as the Bonhoeffers "and enjoyed travelling with young Bonhoeffer on the city train from Halensee Station to the university" (Schlingensiepen, *Dietrich Bonhoeffer 1906–1945*, 27).

66. Pfeifer, "Editor's Afterword to the German Edition," DBWE 9:574–75.

67. Ibid., 575. It was perhaps with this diverse set of influences in the background that Bonhoeffer, writing to E. Sutz in 1931, could refer to himself as having "theological *bastard origins*" (see DBWE 11:36).

interpreting Luther.[68] The significance of this change is demonstrated in that Christology becomes the central category for Bonhoeffer's understanding of the church; with that new focus, we also see that the church is not discussed in terms of morality and consciousness, but as the place where Christ is present.

68. See von Soosten, *Sozialität der Kirche*, 168–72, for a detailed analysis of his transformation.

# 4

# Dissertations

The culmination of Bonhoeffer's student career came with the writing of his doctoral dissertation (*Sanctorum Communio*) in 1927 and his habilitation (*Act and Being*) in 1929. In between the writing of these two works, Bonhoeffer spent a year in Barcelona serving as a vicar in a parish composed of German expatriates. These works, while still written by a young theologian, display both Bonhoeffer's theological skills and his overall orientation. They also point to a marked change in his theological development. Whereas his student papers showed an interest in Luther and some hints at his christological orientation, they still display a student under the influence of his teachers. What we see in the writings that follow, however, is a marked independence.

The significance of Bonhoeffer's final academic writings has already been well established. Clifford Green, for example, has noted that the period 1927–1933 is the formative period of Bonhoeffer's theology. In the writings and lectures of this period we find the "systematic foundations" that, "while supporting later creative building, continued to shape and characterize his theology to the end."[1]

One of the mistakes of early interpretations of Bonhoeffer's theology, especially those that saw in *LPP* something radically new, was that they overlooked the foundations of Bonhoeffer's theology as found in his early writings. When attention is paid to his early writings, what is discovered in his later writings, such as *LPP*, is not a radical departure, but the logical working out of concepts and ideas that had been introduced earlier. His doctoral dissertations, therefore, provide a wealth of information to help us understand the totality of Bonhoeffer's theological enterprise. Here we find the "central ideas that inform all his writings—and, indeed, his life."[2]

Part of what is revealed in an examination of these works is the unique or independent position Bonhoeffer carved out for himself. While it is clear that he sided with Barth over against liberal Protestant theology, following the method of revelation laid out by Barth, he remained fiercely independent at the same time. Even though he had already made a conscious decision to follow Barth's theology of revelation, he "severely criticizes Barth's interpretation in *The Epistle to the Romans* of love of the neighbor, as though the neighbor were merely a cipher for God. A similar criticism of Barth's interpretation of the freedom of God would appear in Bonhoeffer's next book, *Act and Being*."[3] In both cases, the position Bonhoeffer took more closely resembles that of Luther than that of Barth.

1. Clifford Green, *Bonhoeffer: A Theology of Sociality* (Grand Rapids: Eerdmans, 1999), 5.
2. See Clifford Green, "Editor's Introduction to the English Edition," *Sanctorum Communio*, DBWE 1:1.
3. Ibid., 3. Cf. Joachim von Soosten's examination of the Barth/Bonhoeffer relationship for a similar view ("Editor's Afterword to the German Edition," DBWE 1:292ff).

### *Sanctorum Communio*

Having had the opportunity to examine Bonhoeffer's personal copy of Luther's works,[4] Joachim von Soosten has been able to determine which works of Luther Bonhoeffer had read, and by examining Bonhoeffer's notes has concluded that Luther's early works, and the sermons and treatises of 1519 specifically, were of particular importance for Bonhoeffer's dissertations.[5] In commenting on the social structure of the church, for example, Bonhoeffer, in making direct reference to Luther's 1519 treatise, "The Blessed Sacrament of the Holy and True Body of Christ, and the Brotherhoods," says, "Here Luther expresses wonderful and profound thoughts on this question."[6]

Further evidence of what was influencing Bonhoeffer's thought at this time can be discerned from his announced intention in writing his dissertation. In a letter to his parents, written September 21, 1925, Bonhoeffer announced his decision to work with Reinhold Seeberg on his doctoral dissertation, telling them that he had proposed a "half historical and half systematic" project to him; Seeberg accepted the proposal.[7] The method that Bonhoeffer would use to approach the subject of the church already marks a distinction between Bonhoeffer and his theological teachers, who would have "assumed an approach which sought access, by way of historical criticism, to the past witness of faith. Such an approach refrains as long as possible from systematic-theological interpretation, which comes into play only after the historical-critical analysis."[8] This, in part, accounts for the

4. The edition of Luther's works that was widely used in the universities of Germany at the time was the four-volume collection from 1912, edited by Otto Clemen.

5. See chapter 2. It should be noted, however, that Bonhoeffer does not limit himself to the young Luther. For the development of his argument in *SC*, Bonhoeffer refers to several writings of Luther that encompass the entirety of Luther's career.

6. DBWE 1:179n41.

7. DBWE 9:148.

8. Von Soosten, "Editor's Afterword," DBWE 1:290.

differences between Bonhoeffer's theology and his teachers; it is also a source of the tension that characterizes his thinking at the time. To be sure, he is using a variety of sources—Berlin teachers, Barth, and Luther; but there is tension on another level as well. Even more important than the historical-systematic formulation is the basic question that drives Bonhoeffer's theology as a whole: "Where within the reality of the world does the reality confessed by the Christian faith manifest itself and become concrete?" Bonhoeffer is convinced that faith "must have a concrete locus within the reality of the world. This is the leitmotif which he is to pursue throughout his entire life, and which in turn will always remain an unsettling issue for him."[9]

This quest for concreteness, which has been identified by many scholars as a particular concern of Bonhoeffer's, can be seen as having its initial impulses from Luther. It was Luther in his statements on the *theologia crucis*, more than any other theologian with whom Bonhoeffer was familiar, who stressed the concreteness of God's revelation in Jesus Christ. What we know about God is what we know through Jesus' death on the cross. This is specifically earthbound and inherently concrete. Sharing the same orientation as Luther, the "question of the reality of God in the world is evident"[10] already in *Sanctorum Communio* and remains a constant through all his works.

Even though Bonhoeffer found Barth's theological approach conducive to his own way of thinking, the drive toward concreteness is what brings Bonhoeffer to the point of questioning Barth's theology.[11] Not content with Barth's dichotomy between revelation and history, Bonhoeffer "seeks to correct Barth's fundamental

9. Ibid., 290–91.
10. Ibid., 291–92.
11. In his evaluation of Bonhoeffer's dissertation, regarding his use of Barth, Seeberg observed, "Here and there one finds allusions to Barth. . . . Yet these influences are neutralized by others and do not determine the author's thought formation" (DBWE 9:176).

theological decisions." Both by his theological approach and his content, "it can be safely assumed, moreover, that Bonhoeffer consciously intends this controversy with Barth." In order to overcome the limitations of Barth's approach, Bonhoeffer's argument "runs strictly opposite. . . . Bonhoeffer's proposal for the overall design of systematic theology can be understood as a direct criticism of Barth."[12]

As a source for support in this debate, Bonhoeffer turned to Luther.[13] But now, rather than simply relying on the resources taken from Holl, he "now draws on Luther's own writings, in which this link between the christological basis and the social structure of the church-community is developed intensively." As a result, von Soosten remarks, "the importance of the sacrament and the related concept of vicarious representative action [*Stellvertretung*] now move into the center of Bonhoeffer's theology," becoming the "structural principle of the Christian church-community."[14] As a student of Luther's theology, Bonhoeffer wed ecclesiology to Christology, since both have their foundation in Christ's vicarious act of suffering for the sake of the world. This connection, "which is already present in

12. Von Soosten, "Editor's Afterword," DBWE 1:292.

13. Ibid., 292–93; cf. *DB-ER*, 83. See also Joachim von Soosten, *Die Sozialität der Kirche: Theologie und Theorie der Kirche in Dietrich Bonhoeffers "Sanctorum Communio"* (Munich: Chr. Kaiser, 1992) where he points to a major difference between the early Barth and Bonhoeffer in *SC*. The key to Barth's early theology is the *extra Calvinisticum*, which, while acknowledging that God became man in Jesus Christ, at the same time, can understand God apart from the incarnation, *finitum non capax*. Therefore, even though God has bound himself to the world in Jesus Christ, God cannot be identified with the world. Bonhoeffer, on the other hand, places an emphasis on the *finitum capax infiniti*. This difference leads Ralf Wüstenberg, *A Theology of Life: Dietrich Bonhoeffer's Religionless Christianity* (Grand Rapids: Eerdmans, 1998), 39, to conclude, "He follows the Lutheran tradition against the *extra Calvinisticum* in whose tradition he believes Barth to be standing." Cf. Andreas Pangritz, *Karl Barth in the Theology of Dietrich Bonhoeffer* (Grand Rapids: Eerdmans, 2000), 27. Even though Pangritz insists that Barth remains the determinative lifelong influence on Bonhoeffer, he admits the essential difference between the two on this point: "There is no doubt; this is a Lutheran protesting against the Calvinian '*non capax*.'"

14. Von Soosten, "Editor's Afterword," DBWE 1:293–94.

Luther, can be pressed by Bonhoeffer to the point where the two become indistinguishable."[15]

Since a full explication of Bonhoeffer's concept of the church, the subject proper of *Sanctorum Communio*, is not the focus of the present work, the focus here will be on the specifically christological character of his thinking, thereby limiting our discussion to Bonhoeffer's view of Christ. However, since not all Bonhoeffer scholars are in agreement about the nature of Bonhoeffer's Christology or the role it plays in his theology at this time, it is important to note this disparity before proceeding. Ernst Feil has been one of the most prominent scholars to insist that Christology does not play a significant role before *Act and Being*.[16] Until that point, he insists that Bonhoeffer's theology concentrates on ecclesiology. In response to Feil's assertion, a range of scholars have attempted to answer his claims, challenging the very contention of Christology's significance for shaping the whole of Bonhoeffer's theology.[17] What emerges from this exchange is not only the central place Christology holds in Bonhoeffer's theology, but the particular nature of that Christology is noted as well. Bonhoeffer's understanding of Christ is one in which the cross is the key to both Christ's identify and God's presence in the world.[18]

15. Ibid., 294.
16. See Feil, *TDB*, part 2. Feil directly challenges Eberhard Bethge's claim that Bonhoeffer's argument in *Sanctorum Communio* is christologically structured. Cf. Feil, *Die Theologie Dietrich Bonhoeffer: Hermeneutik, Christologie, Weltverständnis* (Munich: Chr. Kaier, 1979), 147n26 (this footnote in the English translation was edited to exclude Feil's reference to Bethge).
17. Cf. Wolfgang Huber, "Wahrheit und Existenzform. Anregungen zu einer Theorie der Kirche bei Dietrich Bonhoeffer," in *Konsequenzen: Dietrich Bonhoeffers Kirchenverständnis heute*, ed. Ernst Feil and Ilse Tödt, International Bonhoeffer Forum 3 (Munich: Chr. Kaiser, 1980), 133n15; Hans-Jürgen Abromeit, *Das Geheimnis Christi: Dietrich Bonhoeffers erfahrungsbezognene Christologie* (Neukirchen-Vluyn: Neukirchener, 1991), 28ff; von Soosten, "Editor's Afterword," DBWE 1:294; von Soosten, *Sozialität der Kirche*, 64ff; Jonathan Sorum, "The Eschatological Boundary in Dietrich Bonhoeffers 'Nachfolge'" (ThD diss., Luther Northwestern Theological Seminary, 1994) 48nn50–51; and Hans-Walter Krumwiede, "Dietrich Bonhoeffers Luther Rezeption," in *Die Lutherischen Kirchen und die Bekenntnissynode von Barmen: Referate des Internationalen Symposiums auf der Reisenburg* (Göttingen: Vandenhoeck & Ruprecht, 1984).

Throughout his discussion of the church, both in terms of its foundation and its nature and witness, Bonhoeffer's thought is clearly christocentric. He cannot talk about the church without talking about Christ. For Bonhoeffer, it is impossible to understand the church apart from Christ: "The church is established in reality in and through Christ—not in such a way that we can think of the church without Christ himself, but he himself 'is' the church. He does not represent it, for only what is not present can be represented. But in God's eyes the church is present in Christ."[19]

For Bonhoeffer, the church can only be properly understood as a theological, not a sociological or historical entity. The study of the church "does not properly belong to the sociology of religion, but to theology. . . . Hence our purpose is to understand the structure of the given reality of a church of Christ, as revealed in Christ. . . . But the nature of the church can only be understood from within, *cum* ira et studio [*with* passionate zeal], never by nonparticipants."[20] At the same time, the church is not merely a theological construct, but a reality that has been created by God through Christ. We know God through Christ,[21] and Christ is the foundation of the church. So Bonhoeffer concludes: "*The reality of the church is a reality of revelation, a reality that essentially must be* either believed or denied."[22]

For Bonhoeffer, the only proper way to understand the true nature of the church is through the revelation of God in Christ. When understood theologically, as opposed to either sociologically or historically, the church is a reality created by God through Christ; in that sense, there can be no proper discussion about the church

18. Cf. Abromeit, *Geheimnis Christi*, 227.
19. DBWE 1:157.
20. Ibid., 32–33. This was Heinrich von Sybel's (Berlin history professor) phrase for how history should be written as opposed to Leopold Ranke's method of objective detachment. Ranke held that history should be written *sine ira et studio* (without anger and zeal).
21. Cf. ibid., 60.
22. Ibid., 127 (emphasis is Bonhoeffer's).

without reference to Jesus Christ. For "Christ is thus the sole foundation upon which the building of the church rests, the reality from which the historical 'collective life' originated."[23] That which was torn asunder because of sin through Adam has been reunited by God in Christ. "It is 'Adam,' a collective person, who can only be superseded by the collective person 'Christ existing as church-community.'"[24] For Bonhoeffer, ecclesiology and Christology belong together, because they have the same theme. They both have their foundation in the presence of Christ.[25] Only where Christ is present is the church the church. It is not the church as an institution that defines "where Christ is communally present. On the contrary, it is not a church organization that defines Christ, but Christ who defines the church."[26]

When it comes to Bonhoeffer's understanding of Christ present in the church, two concepts that are introduced here, but find expression throughout Bonhoeffer's corpus, are critical. *Stellvertretung* (vicarious representation), which describes the work of Christ, and *Christ existing as church-community*, a phrase that connects the vicarious representation of Christ to the vicarious representational nature of the church-community, are ways that Bonhoeffer expresses his Lutheran commitments. *Stellvertretung* can best be understood as an expression of both the *communicatio idiomatum* and "the happy exchange," both of which Bonhoeffer takes over from Luther. As has been widely acknowledged, the phrase *Christ existing as church-*

23. Ibid., 153.
24. Ibid., 121. Bonhoeffer's term here is *Gemeinde*, which he uses in distinction from *Kirche*. While *Gemeinde* can be understood as "community," because Bonhoeffer specifically uses it as a "theological term that emphasizes the communal character of the sanctorum communio," the translators of the Dietrich Bonhoeffer Works have chosen to translate it as "church-community," thereby maintaining the distinction between *Gemeinde* and *Kirche* while noting an inherent connection between the two. See Green, "Editor's Introduction," DBWE 1:16.
25. Huber, "Wahrheit und Existenzform," 93.
26. Green, "Editor's Introduction," DBWE 1:15. This distinction will enable Bonhoeffer to critique the German Christians during the German church struggle.

*community* is one Bonhoeffer borrowed from Hegel, then transformed. Hegel's phrase was *God existing as community*.[27] The christological rephrasing on the part of Bonhoeffer became the foundation for his understanding of the church and, according to Bethge, was the way Bonhoeffer "achieved a third standpoint that transcended the Troeltsch-Barth antithesis."[28]

The core of Bonhoeffer's Christology in *Sanctorum Communio* is laid out in chapter 5.[29] Before turning to Bonhoeffer's explication, however, we will begin with a review of Luther's influential treatise, "The Blessed Sacrament of the Holy and True Body of Christ, and the Brotherhoods," from 1519,[30] a document that Bonhoeffer relied on heavily for his own christological understanding of the church.

Luther's treatise on Holy Communion, written for the laity and the first in which he expounds the significance of the sacrament for Christian living, focuses on the communion or fellowship of saints established through the sacrament of Holy Communion. As Luther understands it, participation in the sacrament makes one a part of the fellowship in which "Christ and all saints are one spiritual body, just as the inhabitants of a city are one community and body, each citizen being a member of the other and of the entire city. All the saints, therefore, are members of Christ and of the church, which is a spiritual and eternal city of God."[31] Participation in the sacrament means nothing other than to receive "a sign of this fellowship and incorporation with Christ and all saints," that is, "all the spiritual possessions of Christ and his saints are shared with and become the common property of him who receives this sacrament."[32] Through

27. See Bonhoeffer's own comments on Hegel in this context, DBWE 1:198.
28. *DB-ER*, 83.
29. Chapter 5 comprises the heart of Bonhoeffer's argument, occupying over half of the total work.
30. "The Blessed Sacrament of the Holy and True Body of Christ, and the Brotherhoods," *LW* 35:47–73.
31. Ibid., 51.
32. Ibid.

the sacrament, believers receive "a sure sign from God himself that he is thus united with Christ and his saints and has all things in common [with them], that Christ's sufferings and life are his own, together with the lives and sufferings of all the saints."[33] As members together they share one another's joys and sorrows, and there find sustenance and strength for life in the world.

In and through the sacrament of Christ's body, believers are united with Christ and with one another in fellowship. It is through this fellowship created in Christ that they are nurtured and strengthened in their fight against sin.

> The immeasurable grace and mercy of God are given us in this sacrament to the end that we might put from us all misery and tribulation [*anfechtung*] and lay it upon the community [of saints], and especially on Christ. Then we may with joy find strength and comfort, and say, "Though I am a sinner and have fallen, though this or that misfortune has befallen me, nevertheless I will go to the sacrament to receive a sign from God that I have on my side Christ's righteousness, life, and sufferings, with all holy angels and the blessed in heaven and all pious men on earth. If I die, I am not alone in death; if I suffer, they suffer with me. [I know that] all my misfortune is shared with Christ and the saints, because I have a sure sign of their love toward me."[34]

For Luther, it is a sacrament of love in which those who partake of the sacrament share in the sufferings of Christ and one another. Real community is formed, and life is therefore transformed. Drawing on the imagery of the elements of bread and wine, Luther describes the nature of this new community:

> Christ with all saints, by his love, takes upon himself our form [Phil. 2:7], fights with us against sin, death, and all evil. This enkindles in us such love that we take on his form, rely upon his righteousness, life, and blessedness. And through the interchange of his blessings and our

33. Ibid., 52.
34. Ibid., 54.

> misfortunes, we become one loaf, one bread, one body, one drink, and have all things in common.[35]

In other words, Christ becomes us and we become him. While humanity should stand guilty before God, Christ substitutes himself, taking our place, conferring on us instead his righteousness. In another place, Luther refers to this as the "happy exchange,"[36] which indeed represents a central christological tenant of Luther's theology.

Bonhoeffer encapsulated Luther's critical point with the term *Stellvertretung*, Christ's vicarious representative act on the cross. "Though innocent, Jesus takes the sin of others upon himself, and by dying as a criminal he is accursed, for he bears the sins of the world and is punished for them. However, vicarious representative love triumphs on the criminal's cross, obedience to God triumphs over sin, and thereby sin is actually punished and overcome."[37] By submitting to the law, Christ substituted himself for sinful humanity, bearing God's judgment on the cross. Having been separated from God through sin, humanity is now reconciled to God and placed in a new community.[38]

Bonhoeffer, building on Luther's understanding of Christ's presence in the sacraments, claimed that through the sacraments we become Christ-like. As with Luther, for Bonhoeffer, the believer becomes Christ for others.[39] Through the fellowship of the faithful, Christ is made real. Having been divided by sin, humanity-in-Adam lives in isolation from one another. Now, however, as is God's will, humanity is restored to fellowship and community through Christ. Therefore, the church, humanity-in-Christ, is the lived reality of what God has done through Christ.

35. Ibid., 58.
36. Cf. Luther, "The Freedom of a Christian," *LW* 31:351.
37. DBWE 1:155–56.
38. Ibid., 150–51.
39. See ibid., 184 and 187.

> The cord between God and human beings that was cut by the first Adam is tied anew by God, by revealing God's own love in Christ, by no longer approaching us in demand and summons, purely as You, but instead by *giving God's own self as an I, opening God's own heart. The church is founded on the revelation of God's heart.* But since destroying the primal community with God also destroyed human community, so likewise when God restores community between human beings and God's own self, community among us also is restored once again.[40]

Using direct quotes from Luther's 1519 treatise, Bonhoeffer developed his understanding of the church, the body of Christ, the new humanity formed in and through Christ's suffering and death on the cross. Through that event, God reconciles humanity to himself, but also to one another. The church, therefore, becomes the place where God's new will for humanity and the world becomes a reality in the here and now.

> The new humanity is entirely concentrated in the one single historical point, Jesus Christ, and only in Christ is it perceived as a whole. For in Christ, as the foundation and the body of the building called Christ's church-community, the work of God takes place and is completed. In this work Christ has a function that sheds the clearest light on the fundamental difference between Adam and Christ, namely *the function of vicarious representative* [*Stellvertreter*].[41]

For Bonhoeffer, as for Luther, the church is founded on and is an expression of God's love for the world in Christ. United in fellowship, believers are nurtured in word and sacrament, the means through which Christ is truly present for them. In the same manner in which Christ has borne the sins of the world, substituting himself for guilty humanity, so that humankind could stand righteous before God, fellow Christians now bear one another's burdens.

40. Ibid., 145 (the emphasis is Bonhoeffer's).
41. Ibid., 146 (the emphasis is Bonhoeffer's).

When Bonhoeffer developed the concept, *Christ existing as church-community*, he drew directly on Luther's 1519 treatise. In a document that is so highly christological, one can see the direct influence of Luther's christological understanding in reformulating Hegel's *God existing as community*.[42] The church is the real body of Christ, and the benefits humanity received through Christ's vicarious representative act on the cross become real for the individual believer. As Bonhoeffer showed, his christologically-formulated understanding of the church reflects the position of Luther.

> It [the church-community] bears the sins by receiving forgiveness through the word and seeing its sins wiped out on the cross. It indeed lives *by the word* alone, but in doing so it has the Spirit. It is bearer of the word, its steward and instrument. It has authority, provided it has faith in the authority of the word; it can take the sins of individuals upon itself, if it builds itself on the word of the cross, and knows itself reconciled and justified in the cross of Jesus. It has itself died and risen with Christ, and is now the nova creatura [new creation][43] in Christ. It is not merely *a means to an end but also an end in itself. It is the present Christ himself, and this is why 'being in Christ' and 'being in the church-community' is the same thing*; it is why Christ himself bears the sins of the individuals, which are laid upon the church-community.[44]

Because of the close identity between Christ and the church-community making Christ's vicarious representative act a present reality, Bonhoeffer can clearly call the church *Christ existing as church-community*. The church embodies the forgiving love of God. In fact, central to Bonhoeffer's understanding of community (reflecting the position of Luther), which rests on and reflects God's love, is the nature of its members to live for one another, bearing each

42. The significance of this change cannot be overlooked. Hegel was talking about the "absolute spirit" incarnated in human beings through reason; his phrase was void of any Christian content.

43. This is an image Bonhoeffer takes from another of Luther's writings; see DBWE 1:190n65.

44. Ibid., 190 (the emphasis is Bonhoeffer's).

other's burdens. Because Christ suffered and died on the cross for the church-community, it is now able to live with and for one another. "Being-for-each-other" is lived out through acts of love in which the members give up "self 'for' my neighbor's benefit, with the readiness to do and bear everything in the neighbor's place, indeed, if necessary, to sacrifice myself, standing as a *substitute* for my neighbor."[45] This "being-for-each-other" comes not as a result of the initiative of the members, but has its very foundation in Christ's vicarious representative action.

> One person bears the other in active love, intercession, and forgiveness of sins, acting completely vicariously. This is possible only in the church-community of Christ, and that itself rests, as a whole, on the principle of vicarious representation, i.e., on the love of God. But all are borne by the church-community, which consists precisely in this being-for-each-other of its members. The structural being-with-each-other [Miteinander] of church-community and its members, and the members acting-for-each-other [Füreinander] as vicarious representatives in the power of the church-community, is what constitutes the specific sociological nature of the community of love [Liebesgemeinschaft].[46]

In summary, Christ and his cross cannot be separated in Bonhoeffer's mind. When Bonhoeffer talked about Christ, he referred to the cross and its significance. In a myriad of images, from "the cross of Christ," "justification in the cross of Jesus," "death of Jesus on the cross," "cross of Jesus still stands at the center of the church-community," "the suffering of Jesus," to "the community-of-the-cross,"[47] there is one dominant understanding of Christ that becomes present in the church. Therefore, for Bonhoeffer, Christ is more than the founder of a religious movement in which his moral teachings or example become models for believers to emulate. Instead, Christ,

45. Ibid., 184.
46. Ibid., 191.
47. Cf. ibid., 150, 151, 154, 155, 161, 167, 190, 204, and 205.

by his suffering and death on the cross, creates a new reality. In describing the New Testament's concept of the church, Bonhoeffer began by laying out the scriptural understanding of love, which is the basis of community. By contrasting God's love and human love, he insists that there can only be one starting point for a proper understanding of love.

> Thus our starting point must not be our love for God or for other human beings. Nor do we really know what love is from the dangers of war, the sacrificial death of our brothers, or from personal experiences of love shown to us; we know love solely from the love of God that manifests itself in the cross of Christ, in our justification, and in the founding of the church community.[48]

God, church, and love all find their expression in the cross of Christ.

In *Sanctorum Communio* we find the foundations of Bonhoeffer's understanding of the church, which never changed in its essential points. But even there his chief interest was in "Christ existing as community." According to Bethge, this emphasis "indicated that the Church can never be traced back to human need, to some religious *a priori* or meaning in man, or to his instinct for sociality. It can only be traced back to Christology. And Christology cannot be complete without an ecclesiology."[49] Christology retained its "critical function . . . beside all ecclesiological realities."[50]

For Bonhoeffer, because God has identified himself with the world, the church is necessary. It remains the visible expression of God's presence. It is where God's word is spoken and where through fellowship people experience the love of God in the world. The

48. Ibid., 167. From this statement we can clearly see how far Bonhoeffer has moved beyond Holl's religion of conscience.
49. Eberhard Bethge, *Bonhoeffer: Exile and Martyr* (New York: Seabury, 1976), 62.
50. Ibid.

church is a visible sign of God's being free, not from, but for the world.

In a statement that shows the radical concentration on Christology as the source for the church as well as our knowledge of God, Bonhoeffer states, "Community with God exists only through Christ, but Christ is present only in his church-community, and therefore *community with God exists only in the church.*"[51] Not only can this be seen as a summary of Bonhoeffer's thinking at this time, it reflects his later commitments as he moved into the struggles with the German Christians in the 1930s. Here one can see the marks of Luther's *theologia crucis*, especially when we see the role the cross places in Bonhoeffer's understanding of Christ.

## Barcelona Interlude

The christological orientation already spelled out is given expression again and becomes even more clearly defined by the cross during the year Bonhoeffer spent as a vicar to an expatriate German congregation in Barcelona in 1928–1929. It was there, separated from his own family and culture, that he became aware of the problems of an entirely different class of people:[52]

51. DBWE 1:158 (the emphasis is Bonhoeffer's). With this statement as background, one can see why Bonhoeffer, in the midst of the church struggle, stated unequivocally that "those who separated themselves from the confessing church, separated themselves from God." Likewise, simply because the church declares itself to be the church, did not make it so. The church exists only where Christ is present.

52. Bethge, *DB-ER*, 97, describes Bonhoeffer's new environment in the following terms: "His new position brought him into contact with a kind of person unfamiliar to him. In Grunewald, he had practically no contact with the type represented by these Germans living abroad: businesspeople with a petit bourgeois outlook. Here there was little sign of the hectic postwar years in Germany and the thirst for novelty and experiment that prevailed in Berlin; the small Protestant community in Barcelona clung to its old patterns and ways of thought." This experience also brought him into contact with a culture with which he had had no previous background; even the Roman Catholic Church he encountered in Barcelona was different from the one he had discovered in Rome years earlier. Cf. *DB-ER*, 100ff.

> I'm getting to know new people each day, at least their life stories. . . . One encounters people here the way they are, far from the masquerade of the "Christian world"; people with passions, criminal types, small people with small goals, small drives, and small crimes—all in all, people who feel homeless in both senses, people who thaw a bit when you speak to them in a friendly manner—real people. I can only say I have the impression that precisely these people stand more under grace than under wraith, but that it is precisely the Christian world that stand more under wrath than under grace. [53]

It was an experience that challenged his presuppositions, tested his theological position, and in turn led him to new insights.[54] It was a time in which Bonhoeffer found himself in a situation where Luther's theology could certainly affect him. Even though Bonhoeffer's questions and concerns in Barcelona were not the same as Luther's—that is, "How to find a gracious God?"—the answers both Luther and Bonhoeffer arrived at were essentially the same. In Bonhoeffer's situation, the concern was not on the individual guilty conscience as it was for Luther, but rather, on the social dimension, on how God relates to forlorn, alienated people of this earth.[55] Nevertheless, Bonhoeffer, like Luther, located the connection between God and the world in the cross of Christ.

During this period, Bonhoeffer presented lectures and preached sermons, all of which offer us insights into the further development of his theology along the lines of Luther's *theologia crucis.* Noting the contrasts Bonhoeffer encountered between the academic world of Berlin and this new world filled with new and unfamiliar types of

53. August 7, 1928, letter to Helmut Rößler: DBWE 10:127

54. See *DB-ER*, chap. 3; Thomas Day, *Dietrich Bonhoeffer on Christian Community and Common Sense*, Toronto Studies in Theology, vol. 11, Bonhoeffer Series, no. 2 (New York: Edwin Mellen, 1982), 33ff; and Clifford Green, *The Sociality of Christ and Humanity: Dietrich Bonhoeffer's Early Theology, 1927–1933* (New York: Edwin Mellen, 1982), 105ff, for insights into Bonhoeffer's experiences at this time that might have had an effect on his theological development.

55. See Day, *Dietrich Bonhoeffer on Christian Community*, 34.

people, Bethge says that Bonhoeffer expended a great deal of time getting to know his parishioners and understanding their problems and anxieties. It was in this context that he committed himself to finding ways to address people in their particular context.[56] As the themes of his work indicate, he continued to focus on the distinctions between religion and Christianity, and on the concrete, this-worldly character of the Christian faith; these are themes that are highly christological and find their expression in a cross-dominated theology.[57]

### Jesus Christ and the Essence of Christianity

In a Berlin prison cell where he sat as a political prisoner in1944, Bonhoeffer posed the question, "Who is Christ actually for us today?" This question comes at the end of his life. Nearly twenty years earlier, however, he posed a similar question that may well set the context for the latter question. In his December 11, 1928 lecture, "Jesus Christ and the Essence of Christianity,"[58] he asked, "What does the cross have to say to *us, today*?"[59] Taken together, these two questions form the front and end pieces of his theology, holding it together much like bookends in which Christ and the cross inform and support all the thoughts in between.

This was the second in a series of three lectures Bonhoeffer presented to his congregation during the winter 1928. It is significant because it represents one of "Bonhoeffer's earliest attempts to grapple with the centrality of Jesus Christ for one's faith commitment within the Christian community"[60] and "contains nuances and insights that

56. According to Bethge, *DB-ER*, 97, "Now his time was consumed by local choirs or gymnastic societies, committee meetings, and consultations in the German colony. He devoted the rest of his time to visiting parishioners or preparing for services."

57. See ibid., 112–13.

58. DWBE 10:342–59.

59. Ibid., 358.

had not been explicitly stated before, which were to make a powerful resurgence in Bonhoeffer's final working period."[61]

It is on the cross, "the historically visible form" of God, Bonhoeffer pointed out, that one learns that God's greatest gift is not religion but the love and mercy God has shown in Christ. In contrast to religion where people seek to find ways to God, "the Christian idea is the way of God to people and has as the visible objectification of this, the cross." Christianity gives new hope to the hopeless, brings value to the valueless, strength to the weak, and life to the dying, all of which comes to light in God's way to people that has its "visible objectification" in the cross. "Jesus wants to be where human beings are no longer anything. The meaning of Jesus's life is the documentation of this divine will toward the sinner, toward the unworthy. God's love is wherever Jesus is."[62]

The presence of God in such a manner, however, is not God merely suffering along with suffering humanity; that would only leave humanity in its misery. God's love is shown in that God brings sin and suffering to an end on the cross:

> Only when Jesus or God's love not only is present where human beings are mired in sin and misery, but when Jesus also takes upon himself that which stands above every person's life, namely, death; that is, when Jesus, who is God's love, genuinely dies. Only thus can human beings be assured that God's love will accompany and lead them through death. Jesus's death on the cross of the criminal, however, shows that divine love extends even to the death of the criminal, and when Jesus dies on the cross with the cry, "My God, my God, why have you forsaken me?" it shows once more that God's eternal love does not abandon us even when we despair and feel forsaken by God. Jesus genuinely dies despairing in his own work and in God, and yet precisely that situation constitutes the crown of his message; God loves us so much that with us,

60. Kelly and Nelson, *TF*, 47.
61. *DB-ER*, 116.
62. DBWE 10:357.

> for us, and as a documentation of that love, God accepts and experiences death itself. And only because Jesus in the humiliation of the cross proves both his own love and God's love does resurrection follow death.[63]

In a more explicit reference to the theology of the cross, Bonhoeffer continued by saying that the cross is central to the Christian faith:

> The meaning of Good Friday and of Easter Sunday is that God's path to human beings leads back to God. Thus Jesus's idea of God is summed up in Paul's interpretation of the cross; thus the cross becomes the center and the paradoxical emblem of the Christian message. A king who dies on the cross must be the king of a rather strange kingdom. Only those who understand the profound paradox of the cross can also understand the whole meaning of Jesus's assertion: my kingdom is not from this world. Remaining faithful to the idea of God that led him to the cross meant declining the royal crown offered to him and renouncing the idea of the "Imperium Romanum" that tempted him on that path.[64]

The cross distinguishes Christianity from religion because it marks off the way of God from the ways of the world. But, in addition, the cross marks the profound identification God has with sinful humanity. It is on the cross that God embraces all of humanity by undergoing death that "hangs over every life." By embracing death, and overcoming it, Jesus' death on the cross is proof that God's desire to love has no limits. As a result, for Bonhoeffer, there is a clear distinction between religion and Christianity.

> Christ is not the bringer of a new religion, but the bringer of God. Hence as the impossible path from human beings to God, the Christian religion stands alongside other religions. Christians can never boast of their own Christian religiosity, for it, too, remains humanly all-too-human. Christians do, however, live from God's grace, grace that comes to us and to every person who opens up to it and comes to understand it in Christ's cross. Thus Christ's gift is not the Christian religion but God's grace and love, which culminate in the cross.[65]

63. Ibid.
64. Ibid.

What is significant about this statement is not only what it reveals about Bonhoeffer's theology, but, as Bethge points out, "This sentence is almost identical to Bonhoeffer's 1944 statement in *Letters and Papers from Prison*: 'Jesus calls us, not to a new religion, but to life.'"[66]

After having pointed to the centrality of the cross, Bonhoeffer went on to answer the question about its significance: "What does the cross say to us?" He acknowledged that there is a problem, but the problem is not the cross; rather, it is the modern world that has created no room for God. Informed by humanism and mysticism, both of which are expressions of the Greek spirit, modernity is an enemy of Christianity. Since this is the case, the world cannot grasp the ways of God that culminate on the cross. But in addition, the modern world has produced longings and desires that cannot be satisfied; as a result, people thirst for release. The presence of cults, sects, and anthroposophy, the preoccupation with the occult and mystery religions, as well as the presence of youth movements—all are signs pointing to an absence, a longing, through which people seek to bring themselves to God. It is in this context of hopelessness that the cross provides hope. In contrast to religious attempts, Christianity

> speaks of God's grace toward the sins of the big cities, about God's love where misery and guilt accumulate in frightening proportions, where calloused hands perhaps are clenched fists, in defiance of fate. You, human being, no matter who you are, you are God's child, you are included in God's love, out of the pure, incomprehensible grace of God; accept this word, believe in it, trust in his rule rather than in yourself or in your own party, rather than in your own work or your own religion. God does as he wills. Turn your misery into God's blessed presence, and

65. Ibid., 358.
66. *DB-ER*, 118. DBWE 8:482, translation altered to read, "Jesus calls not to a new religion but to life."

> from within your guilt and distress hear the voice of the eternal, living God.[67]

From these early assertions a straight line leads to the theology of the cross of the Tegel prison letters. For Bonhoeffer the cross forms the inner core of the Christ event and stands at the center of what he understands by the Christian faith and about God. The cross defines who Jesus is and what he does.

One further example of this characteristic approach that defines Bonhoeffer's theology comes from the third and final lecture, "Basic Questions of a Christian Ethic," given on February 8, 1929. There he concluded that Christianity is basically amoral and, therefore, does not have an ethic because Christianity "stands beyond good and evil"; it is not primarily about human acts that can be judged in ways that might make them appear pleasing to God, but rather is about God and God's ways to humankind. Making the same distinction between Christianity and religion he had made in the previous lecture, he drew a clear line of demarcation, where the cross of Christ is once again the key:

> Because Christianity speaks of the exclusive path from God to human beings from within God's own compassionate love toward the unholy, the sinful, while ethics speaks of the path from human beings to God, about the encounter between the holy God and the holy human being; in other words, because the Christian message speaks of grace while ethics speaks of righteousness.
>
> Because there are innumerable human paths to God, there are also innumerable ethics. But there is but one path from God to human beings, and that is the path of love in Christ, the path of the cross.[68]

This is a consistent theme repeated by Bonhoeffer hereafter. In sermons and works that follow thereafter, it becomes clear that this

67. DBWE 10:359.
68. Ibid., 362–63.

emphasis is not an isolated incident. In fact, this remains a continuous theme throughout his life, culminating in the work from prison.

Before leaving this essay, it should be noted that Bonhoeffer's presentation has also raised a question, so it would be a failure to not point out one aspect of this lecture that remains problematic, marked as it was by "völkish lebensraum theology"[69] in its concept of power and its justification of war. His position in this lecture reflected the traditional Lutheran position at the time and, according to Bethge, "it did not take long for Bonhoeffer to discover the self-deception that lay in this unquestioned loyalty to the world." In fact, his experience in America and involvement in the ecumenical movement "helped him see that the strange link he had made between Barth's systematic theology and the conventional Lutheran ethic was at least in need of revision." Had it not been for the *theologia crucis* he would not have broken out of that mold.[70]

## Sermons

The sermons[71] Bonhoeffer delivered in Barcelona, based mostly on New Testament texts, offer another view into his developing theology. As a sampling of his sermons shows, he continued to develop themes that come to dominate his theology: the antithesis between religion and faith, the cross and justification, and concrete reality.[72] The distinction he had made between Luther's theology and modern theology that took shape in his discussions with Karl Holl became even more sharply defined when viewed from the perspective of the cross.

69. Clifford Green, "Editor's Introduction," DBWE 10:11.
70. *DB-ER*, 120. See Reggie Williams, "Developing a *Theologia Crucis:* Dietrich Bonhoeffer and the Harlem Renaissance," *Theology Today* 71, no. 1 (2014): 43–57.
71. See Green, "Editor's Introduction," DBWE 10:6ff for a description of Bonhoeffer's sermons.
72. Cf. *DB-ER*, 112–13.

In his first sermon, given on March 11, 1928, Bonhoeffer distinguished between religion and justification. Based on Paul's understanding of grace in Rom. 11:6, he distinguished between works and grace, two different, opposing ways to talk about the relationship between God and humankind. "In other words, one line leads from human beings up to God, the other from God down to human beings, and both exclude each other—and yet belong together."[73] Citing the well-known line from Augustine's *Confessions*, "Our hearts are restless until they find their rest in you," Bonhoeffer noted that it is humanity's awareness of its relationship to God that creates great anxiety that, on the one hand, is credited with producing great works of beauty or thought and, on the other, systems of morality and religion, which are the greatest attempts by humanity to secure eternity for themselves. All such attempts are, according to Luther, "part of human flesh"; they are nothing but human works, which are exposed for what they are in light of God's grace.[74]

This again points to a recurring theme in Bonhoeffer's theology, the difference between Christianity and religion. In contrast to religion,

> another path emerges, the path of God to human beings, the path of revelation and of grace, the path of Christ, the path of justification by grace alone. "My ways are not your ways" is what we now hear; it is not we who go to God, but God who comes to us. It is not religion that makes us good before God, but God alone who makes us good. It is God's deed that is important here, God's deed before which all our claims sink.[75]

73. DBWE 10:481.
74. Ibid., 484. It should be noted that this attitude on Luther's part does not mean there is no appreciation for human works, including reason. Luther, in distinguishing between "two kingdoms," acknowledges the positive role of reason in ordering things of this world, including the church.
75. Ibid., 483.

We wanted to be the lords of our own eternity, but instead we've been enslaved and our situation, based on our own concepts of morality and religion, has become hopeless. We need to be rescued and there is only one way—all that remains is God's way. Therefore, "not religion, but rather revelation, grace, love; not the path to God, but rather God's path to human beings, that is the sum total of Christianity."[76] The way of God is the "way of Jesus Christ," whose death on the cross is God's powerful act in history; it is where justice and grace become visible to all the world. It is on that act, and upon it alone, that is our hope. Quoting from the dying Luther, "We are beggars, it is true,"[77] Bonhoeffer concluded that there is nothing we can do to gain our salvation; it rests on God and God's act alone.[78]

A similar emphasis emerged in other sermons given during the year. In a August 26, 1928 sermon on 1 John 2:17, Bonhoeffer made the point that all our efforts, no matter how grand, will come to an end and will eventually pass away. Everything that happens in this life will eventually result in death. The end of this world will result in the beginning of a new eternal world. This eternity is not far from us, however; God in Christ has stretched out his hand and we can grasp the hand of God. This takes place none other than on the cross.

> This is the miracle of the revelation in Jesus Christ. Here amid all transitoriness and darkness stands a sign from eternity, serious and mighty, bathed in the radiance of the divine sun of grace and light—the cross. And there He hangs, his arms outstretched as if to embrace the entire world in love and lead it to his Father. He who was God's love among human beings. Come to this cross, the sign of divine love, come into its light, cling to it, and it will shed its light on you as long you remain with it. And thus it has happened that you yourselves have now become eternal.[79]

76. Ibid.
77. See "Luther's Last Observation Left in a Note, February 16, 1546," *LW* 54:476.
78. DBWE 10:485.
79. Ibid., 519–520.

In another sermon based on the text of 1 Cor. 12:9, preached on September 9, 1928, his theme again was the difference between Christianity and religion; the distinguishing mark of the former is the presence of the cross. He began with the question, "Why is there religion?" for which there was only one answer: "To make human beings happy, both externally and inwardly. Happiness and religion belong together like brilliance and gold; religion that does not make a person happy is not religion. This means, however, that religion is conceived from the perspective of human beings and only in reference to human beings as the center of the world." But the Bible turns this basic orientation around to present a different picture: "It puts its finger on one single event, one single sign, and leaves it to us to reflect: on the cross of Jesus. Here something unprecedented happened; the equation between religion and happiness is sundered once and for all on the cross, where God dies in love for human beings."[80] The cross of Christ "clearly distinguishes Christianity from all other religions from the outset. Here is grace, there happiness; here the cross, there the crown; here God, there the human being."[81] For Bonhoeffer, the issue was the very nature of the Christian confession and the key was the cross of Christ. In contrast to the world, God's power is displayed in weakness; it is on the cross that God's love for human beings is expressed most clearly and explicitly.

In a sermon given a couple of weeks later, September 23, 1928 (sixteenth Sunday after Trinity), he focused on the this-worldly aspect of Christian faith. God is not to be found in otherworldly speculation; instead, Bonhoeffer claimed, "*If you want God, focus on the world.*"[82] The world is where God chooses to locate himself and reveal himself.

80. Ibid., 522–23.
81. Ibid., 523.
82. Ibid., 528; this line is borrowed from Friedrich Christoph Oetinger. It was one of Bonhoeffer's favorite quotes, to which he made frequent and regular reference.

The contours of Bonhoeffer's Christology were also evident in a sermon from December 2, 1928 (second Sunday of Advent), in which he declared that God is present for us in the very human Jesus who comes to us not as one clothed in power but as one who is weak and on the margins. He put it this way: we are "confronted with the terrifying reality; Jesus is at the door, knocking, in reality, asking you for help in the figure of the beggar, in the figure of the degenerate soul in shabby clothes, encountering you in every person you meet."[83] This exhortation would be echoed later in a section of his Christology lectures in which Bonhoeffer reminded his students that Jesus "comes among us humans not in μορφῇ θεοῦ [godly form] but rather incognito, as a beggar among beggars, an outcast among outcasts; he comes among sinners as the one without sin, but also as a sinner among sinners."[84]

Commenting on this and other sermons from this period, Bethge states, "In several ways, these first sermons revealed the full scope of his theological work and perspective."[85] As such, they are prime examples of Bonhoeffer's thinking and throughout one theme dominates: the cross of Christ. This point is emphasized by Green in his analysis of the sermons. "In the theology of the sermons, the love of God is a recurrent note: Christ is 'God's love among human beings,' the cross is a 'sign of divine love,' it is 'where God dies in love for human beings.'"[86]

As was already seen in the discussion of Luther, the *theologia crucis* had as much to say about how one does theology as it does about the content of theological reflection. Regarded in this way, the theology

83. Ibid., 545. The image of the beggar here draws on Luther's vocabulary. See note 77 above. While such language is an apt description of our status before God, it is also an image appropriate for understanding the incarnation, the manner in which God comes to humankind, in human form and in weakness.

84. Cf. DBWE 12:356.

85. *DB-ER*, 112.

86. Green, "Editor's Introduction," DBWE 10:7.

of the cross is an alternate way of doing theology. This same understanding is helpful in getting at the heart of Bonhoeffer's theology, especially as he begins to make a clear-cut distinction between Christianity and religion.[87] According to Bonhoeffer, Christianity is God's way to us. In contrast, religion is our way to God. This is alternative language to describe the difference Luther made between a theology of the cross and a theology of glory. Translated into Luther's terminology, religion (a theology of glory) is any theological attempt or justification that seeks to emphasize our goodness, piety, or some such achievement that brings us up to the level of God. Christianity, on the other hand, is used in the same manner as Luther used the theology of the cross; it bypasses all of that and goes directly to the work of God on us, a work that kills and makes alive.

Even though Bonhoeffer did not provide references, the language he used corresponded to the language of Luther and the Bible. For example, compare what Bonhoeffer said in these sermons to the following words from Luther:

> This is why Paul makes such a frequent practice of linking Jesus Christ with God the Father, to teach us what is the true Christian religion. It does not begin at the top as all other religions do; it begins at the bottom. . . . Therefore, whenever you are concerned to think and act about your salvation, you must put away all speculations about the Majesty, all thoughts of works, traditions, and philosophy—indeed, of the Law of God itself. And you must run directly to the manger and the mother's womb, embrace this Infant and Virgin's Child in your arms, and look at Him—born, being nursed, growing up, going about in human society, teaching, dying, rising again, ascending above all the heavens, and having authority over all things. In this way you can shake off all terrors and errors, as the sun dispels the clouds. This vision will

87. See Wüstenberg's detailed description of Bonhoeffer's understanding of religion, which parallels the development in Bonhoeffer's christological orientation, in *Theology of Life,* passim.

> keep you on the proper way, so that you may follow where Christ has gone.[88]

In conclusion, this text will remain an important one for Bonhoeffer. As we turn to his next work, *Act and Being*, we will see that it will play a role in the development of his argument.

### *Act and Being*

What was true for *Sanctorum Communio* is also true for his habilitation, a second dissertation that would qualify him for an academic position; his announced intention sheds light onto the subject of his work. While he immersed himself in his parish obligations in Barcelona, he was at the same time thinking of his return to Berlin and his next project, which was to engage Luther's theology more directly. In a letter to Reinhold Seeberg he laid out his initial thinking on the project:

> At the same time my thoughts are already busy with another project, albeit again not historical but rather systematic. It picks up the question of consciousness and conscience in theology and also several Luther citations from the big Galatians commentary. You also brought up the question of consciousness once in your seminar; but this will be a theological study rather than a psychological one. Perhaps when I am a bit further along you'll permit me to write to you about it in a letter.[89]

The language here indicates that Bonhoeffer was still grappling with the heritage of Karl Holl; but at the same time, now drawing on Luther's works, he wanted to lay out a theological as opposed to a psychological approach to the subject. There is also another difference that can be noted. According to Wayne Floyd, while Bonhoeffer had shown "deference to Seeberg, who was facing

88. Martin Luther, "Lectures on Galatians 1535," *LW* 26:30.
89. Letter of July 20, 1928, DBWE 10:122; see *DB-ER*, 122.

retirement in the near future," by agreeing on a topic that was "half-historical and half-systematic" for his first dissertation, "now he wanted to turn to theology per se, and to do so with a writing project that would be the entree to a serious academic career, not just a stepping stone to ecclesiastical life."[90]

When Bonhoeffer returned to Berlin in February 1929, he returned to a world that was rapidly changing. It was in the midst of this context that his next work, "despite its seemingly abstract philosophical cast," needs to be understood and interpreted "within the concrete, historical context of the cultural crisis in Germany between the world wars, which eventuated in the National Socialist rise to power in 1933."[91] With new responsibilities at the university as a voluntary assistant lecturer (*Privatdozent*) under Wilhelm Lütgart, Reinhold Seeberg's successor, Bonhoeffer set out to write his habilitation, *Act and Being*. In this work we see Bonhoeffer's continuing struggle to come to terms with his theological heritage, while at the same time attempting to find his own theological voice. Seeking to find a theological method adequate to theology's subject, Bonhoeffer set out to survey recent theological and philosophical attempts at epistemology, all of which he judged to be inadequate in dealing with God's revelation. Again, even though he was attracted to Barth's theology of revelation and had sided with Barth over against other modern theological voices, Barth's reliance on Kant's philosophy had become problematic for him. With this as background, Hans-Richard Reuter states, "*Act and Being* shows Bonhoeffer in search of a theological form of thought that would free theology from the remaining hidden premises of metaphysics." He thereby concludes,

90. Wayne Floyd, "Editor's Introduction to the English Edition," *Act and Being*, DBWE 2:3.
91. Ibid., 7.

> Bonhoeffer seeks to make the thematic of act and being fruitful anew for the interpretation of reality, which, this time is not understood metaphysically. He finds this reality in God's self-binding to the historical revelation in Jesus Christ; hence Bonhoeffer consistently has repudiated the preeminence of the category of "possibility" in theology as a rebirth of the nominalist *potentia Dei absoluta*."[92]

At the heart of his argument is an attempt to deal with questions of theological method in such a way as to allow theology to speak with integrity, while not falling victim to modern thought patterns. Hence, seeking to avoid modern thinking's subject/object split on the one hand, and removing God from the world on the other, Bonhoeffer sought to locate the foundations of theological reflection in God's revelation in Christ, which is a revelation that occurs in this world in ways to be grasped by human beings. Unlike modern philosophy that seeks to understand God in terms of "like can be known only by like," or dialectical theology that understands God as "totally Other" with no contact with the world, Bonhoeffer insisted on an understanding of revelation and God in which "unlike can be known by unlike" in a "contingent revelation" that takes place in the world. To accomplish this task, he turned to Luther's theology.

Here, there is a marked development beyond his student essays, in which he had continued along the lines of Holl's interpretation of Luther's faith in terms of a "religion of conscience." Now Bonhoeffer moves beyond that paradigm. In response to Holl's approach, he declared that conscience was not an adequate foundation for theology.[93] This continues the line of thought he had already

92. Hans-Richard Reuter, "Editor's Afterword to the German Edition," *Act and Being*, DBWE 2:164–65.

93. See DBWE 2:141 and n11 in particular. Here he based his defense, in part, on his reading of Luther's "A Sermon on Preparing to Die," *LW* 42; *Lectures on Galatians*, *LW* 26 and 27; and *The Bondage of the Will*, *LW* 33, where he found a different understanding of conscience. Cf. also Wüstenberg, *Theology of Life*, 46: "Whereas Holl and Seeberg were determinative figures for the student's and doctoral candidate's interpretation of Luther, Bonhoeffer abandons this understanding of Luther after *Act and Being*."

expressed in Barcelona; by contrasting Christianity with religion, the latter originating in the human realm, Bonhoeffer located theology's origin outside of human beings.

What he envisioned was a theological epistemology that was able to break out of modern conceptualities in which the human subject seeks to control its object of knowledge. Given this background, Wayne Floyd says Bonhoeffer's intent in *Act and Being* is clear:

> Bonhoeffer wished theology to speak with all the resources of modern thought, yet with its own distinctive voice, including the prophetic tone of the critique of idolatry. Bonhoeffer therefore approached his chosen topic for *Act and Being*, a theology of consciousness, from within the perspective of the Reformation tradition's insights about the origin of human sinfulness in the *cor curvum in se*—the heart turned in upon itself and thus open neither to the revelation of God, nor to the encounter with the neighbor.[94]

Therefore, even though the tone of his argument is couched in philosophical language, it is clearly christologically conceived.[95] Again, this comes through in his argument with Karl Barth, where he critiqued Barth's formalistic understanding of God's freedom. Desiring to understand how revelation becomes concrete in this world, which had been the theme of *Sanctorum Communio,* Bonhoeffer now placed revelation in the context of the theological discussion of the time and found Barth's position, among others, to be inadequate.[96] And again, Luther became his ally in the debate.[97]

94. Floyd, "Editor's Introduction," DBWE 2: 7–8. Cf. n29, where, in commenting on Bonhoeffer's topic, he says, "One of the surprising discoveries of a careful reading of *Act and Being* may be the discovery of the extent to which the central philosophical sections of the book are deeply indebted to the theological insights from Martin Luther, especially his *Lectures on Galatians*."

95. Ibid., 4ff. Floyd insists that despite Bonhoeffer's announced intentions, a close reading of the text reveals something altogether different. When read in conjunction with the two essays from 1931, written during his time in New York, Bonhoeffer wants to express the theological insight of Luther and the Reformers who stressed that human beings are *cor curvum in se* and are, therefore, unable to break out of their own circle of thought to comprehend God in God's reality.

Bonhoeffer did not refrain from directly identifying Karl Barth as one of his primary targets and it becomes apparent that the difference is one between Bonhoeffer's Lutheran understanding of *finitum capax infiniti* and Barth's Reformed position, with its emphasis on the *finitum non capax infiniti*; the result of the latter was that at least a small sphere remained in which God was hidden in mystery, standing outside what we might know of God through God's revelation on the cross. In contrast to Barth, Bonhoeffer argued that the historical nature of revelation is described as "a contingent revelation of God in Christ." For Bonhoeffer this meant simply "that God has revealed himself in the personal history of Jesus Christ and continues to reveal himself in the personal history of each believer. Revelation was historical for Bonhoeffer because he associated it with the central event of history, the incarnation of Jesus Christ." The "self-binding of God to the historical revelation in Jesus Christ" indicates that Christology is inherently central for Bonhoeffer's thought.[98] It is the nature of this Christology to be described as a *theologia crucis*. Bonhoeffer dealt with the theological and philosophical traditions of the West and responded to them, reshaping them in terms of Luther's *theologia crucis*.

Transcendentalism, the term Bonhoeffer used to describe the philosophical tradition of Immanuel Kant, gives priority to act, while ontology, represented by contemporary figures such as Martin Heidegger, gives priority to being; neither perspective, however, did Bonhoeffer find to be adequate for a theological method. It is from this basic premise that Bonhoeffer set out to analyze contemporary philosophy and the theologies based upon them, in order to establish

96. Cf. *DB-ER*, 131.

97. According to Bethge, ibid., 133, Luther was the most highly quoted source in *Act and Being*, to be followed only by Martin Heidigger.

98. Geffrey Kelly, "Revelation in Christ: A Study of Bonhoeffer's Theology of Revelation," *Ephemerides Theologicae Lovaniense* 50, no. 1 (May, 1974): 42.

the need for a genuine theological model that avoids the weaknesses of either approach.

In general, the problem is that philosophy, be it shaped by concepts of "act" or "being," does not allow room for revelation. Every philosophical approach produces a closed system in which truth is defined in terms of "autonomous self-understanding," in which human beings are "capable of giving truth to themselves, of transporting themselves into the truth by themselves, since the 'ground' of existence must somehow surely be in the truth, in the likeness to God."[99] In opposition to such approaches, Bonhoeffer proposed a different method, in which "truth means only that reference to God which Christian theology does not hold possible save in the *word* of God that is spoken about and to human beings in the revelation of law and gospel."[100] In the end, Bonhoeffer's philosophical debate presented a backdrop to the real subject, revelation. He wanted to establish that modern ways of thinking are inadequate to grasp ahold of revelation, which is the only way to apprehend God. For theology to be truly theological, it must come from God. "Only a way of thinking that, bound in obedience to Christ, 'is' from the truth can place itself into the truth."[101]

The problem with transcendentalism is that God cannot exist as an objective entity. God is only real to the extent that the subjective *I* can apprehend God in the conscience. "God is the God of my consciousness. Only in my religious consciousness 'is' God."[102] To a certain extent, God and the *I* are identical; "in philosophical reflection God is not an objective existent but is only in the execution of that philosophizing. . . . I discover God in my coming to myself; I become aware of myself. I find myself—that is, I find God."[103] In turn,

99. DBWE 2:79.
100. Ibid.
101. Ibid., 80.
102. Ibid., 51.

revelation becomes "what reason can perceive from itself" and "God is completely locked into consciousness."[104]

Based on the presupposition that "like is conceivable only by like," God becomes an expression of the self in which there is an inmost identity. "Through living reflection on itself, the I understands itself from itself. It relates itself to itself, and consequently to God, in unmediated reflection. That is why religion = revelation; there is no room for faith and word. . . . 'if God is to come to human beings, they essentially must already be like God.'"[105] But, in actuality, such propositions are theologically untenable. Quite the opposite is true. "It is not because human beings are like God that God comes to them—on the contrary, God then would not need to come—but precisely because human beings are utterly unlike God and never know God from themselves. That is why God comes to them, that they may know God. Then, but only then, do they indeed know God."[106] Theologically, then, the direction from God to humankind, which is *extra nos*, coming from the outside, is not subject to human consciousness.

The problem that makes it impossible to equate revelation and religion is the reality that humanity is *cor curvum in se.* Because humanity is curved in upon itself, it will strive after flesh and will remain flesh. "If revelation is to come to human beings, they need to be changed entirely. Faith itself must be created in them. In this matter, there is not ability to hear before the hearing." In opposition to thinking that equates religion and revelation, "according to Luther, revelation and faith are bound to the concrete, preached word, and the word is the mediator of the contact between God and human beings, allowing no other 'immediateness.'" Therefore, the

103. Ibid., 50.
104. Ibid., 52–53.
105. Ibid., 53.
106. Ibid., 54.

religious a priori, which was the basis for Seeberg's understanding of God, cannot apprehend Christ; rather, "all that pertains to personal appropriation of the fact of Christ is not a priori, but God's contingent action on human beings."[107] Translating the argument into the terms of Luther's debate, Bonhoeffer concluded, "Thinking is as little able as good works to deliver the *cor curvum in se* from itself."[108] As is true of good works, thought places the person at the center, moving God to the margins.

In contrast to philosophical methods, Bonhoeffer posed a theological understanding of truth. Theologically, truth can only be established by revelation, which comes from outside and beyond the human subject.

> Revelation, which places the I into truth, i.e. gives understanding of God and self, is a contingent occurrence which can only be welcomed or rejected in its positivity—that is to say, received as a reality—but not elicited from speculations about human existence as such. It is an occurrence with its basis in the freedom of God, whether positively, as his self-giving, or negatively, as his withholding of himself.[109]

This cursory review of Bonhoeffer's argument in *Act and Being* is necessary because it provides the background by which we can understand his use of Luther and the particular understanding he has of Christ. When he turned to the second part of his work, Bonhoeffer turned to his main theological concern. It is here that his argument with Barth is laid out in greater detail. Barth is faulted, along with the modern philosophers, because Barth's theology is subject to Kant's transcendentalistic epistemology. Because Bonhoeffer wanted to use revelation as the proper method for constructing Christian theology, the distinctions he draws are important. Using the paradigm for

107. Ibid., 58.
108. Ibid., 80.
109. Ibid.

analyzing modern philosophy, Bonhoeffer claimed that Barth's understanding of revelation can be interpreted in terms of a Kantian "act" epistemology. As a result, Barth placed the emphasis on the freedom of God. "God is free inasmuch as God is bound to nothing, not even the 'existing,' 'historical' Word. . . . Never is God at the disposal of human beings; it is God's glory that, in relation to everything given and conditional, God remains utterly free, unconditioned."[110] Barth's dialectical theology, based as it is on the Reformed principle of the *finitum non capax infiniti,* therefore repeated the problems of transcendental philosophy, with the result that "God recedes into the nonobjective, into what is beyond our disposition."[111]

It is in contrast to such an understanding of revelation that Bonhoeffer turned to Luther's 1527 work, "That These Words of Christ, 'This is my Body,' etc., Still Stand Firm against the Fanatics." Rather than emphasizing God's freedom in which God might withhold something of himself in revelation, "It is the honor of our God, however, that, in giving the divine self for our sake in deepest condescension, entering into flesh and bread, into our mouth, heart and bowel and suffering for our sake, God be dishonorably handled, both on the altar and the cross."[112] This distinction, between the

110. Ibid., 82.

111. Ibid., 85. This is another way of stating his earlier criticism of Barth's position, which Bonhoeffer believed neglected "the historicity of Jesus" (DBWE 9:441).

112. From Luther, "That These Words of Christ, 'This is my Body,' etc., Still Stand Firm against the Fanatics," *LW* 37:72 (translation altered); see DBWE 2:82nn1 and 3. In Luther's text, shortly before the section that Bonhoeffer quotes, are the words, "Because it is one thing if God is present, and another if he is present for you. He is there for you when he adds his Word and binds himself, saying, 'Here you are to find me.' Now when you have the Word, you can grasp and have him with certainty and say, 'Here I have thee, according to thy Word.' Just as I say of the right hand of God: although this is everywhere, as we may not deny, still because it is also nowhere, as has been said, you can actually grasp it nowhere, unless for your benefit it binds itself to you and summons you to a definite place. This God's right hand does, however, when it enters into the humanity of Christ and dwells there. There you surely find it, otherwise you will run back and forth throughout all creation, groping here and groping there yet never finding, even though it is actually there; for it is not there for you" (*LW* 37:68–69). Taken

Barthian freedom of God and the Lutheran condescension of God, is of great significance for understanding Bonhoeffer's own theological position as well as providing a way in which to see Bonhoeffer's independent contribution.

This is stated no more clearly than when he questioned the possibility of basing theology on any formalistic understanding of God. In contrast to Barth, he stated,

> In revelation it is not so much a question of the freedom of God—eternally remaining within the divine self, aseity—on the other side of revelation, as it is of God's coming out of God's own self in revelation. It is a matter of God's *given* Word, the covenant in which God is bound by God's own action. It is a question of the freedom of God, which finds its strongest evidence precisely in that God freely chose to be bound to historical human beings and to be placed at the disposal of human beings. God is free not from human beings but for them. Christ is the word of God's freedom. God *is* present, that is, not in eternal nonobjectivity but—to put it quite provisionally for now—"haveable," graspable in the Word within the church.[113]

Bonhoeffer's understanding of God's revelation was the exact opposite as that of Barth's. To place an emphasis on God's freedom apart from God's revelation was to deny Christ. In freedom, and here Bonhoeffer's argument reflects the language of Luther's *theologia crucis*, God does not remain distant and apart from the world. Instead of God being free *from* humanity, God's revelation in Christ means that God is free *for* humanity. Rather than being concerned about protecting God, God through the revelation in Christ becomes vulnerable in the world. In Christ, God is present and can be grasped

together, these statements indicate that for Luther, God's binding himself to the world is far more important than God's freedom in God's person. That same orientation comes into play in Bonhoeffer's theology, and it clearly makes a distinction between a *theologia crucis*, which stresses that we cannot understand or grasp God apart from the world, and Barth's theology that seeks to preserve a place for God outside of the world.

113. DBWE 2:90–91.

in and through the church's proclamation of the Gospel and the fellowship that emerges from this gospel event.

In this statement the differences between Bonhoeffer and Barth were clearly drawn. According to Eberhard Bethge,

> To Bonhoeffer, the old *extra calvinisticum* was in error if it ultimately denied the complete entry of God's majesty into this world. Bonhoeffer suspected it at work when he saw Barth establishing the majesty of God by the methods of Kantian transcendentalism. To greatly oversimplify: while the early Barth, desiring to proclaim God's majesty, began by removing him to a remote distance, Bonhoeffer's starting point, inspired by the same desire to proclaim his majesty, brought him into close proximity.[114]

This judgment corresponds to the distinction between Barth and Bonhoeffer drawn by John Godsey noted earlier; in his language it is a difference between a *theologia gloriae* and a *theologia crucis.*[115]

In contrast to Barth, God's revelation is defined in terms of a "self-binding" act on God's part, in which God is bound to the earth and humankind through Christ. The revelation of God becomes real in Christ, encountered in the congregation where the word is preached and the sacraments administered. There, in that setting, peopled are encountered by the present Christ, who both creates faith and becomes real in faith. There, in faith, human beings become new creations. Developing the understanding of the church ("Christ existing as church-community") along the same lines as presented in *Sanctorum Communio,* Bonhoeffer once again relied heavily on Luther's 1519 treatise in which the present Christ is the basis for the new reality. Here, countering the assumptions of philosophy, he stated,

114. *DB-ER*, 134.
115. See introduction, pg. 8.

> "In faith" people understand themselves as in the church of Christ in their new being, in an existential reality that was not included in their deepest potentiality. They see their existence to be founded solely by the word of the person of Christ. They live in God's sight and in no other way. Being is being in Christ, for here alone is unity and wholeness of life; thus they discover their old being as being in Adam.[116]

Rather than human beings defining God and themselves from within the confines of their own reasoning, they are defined in their encounter with Christ. Their existence is defined "in Christ" and truth is not determined by its correspondence of "like to like." Here "unlike is known by unlike," the mediator of truth standing beyond the grasp of any "autonomous self-understanding." In this new setting,

> unlike gives itself to be known by unlike: Christ, the crucified and risen one, gives Christ's own self to be known by human beings, who live to themselves. It is in being known by God that human beings know God. But to be known by God means to become a new person. It is the justified and the sinner in one who knows God. It is not because the word of God is in itself "meaning" that it affects the existence of human beings, but because it is *God's* word, the word of the creator, reconciler, and redeemer.[117]

Accordingly, theology is impossible without the church, because the church is where God in Christ is revealed. It is because of God's contingent revelation, in which God has bound God's self to human beings, that the church is a necessity. And what takes place there is through the proclamation of the word, the crucified, risen, and ascended Christ is a present reality.

A new humanity emerges through Christ's death on the cross. If sin is the human will turned in upon itself (*cor curvum in se*), in order to break out of that cycle of death, salvation can come only from the

116. DBWE 2:134.
117. Ibid.

outside, from beyond. Drawing on extensive references from Luther, Bonhoeffer declared that in Christ,

> the person *in se conversus* [turned in upon itself] is delivered from the attempt to remain alone—to understand itself out of itself—and is turned outwards towards Christ. The person now lives in the contemplation of Christ. This is the gift of faith, that one no longer looks upon oneself, but solely upon the salvation that has come to one from without. One finds oneself in Christ, because already one is in Christ, in that one seeks oneself there in Christ.[118]

In spite of the philosophical language in which his argument is framed, Christology is at the heart of Bonhoeffer's thinking. Human beings in sin are curved in upon themselves, and cannot think beyond the boundaries of their experience. This theological understanding of humanity in Adam, Bonhoeffer claimed, corresponds to modern philosophy, which by its own definitions cannot understand God. God is available to human beings only because God is revealed in Christ. Faith and salvation come from outside and beyond human limitations, and is the result of God's own act of revelation which is Christ.

It is for that reason that conscience is not adequate for our understanding of God, because, as Bonhoeffer made clear, conscience is only where sin is. "Human beings in Adam are pushed to the limits of their solitude but, misunderstanding their situation, 'they seek themselves in themselves' (Luther), hoping that in being repentant they may yet save their sinful existence."[119] Contrary to much Christian thinking that identifies conscience as the voice of God, Bonhoeffer said, "Conscience primarily is not God's but the human

118. Ibid., 150. As extensive editorial notes make clear, Bonhoeffer draws heavily on Luther's works for both his basic orientation as well as specific concepts. This section is informed particularly by Luther's "A Sermon on Preparing to Die," and *Lectures on Galatians*. The former was discussed in chapter 2.

119. Ibid.,139. His reference is to Luther, "A Sermon on Preparing to Die": "Search for yourself only in Christ and not in yourself, and you shall find yourself for ever in him;" see DBWE 2:139n8.

being's own voice. If being-in-Christ means being oriented towards Christ, reflection on the self is obviously not part of that being."[120] Whereas "conscience can torment and drive to despair,"

> only when Christ has broken through the solitude of human beings will they know themselves placed into truth. It matters not whether, in the offense that the cross causes the sinner, human beings die forever and remain in solitude, or whether they die in order to live with Christ in the truth (for die they must, as Christ died). In both cases, true knowledge of themselves in given here only through Christ.[121]

It is only in Christ that human beings are able to break free of the *cor curvum in se*; through Christ "God turns one's eyes away from oneself, and gives them God's own orientation . . . towards Christ the crucified and risen one who is the overcoming of the temptation to death."[122] It is only in Christ that "human beings know themselves as God's creatures. . . . Being in Christ, as being directed towards Christ, sets Dasein[123] free. Human beings are 'there' for and by means of Christ; they believe as long as they look upon Christ."[124]

Bonhoeffer's christocentric understanding of God and revelation as developed in *Act and Being* is along the lines established in his earlier student essays, bringing to a culmination Bonhoeffer's theological formation and in its contours the foundations for the rest of his theology. Of this period, Bonhoeffer himself admitted in a letter to his church superintendent Max Diestel that with his assistance,

120. DBWE 2:155.
121. Ibid., 140–41.
122. Ibid., 149–50.
123. See Floyd, "Editor's Introduction," ibid., 2n13: "Bonhoeffer throughout *Act and Being* uses Dasein in a technical sense denoting the qualitatively distinctive mode of the being-there [Da-Sein] of human beings, in contrast to the being of all else that is. The 'there' of Dasein calls attention to human finitude, the fact that we find ourselves always already situated in time. But the finitude of Dasein is also disclosed to human beings; for only Dasein 'ex-ists', stands out, from all that is around it, aware of itself, aware that its being is for itself an issue, a responsibility."
124. DBWE 2:151 and 153.

beginning in 1927, that his "entire thinking" had been set "on a track from which it has not yet deviated and never will." [125] Eberhard Bethge, in noting the significance of these works, says, "From our biographical point of view, the importance of *Act and Being* was that—taken in conjunction with *Sanctorum Communio*—it contained many of the ideas that were to be applied to the 'nonreligious interpretation' in the letters from prison fifteen years later."[126] Floyd concurs with Bethge in spelling out the implications of Bonhoeffer's work in *Act and Being* for his subsequent theology. He insists that we see these early works, through his Christology lectures, as a whole.[127]

125. DBWE 16:367. Cf. Green, "Editor's Introduction," DBWE 10:1.

126. *DB-ER*, 135. See also Green, *Bonhoeffer: A Theology of Sociality*, 86, where he states the importance of these early works for properly understanding Bonhoeffer's later works.

127. See Floyd, "Editor's Introduction," DBWE 2:13ff.

# 5

# New York and Berlin

## New York 1930–1931

During the academic year 1930-31, which he spent in New York City, the shape of Bonhoeffer's Christology sees further development. Still too young to hold a position on the faculty in Berlin, Bonhoeffer took the opportunity of a student fellowship to go to New York's Union Theological Seminary. He set sail for New York on September 5, 1930, returning to Germany on June 20, 1931. While he spent a relatively short time in America (he did not spend all of his time in New York; he managed to travel at great deal, taking trips that included Mexico and Cuba), it was nevertheless filled with experiences and insights that were transformative.[1] His experience served both to clarify his thinking and to provide the foundations for his theological engagement with the world. It was during this interlude that he wrestled with Barth's theology in more detail, even

1. See Clifford Green, "Editor's Introduction to the English Edition," *Barcelona, Berlin, New York: 1928–1931*, DBWE 10, and Reggie Williams, *Bonhoeffer's Black Jesus: Harlem Renaissance and an Ethic of Resistance* (Waco, TX: Baylor University Press, 2014).

to the point of making plans to visit him in Bonn on his return to Berlin at the end of his New York stay.

Many of Bonhoeffer's experiences in America were pivotal for his theological development. His diary makes mention of his impressions of American churches; whereas he found the white churches wanting in their proclamation of the gospel, he found the black churches, and Abyssinian Baptist Church in Harlem in particular, to be places where the gospel came to life in ways that he had not seen before.[2] It was through his regular attendance at Abyssinian Church that he became aware of the insidious problems connected with racism; this experience, perhaps more than any other in America, contributed to his identifying with "the underside of history."[3]

> What was so impressive was the way in which he pursued the understanding of the problem to its minutest detail through books and countless visits to Harlem, through participation in Negro youth work, but even more through a remarkable kind of identity with the Negro community, so that he was received there as though he had never been an outsider at all.[4]

As for Union Seminary's influence, the young German theologian was appalled "by the American lack of concern for what to him were the genuine problems of theology." For someone like Bonhoeffer, who had been trained in Berlin, very little serious theology seemed to be taking place in America. As the course offerings from that year indicate,

2. See his correspondence, DBWE 10:241–322. In addition, see Bethge, *DB-ER*, 149ff. This influence is also hinted at in Josiah Ulysses Young III, *No Difference in the Fare: Dietrich Bonhoeffer and the Problem of Racism* (Grand Rapids: Eerdmans, 1998), 115ff.
3. See Ruth Zerner,"Dietrich Bonhoeffer's American Experiences: People, Letters, and Papers from Union Seminary," *Union Seminary Quarterly Review* 31, no. 4 (Summer 1976): 261–82, for additional details on Bonhoeffer's American experience.
4. Paul Lehmann in a March 13, 1960 BBC program; quoted in *DB-ER*, 155.

> there was an almost complete lack of exegesis or dogmatics. To compensate, there was a great deal of ethics, and an abundance of courses devoted to the analysis and explanation of contemporary American philosophy, literature, and society. Future ministers were expected to master these things, not the loci of the creeds or the history of dogmatics.

Bonhoeffer "regarded what he heard not as theology, but as long outdated religious philosophy." This state of affairs led him to portray what he had experienced as "hopeless," when he reported to his church at the conclusion of his year-long visit:[5] "Americans have absolutely no understanding for Pauline and Lutheran Christianity. They are not only the purest Pelagians but also adherents of Protagoras."[6]

Bonhoeffer visited America briefly again in 1939 at the urging of friends who wanted to provide for his safety away from Nazi Germany. After a few short weeks, however, he came to realization that he could not live out the war in safety while his fellow citizens suffered. He also felt that if he were to contribute to the rebuilding of German society and the church after the war, he needed to share in the experiences of his people during the war. With such thoughts in the background, he returned to Germany. As he did so, however, he wrote a report on his perceptions of the American church; they had

5. *DB-ER*, 157–59. It should be noted that while Bonhoeffer's reflections were based on his experiences in America, he was exposed to a small segment of America's religious life and theology. The theological landscape was far richer and more diverse that Bonhoeffer was able to acknowledge.

6. "Report on My Year of Study at Union Theological Seminary in New York, 1930/31," DBWE 10:311. Note Bonhoeffer's assessment of Union Seminary in that same report: "The theological spirit at Union Theological Seminary is accelerating the process of the secularization of Christianity in America. Its criticism is directed essentially at fundamentalism and to a certain extent also at the radical humanists in Chicago; such criticism is healthy and necessary. But the foundation on which one might rebuild after tearing down is not able to support the weight. The collapse destroys it as well. A seminary in which numerous students openly laugh during a public lecture because they find it amusing when a passage on sin and forgiveness from Luther's *de servo arbitrio* is cited has obviously, despite its many advantages, forgotten what Christian theology in its very essence stands for." (DBWE 10:309–10).

not changed in the intervening years. Again, he attacked American Christianity, this time labeling it as "Protestantism without Reformation." The reason for his harsh judgment stemmed from his perception of a failure in Christology in American theology. He believed that "a doctrine on the person and work of salvation of Jesus Christ is missing," that while God had provided America with revivalist preachers, "God did not grant a Reformation to American Christendom." And even the "churches of the Reformation that came to America either stand in deliberate seclusion and distance from general church life or have fallen victim to Protestantism without Reformation." He concluded his observations with the following:

> Christendom in American theology is essentially still religion and ethics. Hence, the person and work of Jesus Christ recedes into the background for theology and remains ultimately not understood, because the sole foundation for God's radical judgment and radical grace is at this point not recognized. The decisive task today is the conversation between the Protestantism without Reformation and the churches of the Reformation.[7]

Bonhoeffer's comments on the conditions of the church and theology were made precisely because of what was missing: the fact that Jesus Christ was not at the center of American theology had reduced it to religion and ethics, things that have to do with human activity and achievement but that can easily exclude God. But in that case, it then ceases to be Christian, because by definition Christianity has to do with God's way to humanity and not human ways to God. Therefore, in these words coming from both 1931 and 1939, Bonhoeffer's theological task was to develop a theological witness that had Christ at the center.

7. August 1939 report, "Protestantism without Reformation," DBWE 15:460–62. Cf. H. Richard Niebuhr's 1937 oberservations of American church life: "A God without wrath brought men without sin into a kingdom without judgment through the ministrations of a Christ without a cross" (*The Kingdom of God in America* [New York: Harper, 1937], 193).

In spite of Bonhoeffer's own reservations about the shortcomings of American theology, the year and the experiences it provided were not lost on him. In fact, the work he did while at Union is important to the ongoing development of Bonhoeffer's theology. Through an examination of two works written at the time, his theological orientation remained consistently christocentric and bore the marks of the *theologia crucis.* This is seen in an article entitled "Concerning the Christian Idea of God," written for *The Journal of Religion*,[8] where the cross of Christ takes center stage. Again, the emphasis is on the hidden presence of God in the cross of Christ that is decisive for Bonhoeffer's understanding. Bonhoeffer's overall theological orientation is displayed in a second work, "The Theology of Crisis," a lecture on Karl Barth prepared for an American audience, for whom Barth's theology was still relatively unknown.

## "Concerning the Christian Idea of God"[9]

In the essay, "Concerning the Christian Idea of God," Bonhoeffer describes God in terms of the theology of the cross. In the first place, he insisted that God remains transcendent to all our attempts to understand God. "God as the absolutely free personality is, therefore, absolutely transcendent. Consequently, I cannot talk about him in general terms; he is always free and beyond these terms."[10] Given the nature of God, the theological task "must be to make room for the transcendent personality of God in every sentence."[11] And does God, who remains hidden from my thinking, speak? How can we know anything about this transcendent God? "The answer is given

8. DBW 10:451–61. The essay appeared in *The Journal of Religion* 12 (1932): 177–85.
9. Note that both this and the following essay were written by Bonhoeffer in English, which accounts for the awkward style and mistakes in spelling, particularly in the latter case, and are not the result of faulty translation.
10. DBWE 10:455.
11. Ibid.

and must be given by God himself, in his own word in Jesus Christ, for no one can answer this question except God himself, in his self-revelation in history, since none can speak the truth except God."[12] Thus God speaks through his own "self-revelation" that "is executed in history. . . . That happened according to the testimony of the Bible and the present Christian church in the revelation of God in Christ."[13]

In language similar to that which he uses elsewhere, the significance of Christ is at the core of the Christian faith. But, again, it is not the Jesus of liberal Protestant theology, but the Christ of the *theologia crucis*. "Thus, Christ becomes not the teacher of mankind, the example of religious and moral life for all time, but the personal revelation, the personal presence of God in the world."[14] In another significant difference from the thought that dominated the theology at both Union Seminary and Berlin, Bonhoeffer based this appraisal not on Jesus' self-understanding or consciousness, but he reflected the Christology of Luther and the reformers:

> It is not Jesus who reveals God to us . . . , but it is God who reveals himself in absolute self-revelation to man. Since God is accessible only in his self-revelation, man can find God only in Christ. That does not exclude God's being elsewhere too, but he cannot and should not be grasped and understood except in Christ. God entered history and no human attempt can grasp him beyond this history.[15] This is the greatest stumbling-block for all general religious thinking, God revealed himself in "once-ness" from the year one to the year thirty in Palestine in Jesus."[16]

12. Ibid., 456; cf. Hans-Jürgen Abromeit, *Das Geheimnis Christi: Dietrich Bonhoeffers erfahrungsbezognene Christologie* (Neukirchen-Vluyn: Neukirchener, 1991), 56, who says that Bonhoeffer reached the height of his christological understanding with this sentence.
13. DBWE 10:456.
14. Ibid.
15. This statement can be compared to Luther's statement in his treatise, "That These Words of Christ, 'This is my Body,' etc., Still Stand Firm against the Fanatics," concerning Christ's presence. Luther said that Christ is indeed present everywhere, but unless he is present for you, you cannot experience it as grace: "In this art I am bold enough to boast that by God's grace I am a master. For if Christ remains mine, everything remains mine; of this I am sure" (*LW* 37:103)

Continuing the distinction made by Luther between true and false theology, Bonhoeffer pointed out the differences between a theology based in human ideas and a theology based in a "revelation in 'oneness.'" In the former, people will always come up with new ideas into which they will attempt to fit their conceptions of God. In such a scheme, Jesus becomes a mere "symbol of God's love, . . . a transient bearer of the general new truth."[17] In the latter approach, however, this is an impossibility. "That is the reason why God reveals himself in history: only so is the freedom of his personality guarded. The revelation in history means revelation in hiddenness."[18] Continuing this same line of reasoning, which concludes that all human attempts to understand and know God are futile, he asked, "How can I know anything about God?" This is something we know only through God's own self-revelation that we receive in faith. "In my faith God reveals himself through Christ in me."[19]

Then, in a clear expression of the *theologia crucis,* Bonhoeffer described how this revelation takes place; faith remains central, because the God who enters history in Jesus Christ remains a hidden God, accessible only by faith. He continued,

> God entered history in Jesus, and so entirely that he can be recognized in his *hiddenness* only by faith. God gives an amazing proof of his *sole authority in the cross of Christ.* In the very same moment when Christ dies upon the cross, the whole world dies in its sinfulness and is condemned. That is the extreme judgment of God upon the world. God himself dies and reveals himself in the death of a man, who is condemned as a sinner. It is precisely this, which is the foolishness of the Christian idea of God, which has been witnessed to by all genuine thinking from Paul, Augustine, Luther, to Kierkegaard and Barth.[20]

16. DBWE 10:456–57.
17. Ibid., 457.
18. Ibid.
19. Ibid., 459.
20. Ibid., 460 (emphasis added).

In a similar statement reflecting this same theological orientation, now describing God's act of justification, he concluded that this is the only way, because

> no religion, no ethics, no metaphysical knowledge may serve man to approach God. . . . That is the foolishness of the revelation of God and its paradoxical character—that just there, where the power of man has lapsed entirely, where man knows his own weakness, sinfulness, and consequently the judgment of God upon him, that just there God is already working in grace, that just and exactly there and only there is forgiveness, justification, resuscitation. There, where man himself no longer sees, God sees, and God alone works, in judgment and in grace. There, at the very limits of man, stands God, and when man can do nothing more, then God does all.[21]

This act of God leads to new life and is the ground of faith. "In this justification man becomes a new personality by faith, and he recognizes here—what he never before could understand or believe—God as his creator."[22]

Each of these statements lifts up Bonhoeffer's theological orientation, and when taken together clearly indicate to what extent his theology is shaped by the *theologia crucis.* In many respects, this last statement in particular is a summary statement of Bonhoeffer's theological position, containing several themes that are of concern to him. In these reflections are also found the foundations of Bonhoeffer's "radical" thinking in prison, thus displaying continuity in his thought rather than disruptions or breaks. But again, it must be pointed out that the cross of Christ stands at the center, providing Bonhoeffer with his theological orientation, serving as the hermeneutic for understanding all other aspects of theology.

21. Ibid., 461; cf. Geffrey Kelly, "Revelation in Christ: A Study of Bonhoeffer's Theology of Revelation," *Ephemerides Theologicae Lovaniense* 50, no. 1 (May, 1974): 60–61, where he relates Bonhoeffer's thinking here directly to Luther's *theologia crucis.*

22. DBWE 10:461.

### "Theology of Crisis"

In that same year, in a seminar paper on Barth's "theology of crisis,"[23] which served as an introduction to Barth's thought to an American audience, his language became even more radically centered on the weakness and suffering of God; in the paper, he placed the emphasis on the suffering of the human Jesus on the cross. In this suffering God is both revealed and comes closest to humankind. Distinguishing between philosophy and theology,[24] the latter being based on the premise of God's revelation in Christ, he lays out the essential character of Christian theology, which has Christology as its distinctive mark; it is both the content of God's revelation and the beginning point for theology. God has entered into history; "God himself was made flesh." In Christ made flesh God's will of judgment and grace is revealed. This means that theology deals not in the realm of ideas but in reality.

> Christ's cross is the judgment of God upon the world, Christ's resurrection is his grace. That is to say, the revelation of God in Christ is not a revelation of a new morality, of new ethical values, a revelation of a new imperativ [*sic*], but a revelation of a new indicativ [*sic*]; It is not a new "you ought," but "you are." In other words the revelation of God is executed not in the area of ideas, but in the area of reality.[25]

The fact that God comes into the world in Christ says something about God and God's ways. It also is a statement that reemphasizes the impossibility of religion, no matter how good, to reach God or

23. "The Theology of Crisis and Its Attitude toward Philosophy and Science," DBWE 10:462–76. Even though Bonhoeffer willingly takes on the assignment to introduce American students to Barth's theology, this did not mean that he gave up his criticisms of Barth. See *DB-ER*, 153.
24. Even his language introducing Barth to this American audience is clear. Barth, he said, is a not a philosopher, "just a christian [*sic*] theologian. This at least has to be clear, what we intend to be, Christian theologians or philosophers" (DBWE 10:463). Note that as with the previous essay, Bonhoeffer wrote this essay in English and it appears as he prepared it.
25. Ibid., 464.

humanity's ability to make itself right before God. That is something only God can do, and the presence of Christ in the world is a visible sign of that fact.

> The *fact* that God himself comes into the world convicts the world of impossibility to come to God by itself; the fact, that God's way in the world leads to the cross, that Christ must die condemned as a sinner on the cross, convicts the world that this impossibility to come to God is its condemnation, its sin and its guilt. The fact of Christ's resurrection proves to the world that only God is right and powerfull [*sic*], that the last word is his, that by an act of his will alone the world can be renewed.[26]

It is the very presence of Jesus that is a sign to the world that its attempts at justification are futile. But, at the same time, that presence is the revelation that allows the world to see that God is a God of grace.

> In short, the fact of God's coming into the world in Christ makes the world see, that here in the life of Jesus of Nazareth God is acting with mankind in an eternal way, that in this life the decision upon the world fells, and that in this decision God does everything, man nothing. Yet it is exactly the fact, that God really entered history, which makes him invisible for human eyes. . . . The fact of God's encarnation [*sic*] in Christ, the fact of Christ's suffering and death, the fact of his resurrection are the revelation of God.[27]

That God, even though revealing himself in Christ, remains hidden, "invisible for human eyes," means that unlike a "revelation of new ideas" that everyone could recognize, Christian revelation is "revelation because it is not congenial to our deepest essence, but entirely beyond our whole existence." In fact, all such claims are foolishness and it is for that reason "that God's revelation in Christ is

26. Ibid.
27. Ibid., 464–65.

revelation in concealment, secrecy, all other socalled [*sic*] revelation is revelation in openness."[28] In contrast to philosophy, which for all its attempts cannot escape the bonds of human thinking *cor curvum in se,* the Christian message comes "entirely from outside of the world of sin God himself came in Jesus Christ, he breaks as the holy Ghost into the circle of man, not as a new idea, a new value but virtue of which man could save himself, but in concreteness as judgment and forgiveness of sin, as the promise of eschatological salvation."[29] And the Christian message is nothing other than

> God revealed in the poor life of a suffering man; God revealed on the cross; God revealed in the depth of history, in sin and death;—is this a message worth hearing by a wise man, who really would be able to invent a nobler and prouder God?. . . . [It is a] faith which sees God coming most closely to man where a man hanging on the cross dies in despair with the loud cry: "My God, my God, why hast Thou forsaken me?" . . . This is the real world of biblical faith, which sees God's work not on the top, but in the depth of mankind; and because faith sees God in Christ it sees God, the same God of Christ, in man's own sin, weakness and death as judgment and as grace.[30]

That Bonhoeffer sides with Barth over against liberal theology in the early 1930s is evident from his writings; this emphasis is already present in the 1925 seminar paper Bonhoeffer wrote for Seeberg. Both in his lecture prepared for Union Seminary, and again in Berlin in his survey of twentieth-century theology, there is a noticeable affinity between Bonhoeffer's own theology and Barth. However, there is also an additional quality to Bonhoeffer's language that

28. Ibid., 465.
29. Ibid., 473.
30. Ibid., 465–66. These statements, when compared to those of *LPP*, where Bonhoeffer concentrates not on the omnipotent, but on the suffering God who is pushed out of the world on a cross, again demonstrates the continuity in Bonhoeffer's thought between 1931 and 1944. Cf. the July 16, 1944 letter, *LPP*, DBWE 8:473–80. See chapter 10 below for more on Bonhoeffer's theology from that period.

indicates both his reservations about Barth and his going in another direction. At the center of his theology, there is an influence that does not come from Barth. Even though the Barthian revolution is one that Bonhoeffer welcomed, Bonhoeffer's language does not remain Barth's.

Bonhoeffer was not content with Barth's diastasic understanding of the relation between God and the world. Rather than limiting his talk to the impossibilities of speaking God's word, Bonhoeffer broke the impasse by pointing to Jesus Christ as the Word of God. Note the christological concentration in Bonhoeffer's words a year later in his 1932 lecture on "The History of Twentieth-Century Systematic Theology":

> This is not a concept of revelation postulated after the fact; only from the revelation itself do we know God as the absolute beginning of self-revelation in Jesus Christ, in a generally understandable way. This word is really God's as such, wholly free, but at the same time shrouded in the garment of history, in humanity. God is indeed something entirely different from humankind, but when God speaks, the speech is veiled; my hearing is shrouded by religion. . . . We would know nothing about God if God did not come in this way. That God comes in such a way is the mystery of God. . . . God's word [is] the absolute *petitio principia* [necessity of evidence]. *Deus dixit* [God has spoken]—to accept this is the beginning of all genuine theological thinking, to allow space for the freedom of the living God.[31]

For Bonhoeffer, God is located in the human Jesus, coming to us in this world, in forms and ways that we can understand. There is no longer a gulf separating God from humankind; the gulf has been bridged by God in the person of Jesus.

31. DBWE 11:230–23.

## Berlin 1931–1933

Bonhoeffer's return to Berlin in the summer of 1931 marked a significant change in his life.[32] He was no longer a student, but instead joined the ranks of the theological faculty, served as a student chaplain at the university and taught confirmation classes in Wedding, a poor Berlin neighborhood. That same fall, he was ordained on November 15 at the Matthais church in central Berlin.[33] Bethge describes Bonhoeffer's changed situation, briefly, as follows: "The period of learning and roaming had come to an end. He now began to teach on a faculty whose theology he did not share, and to preach in a church whose self-confidence he regarded as unfounded. More aware than before, he now became part of a society that was moving toward political, social, and economic chaos."[34]

In that context, Bonhoeffer's basic theological orientation continued to develop along the lines begun in his student works, but now was sharpened to respond to the new political and social realities. From the moment he returned to Berlin, it is apparent that he saw challenges before him and all others who were called to proclaim

32. It should be noted that one of the first things he did after returning to Berlin was to make a trip to Bonn to visit Karl Barth in person. What he discovered was a man "'who had gone beyond his own books' and was hungry to hear from others who were grappling with the same problems." During that visit Bonhoeffer was invited to one of the "open evenings" at Barth's house to which Barth invited his students for theological discussion. In the midst of the discussion, Bonhoeffer quoted Luther, which, in turn, earned him a personal invitation from Barth. See Ferdinand Schlingengsiepen, *Dietrich Bonhoeffer 1906–1945: Martyr, Thanker, Man of Resistance* (New York: T & T Clark, 2010), 76–77.

33. At the time, his ordination held little significance for Bonhoeffer. "He did not choose those who ordained him; none of them were especially close to him either spiritually or personally, and later he hardly ever mentioned the occasion. That Sunday was not treated as an unusual one in the family. That afternoon he went to see his friend Franz Hildebrandt, who was now assistant minister to Fendt in Heilsbronnen, and listened to his sermon on the centenary of Hegel's death" (*DB-ER*, 222). In the course of a few years the significance of ordination would change for Bonhoeffer: "Later he made the occasion and preparations for it an unforgettable experience for his ordination candidates, and by then it meant a great deal when the assurance of commission came from the legal church administration!" (ibid).

34. Ibid.,173. Cf. Schlingensiepen, *Dietrich Bonhoeffer 1906–1945*, 78–81.

the gospel. In an October 18, 1931 letter to his university friend Helmut Rössler, Bonhoeffer revealed his discomfort with the church and society, wondering if it was possible that the church was dead and the gospel had been given to another people. Reflecting on the state of the church and his new role as chaplain at the Technical College in Charlottenburg, he identified the difficulties he perceived to lay ahead:

> Is our time over? Has the gospel been given to another people, perhaps proclaimed with *completely* different words and actions? How do you see the eternal nature of Christianity in light of the world situation and our own way of living? It is becoming less and less understandable that for the sake of *one* just man "the city should be spared." I am presently the pastor for the students at the Technical College. How should I preach such things to these people? Who still believes that anymore? Invisibility is ruining us. If we cannot see in our personal life that Christ has been here, then we want at least to see it in India, but this madness of being constantly thrown back to the invisible God himself—no one can stand that anymore.[35]

Bonhoeffer could not bear any abstract understanding of God. If that was what the church was offering, then it was highly likely that the church would be dead. Thus emerges Bonhoeffer's concern that is later expressed in *LPP* in terms of "non-religious interpretation." In the same way that his developing theology had been marked by the historical, concrete presence of God in Christ, this theme moves to the forefront as he takes on positions of leadership within the church. It, therefore, serves as a programmatic statement that shapes the remainder of Bonhoeffer's career both in Berlin and the German Church Struggle, for his answer to any conceptions of an invisible God, far removed from earthly life, was to be found in Jesus Christ.

35. DBWE 11:55. Ernst Feil, *TDB*, 27, sees in this letter the elements pointing forward to the themes that are central to *LPP*.

With such an understanding of the context and the challenges before him, Bonhoeffer continued to develop a theological perspective that would speak to the world as it was in the 1930s. Working as a university lecturer, student chaplain, and ecumenist, Bonhoeffer worked out a theology that continued to grow out of an orientation shaped by Luther's *theologia crucis.*

The strength of Luther's influence is seen in that one of the first things Bonhoeffer did upon his return to Berlin was to write a Lutheran catechism with his friend Franz Hildebrandt. Before taking up his official responsibilities at the university they spent the month of August working on this new catechism, hoping to find a way to speak the words of the gospel in a credible way in this new context; in this way, not only can this attempt at writing a catechism be viewed as a theological work, but as a summary of the Christian faith as well. To be sure, while they were writing it for "students in a confirmation class," with the stated goal "to formulate what the Lutheran faith is saying today,"[36] it also stated clearly their own understanding of the Christian faith, which was based on their understanding of Luther's theology. Taking a phrase from Luther as the title, "As You Believe, so You Received," they used Luther's own confession of faith as a basis for their understanding of the gospel.[37]

> I believe in God, that he is my creator, in Jesus Christ, that he is my Lord, in the Holy Spirit, that he is my sanctifier. God has created me and given me life, soul, body, and all goods; Christ has brought me into his lordship through his body; and the Holy Spirit sanctifies me through his Word and the sacraments, which are in the church, and will sanctify us wholly on the last day. [. . .] This is the Christian faith: to know what you must do and what has been given to you."[38]

36. DBWE 11:258–59. According to Bethge, at Hildebrandt's suggestion, Bonhoeffer committed himself to this task because he was "convinced of the need for new catechisms" (*DB-ER*, 186).

37. See DWBE 11:258–59nn1–2; the editors point out the references from Luther the authors were drawing on.

In addition, the catechism is filled with quotes from Luther, from whose writings they took their understanding of the Lutheran tradition. One Luther quote, in particular, stands out because Bonhoeffer returned to it again in several of his writings. In discussing their confession of Christ as Lord, they ask, "How can a man be God?" They gave the following answer, which ends with a quote from Luther:

> In no other way than that God miraculously humiliates himself in order to share everything with us. The human Jesus, born of his mother, Mary, through temptation and suffering until death on the cross, is the miracle and word of God. He himself says this, and on this authority he acts. "This is the person to whom you should point and say: Here is God" (Luther)[39]

Far from being a work from which Bonhoeffer simply moved on to other tasks once completed, these words can serve as a lens through which to view Bonhoeffer's writings and lectures from this time. As we turn to other writings, we see that same emphasis. As a young lecturer at the university, the cross continued to be of significant importance for Bonhoeffer. As a pastor, his sermons were filled with images where Christ on the cross is central. If anything, because of

38. DBWE 11:259–60. Luther's words are from a December 1528 sermon on the catechism (see Luther, "Ten Sermons on the Catechism (1528)," *LW* 51:169). Bonhoeffer liked this text of Luther's "so much that he kept it in his daily prayer and service book for the rest of his life, and occasionally used it instead of the Apostles' creed even in the most orthodox confessional services" (*DB-ER*, 187).

39. DBWE 11:264. Cf. *DB-ER*, 187. According to the editors (DBWE 11:264n15), the Luther citation is actually a combination of two different quotations; the first is from Luther's 1520 treatise, "The Babylonian Captivity of the Church," where Luther, in discussing the two natures of Christ, says, "Both natures are simply there in their entirely, and it is truly said: 'This man is God, this God is man.'" (*LW* 36:35); the second comes from Luther's 1528 "Confession concerning Christ's Supper": "I point to the man Christ and say, 'This is God's Son' or 'this man is God's Son'" (*LW* 37:297). These references had been discovered by Franz Hildebrandt and used by him in his doctrinal dissertation, *EST. Das Lutherische Prinzip* (Göttingen: Wissenschaftliche Buchgesellschaft, 1931). Such language can be found in other writings by Luther as well; he used it in sermons and other treatises to express the christological formulation *communicatio idiomatum*.

the perceived state of the church and the future of Christianity itself, at least in the western world, the theme of the cross took on more urgency. In fact, as the political forces that came to dominate life in the 1930s begin to emerge, the need to speak clearly and forcefully of the cross and God's hidden presence in the world became more important than ever. When the Christian message is reduced to its core, what Bonhoeffer found is the message of hope that comes through Christ's death on the cross. In that event is where believers find God.

The same themes that had come to occupy him earlier are expressed now even more concretely than before. The church is called into being by Christ and is realized at the foot of the cross. It is because the church is called into existence by the crucified Christ that it exists for the world;[40] it is always the church for others, as Christ is the man for others. The crucified and risen Christ, and the Christian in a life of faith, share in the sufferings of God in the world. Such images were the voice of the young theologian, expressed in both lectures given and in sermons preached.

## Sermons

In a sermon preached on evening of February 21, 1932, the national day of mourning (the German Memorial Day), using Matt. 24:6–14 as his text, Bonhoeffer used the cross as a means of making sense of all the war dead and understanding God's role in such a horror. Acknowledging that there are different ways of observing Memorial Day, when the church observes it, "it must have something special to say." Its message was to be different: it must recognize and speak

40. Bonhoeffer stated it in the following manner in his lecture, "The Nature of the Church:" "[The] church has become quite worldly for our benefit. It denies itself everything except Christ's word. The church existing in the world knows that it must renounce everything else" (DBWE 11:328).

of the suffering war has caused; its message is shaped by the cross. Instead of joining the chorus of heroic celebration, the church, like a seer of old, "sees deepest, sees the great danger." And the answer of the church: "Christ goes through the cross, only through the cross to life, to the resurrection, to the victory. It is the wonderful theme of the Bible, so frightening for many people that the only visible sign of God in the world is the cross." Instead of separating God from such agony, he identified God with it. The cross is God's way in the world. It is there that God comes most closely to identifying with the suffering of the world. It is precisely there "where everyone begins to doubt God, where everyone falls into despair about God's power, there God is fully, there Christ is alive and near."[41]

The Christ that Bonhoeffer sees as determining all of reality is the Christ of Luther's *theologia crucis*. "Christ, who knows that his path leads to the cross, knows that the path of his disciples also does not lead peacefully and safely straight into heaven; rather, they too must pass through the darkness, through the cross. They too must struggle."[42] Even so, Christians are not afraid, nor need they be alarmed. For "God's way in the world leads onto the cross and through the cross to life."[43] That is an explicit statement of the *theologia crucis*.

Later that spring, on May 8, Bonhoeffer preached on 2 Chron. 20:12. Using the text, "We do not know what we should do, but our eyes are on you," he contrasted what we might expect from a speech of a leader—one who lays out a vision, a program, and who shows determination—with this "uninspiring" man of the Bible. He really is not appealing, for we would prefer one who would say, "We know what to do." But the reality, given the circumstances, is that

41. Ibid., 420–27.
42. Ibid., 423.
43. Ibid., 426.

we do not know what we should do. Even God's commandments are hidden "and a terrible fear comes over us. . . . And we know in all our not knowing that it is the wrath of God that [has] come over us." Thankfully, however, God has recreated the world, giving us the chance to start over. This new creation is called "the cross of Christ and resurrection. In the cross of Christ, the fallen world is brought to its end and judged, with its knowledge and its deeds." So we look to the one who "creates life in death, resurrection in the cross." Therefore, "in this world we *see* only the cross"; but know that there we receive forgiveness of sin and new life. At the foot of the cross, "we see ourselves as those who stand condemned under the cross, as those who do not know what they should do." There, at the foot of the cross, "we believe in life, . . . we believe in God." So while we may not know what to do, "our eyes are on you, on the Lord, on the risen Lord." And having heard this word proclaimed,

> now we go home to our work—workers, civil servants, merchants, students, pastors—back to our work in which we do not know what we should do. But now we know that our work takes place under the cross, under the judgment of Christ, that the ground on which we stand has become unstable, that we cannot stand still on that ground without sinking in. And now we must go forward and—especially if we know only that we don't know what we should do—must not put our hands in our laps and rest up until God does his part.[44]

Then later, in a sermon preached on July 24, 1932 for the closing worship service of the semester, using John 8:32 as a text, Bonhoeffer described a "crucified Truth."[45] Here again the cross became the key to understanding God's truth and our relationship to that truth. God's truth and freedom come to us in an unexpected way, in a way different from popular culture. Truth happens to us in the form of

44. Ibid., 435–39.
45. Ibid., 465–72.

crucified truth, as the crucified Christ. "The path that God's truth took in the world leads to the cross. From then on, we know that all truth that wants to stand up before God must go to the cross. The congregation that follows Christ must go with him [on] to the cross."[46]

In a sermon (based on Rev. 2:4–5, 7) preached for Reformation Sunday, November 6, 1932, at Dreifaltigkeitskirche in Berlin, Bonhoeffer related the Reformation celebrations to what was going on in Germany at the time and, in a sense, called for a new reformation. Through his words we note that Bonhoeffer saw this as a critical time in which the word of God must be spoken. Using this opportunity, he stated at the beginning of the sermon that it should be clear to everyone that there is not much time remaining for the church, which is in its final hour.[47] The reason for the crisis is because of the church itself. The Reformation was celebrated with great fanfare in Germany, but the problem was that the church celebrated the Reformation and Luther; in so doing, it had lost sight of the principles of the Reformation and had failed to hear God's word.

> In celebrating the Reformation, the church can't leave old Luther in peace. He has to suffer for all the terrible things that are going on in the church today. Though he is dead, we prop him up in our church and make him hold out his hand, gesture toward the church, and keep saying over and over those same self-confident words with all their pathos, "Here I stand—I can do no other." We fail to see that this is no longer Luther's church.[48]

It is simply not enough for the church to barricade itself behind Luther's words and insist that it "can do no other," for the church "can and should do otherwise. It must have resounded from pulpits

46. Ibid., 472.
47. DBWE 12:439.
48. Ibid., 440.

thousands of times today: 'I cannot do otherwise; here I stand.' God, however, says, "But I have this against you."[49] The church sings "A mighty fortress is our God" and "If God is for us, who is against us," but God responds, "I have this against you." It "fails to see that every time it says 'God,' God actually turns against it."[50] While the church of the Reformation had come to pride itself on its protest against all that was wrong in the world, it had failed to hear God's clear word to it, collectively and individually. The time has come to "lay the dead Luther to rest at long last, and instead listen to the gospel, reading his Bible, hearing God's own word in it. At the last judgment God is certainly going to ask us not, 'Have you celebrated Reformation Day properly?' but rather, 'Have you heard my word and kept it?'"[51] The true church of the Reformation is the church that hears the call of God, which was Luther's call as well, to repent. Instead of placing its trust in such outward celebrations, "our church stands on God's Word alone, and it is that Word alone that makes us those who stand facing the right direction. The church that stands in repentance, the church that lets God be God, is the church of the apostles and of Luther."[52]

According to Christian Gremmels, this sermon was an early indication that Bonhoeffer was fighting for genuine Lutheranism in 1930s Germany. Making the distinction between the church that used Luther's name and Luther himself, Bonhoeffer offered up a critique of the church, in a sense using Luther against the Lutherans and, in so doing, attempted to reclaim the church. Coming as it did four months after the Deutsche Christen (the German Christians) had declared that they embodied "the German spirit of Luther," which carried the attending implication that there was a direct line

49. Ibid., 441.
50. Ibid., 440.
51. Ibid., 442.
52. Ibid., 444.

from Luther to Hitler, Bonhoeffer's sermon was a direct critique of such thinking.[53] Rather than discarding Luther in favor of some other authority, by drawing a clear line, Bonhoeffer laid claim to the true Luther over against any false claims being made by the German Christians. But at the same time, Bonhoeffer was not simply advocating a return to Luther; as he would do several times over the next few years, he would acknowledge that there was a real difference between Luther's time and 1930s Germany. Therefore, what was called for was not a mere repetition of Luther's words, but a reformulation of Luther's ideas. The "Here I stand" language of Luther had become "cheap." What was needed was something more costly; instead of saying, "As Luther says," the word now needs to be "other than Luther: We can do something other."[54]

Geffrey Kelly and John Godsey also see this sermon as an expression of Bonhoeffer's belief that the church had twisted Luther's heritage and could no longer be trusted. By giving glowing support to the growing nationalistic sentiments in Germany, the church, under the banner of Luther and his heritage,

> had turned from the light of Jesus Christ toward a new, glowing light of the nation. The church had come perilously close to transforming itself into a national church that honored the Teutonic gods of blood, soil, and conquest, all under the banner of Martin Luther in the 'mighty fortress' of Nazi Germany. This prompted Bonhoeffer . . . to decry Germany's revival of triumphalist nationalism, which he viewed as part of a lethal illness and as evidence of the church's slow death as an

53. Christian Gremmels, "Rechtfertigung und Nachfolge: Martin Luther in Dietrich Bonhoeffer's Buch 'Nachfolge,'" in *Dietrich Bonhoeffer heute: Die Aktualität seines Lebens und Werkes*, ed. Rainer Mayer and Peter Zimmerling (Giessen/Basel: Brunnen Verlag, 1992), 83–84. See also Larry Rasmussen, "Editor's Introduction to the English Edition," DBWE 12:2: Finding intolerable what was playing out in Germany in late 1932–early 1933, Bonhoeffer and his family knew "they could not withdraw from the challenges facing them." In fact, they were searching for "alternatives amid unrelenting crises." Finding neither the church nor the university satisfying in that regard, Bonhoeffer's search eventually lead him down a different path—but the seeds were already present before Hitler emerged on the scene.
54. Gremmels, "Rechtfertigung und Nachfolge," 86.

> effective voice in German society. That sermon expresses clearly Bonhoeffer's way of setting straight the theological record on what Luther really thought about Christian 'works' and the present, attractive "work" of building a new earthly kingdom in tandem with the growing glorification of the Nazi nation.[55]

Additional insights into Bonhoeffer's theology are provided in two sermons he preached in 1933. The first, preached on February 26, his first sermon after Hitler's rise to power, ended with the words, "Lord on the cross, be our only Lord."[56] Preaching on reluctant Gideon, contrasted with the Germanic heroic figure Siegfried, Bonhoeffer drew direct parallels to his context.[57] In direct contrast to the intimations of power exhibited by the Reich church, Bonhoeffer proclaimed that God exhibits power through the cross of Jesus Christ, leaving no room for any other god. "In the church we have only *one* altar. . . . In the church we also have only *one* pulpit, from which faith in God is preached and not any other faith, not even with the best intentions."[58] Because of its timing, this sermon also fits with the message of his radio address given shortly before, in which he warned people of the "Führer principle."[59]

The second sermon, preached on May 28, while giving his Christology lectures, is also helpful. Coming as it did during the summer of 1933, after Hitler had come to power and after a victory for the Deutsche Christen for leadership of the church, it provides theological insights that shape Bonhoeffer's political positions.

55. Geffrey B. Kelly and John D. Godsey, "Editors' Introduction to the English Edition," *Discipleship*, DBWE 4:9–10.

56. DBWE 12:461–67.

57. See Rasmussen, "Editor's Introduction," DBWE 12:23–24, where he points out the contrast with the sermon preached at the Magdeburg Cathedral, in which the swastika flag was lifted up as a symbol of hope for Germany.

58. DBWE 12:462–63.

59. "The Younger Generation's Altered View of the Concept of Führer," DBWE 12:266–268. See also his expanded written version, "The Führer and the Individual in the Younger Generation," ibid., 268–82.

Preaching on Exodus 32, Bonhoeffer raised the question about the church: Is it a church of the word or a church of the world? Moses and Aaron, two brothers called by God to different responsibilities, one a prophet, the other a priest, stand in conflict at the foot of Mount Sinai. Moses represents the church of the word. He is called up the mountain by God, where he fights, prays, and suffers for the people of Israel. "He wears no purple robe, he is not a priest; he is nothing, nothing at all but the servant who waits on the word of his Lord, who falls ill if he cannot listen to that word. He is nothing—but the prophet of his God."[60] While this is going on up on the mountain, the church of the world, which is in Aaron's hands, grows impatient and anxious. Because it cannot see Moses, "it must go to go ahead and do something itself, take action itself, since God and the prophet are not doing so." Feeling as though God had abandoned it, it wants Aaron to do something. "God has left us alone here, but we need gods! We need religion! If you can't prevail with the living God, then make us gods yourself!"[61] And so it is that under Aaron's leadership the people of God create their own god, one to which they are prepared to worship and offer sacrifice. "The human race and the worldly church fall on their knees joyfully, and with smiles, before the god whom we make as it pleases us." But while they celebrate their achievement, "there is rumbling on Sinai";[62] God judges the worldly church, bringing it to an end.

This, however, is not just something that happened at an earlier time in a faraway place; Bonhoeffer insisted that the same conflict was being repeated "in our church, day by day, Sunday by Sunday. As the worldly church, which doesn't want to wait, which doesn't want to live by something unseen; as a church that makes its own gods,

60. Ibid., 473.
61. Ibid., 474.
62. Ibid., 475.

that wants to have a god that pleases it rather than asking whether it is itself pleasing to God." Falling prey to the ideology of the Nazis, the German church was no different from the church of Aaron. This church, too, will receive the same judgment from God as did the worldly church under Aaron's leadership. But this time, rather than Moses offering a sacrifice, the expiation comes from Christ, who is both priest and prophet:

> The man in the purple cloak and the crown of thorns, who stands before God and makes intercession for us, the crucified Son of the Father. Here on his cross, all idolatry comes to an end. Here the whole human race, the whole church, is judged and pardoned. Here, God is wholly God, who does not tolerate any other gods but himself, but who is also wholly God in boundless forgiveness. We point to the cross as the church that is always both church of Moses and church of Aaron; we point to the cross and say: See, O Israel, this is your God who brought you up out of slavery, and who will lead you again. Come, believe and worship.[63]

Reflecting on the state of the church in Germany at this time, by recalling the story of Moses and Aaron, he reminded his listeners that the church was not the church simply because it bears the name. The church is either of God, and therefore waits on God and God's word, or it creates gods in its own image. One is the true church, the other is the false church. The church exhibits power and fights for standing in the world, or it can wait on God and listen to the word of God. Bonhoeffer knew which one was the true church, and the one to which he must listen. It is the church of the word, created by the cross of Christ. In a short time, he would abandon his positions in Berlin and after spending time in London, would return to Germany to lead the underground seminary at Finkenwalde; for him this move was the means to both form an alternative to the church corrupted

63. Ibid.

by Nazi ideology and to ensure that the gospel provided the sole foundation for the true church.

## University Lectures

Bonhoeffer set about his teaching at a time of political turmoil and change.[64] Even though he began as non-salaried lecturer and was a relatively unknown newcomer to the faculty, because of his ability to relate theological themes to the practical issues that were affecting the daily lives of his students, he quickly developed a following. What became clear to his students was his unwavering faith commitment, which was christocentric in shape and content. By all appearances, Bonhoeffer should have had a long career as a university professor. At the same time as he began his teaching responsibilities, he became involved in the church as both a pastor and participant in the ecumenical movement. These activities, together with his Christian faith and the political influences from his family, led him to become involved in the Confessing Church; it was this latter association, in particular, that led to his dismissal from the theological faculty in 1936, cutting short an academic career but opening another. His work during his short time in Berlin became the foundation for his work in the Confessing Church and led to his involvement in the resistance movement. His lectures provide the insights into how his christologically-shaped theology, a theology that pushed him to take reality seriously, drove him into the political realm.

In "The History of Twentieth-Century Systematic Theology," a series of lectures Bonhoeffer gave between November 2, 1931 and February 29, 1932, several christological themes emerge that show his independent stance vis-à-vis his colleagues.[65] Through them Bonhoeffer shows where he stands. It is here that he identifies

64. See Rasmussen, "Editor's Introduction," DBWE 12:2–3, and Schlingensiepen, *Dietrich Bonhoeffer 1906–1945*, chapters 4–5, for details on life in Berlin and Germany at this time.

liberal theology's understanding of God as a sentimental one in which the Bible has no interest. The Bible's, and the Reformation's, concern was, "How can I have a merciful God?"[66] This was Luther's question and the answer comes in the form of justification, which has its foundation in the cross of Christ. Unfortunately, "the issue of the Reformation had faded away by the turn of the century," because everything that theology deals with is related to the question of justification, which is intimately tied to Christology.[67] In these early lectures, Bonhoeffer showed his independence from both the liberal theological tradition of his teachers and Karl Barth, and, in the end, after concluding his review, he asked, "*Who will show us Luther!*"[68] In this case, too, Luther is Bonhoeffer's authority.

During the summer of 1932 Bonhoeffer lectured on "The Nature of the Church."[69] Given at a time of political and ecclesial tension that "had led people cynically to question whether there was any need at all for a church. . . . Bonhoeffer depicted the church's location and mission within the everyday reality of secular life. The church, he insisted, is not called to be a tiny, sacred haven from the world but, like Jesus, a presence in the very midst of the world."[70]

Bonhoeffer's understanding of the church introduced in *Sanctorum Communio* and developed in *Act and Being* is here seen in the same

65. According to Bethge, the significance of these first lectures lies in what they reveal about Bonhoeffer's own theological position. Given the fact that he was free to pick the topics of his courses, both the content and organization of this course provide an outline of Bonhoeffer's perception of his standing among his contemporaries: "The course undertook a solid sketch of his own position on the theological map. Bonhoeffer's assessment that he had arrived at a significant turning point in theological history was the central point of the entire course" (*DB-ER*, 211).
66. DBWE 11:213.
67. Ibid., 213, 215.
68. Ibid., 244.
69. DBWE 11:269–332; these lectures, like most of the lectures Bonhoeffer gave at the University of Berlin that were not published during his lifetime, have been reconstructed from student notes.
70. Kelly and Nelson, *TF*, 82.

light. The church has its foundations in Christ, but now with an added emphasis. Now it is more specifically Christ, the crucified one, who produced a more concrete understanding of the church. This church, where Christ is present, belongs in the world. He specifically noted that the church is not a refuge from the world (which is reiterated during his Finkenwalde years), but rather exists for the world. The christological grounding of the church ties it to the world in the same way that Christ lived and died for the world.

Given the circumstances, Bonhoeffer began with an analysis of the church's place in the world. He acknowledged that the church had become problematic, due to the its loss of place. This loss was not the fault of culture, but rather was the result of the church's own loss of its mission: "[The] desire of our church to be everywhere results in its being nowhere. That which is tangible becomes unassailable! The church is never and nowhere itself anymore. Existence without a place is the existence of Cain, of the refugee. Therefore despised!"[71] The church did this because it did not want to be "isolated" from culture; rather, it "wanted to fit in." But having lost its place, the church has "become acculturated, . . . has made itself harmonious with culture" and, as a result, "has become a slave to culture." Having forfeited its place and, therefore, its mission, the church was now found only in privileged places, where its services, rituals and symbols were used to bolster the support of the privileged, the *petite bourgeoisie*, while ignoring the needs of the less privileged.[72]

All of this stands in direct contradiction to the proper place of the church, which "is the place of the present Christ in the world." Established by God, the church's place is not a privileged place set aside for it, but is the "*place of God himself*." "Then the church [will be] loved or hated only because of its own cause (the gospel)." When

71. DBWE 11:276.
72. Ibid., 277–78.

the church waits on God to establish its place, it will not be "on the periphery of life, but in the center." For "God is not [an] aspect of reality! . . . God penetrates the entire everyday reality and must be felt in everything!" And because God is at the center "Christianity is not removed from the world. [It] is in the everydayness of the world. Therefore, the word must stand in [the] sphere of the everyday. [The church is] not an 'exceptional light' outside the profane realm, not a separation of church and the world."[73]

The church exists in the world because God is in the world. As Bonhoeffer had already stated in both *Sanctorum Communio* and *Act and Being*, God created the church through Christ, who is its foundation. Through his vicarious representative act on the cross, namely, through his incarnation, crucifixion, and resurrection,[74] a new humanity, which is the church, is created and finds its place in the world. Hence, like Christ himself, who takes his place not in privileged places but is found on the cross, the church, the body of Christ, finds itself in that same worldly place.

Therefore, the real church exists in and for the world. But in this case, the church is worldly, not as a result of its own doing but because of God's presence in Christ. The incarnation of Christ drives the church into the world. It does not have a place in the world because of its abilities to carve out a space for itself; but because Christ is its foundation, it follows Christ into the world, taking on the burdens and suffering of the world, not for its own sake, but for the world's sake. By living solely in Christ, the church is free to give up its privileges, give its very self up for the world all because of Christ, its foundation.

73. Ibid., 278–81.

74. It should be noted at this point that even though Bonhoeffer's Christology follows the lines articulated earlier, one development beyond his description of Christ that appears in *SC* and *AB* is the threefold formula, which is used to describe the work of salvation in Christ. See Abromeit, *Geheimnis Christi*, 229ff.

> Our church is here. [It is] not an ideal; otherwise we would still be in Advent. Christ is present in his church today. [That is] no ideal but rather reality. [The] worldliness of the church is real, not only illusion [Schein]. [The] church is wholly world! Furthermore, where [the] church [has] become homeless, this must be so. [The] church has become quite worldly for our benefit. It denies itself everything except Christ's word. The church existing in the world knows that it must renounce everything else.[75]

Rather than seeking a privileged place or reserving a holy place as the church, the church is completely in the world. The church is not a place one goes to escape the ravages of the world, a refuge from the world, but rather is the very presence of God in the world. This follows from Bonhoeffer's own Christology, which takes the humanity of Jesus seriously. Building on the Adam-Christ typology of *Sanctorum Communio,* Bonhoeffer insisted that it is Christ's act of dying on the cross that brings about humanity's justification. By dying on the cross, Christ puts the old Adam to death, and through his resurrection a new humanity is created.

The influence of these lectures was seen in a presentation Bonhoeffer gave later that summer to the International Youth Conference of the Universal Christian Council on Life and Work and the World Alliance for Promoting International Friendship through the Churches, held in Gland, Switzerland, on August 29, 1932.[76] Beginning with the assertion, "The church is dead," Bonhoeffer used this occasion to condemn National Socialism's ideology. When the church is compromised by such worldly values as were becoming commonplace in culture, the church is on the verge of death. The church, however, called into being by the cross of Christ, offers a life-giving word to the dying. In spite of what

75. DBWE 11:328–29.
76. "Address in Gland," DBWE 11:375–81.

the world might see, Bonhoeffer has hope in the church because it is founded on the cross of Christ.

In contrast to the world that declares the death of the church, the believer announces, "The church lives in the midst of dying, solely because God calls it forth out of death into life, because God does the impossible against us and through us."[77] The true nature of the church exists "beneath the cross." When one sees

> how the New Testament proclaims life to the dying man and how in the cross of Christ death and life collide, and how life swallows up death—only where one sees this does one believe in the church beneath the cross. Only with clear eyes on reality, without any illusion about our morality or our culture, can one believe. Otherwise, our faith becomes illusion. The believer can be neither a pessimist nor an optimist. Both are illusory. The believer does not see reality in a particular light but rather sees it as it is and believes against everything and beyond everything that he sees *solely in God* and God's power. He does not believe in the world, not even in a world capable of development and improvement. He does not believe in his world-improving power and his goodwill. He does not believe in humanity or in the human good that must finally triumph. He does not believe in the church in its human power, but rather the believer believes solely in God, the God who creates and does the impossible, the God who creates life out of death, the God who has called the dying church into life against and despite us and through us, the God who alone does this.[78]

This is the true church and it was the church needed for his world. So Bonhoeffer insisted, "Christ must again become present among us in preaching and sacrament, just as Christ as the crucified one made peace with God and humanity. The crucified Christ is our peace. Christ alone adjures the false gods and the demons. Only before the cross does the world tremble, not before us."[79]

77. Ibid., 376.
78. Ibid.
79. Ibid., 379.

This is a church planted in the midst of the world, ready to do battle if necessary, for Christ's cross stands in judgment over worldly values. Where Christ is, there the true church must be. And that means being at odds with the world, which, in this case, means standing for peace in opposition to war.

> And now the cross places us in the midst of a world that has gone haywire. Christ is not distant from the world or in an otherworldly dimension of our existence. Christ went into the deepest depths of the world; his cross is in the midst of the world. And now this cross of Christ calls forth wrath and judgment upon the world and proclaims peace. Today there should no longer be war—the cross does not want it. One must make a distinction: in the world that has fallen away from God, struggle is inevitable, but there should be no war. War in its present-day form lays waste to God's creation and obscures the view of revelation. As little as one can justify torture as a means of justice out of the necessity for justice, one can just as little justify war as a means of strife out of the necessity of strife. The church forsakes obedience whenever it sanctions war. The church of Christ stands against war in favor of peace among the peoples, between nations, classes, and races.[80]

During the winter semester, from November 8, 1932 through February 21, 1933, Bonhoeffer lectured on the Bible, seeking to understand his world according to Genesis 1–3.[81] The response to these lectures was so great that, at the request of his students, they were published; as such, these lectures are the only ones that survive in Bonhoeffer's own words. All other remaining lectures he gave having been reconstructed from student notes.

According to John W. de Gruchy, there was a reason for the lectures' success:

> It was a winter of profound discontent in Germany; it was also a time of confusion, anxiety, and, for many, false hope, as social and political upheavals led to the demise of the Weimar Republic and the birth of the

80. Ibid., 379–80.
81. *Creation and Fall: A Theological Exposition of Genesis 1–3*, DBWE 3.

> Third Reich. In the midst of these events Bonhoeffer called his students to focus their attention on the word of God as the word of truth in a time of turmoil.[82]

Not only were these lectures on Genesis important to the students who attended Bonhoeffer's classes, they serve as a turning point in Bonhoeffer's career as well, representing a link between his earlier academic writings and his later theological reflections that grew out of his life and work in the church. What is displayed in these lectures is "a turning point in Bonhoeffer's development from an abstruse academic theologian whose context was solely the university to a theologian for preachers."[83]

But in addition to their focus on a biblical text, it was Bonhoeffer's particular emphasis or approach that caught the students' attention. At a time when the role of the Old Testament was downplayed in the Christian church, Bonhoeffer wanted to make the point that the Hebrew Bible was also a part of the Christian canon; "therefore it had to be read in the light of God's self-disclosure in Jesus Christ." Throughout history, according to Bonhoeffer, any attempt to downplay the role of the Old Testament always resulted in

> a dualistic separation of creation and redemption and of the public and the private spheres of life. . . . The practical consequences have been far-reaching and destructive. In Bonhoeffer's own situation such an attitude to the Old Testament led inevitably to the reinforcement of German anti-Semitism. More universally this dualism had bred a perverse attitude to human sexuality, a piety that denies the social and political responsibilities of Christians, and an attitude toward the environment that has allowed its destruction. Bonhoeffer's own growing love for the Old Testament contributed a great deal to his quite different approach. . . . For Bonhoeffer the God of Israel and of Jesus Christ is always in the midst of the world and can only be encountered there.[84]

82. John W. de Gruchy, "Editor's Introduction to the English Edition," DBWE 3:1.
83. Ibid., 8.

One of the elements that contributed to Bonhoeffer's "different approach" was that he interpreted these texts through a christological lens.[85]

In his discussion of humankind having been created in the "image of God," Bonhoeffer said freedom is the character that sets humanity apart from the rest of creation, aligning them with God. But human freedom is like God's freedom. In words echoing *Act and Being*, he stated,

> The answer is that it is the message of the gospel itself that God's freedom has bound itself to us, that God's free grace becomes real with us alone, that God wills not to be free for God's self but for humankind. Because God in Christ is free for humankind, because God does not keep God's freedom to God's self, we can think of freedom only as a "being free for . . ." For us in the middle who exist through Christ and who know what it means to be human through Christ's resurrection, the fact that God is free means nothing else than that we are free for God.[86]

In his interpretation of creation, everything is read through the prism of Christ, who is the only way to understand and know God and the world. Rather than being satisfied with a highly abstract concept of God, the anthropomorphic manner of speaking about God, as Genesis does, helps humankind conceive of God as God really is. And the way humanity has God is through his name. "Indeed the proper name is God as such. We have God in no other way than in God's name. This is true today as well. Jesus Christ—that is the name of God, at once utterly anthropomorphic and utterly to the point."[87] Creation and cross are bound together in God's name.

84. Ibid., 9–10.
85. Bonhoeffer is not unlike Luther in this regard. Luther, too, easily approached the Old Testament from a christological point of view. In addition, Bonhoeffer, like Luther, came to love the Old Testament's down-to-earth quality.
86. DBWE 3:63.
87. Ibid., 75.

In a highly christocentric move, he ended his lectures by describing the cross as the tree of life. There all the sin that has been a burden weighing down humanity since the time of Adam and Eve is canceled. The old Adam is put to death and a new humanity is created. The cross brings about a new reality, one which is firmly planted in this world.

> The end of Cain's history, and so the end of all history, is Christ on the cross, the murdered Son of God. That is the last desperate assault on the gate of paradise. And under the whirling sword, under the cross, the human race dies. But Christ lives. The trunk of the cross becomes the wood of life, and now in the midst of the world, on the accursed ground itself, life is raised up anew. In the center of the world, from the wood of the cross, the fountain of life springs up. All who thirst for life are called to drink from this water, and whoever has eaten from the wood of this life shall never again hunger and thirst. What a strange paradise is this hill of Golgotha, this cross, this blood, this broken body. What a strange tree of life, this trunk on which the very God had to suffer and die. Yet it is the very kingdom of life and of the resurrection, which by grace God grants us again. It is the gate of imperishable hope now opened, the gate of waiting and patience. The tree of life, the cross of Christ, the center of God's world that is fallen but upheld and preserved—that is what the end of the story about paradise is for us.[88]

## Christology Lectures

The last university lectures Bonhoeffer gave were held in the summer of 1933. In the midst of radical changes taking place in Europe as a result of Hitler's ascension to power earlier that year and the struggles emerging in the church over the question both of loyalty and the proclamation of the gospel, Bonhoeffer chose to lecture on the topic that for him got to the core of the Christian faith. At such a time—a time of crisis—there was no more important issue than clarity on

88. Ibid., 146.

what the church believed and confessed. Confession of Jesus Christ was the most important question; that was the subject he took up.

Given that orientation, his decision to give a series of lectures on Christology, even though such a course was not the norm from the Berlin faculty, is indicative of both Bonhoeffer's independent thinking and the importance the subject matter held for him.[89] These lectures both represent the peak of Bonhoeffer's academic achievement and lay the foundation for his future work.[90] It was stated with regard to *Creation and Fall* that those lectures represented a transition for Bonhoeffer, but this is even more true with these lectures. The significance of these lectures has been summarized in the following manner:

> The insistence on Christ as the center of history, which runs from the beginning to the end of Bonhoeffer's theological legacy, means that his political commitments are informed by his Christology while his Christology is only realized in political engagement. In this way these early lectures on Christology continue to lay the foundation for both Bonhoeffer's later writings on the cost of discipleship and his decision to participate in the conspiracy to assassinate Adolf Hitler.[91]

Here the themes that emerged in Bonhoeffer's thinking are developed more systematically, where his christological orientation pushed him to identify ever more strongly with the "humiliated" Jesus who takes on sinful human flesh. Rejecting any discussion of purely doctrinal formulations, he insisted on answering the question, "Who is this Jesus?" And his answer was that he is the "God-human." In Jesus Christ, fully God and fully human, God is present for us. From the side of faith ("Jesus Christ is God . . . in our faith alone"),[92]

89. His lectures were also very popular with students, attracting as many as two hundred who came to hear him. See Rasmussen, "Editor's Introduction," DBWE 12:3.

90. See Ernst-Albert Schaffenorth, "Editor's Afterword to the German Edition," DBWE 12:488ff.

91. Craig Nessan, "Foreword to the English Edition," in Dietrich Bonhoeffer, *Who Is Christ for Us?*, ed. Craig L. Nessan and Renate Wind (Minneapolis: Fortress Press, 2002), 2.

which is the only place that the christological question can be asked, the *who* question" is the important question; it is the one that deals with the real presence of God and of God in relation to the world. That faith is the framework for approaching Jesus is obvious for Bonhoeffer:

> There are only two possibilities when a human being confronts Jesus: the human being must either die or kill Jesus. Thus the question, Who are you? remains ambiguous. It can also be the question of those who realize, as soon as they ask the question, that they themselves are meant by it, and instead of hearing the answer, hear the question in return: Who then are you? Only then is it the question of those judged by Jesus. The "who question" can only be asked of Jesus by those who know that it is being asked of them. But then it is not the human beings who are finished with Jesus, but rather Jesus who is finished with them. Strictly speaking, the "who question" can be asked only within the context of faith, and there it will receive its answer.[93]

In these lectures Bonhoeffer once again is concerned primarily with God present in Christ, now described as the humiliated Christ. Without detracting from Christ's divinity, Bonhoeffer, like Luther, said, "For our sake [God] made him to be sin. Christ is the very *peccator pessimus*. Luther even said that Christ was a robber, murderer, and adulterer like ourselves, because he carries our sins. But *he* is at the same time the One who is without sin, the Holy One, the Eternal, the Lord, the Son of the Father."[94]

92. DBWE 12:354.

93. Ibid., 307.

94. Ibid., 357. Bonhoeffer's Luther reference here is from Martin Luther, Psalmus XXII (21) "Operationes in psalmos," 1519–21 (*WA* 5:602, 21–35); this text was not translated for inclusion in *Luther's Works*.

These lectures have been reconstructed from student notes. The earlier version of these lectures, which were the basis for previous English translations, *Gesammelte Schriften* III, 166–242, and upon which the previous English translations were based, were based on the notes of Gerhard Riemers. The latest edition draws not only on Riemers's notes but on those of several other students as well. See DBWE 12:279n1.

Rather than addressing the topic of Christology from a purely academic position, which would have engaged in all the questions that had occupied Christian thinkers over the centuries (questions such as how the incarnation is possible, how God could become human, how the two natures of Christ are united, how a human being could save us, etc.), Bonhoeffer pushed such concerns aside to get at the heart of the Christian proclamation. While these were important points for discussion, Bonhoeffer's concern was more immediate. He wanted to concentrate on the person of Jesus. Therefore, for him, the most important christological questions were not about the *how* of the incarnation, but rather *who* the one is who saves us. "Who" is it that we encounter in the church? Beginning with the confession that Christ is present "as the Crucified and Risen One," Bonhoeffer located the basis of his exploration: "Only because Christ is the Christ who is present are we still able to inquire of him. Only because proclamation and the sacraments are carried out in the church can we inquire about Christ."[95] This presence, which is the starting point of Christology, however, is more than an "influence that emanates from him" or the attempts "to reach across history to keep bringing the image of Christ into view." Instead, drawing on Luther to counter the mistakes of modern theology, he stated it as follows:

> To be present means to be in the same place at the same time (presence). We are talking about Christ's ability to be simultaneously present to us all. Even as the Risen One, Jesus remains the human Jesus. Only because he is human can he be present to us. But that he is eternally with us here, eternally with us in the now—that is his presence as God. Only because Jesus is God can he be present to us.
>
> The presence of Jesus Christ compels the statement that Jesus is wholly human, as well as the other statement that Jesus is wholly God—otherwise he would not be present. Thus, from the presence of

95. Ibid., 310.

> Christ arises the twofold certainty that he is both human being and God. Therefore it is impossible to ask how the human Jesus can be simultaneously with each of us—as if this Jesus could exist in isolation! It is just as impossible to ask how God can enter into time—as if such an isolated God could exist! The only question that makes sense is: who is present, who is with us here and now? The answer is: the human-God Jesus. I cannot know who the human Christ is if I do not simultaneously think of the God-Christ and vice versa. God in his timeless eternity is *not* God. Jesus Christ in his humanity, limited in time, is *not* Jesus Christ. Instead, in the human being Jesus Christ, God is God. Only in Jesus Christ is God present. The starting point for Christology has to be the God-human.[96]

For Bonhoeffer, the christological question was not how "the relation of God and human in Jesus Christ";[97] ultimately the *how* question is doomed to failure because it cannot adequately explain the union between God and human being; it "is impossible to think through." Because of its very nature, therefore, it cannot be the starting point for Christology. Instead, at most, it can only point to the "One Who Became Human"; it can only point to the *who* question: "Who is this God?"[98]

For Bonhoeffer Christology has to do with the whole God-human, rather than with either God or humanity alone. In that way, Christology begins from the perspective of faith. One can never get at the heart of Christology or hope to arrive at christological answers outside of faith. For Bonhoeffer, the christological question did not "attempt to unite two isolated existing realities."[99] Rather, beginning with the confession that Jesus is fully God and fully human, and that in him God is fully present for the world, albeit in hidden form, in

96. Ibid., 312–13. Cf. Luther's teaching of the ubiquity of the body of Christ. Bonhoeffer, drawing extensively on Luther and Lutheran eucharistic theology, uses this same notion to establish the bodily presence of Jesus for us. See 320ff.

97. Ibid., 313.

98. Ibid., 353.

99. Ibid., 354. The *communicatio idiomatum* assumes the unity of the divine and human.

the "likeness of flesh," the christological problem is shifted from *how* to *who*: "It is not the relation of God and human in Jesus Christ, but rather the relation of the God-human, as already given, to the ὁμοίωμα σαρκός. The God-human is present in the form of the σάρξ, the form that is a stumbling block."[100]

Bonhoeffer viewed the *how* question as a false christological question because it sought to get to the core of the Christian faith outside of faith. This ultimately is what separates a false Christology from the true Christology. In fact, the "'how' question shows how we are chained to our own authority. It is the *cor curvum in se* (Luther)."[101] Since the New Testament is already written from the perspective of faith, Bonhoeffer believed it was impossible to get behind "belief in the Christ as Lord." Believing that it is not possible to go behind the confession "that God was revealed in Christ," he concluded that liberal theology's attempts to identify the historical Jesus failed.

Therefore, siding with Martin Kähler over against the early liberal quests for the historical Jesus, Bonhoeffer saw two divergent paths by which theologians have sought to focus their christological inquiry. It is also equally clear with whom he aligned himself:

> So the christological question is in its essence an ontological question. Its purpose is to bring out the ontological structure of the *who*, without getting caught in either the Scylla of the "how question" or the Charybdis of the "that question." The early church foundered on the "how question," modern theology since the Enlightenment on the "that question." Luther, Paul, and the New Testament stayed on track through the middle.[102]

100. Ibid., 313. See also 313n35, for an extended commentary on the difference Bonhoeffer drew between the incarnation, God becoming human, and the humiliation of the God-human; it is the latter, which is a reference to Paul in 1 Cor. 1:23, Christ's death on the cross, that for Bonhoeffer is more significant.
101. Ibid., 303.
102. Ibid., 304.

Said in another way, his Christology lectures point to the same understanding of God in Christ that had emerged in his earlier work. Bonhoeffer rejected outright any discussion or speculation on doctrinal formulations, especially the *how* question and, instead, focused on the question of who this Jesus is. That is the important question, for it is the one that confronts us with the real presence of God. What these lectures reveal, therefore, is Bonhoeffer's interest in humanity's encounter with God and, as with all his writings, this encounter is centered on Jesus Christ.

"Who are you?" That is the christological question. It is related to the soteriological question (the question of Jesus' work); yet the two questions must be kept separate, with priority given to the christological one. The question about person has precedence because Christ's work all by itself is not unambiguous.

> Even the works of Christ are not unambiguous. They are open to the most varied interpretations. Christ's works permit the interpretation that he is a hero, that his cross represents the consummate act of a courageous man who is true to his convictions. There is no point in the works of Jesus to which one can unambiguously refer and say that here Jesus can truly be recognized, unambiguously and without doubt, as the Son of God on the basis of his works. This is the issue, that the Son entered into the flesh, that he wants to do his work within the ambiguity of history, incognito. This incognito is the basis for the two reasons why it is impossible to recognize the person of Jesus through his work; . . . In this way, the christological question is shown to have theological priority over the soteriological question. I must first know who it is who does something before I can know what it is that the person has done. Nevertheless, it would be wrong to conclude that person and works should be considered separately. We are talking here only about the connection between the knowledge of works and the knowledge of the person, not about the real connection between person and works. The separation is only necessary for reasons of theological method. For the theological question, by nature, can only be asked of Christ in his whole being. It is the Christ of history, the whole Christ, whom we ask and who answers. But Christology asks not about what Christ has done but

> rather who Christ is. To put it in the abstract: The personal ontological structure [personale Seinstruktur] of the whole, historical Christ is the subject matter of Christology.[103]

Therefore, following Luther, Bonhoeffer insisted that the person interprets the work, rather than vice versa. In this way he contradicts both Schleiermacher and Ritschl.[104]

On the other hand, because we know who Jesus is his work becomes effective.

> But if the works of Christ are God's own works, then I am not called to do exactly as God does, to emulate God; instead, I am affected by these works as one who could in no way perform them myself. At the same time, through this discovery, through these works, through this Jesus Christ, I have found the God of mercy. My sin is forgiven me, and I am no longer in the realm of death, but rather in that of life. Thus it depends on the person of Christ, whether his works perish in the old world of death or last eternally in a new world of life.[105]

Focusing on the weak, human Jesus, there is a decidedly Lutheran quality to his argument. Quoting Luther, he said, "This is the human being to whom you should point and say, this is God."[106] Together with Luther, he insisted that the baby in the manger and the man on the cross are wholly God present for us. In fact, all that we know about God we know only through the encounter with the "humiliated Christ."[107] Conversely, when speaking of Jesus as God, "we would not speak of his being all-powerful or all-knowing; we should speak of his birth in a manger and of his cross. There is no 'divine nature' as all-powerful and ever-present."[108] In a clear

103. Ibid., 309–10.
104. Ibid., 311. See Kelly, "Revelation in Christ," 45.
105. DBWE 12:309.
106. Ibid., 318. Returning to this quote from Luther that he learned earlier from Franz Hildebrandt, Bonhoeffer used it repeatedly during the course of his lectures.
107. Ibid., 360.
108. Ibid., 354.

statement reflecting the *theologia crucis,* Bonhoeffer insisted that Jesus Christ as the God-human is the *deus absconditus*, who enters the world incognito: "He comes among us humans not in μορφὴ θεοῦ [godly form] but rather incognito, as a beggar among beggars, an outcast among outcasts; he comes among sinners as the one without sin, but also as a sinner among sinners. This is the central problem for all Christology."[109] This God does not hold anything back, but rather enters totally into this fallen creation, taking our sinful nature upon himself. Reflecting Luther's concerns stated in the *Heidelberg Disputation*, Bonhoeffer continued by insisting that there is no way around the incognito:

> If Jesus's human nature had been deified, people would have accepted this claim. If he had done signs and wonders on demand, people would have believed him. But when it comes down to cases, he withdraws. That creates a stumbling block. But everything depends on the fact that he did so. If he had replied to the question, are you the Christ? by doing a miracle, then the statement that he became a human being like us would no longer be true, since at the decisive moment an exception would have been made. That is why Christ's incognito had to become even more impenetrable, the more urgently people asked whether he were the Christ.
>
> This means that the form of the stumbling block is the form that makes possible all our faith in Christ. That is, Christ in the form of stumbling block is in the form of *Christus pro nobis*. Because Jesus wants to be our freedom, he must first become a stumbling block for us before he can be our salvation. Only by being humiliated can Christ become *pro nobis*. If he had documented himself by performing miracles, we would indeed believe, but then Christ would not be our salvation, because that would not be faith in God become human but only recognition [of a supposedly supernatural event]. But that is not faith. Faith exists when I yield myself to God, [to the extent that] I will wager my life on God's Word, even and especially there where it goes against all visible appearances. Only when I give up having visible

109. Ibid., 356.

> confirmation do I believe in God. The only guarantee that faith can bear is the Word of God itself.
>
> *Christus pro nobis* is the Christ who reconciles me with God, and that is only possible through this stumbling block and through faith. The stumbling block, which we accept, is that our faith is continually tested. But this teaches us to pay attention to the Word. Faith comes through temptation.[110]

Throughout Bonhoeffer displayed a real preference for Luther's Christology in giving emphasis to both the *finitum capax infiniti* and the *communicatio idiomatum*. It follows from this that the whole person of Christ, both human and divine, must be viewed together. This is what ultimately renders the *how* question pointless and irrelevant. Together with Luther he declared, "I cannot know who the human Christ is if I do not simultaneously think of the God-Christ and vice versa. God in his timeless eternity is *not* God. Jesus Christ in his humanity, limited in time, is *not* Jesus Christ. Instead, in the human being Jesus Christ, God is God. Only in Jesus Christ is God present."[111] Elsewhere he can say, "If we know anything about God it is because God has revealed himself through Christ."[112] Such statements, when combined with those that stress Jesus is wholly God, show the extent of that influence.

In formulating the *who* question, what becomes important is the encounter with the living Christ. This is important because it is easy to formulate our own ideas in advance, to set Jesus up as an image that resonates with us; when this happens, however, we miss him entirely. Christ then becomes the object of human inquiry and is no longer the living God who comes to us, acts upon us, and justifies us.

This encounter with the living Christ is understood along the same lines that Bonhoeffer had laid out earlier. Christ is present in the

110. Ibid., 358.
111. Ibid., 313.
112. See Kelly, "Revelation in Christ," 45.

church through the preaching of the word and the administration of the sacraments. And here, again, he relied heavily on Luther's understanding of the present Christ, defined in terms of ubiquity, which stands contrary to the Reformed church's emphasis on the *extra Calvinisticum*.[113]

Drawing on the language of *Act and Being*, Bonhoeffer repeatedly stated that God has bound himself to the world in Jesus Christ. He maintained that "both the being and the works of Christ" are present in the *pro me* structure, which is understood "according to Luther, 'Because it is one thing if God is present, and another if he is present in you.'"[114] And in describing the presence of Christ as the preached Word of God, he says, "The sermon is the form of the present Christ to whom we are committed, whom we are to follow. If Christ is not wholly present in the sermon, the church breaks down. The human word and God's Word are not simply mutually exclusive; instead, God's Word, Jesus Christ, as the Word of God that has taken human form, is the Word of God that has humbled itself by entering into the human word." Here again, he refers to Luther's quote, "This is the human being to whom you should point and say, this is God." But in case of preaching, he notes it should be altered to read, "This is the human word to which you should point and say, this is God! The two statements mean the same thing. For I cannot point to the human being unless I am pointing to this Jesus."[115] Noting that God is present not only in the preached word but in the sacraments as well, he said that the word of God "in the sacrament is the Word in bodily form. The sacrament does not represent the 'Word,' for only that which is not present can be represented. The sacrament is the form of the Word." For by his word, "God has bound himself

113. See DBWE 12:320.
114. Ibid., 314.
115. Ibid., 318.

to the sacrament, that is, Jesus Christ is one who is bound by the sacrament. The God-human Jesus Christ is wholly present in the sacrament."[116] All of this led him to the same conclusion that he had already reached in *Santorum Communio*, namely, that "Christ exists as church-community," but in this case with the added identifier: the one "who is present, exalted and humiliated."[117] Christ *pro me*, the humiliated and risen Christ existing as church-community, is the center of human existence. Standing between God and humanity, in fact standing in humanity's place before God, Christ stands at the center of the new humanity, at the center of human existence and history. As the hidden center of human history, fulfiller of all messianic hopes and promises, means that "in Christ the messianic expectation of history is crushed as well as fulfilled. It is crushed because its fulfillment is hidden. It is fulfilled because the Messiah has truly come. The meaning of history is swallowed up in an event that takes place in the deepest desolation of human life, on the cross. History finds its meaning in the humiliation of Christ."[118]

There is an interesting dialectic that shapes Bonhoeffer's Christology. On the one hand, he rejected the liberal Protestant historical Jesus as a basis for Christology. On the other hand, while his Christology is based on the doctrinal traditions of the church, he makes clear that Chalcedon, as important as it is for setting the parameters for christological reflection, does not limit, but rather sets the bare minimum necessary for defining Christology. This position may indeed make Bonhoeffer a modern theologian, but one set apart from the liberal nineteenth-century Protestant theologians. Rather, by reaching back to the formulation of the sixteenth century, he recasts the tradition in light of modern thought patterns.

116. Ibid., 318–19.
117. Ibid., 323.
118. Ibid., 325.

For Bonhoeffer, the central problem of Christology was that even after the resurrection, Christ remains incognito. We know him only as the humiliated one. Incognito (God hidden, known under the opposites) and humiliation (weakness and the cross) are characteristics of the *theologia crucis.* "We can have the Exalted One only as the Crucified One. The resurrection of Christ does not get us around the stumbling block. Even the Risen One remains the stumbling block for us. If it were not so, he would not be for us. Jesus's resurrection does not jeopardize the incognito."[119]

When sifting through the academic language geared to unraveling the contours of the christological controversy, Bonhoeffer's concern remained focused clearly on the human, weak Jesus. There can be little question that Bonhoeffer's radical "this-worldly" orientation has its foundations firmly rooted in the cross of Christ; there we know that God has not abandoned the world. On the contrary, God has taken the human situation seriously—indeed, has taken the world so seriously as to have identified with its pain. This God who is present in the suffering Jesus does not hold anything back, but rather enters totally into this fallen creation, taking our sinful nature upon himself. The cross is the place, the only place, where God is to be found in the world.

As was true for Luther, is true for Bonhoeffer as well. The *theologia crucis* is a way of talking about the whole Christ-event, and is not limited only to the cross. In fact, Bonhoeffer says without the resurrection there would be no possibility of talking about the present Christ. If talk were limited to the cross alone, then all talk would stop with the historical Jesus and an encounter with the living Lord would not be possible. The presence of the living Lord is all important;

119. Ibid., 359.

without the resurrection of Christ, Jesus would be seen "only as dead and gone, the way we might think about Goethe or Socrates."[120]

These lectures were "the high point of Bonhoeffer's academic career." But even more than that, they

> bring together all the disparate threads of his new understanding of both himself and of his commitment to Jesus Christ. In these lectures his life and his theology appeared to converge. What is more, his Christology had become the interpretive key to reading the Bible and to his vinegary judgments on church and society, on contemporary ethics, and on the liberal reduction of dogmatics to what Barth correctly detected to be merely a humanistic domestication of God himself.[121]

Given the context, these lectures were not merely of academic interest for either Bonhoeffer or his hearers. They both summarized his thought to this point and "provided the foundation for his own professional life as he moved Christology to the still center of all his thought." As a result, they become the means by which Bonhoeffer addressed the challenges facing the church. Therefore, Larry Rasmussen concludes, "It is not too much to say that Bonhoeffer's Christology was not only the ground for his critique of National Socialism; it was the basis for his efforts to find a way beyond the present crisis and beyond the church as well as within it." When the Confessing Church failed to live up to the early expectations he had in it, "Bonhoeffer's Christology led him to the conspiracy as the other viable community open for the exercise of vicarious representative action and genuine responsibility."[122]

120. Ibid., 312.
121. Kelly and Nelson, *TF*, 11.
122. Rasmussen, "Editor's Introduction," DBWE 12:37–38.

## Summary

It is not an understatement to say that for Luther, Christ as the Word of God is essential. Without this christocentric core, justification of sinners would be impossible and one would be talking about a different gospel. For him, the *sola scriptura, sola fides, sola gratia*, his key Reformation insights at the heart of his teaching on justification, have their foundation in the *solus Christus*. Without Christ any talk of justification would be empty, and the result would be that humanity is thrown back upon itself. The biblical message, however, moves in the opposite direction. Through Christ, God accomplishes the reconciliation that was impossible by human beings when left on their own. Luther, therefore, could not conceive of justification or a renewed relationship with God without understanding it from the perspective of Jesus' death on the cross.

What Bonhoeffer's thinking reflects up to this point are the commitments, concerns, and viewpoint of Luther. Like Luther, Bonhoeffer's thinking can be summarized in terms of *solus Christus*. It is in Christ alone that we know God. It is in Christ alone that the world and the church are judged and it is in Christ alone that a new humanity is created. It is Bonhoeffer's commitment to Jesus Christ that gives him the perspective from which to critique the church's action in the world. Rather than focusing on the ethical or political questions, it comes to down one thing: Christ.

Unlike both his teachers in Berlin, for whom Jesus Christ was not central, and Karl Barth, who reserved space outside of Christ for knowledge of God, Bonhoeffer sided with Luther and found God completely present in Christ. From his own statements, for him one cannot properly understand God, the church, justification, or the world without direct reference to Jesus Christ. This remains true throughout the remainder of his life.

Christ is present, but only as the humiliated one. Through Christ on the cross we know the reality of God and the world. Hence, what we have at the center of Bonhoeffer's christological thinking is a cross of reality. Because one cannot perceive God without the world, or properly conceive of the world without God, Bonhoeffer's cross of reality is this-worldly in orientation and content. This does not mean that one turns away from the church for the world, but rather one finds God only in the world and encounters God only as one goes about one's day-to-day life. Those with eyes of faith recognize this, so it is in and through the church, where the gospel is proclaimed and the sacraments are celebrated, that it is known that God is present for us.

Therefore, to renounce the world is to renounce God, its Creator. The world, though fallen, has been redeemed by God in Christ. Christian life, therefore, should reflect the same care and concern for the world that God has exhibited. Living faithfully in the world, taking responsibility for the world, is the Christian's calling. These themes will be developed further in chapter 9.

As a result of his christological orientation, Bonhoeffer holds a high view of the world, which has been created and redeemed by God. Likewise, Bonhoeffer's charges against the church (which emerge during the Church Struggle) came as a result of the church's not living up to its responsibilities as the people of God—the body of Christ. Seeking refuge from the world, or by seeking to secure a place for itself in the world, was contrary to God's act in Christ.

Cliff Green has stated that *Sanctorum Communio* is a foundational work, without which it is easy to misunderstand Bonhoeffer's later theology;[123] the same might be said of this whole formative period. Elements of Bonhoeffer's thinking come together (albeit in stages)

123. See Clifford Green, "Editor's Introduction," *Sanctorum Communio,* DBWE 1:7.

in these early writings that will form the core for his theological reflections in what is to come.

After reviewing Bonhoeffer's early work, we can draw the following conclusions: First, the earliest evidence available from Bonhoeffer's student years shows that he had a fascination with Luther. Second, at the same time, questions centered on Christology are present in his thinking from the beginning. Third, his early study of Luther parallels and reflects Karl Holl's own study, which shows the extent of Holl's influence. Fourth, Bonhoeffer created a personal identification with Luther through these studies, seeing Luther's struggles as his own. But fifth, there are stages of development in Bonhoeffer's own Luther interpretation. In his seminar papers, he relied almost exclusively on Holl for both the content and structure of his papers. But when he began reading Luther on his own, readings that concentrated on the early Luther, changes emerge that will eventually separate Bonhoeffer's interpretation from that of Karl Holl. This brings Bonhoeffer to his own independent reading of Luther and when he does, Christology, which is increasingly focused on the cross of Christ, becomes the norm for both his theological reflection and his life of faith. And finally, throughout his career, Bonhoeffer treats Luther with great reverence and finds in him a positive theological authority.

It will be the task of part 3 to show how these themes are expressed in Bonhoeffer's theology as he entered the German Church Struggle and, later, the resistance.

PART IV

# Christological Development and Witness: 1933–1945

# 6

# The German Church Struggle

In the first of his Finkenwalde newsletters on November 15, 1935, Bonhoeffer told his former students, "The summer of 1935 was, I believe, the most fulfilling period in my entire life thus far both professionally and personally."[1] These words are telling in that they reveal a great deal about how Bonhoeffer saw his vocation. Finding himself in a ministry far different than he could have imagined years earlier, what he discovered was that the underground seminary at Finkenwalde was perhaps his highest calling. "Being director of Finkenwalde matched his skills and was a platform for his theological concerns. Instead of moving him to the fringes of the Church Struggle, Finkenwalde served to place him at the center of the struggle and positioned him to lay the foundation for the renewal of the church."[2]

His time at Finkenwalde prepared him to answer his own question from his prison cell a few years later: "Who is Christ actually for

1. DBWE 14:119.
2. H. Gaylon Barker, "Editor's Introduction to the English Edition," DBWE 14:1.

us today?" In one sense, everything to that point was preparing and pointing him in that direction. From what we have seen from Bonhoeffer's writings thus far, this concern represents the continuation and fulfillment of his christocentric preoccupation that began while a student. What emerges during this period is his concern to find more specific ways to relate that faith to his context.

As he sought to locate God in the concrete reality of this world and attempted to live out the implications of such a faith, he was never content with living by a set of principles or ideals. In defining his life in terms of Christian discipleship, it was a matter of living out his faith in Jesus Christ in the concrete realities of life in the here and now. Because faith is a relationship with Jesus Christ, it is a living, dynamic reality and becomes an expression of one's life. As a result, faith is always probing and asking questions, never assuming that discipleship was a fixed commodity to be lived out by repetition.

Christology, therefore, was more than an academic question for Bonhoeffer. First and foremost, it was a faith question. Therefore, when changes took place in his world, he found that he had to wrestle with the implications of his faith as well. It is this faith question, and his constant reflection on its implication, that moves Bonhoeffer from a preoccupation with the academic theological questions to living out the faith implied in those questions.

In finding himself immersed in the emerging German Church Struggle, he could no longer remain behind the safety and security of the lecturer's podium; for that reason, upon the completion of the summer semester 1933, he took leave of his university responsibilities. Just months after Hitler's election as chancellor of Germany, several changes were made and laws implemented that threatened the life of the church.[3] In that context and for that reason, he worked with

3. For background on the historical context, see Larry Rasmussen, "Editor's Introduction to the English Edition," DBWE 12:3ff; Barker, "Editor's Introduction to the English Edition," DBWE

Martin Niemöller and others to help form the Pastors' Emergency League, the group that would become the Confessing Church months later. However, by the fall of 1933 his direct involvement in the Church Struggle took an odd turn, when he left Germany to serve two German-speaking congregations in London.

His decision to go to London was due in part to his increasing feelings of isolation within the church struggle. The majority of the Young Reformers and the Pastors' Emergency League did not share his sense of urgency; indeed, many thought he was too radical in his stance toward the German Christians. Bonhoeffer, however, believed that nothing should compromise the church's confession of Christ alone, which is precisely what he identified as the core issue. Acknowledging the tensions between Bonhoeffer and his colleagues in the church struggle, John de Gruchy points out, "Bonhoeffer already in 1933, right at the outset of Hitler's rise to power, was only too aware of the dangers ahead and of the extent to which the church could not remain aloof from the burning ethical issues of the day by recourse to a misappropriation of Luther's teaching on the two kingdoms."[4] He goes on to describe the conditions that led to Bonhoeffer's uncompromising position: "In the land of the Reformation the doctrine of the two kingdoms was operative in such a way that the church was prevented from exercising any politically critical or prophetic function."[5]

Finding refuge in London provided Bonhoeffer with a perspective from which to view what was happening to his church and his country from a new angle. This new perspective and the actions

14:2ff; and Ferdinand Schlingensiepen, *Dietrich Bonhoeffer 1906–1945: Martyr, Thinker, Man of Resistance* (New York: T & T Clark, 2010), chapter 3.

4. John de Gruchy, "*Sanctorum Communio* and the Ethics of Free Responsibility: Reflections on Bonhoeffer's Ecclesiology and Ethics," in *For All People: Global Theologies in Contexts*, ed. Else Marie Wilberg Pedersen, Holger Lam, and Peter Lodberg (Grand Rapids: Eerdmans, 2002), 88.
5. Ibid., 101.

that grew out of it continued to be informed by his faith in and commitment to Jesus Christ. Because of the way in which he conceived of God relating to the world in the *theologia crucis*, it was not possible to separate the issues facing the church from the rest of the world; instead, his worldly concerns and commitments became all the more intensified because of his faith.

During this period, 1933–1945, Bonhoeffer's academic interests fall into the background as his theology is placed in the service of the church; this means that his writings from this period are now written under different circumstances and take on a different character. Even the more systematic writings, such as *Discipleship*, are written to address issues arising out the German Church Struggle. Bonhoeffer's cross of reality will emerge as the thread that holds his life and theology together.

## The Impending Crisis

Upon the completion of his teaching responsibilities at the end of the summer semester 1933, Bonhoeffer prepared to depart for London, where he would spend the next eighteen months serving two congregations in the German-speaking community. Prior to his departure for London, however, he spent the month of August at Bethel, Germany, where he went to work on the Bethel Confession, one of the foundational documents of the emerging Confessing Church, along with Franz Hildebrandt, Hermann Sasse, and others.[6] Bethge has alluded to the urgency of this task in his description of the events and turmoil that marked the summer of 1933. The growing power of the German Christians created a situation in which there was a demand for clarity on the basic confession of the church.

6. *DB-ER*, 300ff. For more on the Sasse/Bonhoeffer relationship, see Maurice Schild, "Hermann Sasse and Dietrich Bonhoeffer: Churchmen on the Brink," *The Bonhoeffer Legacy: Australasian Journal of Bonhoeffer Studies* 2, no. 1 (2014): 45–56.

Given the circumstances, "In Bethel, Sasse and Bonhoeffer began work on the document that was to confront these same German Christians with the question of truth. The time seemed ripe for such a move. Throughout the country people were working on drafts for confessions,"[7] all intended to address the heretical teachings of the German Christians.

This task was viewed as necessary, because a majority of the people, including leaders of the church, was either supportive or uncritical of National Socialism. Those who supported Hitler did so because they believed he would restore traditional moral values to Germany. Heinz Eduard Tödt, for example, points out that "a large majority believed that they could stand for the cause of the church, and yet remain unpolitical but affirmative of the state. They lived in an enormous delusion as to the true character of National Socialism, because they did not want to interfere in politics and did not look for realistic information. Bonhoeffer the theologian did not give in to such delusions."[8]

Kyle Jantzen, in *Faith and Fatherland: Parish Politics in Hitler's Germany*, offers additional insights. He says that even though Hitler and Nazi ideology contradicted almost every core Christian belief, pastors and parishioners were inclined to favor them, primarily because the "protestant pastors feared they were losing their place in society." He goes on to say that they were motivated by four factors: 1) they believed that political renewal would bring about a moral renewal; 2) clergy believed that they were being called to a partnership with Hitler in this process of renewal; 3) they feared Communism; and 4) because of problematic elements in their theology, the clergy were predisposed to authoritarian politics. So it

7. *DB-ER*, 300.
8. Heinz Eduard Tödt, *Authentic Faith: Bonhoeffer's Ethics in Context* (Grand Rapids: Eerdmans, 1993), 8.

was that many warmly embraced Hitler's assent to power, seeing it positively as a way to renewal of the German nation. "With the new state," declared Ravensburg church superintendent Hermann Ströle, "a spiritual change is also being generated. Through this spiritual change, the church will be called to a new great service . . . for our nation."[9]

An example of the church's support for the new Nazi state came from Bavarian Lutheran bishop Hans Meiser; he prepared a proclamation to be read from pulpits on Easter Sunday 1933, in which the new government and the future prospects for the renewal of society and the church were praised.

> A state which brings into being again government according to God's Laws should, in doing so, be assured not only of the applause but also of the glad and active co-operation of the Church. With gratitude and joy the Church takes note that the new state bans blasphemy, assails immorality, establishes discipline and order, with a strong hand, while at the same time calling upon man to fear God, espousing the sanctity of marriage and Christian training for the young, bringing into honor again the deeds of our fathers and kindling in thousands of hearts, in place of disparagement, an ardent love of *Volk* and Fatherland.[10]

The goal at Bethel, therefore, was to produce a confessional document that was "usable and widely accepted by the time the national synod met at the beginning of September."[11] Through their efforts, a clear attempt by members of the nascent Confessing Church to respond to the political and theological challenges before them

9. Kyle Jantzen, *Faith and Fatherland: Parish Politics in Hitler's Germany* (Minneapolis: Fortress Press, 2008), 2, 17–19.

10. Cited in Matthew D. Hockenos, *A Church Divided: German Protestants Confront the Nazi Past* (Bloomington, IN: Indiana University Press, 2004), 17. See chap. 1 for a description of the various positions taken by church leaders. See also Schlingensiepen, *Dietrich Bonhoeffer 1906–1945*, 193–94.

11. DB-ER, 301. See also Christine-Ruth Müller, *Bekenntnis und Bekennen: Dietrich Bonhoeffer in Bethel (1933); ein lutherischer Versuch* (Munich: Chr. Kaiser, 1989), 10ff, for an added perspective on the urgency of a new confession for the church.

was on display. Far from being limited to issues of politics and the church's relationship to and involvement in matters of government, the Confessing Church struggle was centered on the church's confession of faith. Since the very foundation of the church's existence was tied to its confession, it became a matter of truth. And Bonhoeffer, one of the early advocates of the Confessing Church and one of its most avid defenders, was adamant in his insistence on affirming the core confession of Christ.

The debate within the Confessing Church centered on the fight against the German Christians and how to appropriately respond to the challenges their ideology posed. However, since there was no clear consensus, the problem facing the Confessing Church leaders was how to overcome the differences within the Confessing Church and to establish an identity for it. In that regard, the Bethel Confession (and the later Barmen Declaration) became important documents.

The differences within the Confessing Church were the differences between the radicals and moderates in their attitudes and responses to the German Christians. The radicals, such as Bonhoeffer, wanted a confessional identity over against the German Christians. The moderates, including the majority of the Lutherans, on the other hand, wanted a confession that did not exclude anyone. So while the radicals wanted a confession that clearly stated that there was no room for Nazi ideology in the church, the moderates were looking for a common ground that would somehow serve to bring the "misguided" German Christians back into the fold.[12] It is from within this context that Bonhoeffer's work at Bethel in August 1933 and his future work in the Confessing Church must be understood.

12. See Victoria Barnett, *For the Soul of the People: Protestant Protest against Hitler* (New York: Oxford University Press, 1992), 54–55. See also Hockenos, *Church Divided*, chap. 1

The Bethel Confession[13] was Bonhoeffer's early attempt to formulate his theological convictions to serve the church; it was an urgent call for the church to be clear about its faith. That meant, ultimately, drawing distinctions between what might be believed in general and what were the specific teachings, beliefs, and practices of the Christian community. The importance of the work that was set before Bonhoeffer and his colleagues comes through in his own words. Writing to his grandmother, he explained their theological task in either/or terms:

> Our work here is very enjoyable and also very demanding. We want to try to make the German Christians declare their intentions. I rather doubt we shall succeed. Even if, at this point, they make concessions in their official formulations, they are under such strong pressure that sooner or later any promises made are bound to break down. It is becoming increasingly clear to me that what we are going to get is a big, *völkisch* national church that in its essence can no longer be reconciled with Christianity, and that we must make up our minds to take entirely new paths and follow where they lead. The issue is really Germanism or Christianity, and the sooner the conflict comes out in the open, the better. The greatest danger of all would be in trying to conceal this.[14]

13. See DBWE 12:374ff. See also Carsten Nicolaisen, "Concerning the History of the Bethel Confession," in DBWE 12:509–13. See Guy Carter, "Confession at Bethel, August 1933—Enduring Witness: The Formation, Revision and Significance of the First Full Theological Confession of the Evangelical Church Struggle in Nazi Germany" (PhD diss., Marquette University, April 1987), for a detailed study of the Bethel Confession. As Kelly and Nelson, *TF*, point out, despite its shortcomings (one of which, as they note, was the inclusion of language that still blamed the Jews for rejecting Christ), "It expresses new beginnings in the church's attitude toward Jews. . . . This confession remains important because it is so revealing of the theological clash between the German Christians and the group represented by Bonhoeffer and Vischer" (134). Cf. Stephen Haynes, *The Bonhoeffer Legacy: Post-Holocaust Perspectives* (Minneapolis: Fortress Press, 2006), 74–82, for an examination of the Bethel Confession with regard to the Jewish question. According to Klaus Scholder, "The original version of the Bethel confession remains a brilliant, sharp and impressive witness to what theological work was still capable of achieving in summer 1933" and "theologically and politically clearer and more exact in some passage than the famous Barmen Declaration of May 1934" (*The Churches and the Third Reich*, vol. 1, *Preliminary History and the Time of Illusions 1918–1934*, trans. John Bowden [Philadelphia: Fortress Press, 1988], 456).
14. DBWE 12:159.

The high hopes that Bonhoeffer held for this task, however, were short-lived. After they completed their draft, the document went through so many revisions at the hands of others that "their text was watered down to such an extent that he ultimately refused to work on the final edition."[15] It was with great disappointment, therefore, that Bonhoeffer headed to London and continued his participation in the church struggle through ecumenical channels.

Following the major victory of the German Christians in the July 1933 church elections, many church leaders, including Martin Niemöller, saw the need for a new confession that would clearly lay out the core beliefs of the Christian faith. As a result of the German Christians' clear victory, Guy Carter, in his work on the Bethel Confession, characterizes the situation as an emergency: "The time of church-political maneuvering and bridge-building with the German-Christians was decisively over," leaving "theological confession" as "the only path of resistance left."[16]

In a matter of days, the urgency of the challenge was articulated. At a meeting of the Young Reformers on August 2, 1933, Niemöller saw the task as follows:

> That which has been devised by the German-Christian majority must now come to pass in the church. The congregation of Jesus Christ shall be that one which is ready to confess, if a confession is really demanded of it. The task which arises here is set inwardly for us: it is appropriate to assemble the faithful members of the congregation . . . especially with an eye toward determining what the confessional foundation of the church is and must remain . . . in an outwardly articulate manner: It is appropriate to place the new leadership of the church and the

15. *DB-ER*, 303. Kelly and Nelson, *TF*, 134, add, "Because the strengths of the section Bonhoeffer and Sasse wrote were diluted by heavy editing and because of other changes to make the overall text more acceptable, Bonhoeffer would eventually refuse to sign the document at its November 1933 publication by Martin Niemöller." In all, four versions of the Bethel Confession were produced. For a detailed comparison of the four versions, see Müller, *Bekenntnis und Bekennen*, and Carter, "Confession at Bethel."

16. Carter, "Confession at Bethel," 50–51.

> German-Christian movement which is authoritative for it before the confessional question. Is there a theologically fundamental difference between Reformation doctrine and that which the German-Christians proclaim? We fear: Yes! They say: No! This confusion must be clarified through a contemporary confession. If the initiative will not come from the other side–and it does not appear that it will come soon–then it must therefore come from us; and it must come in such a way that the other side must either say "Yes" or No" to it. The relationship of the three articles of the Creed will be decisive in such a confession.[17]

It was with such urgency that Bonhoeffer, Sasse, and others met at Bethel later that month to write a draft of a new confession. Rather than being simply a debate over the church's polity, the context in 1933 Germany created a *status confessionis*[18] that required the church

17. Cited in ibid., 51.
18. In *A Time for Confessing* (Grand Rapids: Eerdmans, 2008), 65, Robert Bertram describes the challenges to the church created by National Socialism, creating a *status confessionis*: "It is a 'time for confessing,' the Formula of Concord calls it, whenever the church is in danger of abdicating its unique authority to an overreaching secular authority. The secular pretender may be the state or the people as a whole or the secular power of the ecclesiastical institution itself or, most likely, all of these together. Against these usurpers the church's confessors must testify, even when the state is immensely popular as under Hitler, even when the people are a defeated and voiceless nationality as the Germans were then, even when the church's own leadership sides with this yearning ethnic folk and their revolutionary government. Against these encroaching secular powers the confessing church must testify, not in order to nullify secular authority, but in order rather to restore the church to its own distinctive priorities, where the authority of Christ's gospel is supreme and where secular authority, even if that also is Christ's, is strictly subordinate." According to Müller, *Bekenntnis und Bekennen*, 11, the "Jewish Question" created this situation for Bonhoeffer, and it was for that reason that Bonhoeffer sought to clarify the theological foundation of the church's confession. Rather than being a political issue, the Aryan Clause and the Jewish Question represented a challenge to the theological heritage of the church. Because the church struggle was defined in theological rather than political terms, it created a *status confessions* and called for a new confessional statement. See Schlingensiepen, *Dietrich Bonhoeffer 1906–1945*, 137, where he describes Bonhoeffer's stance that "the Aryan paragraph as adopted by the church [was] blatantly false doctrine." Heinz Eduard Tödt shares in this judgment, concluding that "Bonhoeffer recognised that with this matter the churches had come to the decisive turning point of unacceptable heresy (*status confessionis*), and called them to stand by their confession. Furthermore, with political foresight he shared the judgment of those who were persuaded that Hitler would mean a new war of extermination" ("Dietrich Bonhoeffer's Decisions in the Crisis Years 1929–33," *Studies in Christian Ethics* 18, 3 [2005]: 108). In addition, Kelly and Nelson, *TF*, 135, make the point that the Bethel Confession is a forthright rejection of the church's anti-Semitism and the church leaders who readily accepted the racist policies of Hitler's government: "We can see that this confession . . . is a sharp repudiation of Aryanism and the Nazi aims to rid the German nation and church of

to state as clearly as possible its beliefs in the face of heretical claims that would distort the church's message.[19] The question of *status confessionis* would become a central issue for Bonhoeffer during the Finkenwalde period;[20] however, in a short essay written at about this same time, he had already articulated its importance, saying that theology should prepare one "to discern the spirits in Christ's church" to distinguish "what is the pure and true teaching of the gospel of Jesus Christ, and which are human teachings, human laws, false doctrines, and idolatry." He went on to say that "one must learn to recognize where and when the church of Christ reaches its hour of decision, when it is time for confession—the *status confessionis*."[21] It seemed as though that time had come. It was deemed no longer sufficient to simply "refer back to the Reformation confession." What

any Jewish presence and influence. In its own way, it represents a major move away from some of the old slogans that have been used to slander the Jewish people and to make the persecution of them seem religiously justified. This confession criticizes the attitudes of church leaders who themselves subscribed to the nation's racist policies and, what is startling, given the long history of Christian anti-Semitism, emphasized God's continued fidelity to Israel and the indestructibility of the Jewish people themselves. These were formulations close to treason in those days of racial hatred."

19. Of the work carried out at Bethel, Bethge, *DB-ER*, 303, says, "With theological conscientiousness, the group in Bethel tried to make its teachings relevant for the times. In an address to German pastors in Bradford, Yorkshire, Bonhoeffer described the nature of the work that had defined Confessing statements from trinitarian doctrine to eschatology. They had made a number of reformulations: in the doctrine of justification, to unmask Ludwig Müller's trite reduction of Christianity to trust in God and being good fellows; in the doctrine of the cross, so as to pillory the reinterpretation of the cross as a symbol of the Nazi slogan 'public interest before self-interest' by Friedrich Wieneke, the German Christian chaplain to the Prussian court; and finally, in the doctrine of the Holy Spirit, from a christological standpoint, with renewed emphasis on the *filoque*, so as to guard against the dangerous emphasis that Hirsch, Althaus, and Fezer put on the revelation in the creation, and to refute its consequences in Stapel's independent notion of the law of race." For additional background on *status confessionis* in the Lutheran tradition, see Edward H. Schroeder, "Forward," in Bertram, *Time for Confessing*.
20. The conditions setting forth a *status confessionis* were spelled out in the Formula of Concord 10 (*The Book of Concord: The Confessions of the Lutheran Church*, ed. Robert Kolb and Timothy J. Wengert [Minneapolis: Fortress Press, 2000], 635ff), a document that became an important resource and part of Bonhoeffer's curriculum at Finkenwalde.
21. "What Should a Student of Theology Do Today?" DBWE 12:434.

was needed was "*a* new confession which would apply *the* confession to the present."[22]

At the heart of this new confession drafted by Bonhoeffer and his colleagues was article 5 on Jesus Christ. After studying the language of the document, Carter concludes that there is little doubt that this comes from Bonhoeffer's hand.[23] While the August draft of the confession was created as a collaborative effort between Bonhoeffer and other theologians, each contributing different parts, the emphasis of article 5 on Jesus Christ was Bonhoeffer's. When compared to his Christology lectures he had just completed, there were obvious points of similarities in the wording and emphases of the Bethel Confession.[24] Even though this article is marked by brevity, according to Carter, it nevertheless plays a central role in shaping the argument of the entire document.[25]

While an analysis of the entire confession is beyond the scope of this work, by drawing attention to Bonhoeffer's influence in terms of its christological affirmation, the Bethel Confession demonstrates the manner in which Bonhoeffer applied his academic interests and faith commitments to the service of the church.

Designed to provide a counter to the stance of the German Christians, article 5 begins by affirming the classic Christian teachings about Jesus: He is the "Son of God and Son of David, true God and true human being;" he is "the end and fulfillment of the law," without whom the world would be lost under the wrath of God. "Jesus was crucified for the sake of the guilt of all people and through their lack of faith."[26] Citing portions of Luther's explanation of the second article of the Apostles' Creed from the *Small Catechism*

22. Carter, "Confession at Bethel," 51 (emphasis in the original).
23. Ibid., 77f. Cf. DBWE 12:374n2.
24. Carter, "Confession at Bethel," 221–22.
25. Ibid., 226.
26. DBWE 12:396.

as a basis for this confessional stance, Bonhoeffer went on to state that the church rejects the false claims that present Jesus as a "flare of nordic light" or his cross as "symbol for a generalized religious or human truth" or "anything whatever." In contrast to any general religious sentiments, Bonhoeffer claimed that Jesus is the Son of God and Son of David "sent to the lost sheep of the house of Israel" and his cross is the "unique revelatory act of God" that brings reconciliation with God.[27] Therefore the crucifixion of Jesus is not to be confused with any other sacrifice, nor can the suffering of Jesus be equated with the suffering of any other person or people: "The passion of Jesus Christ should not be compared with the passion of any other person or people. Christ's passion and cross can only be proclaimed as God's judgment on and mercy for the entire world."[28]

From this confessional basis, what is condemned were the attempts by the German Christians to turn Jesus into an idealized "Aryan type" to fit Nazi ideology. In contrast to that position, Bonhoeffer stressed the Jewishness of Jesus. And rather than accepting the widespread assumption that the Jews were responsible for the death of Jesus, Bonhoeffer, by stressing Jesus' own Jewishness, preferred to call him the "Son of David," and concentrated on the sinfulness of all humankind, implicating not the Jews but all people in the death of Jesus. Therefore, anyone who rejects Christ, regardless of his or her race, is guilty of putting him to death. By the same token, citing Isa. 53:6 and articles 13 and 24 from the *Apology of the Augsburg*

27. According to Carter, "Confession at Bethel," 224, there is "no more characteristically Bonhoefferian section in the entire Bethel Confession than this third condemnation in the fifth article. 'The cross of Jesus Christ is not a symbol for anything whatever, but is rather God's unique act of self-revelation . . .' Just as Bonhoeffer taught that it was impossible to 'penetrate behind God creating . . . to go behind the beginning,' so also here the redemptive act of God on the cross is not to be interpreted by some other reality. It is rather *the* reality of God in the world against which all other reality is to be compared and interpreted and not vice versa."

28. DBWE 12:397–98.

*Confession,* Bonhoeffer claimed that the act of this Jewish man benefits all.[29]

As already noted, the confession was not as warmly received as Bonhoeffer had hoped. Since it was produced early in the church struggle, this was due in part to the fact that some within the leadership were still hoping that some middle ground could be found. For others, however, the document was "too Lutheran."[30] Indeed, it "has a pronounced Lutheran emphasis, including many quotes from the Lutheran confessions. This was due as much to Bonhoeffer as to the more experienced Sasse."[31]

## London 1934–1935

Even though Bonhoeffer removed himself from the German context, he remained an active member of the Confessing Church, hosting visiting theologians in London, working with ecumenical leaders, carrying on regular correspondence, and making regular trips back and forth to Berlin.[32] Since he maintained a busy schedule attending to the many aspects of parish life and participating in the ecumenical movement, the sermons he preached while serving as a pastor in London provide some of the best views into his theological stance at the time. What his sermons reveal was one wrestling with the church's need for clarity. The importance of this theme is captured in the urgency of the language that pervades them. Therefore, they can be seen as a continuation of thinking prior to his departure from

29. Ibid., 398.
30. *DB-ER*, 302.
31. Charles Ford, "Dietrich Bonhoeffer, the Resistance, and the Two Kingdoms," *Lutheran Forum* 27, no. 3 (August 1993): 32. Müller, *Bekenntnis und Bekennen*, 21, states it even more strongly: "Bonhoeffer played the decisive role in the conception and creation of the first draft."
32. See Keith Clements, "Editor's Introduction to the English Edition," DBWE 13:1–10.

Berlin.[33] A sampling of the sermons from this period provides ample evidence of this.

Bonhoeffer preached on Luke 1:46–55, the Magnificat, on the third Sunday of Advent, December 17, 1933.[34] In this sermon he relied on the images of the human infant Jesus in the manger to communicate the message of hope that belongs to the Advent season. Drawing on the language of Mary's Advent hymn, Bonhoeffer proclaimed that God is present not in those places where human strength and goodness are exhibited, but is found where human understanding, human nature, and piety reach their end. Instead of locating God in places that might celebrate human achievement, everything about God points in the opposite direction. "For just this is the miracle of all miracles, that God loves the lowly. God 'has looked with favor on the lowliness of his servant.' God in the midst of lowliness—that is the revolutionary, passionate word of Advent."[35]

Seen in that way, Bonhoeffer could say that Christ is both "the poor son of a laborer from the East End London," and "Christ in the manger." There is a "real world" connection between the incarnation, by which God enters the world as a lowly baby in a manger, and the struggles of real people in the real world. In both instances we see that

> God is not ashamed of human lowliness but goes right into the middle of it, chooses someone as instrument, and performs the miracles right there where they are least expected. God draws near to the lowly, loving the lost, the unnoticed, the unremarkable, the excluded, the powerless, and the broken.

33. According to Ernst Feil, *TDB*, 77, "The sermons Bonhoeffer preached in London show in some measure that the christological orientation had gained momentum."
34. DBWE 13:342ff.
35. Ibid., 343.

That is the blessing of Advent. In fact, Mary can call herself blessed, because "God seeks out not the heights but rather the depths, and that we see the glory and power of God by seeing made great what was small." It is because God comes into the world in the manger at Bethlehem that there is a new ordering of things in this world. What is experienced by those who celebrate Advent and Christmas is nothing other than the judgment and redemption of the world, and it takes place in the manger. Christmas is a time to celebrate the coming of God into the world and the place where God is present is not with the strong and mighty; instead, "the throne of God in the world is not set on the thrones of humankind, but in humanity's deepest abysses, in the manger."[36]

St. Paul's church, the Reformed congregation that Bonhoeffer served in London, had an English language service one Sunday evening per month. Two of the sermons Bonhoeffer preached there in 1934 have survived, and in both instances they show Bonhoeffer's characteristic christocentric approach to the Christian faith. In one such service Bonhoeffer preached on Prov. 16:9. Reflecting on the circumstances that brought him and all the members of his congregation to London, Bonhoeffer asked, "On which way were they led? Which were the multifarious motives and which was the strange destiny that brought them here?"[37] Far too often, he said, people reach the conclusion that life is in their hands, that through their own plans and hard work, they have achieved success or have arrived at the place in life they find themselves. Reflecting common wisdom, we believe, "It lies all with me and you, if we make our life a success or a failure, if we are happy or not, it depends altogether on my willpower, my work, my sacrifices, my temperament and

36. Ibid., 343–45. The language here is a vivid reflection of Luther's use of the *communicatio idiomatum*.

37. Ibid., 397. English original, including grammatical errors.

my gifts, if we are content or if we are always discontented and grumbling against our fate."[38]

Preaching to a community of business people and expatriates who in one way or another saw their success as the result of their own efforts, the gospel message Bonhoeffer wanted to convey was of another sort, one that stood in contradiction to popular wisdom. Both as a means of preserving the uniqueness of the biblical message and of preventing individuals from extracting bits of wisdom from it that one could then apply to one's life, Bonhoeffer insisted that the world of the Bible was different from the modern world. The Bible's message is that people are not in charge of their own lives. Therefore, two options are available. One can either live by one's "own ideas, plans and devices and believes them to be the ultimate reality" or one may realize "that neither his ideas and wishes nor even his highest willpower may destine his life, but that there exists some other unknown, unseen and hidden element which alone matters, which is behind everything, which makes history of men and nations, which is the ultimate reality–called God Almighty." Therefore, contrary to what people might think, it is not simply a matter of believing that they are in charge of their own destiny. In actuality,

> Our life is not a simple straight line, drawn by our own will and mind, but life is something which is composed of two different lines, two different elements, two different powers–life is composed of man's thoughts and Gods [*sic*] ways and in reality there is not even such a thing as man's way at all—for: "a man's heart deviseth his way"—that is to say it is only a devised way, a way of ideas, in theory, in illusion—but there is only one real way which we are bound to go inevitably and this is God's way.[39]

38. Ibid., 398.
39. Ibid.

On this occasion, Bonhoeffer contrasted human yearnings in terms of illusions, on the one hand, and God's ways in terms of reality, on the other. Human ideas seek to relocate life in the realm of the ideal, but God's way, the life of faith, drives humanity back to the world. "Life is beyond the realm of figures and ideas, life laughs at every attempt to calculate it, for life come from God Himself, who cannot be calculated in his plans, who is free to do whatever he pleases." The ways of God, therefore, demand that we live by faith, since God does not allow us to view our entire lives as a whole.

> He wants man to go step by step, guided not by his own ideas of life, but by God's word, which comes to him on every step whenever man asks for it. . . . God's word is new and free today and tomorrow, it is only applicable to the very moment in which we hear it. God wants us to go step by step in order to drive us to Himself for help again and again.[40]

At the same time, through people's day-to-day lives, there is a certain providence to God's way, guiding humankind, sometimes slowly, but certainly always with the hope

> that man finally will understand his moves and surrender his life to him. But once in every man's life . . . God crosses man's way so that man *cannot* go any further, that he must stop and recognize in fear and trembling God's power and his own weakness and misery,–that he must surrender his life to him who is the victor, that he must ask for mercy; for nothing but mercy can help him.[41]

Ultimately, this providential work of God finds its goal in one place. There is only one place where this all becomes clear and God's will is fulfilled. All human illusions come to an end at the foot of the cross.

> Man's plans are crossed by God's way, and this crossing *points to that place* in the world where all human desires, ideas and ways were crossed

40. Ibid., 399.
41. Ibid. 400.

> by God's way—it points to the cross of Christ—two directions, two ways, one crossed by the other;—man's will crossed and crucified by God's will; man's defeat—God's victory; man's end—God's beginning; man's crucifixion—God's kingdom. Only the way which leads to the Cross is the way which is directed by God step by step—and which finally must lead through his Cross to the life everlasting.[42]

In a second evening sermon given that same year, Bonhoeffer preached on 2 Cor. 12:9. This time he asked, "What is the meaning of weakness in this world?"[43] and then talked about the Christian taking a "stand for the weak." In this manner, he presented a clear statement of the *theologia crucis.* The question about human weakness is important because "our whole attitude toward life, toward man and God depends on the answer to this problem." He asked,

> Have you ever seen a greater mystery in this world than poor people, ill people, insane people—people who cannot help themselves but who have just to rely on other people for help, for love, for care. Have you ever thought what outlook on life a cripple,[44] a hopelessly ill man, a socially exploited man, a coloured man in a white country, an untouchable—may have? And if so, did you not feel that here life means something totally different from what it means to you and that on the other hand you are inseparably bound together with the unfortunate people, just because you are a man like them, just because you are not weak but strong, and just because in all your strength you will feel their weakness? Have we not felt that we shall never be happy in our life as long as this world of weakness from which we are perhaps spared—but who knows for how long—is foreign and strange and far removed from us, as long as we keep away from it consciously or subconsciously? (Bethel!)[45]

42. Ibid.
43. Ibid., 401.
44. According to the editors of this volume, these references make it clear that Bonhoeffer had the Nazi ideology in mind. In addition, Bonhoeffer's stay at the Bethel Institute during August 1933, as well as the time spent in Harlem in 1930–31, could have played a role in lifting up these classes of individuals. See ibid., 401n9.
45. Ibid., 401–2.

Even if we have not thought about it, he declared, which would not be all that surprising since it is human nature to avoid "all problems that might make us feel uncomfortable," Christians are confronted by it directly through the word of God. "We are all dealing with the problem of weakness everyday, but we feel it somewhat dangerous to give account of our fundamental attitude. But God does not want us to put our head into the sand like ostriches, but he commands us to face reality as it is and to take a truthful and definite decision."[46]

Rather than seeking solace by escaping from the world's problems, the Gospel confronts us with the reality of our lives. In opposition to Nietzsche, whose negative views toward Christianity stemmed from its preference for the weak, Bonhoeffer stated, "Christianity stands or falls with its revolutionary protest against violence, arbitrariness and pride of power and with its apologia for the weak."[47] Against all such attempts that viewed the weak with pity, even those who might have been moved by Christian love, in which the strong and healthy look down upon the weak, Bonhoeffer proclaimed,

> The Christian relation between the strong and the weak is that the strong has to look *up* to the weak and never to look down. Weakness is holy, therefore we devote ourselves to the weak. Weakness in the eyes of Christ is not the imperfect one against the perfect, rather is strength the imperfect and weakness the perfect. Not the weak has to serve the strong, but the strong has to serve the weak, and this not by benevolence but by care and reverence Not the powerful is right, but ultimately the weak is always right. So Christianity means a devaluation of all human values and the establishment of a new order of values in the sight of Christ.[48]

46. Ibid., 401.
47. Ibid., 402. By noting that this Nietzschean attitude toward Christianity is one that was ongoing in his own day, Bonhoeffer faults the church for "doing too little" to counteract this influence. Even though they are not named, the attempt of the German Christians to mix the Christian tradition together with Nazi ideology, which gave preference to the powerful and strong, had to stand in the background of Bonhoeffer's critique.
48. Ibid., 403.

Why should Christians have this attitude toward the weak? Why is weakness and suffering holy? In words sounding very much like those written a decade later in *Letters and Papers from Prison,* Bonhoeffer concluded his sermon:

> Because God has suffered in the world from man, and wherever he comes, he has to suffer from man again. God has suffered on the cross. It is therefore that all human suffering and weakness is sharing in God's own suffering and weakness in the world. We are suffering: God is suffering much more. Our God is a suffering God. Suffering conforms man to God. The suffering man is in the likeness of God. . . . God glorifies himself in the weak as He glorified himself in the cross. God is mighty where man is nothing.[49]

The themes of the *theologia crucis* that have provided the basic orientation to Bonhoeffer's thought here emerge as a clear statement that identifies God and suffering, God and the world. Because God has entered into the human arena and suffers, Christians share in the suffering of God as well. But most importantly, God is manifest not through glorious displays of power, but in weakness; God rules not from a position of authority, but vulnerability. God's way in the world forms the way of discipleship for those who believe in Christ.

The central themes of his theology are emphasized again in his sermon on Trinity Sunday, May 27, 1934, when he concentrated on the theme of mystery, which is the way God exists in the world. Bonhoeffer began by noting that the lack of mystery is the problem of modern life; this lack of mystery means "decay and impoverishment for us."[50] On the other hand, "respect for mystery" gives meaning to life. He went on to describe it in the following manner:

49. Ibid., 403–4.
50. Ibid., 360.

> Anything *mysterious* is *uncanny* for us—we cannot do anything with it. We are not *at home* with it; it points toward another kind of "being at home." However, to live without mystery means not to know anything about the secrets of our own lives or those of other people, or of the world's secrets. It means passing by that which is hidden within ourselves, other people, and the world, staying on the surface, taking the world seriously only to the extent to which it can be *calculated* and *exploited*, never looking for what is behind the world of calculation and of gain. To live without mystery means not to see the most important things that happen in life, even to deny that they exist. It is our refusal to know that a tree has roots in the dark realm of the earth, that everything living here in the light has come forth from the dark, secret place of the womb, and that all our thoughts, too, all our spiritual life, also come from a hidden, secret, dark place, like our body, like everything that lives. *That the roots of all that is clear and obvious and understandable lie in mystery*, that is what we do not want to hear. . . . However, *mystery does not mean simply not knowing something*. The greatest mystery is not the most distant star; to the contrary, the closer something is to us, the better we know it, the more mysterious it becomes to us. The person farthest away from us is not the most mysterious to us, but rather the neighbor. . . . God lives in mystery. To us, God's very being is mystery, from everlasting to everlasting; a mystery because it speaks of a home in which we cannot—not yet—be at home.[51]

Mystery is not about far-away worlds, but rather is about that which is closest. It is not about God located somewhere in the heavens beyond human grasp, but rather becomes the deepest, most profound mystery in God's entering into the world. The mystery surrounding

51. Ibid., 360–62. According to Feil, mystery ("the mystery of a faith that is beyond complete rational comprehension") is the "leitmotif" of Bonhoeffer's theology, the "center which necessitates the distinction in theory between faith and reason, *actus directus* and *actus reflectus*. . . . It took the directness of preaching for Bonhoeffer to state clearly that mystery is the root of everything comprehensible. The mystery which is close to us was also the original point of departure for Bonhoeffer's theology." (*TDB*, 5–6). Later in his study, 77, he concludes, "The text of Bonhoeffer's sermon about mystery . . . speaks of Jesus Christ as the unrecognized mystery of God in the world, thus conceiving of mystery in terms of christology." See also Hans-Jürgen Abromeit, *Das Geheimnis Christi: Dietirch Bonhoeffers erfahrungsbezognene Christologie* (Neukirchen-Vluyn: Neukirchener, 1991), 102–9, where he discusses "mystery" in Bonhoeffer's theology in more detail, giving particular attention to this sermon.

God has nothing to do with what we don't know about God, but rather is the result of what we do know. The mystery of God is not the God of scholastic theology, the theology of glory, to use Luther's terms, but is in God's self-revelation in Jesus Christ. At the heart of the mysterious presence of God is Jesus Christ whose very presence is the *deus absconditus*.[52]

At the same time, "the world, however, is blind to this mystery"; this is not the kind of God the world wants. It wants a God it can "calculate and exploit" or else it wants no God at all. "The mystery of God remains hidden from the world. The world does not want it. Instead, it makes its own gods according to its wishes and never recognizes the mysterious and hidden God who is near at hand."[53] There is hope, however, because in spite of human inability to recognize and turn to God, "an unmistakable sign" points humankind beyond its blindness to God: "the cross of Christ." God is present in the world, even though God remains hidden, recognized only through the eyes of faith.[54] "That is the unrecognized mystery

52. Althaus's comments on Luther's understanding of the "hidden God" are appropriate for our understanding of Bonhoeffer as well: "The hidden God, his secret will, and his almighty working in man must be preached so that the faith of Christians will really remain faith that humbly fears God. If we had only the picture of the 'preached God' and of his all-inclusive will to save, human reason could control God. The doctrine of the hidden God, however, eliminates this possibility. Now reason cannot control God; on the contrary, man knows that he is in the hand of God who in free grace controls him. This is the end of all presumption and security. The certainty of salvation still belongs to the humble man who receives God's mercy as a pure miracle" (Paul Althaus, *The Theology of Martin Luther* [Philadelphia: Fortress Press, 1966], 285).

53. DBWE 13:362.

54. Here, again, Althaus's commentary on Luther's understanding of the hidden nature of God and the church is helpful in providing a perspective on Bonhoeffer's own appropriation of Luther. As Althaus describes Luther, it can be seen that Bonhoeffer is speaking the same language: "The Church is visible because it can be recognized by its marks. Only faith, however, can recognize its existence. 'The church is a so deeply hidden thing that no one can see or know it but can only grasp and believe it in baptism, the Lord's Supper, and the word.' The eyes of the world cannot see that it is the church of Christ. It shares this hiddenness with the entire content of faith and thus with God's revelation generally and with Jesus Christ. Here Luther's theology of the cross once again makes itself felt. As God meets us 'hidden in the sufferings' of Christ, so the church is also 'veiled in the flesh' and hidden under its opposite. Reason therefore is not able to recognize the church as such. One can, and must, be scandalized by it in the same way that one is scandalized by Christ. For its 'holiness is in heaven where Christ is and not visible

of God in this world: Jesus Christ. That this Jesus of Nazareth, the carpenter, was the Lord of glory in person, that was the mystery of God." This is mysterious and remains hidden, because in this world God was "poor and lowly, small and weak." And because "God became a human being like us, so that we might become divine; because God came to us, so that we might come to God" and "because God did not remain far above human beings but rather comes *close* to us and loves us, *God's love and closeness—that is the mystery of God*."[55]

During his time in London, Bonhoeffer continued his involvement with the ecumenical community. In addition to the sermons he preached at his congregations, his contributions at ecumenical gatherings show the nature of his theological orientation. One significant contribution was a presentation at the ecumenical youth conference meeting in Fanø, Denmark during the late summer 1934, where Bonhoeffer both gave a lecture and preached a sermon. The manuscript for the lecture is missing; the sermon, however, survives. Entitled "The Church and the Peoples of the World,"[56] it "has become known as Bonhoeffer's Fanø 'peace speech'"; according to those present, however, it "was the homily Bonhoeffer delivered during the morning worship."[57] Based on Psalm 85, Bonhoeffer

in the world like merchandise in the marketplace.' It is hidden under many errors and failures, under heresies, divisions and offenses–just as the individual Christian can see only failure and unholiness in himself and is thus even hidden from himself as a Christian" (*Theology of Martin Luther*, 291). As was true for Luther, Bonhoeffer sees Christian faith as a whole; with its center on the cross of Christ, God is present in and through the church community, albeit in hidden form, and it is because of this presence of God that the church does not seek refuge from the world but goes out into the world "for God's sake."

55. DBWE 13:362.

56. An English translation of Bonhoeffer's text appeared in the International Fellowship of Reconciliation, Newsletter no. 60 (Oct 1948) and is included in DBWE 13:307ff.

57. *DB-ER*, 387. According to Otto Dudzus, "From the first moment the assembly was breathless with tension. Many may have felt that they would never forget what they had just heard. . . . Bonhoeffer had charged so far ahead that the conference could not follow him. Did that surprise anybody? But on the other hand: Could anybody have good conscience about it"

addressed the question of world peace; in order to do so, he immediately moved to a christological explanation and rationale.[58]

Peace, he said, is based on the commandment of God. The church shall promote peace, because the people of God are bound together by something stronger than nationalistic sentiments. In obedience to God's command, Christians follow Christ. Peace, therefore, is a must among Christians, because "they cannot take up arms against Christ himself—yet this is what they do if they take up arms against one another."[59] This peace, however, cannot come about through political treaties, financial arrangements, or rearmament. These attempts confuse peace with safety; while they might provide a sense of safety and security, they will not lead to peace. "Peace is the opposite of security. To demand guarantees is to mistrust. . . . To look for guarantees is to want to protect oneself." The way to peace that comes from God is something different. "Peace means to give oneself altogether to the law of God, wanting no security, but in faith and obedience, laying the destiny of the nations in the hand of Almighty God, not trying to direct it for selfish purposes. Battles are won, not with weapons, but with God. They are won where the way leads to the cross."[60]

In Bonhoeffer's words, there is a clear call for peace, not because of the world's needs, but because of Christ. Bonhoeffer's call for peace

(Cited in Kelly and Nelson, *TF*, 22). A paper outlining a series of theses to be discussed in the lecture was prepared in preparation for the conference; it is included in DBWE 13:304–06.

58. Commenting on the significance of this text, Kelly and Nelson, *TF*, 22, say, "Bonhoeffer's words were a challenge to those who were attempting to maintain a good conscience, all the while avoiding the real issue of whether one could be a Christian at all without committing oneself to the gospel of peace. . . . He attacked those attempts to soften [Christ's] command by interjections in favor of national security and legitimate defense needs. . . . The church, he declared, must be in the vanguard of this struggle for peace. . . . The real issue, he argued in that sermon, was whether the churches could justify their existence if they did not take steps to halt the march toward war."

59. DBWE 13:308.

60. Ibid., 309.

was reinforced by the hopes and expectations that he had in the ecumenical movement, whose task, he believed, was to preach Christ.

This christocentric focus is seen again in Bonhoeffer's August 8, 1934 letter to Ove Valdemar Ammundsen, the Danish bishop and ecumenical leader. Writing in conjunction with the Fanø conference, Bonhoeffer said the decision about the German Christians and the future of the German church was clear: "It must be made quite clear . . . that we are immediately faced with the decision: National Socialism *or* Christian."[61] Any effort on the part of the churches to secure peace through accommodation with the Nazis was out of the question. Likewise, any work of the church that was not centered on the proclamation of Christ was a false work. By locating peace in Christ alone, Bonhoeffer was carefully drawing an important distinction that got at the heart of the church's role in the world—proclaiming the presence of Christ.

These are but illustrations of the passion and single-mindedness with which Bonhoeffer drove home his conviction of a *theologia crucis.* God on the cross, God hidden but present, the church's confession of Christ alone: these are all themes that point to Bonhoeffer's theological orientation. And like Luther, Bonhoeffer's *theologia crucis* is not something that can easily be narrowly defined as having only to do with church or Jesus' death; the cross is the means for understanding the hidden presence of God in the world. God's love is for the world, and it is there that Christians must live out their faith. Bonhoeffer's confession of Christ will not allow him to see the gospel or the church segregated into a spiritual reality or relativized by voices clamoring to set the agenda. This God who enters into our world and dies on the cross for us has to do with every facet of life. The gospel, therefore, cannot be confined within the walls of

61. Ibid., 192.

the church. It must be oriented toward the world, because this act of God has brought about a very different situation. It has created a new reality. The cross that has been turned into a religious icon is in actually the cross of reality. The forgiveness of sins that comes with Jesus' death on the cross is not just a religious feeling—it is something that restructures the world. It has to do with the reality of the world—a reality that encompasses all.

In an effort to preserve its witness against other ideologies, this commitment to the church led Bonhoeffer to leave London behind to become the director of one of the five newly formed seminaries of the Confessing Church.

# 7

# Finkenwalde

After eighteen months in London, Bonhoeffer returned to Germany in the spring of 1935 to engage in the battle of the "true church" against the "false" claims of the German Christians. The seminary at Finkenwalde became the setting for this battle to be played out. Bonhoeffer's motivation had already been revealed in a letter months previously, when he admitted to Erwin Sutz, a friend from his days at Union Seminary, that he was tormented about the future course of his life: Should he remain in England, go to India to study with Gandhi, or return to Germany to direct the seminary at Finkenwalde? He confessed,

> I no longer believe in the university; in fact I never really have believed in it—to your chagrin! The next generation of pastors, these days, ought to be trained entirely in church-monastic schools, where the pure doctrine, the Sermon on the Mount, and worship are taken seriously—which for all three of these things is simply not the case at the university and under the present circumstances is impossible. It is also time for a final break with our theologically grounded reserve about whatever is being done by the state—which really only comes down to

> fear. "Speak out for those who cannot speak"—who in the church today still remembers that this is the very least the Bible asks of us in such times as these?[1]

In another letter from this time, November 30, 1933, in this case written by Bonhoeffer and Franz Hildebrandt to Martin Niemöller, Bonhoeffer's conviction about the power and significance of Luther's witness to address the theological challenges becomes evident. Addressing the church crisis, which they identify primarily as a theological issue, they believe that there is little time left "for saving the church. . . . What is indispensible now is for the synod to be dissolved immediately, and for the entire church to be cleansed of this entire plague. . . . Precisely because this is about doctrine and not about jobs, . . . only Luther's language, not Menlanchthon's, can help today."[2]

In the end he returned to Germany and Finkenwalde became his answer to the challenges facing the church. This was a critical time for the Confessing Church. Hitler had passed a series of laws that meant the Confessing Church found itself in direct conflict with the state. Its newly formed seminaries were outgrowths of that very conflict.[3]

As a result of these laws, the Reich Church would no longer ordain pastors to serve in the Confessing Church; therefore, the Confessing Church created "illegal" preachers' seminaries for that purpose.[4] Bonhoeffer was asked to form and direct the seminary for the church of Pomerania, in northeast Germany. It opened its doors in the spring 1935 with twenty-three students in temporary space; later the seminary would move to the Finkenwalde location.

1. DBWE 13:217.
2. Ibid., 52–53.
3. See H. Gaylon Barker, "Editor's Introduction to the English Edition," DBWE 14, for background on this conflict and its impact on Finkenwalde.
4. See *DB-ER*, 419–24.

Many of these students, including Eberhard Bethge, would become instrumental in preserving Bonhoeffer's legacy.[5]

Finkenwalde, located along Germany's northern coast on the Baltic Sea, was organized according to Bonhoeffer's vision for Christian community, a concept he had been developing for several years; it was based on models he had discovered on visits to cloisters and religious communities in England. As such, it was not to be a seminary in the traditional sense; in fact, it was more than a seminary, it was an experiment in communal living. Because Bonhoeffer had charge of the seminary, the community and its curriculum reflected his own priorities and commitments, both theologically and in terms of forming pastors to serve in the Confessing Church. From the beginning, Bonhoeffer never intended to create an isolated community, living a cut-off existence apart from the world, but rather wanted to preserve a place for the authentic church and to nurture its witness. According to Bonhoeffer, "The goal is not monastic isolation but rather the most intensive concentration for ministry to the world."[6] Finkenwalde, then, was not conceived to be an experience that isolated the community from the world, but existed to prepare leaders to engage the world.

The significance of Finkenwalde for Bonhoeffer is hard to underestimate. Prior to the church struggle, seminaries that provided practical theological training for future pastors of the church were not held in high respect. Bonhoeffer was counted among those who viewed them as "a waste of time."[7] All this changed, however, with the church struggle. As Bethge describes it,

5. John de Gruchy has written about Bethge's friendship with Bonhoeffer and, in so doing, has provided a detailed account of Bethge's contribution to the church struggle and to preserving Bonhoeffer's theological legacy. See *Daring, Trusting Spirit: Bonhoeffer's Friend Eberhard Bethge* (Minneapolis: Fortress Press, 2005).
6. DBWE 14:96.
7. *DB-ER*, 420.

> a fundamental change had occurred, and the stepchild became the darling of the church. The severe crises with the university faculties and the regional churches forced the Confessing church to set up new preachers' seminaries. What followed was almost miraculous. Protected by their relative obscurity, the new seminaries were able to turn themselves into remarkable power centers of theology. . . . The seminaries, although they owed their immediate existence to the struggle of the churches of the Old Prussian Union, remained outside the fray for some time. Only after two and a half years of intensive work did the police come to seal their doors.[8]

## Course Materials and Sermons

Part of what remains of Bonhoeffer's literary output from Finkenwalde[9] are a series of sermon outlines prepared for his homiletics classes that span the time Finkenwalde was in existence. Because Christ is present in the proclaimed word and in the sacraments, a reoccurring theme in Bonhoeffer's theology from *Sanctorum Communio* onward that he reemphasized in his Christology lectures, he viewed the sermon as being of central importance in the life of the church. Proper preparation for preaching involved being theologically informed. Therefore, Bonhoeffer gave considerable time to preparing his students for this important task. Here, as previously, these are reconstructed from student notes, and many of them appear without dates. In the majority of them, however, there is a consistent emphasis on themes that reflect his *theologia crucis*. An examination of a selection of this material follows.

From preparation notes and an outline from May 24, 1935 on Rom. 3:23–26, for example, Bonhoeffer identified the cross as the focal point of the text, insisting that the cross is the "demonstration of

8. Ibid., 420–21.
9. The most widely-known works from the Finkenwalde period are *Discipleship* and *Life Together*. However, although they have their genesis at Finkenwalde, they were written after Bonhoeffer's experiment there came to an end.

God's righteousness, which is simultaneously the process of making righteous."[10] Through his act of going to the cross God is justified and we are made righteous to stand before him. The cross is the place where God himself answers the question of righteousness, atoning for human sin. Here, by referring to God on the cross,[11] rather than using the language of Christ, Bonhoeffer clearly intends to convey the message that Jesus Christ is God. This does not signal a retreat from his christological orientation, but is its intensification. Distinguishing himself from those who would limit Jesus to being a moral teacher, Bonhoeffer insisted that God is wholly present in Christ; it is not solely the human Jesus who dies on the cross, but God is the one who suffers and dies. That is the core gospel message.

Similarly, in notes for a sermon on 1 Cor. 1:18, Bonhoeffer pointed to the paradoxical nature of the cross. Perceived as foolishness, it is the power of God: "It is those who become blessed for whom it [is] power of God. 'Power': that God's power and majesty consist precisely in debasement and weakness. God's power is God's power for the cross. But also power for us insofar as we believe—that God abides with God—place us beneath the cross and live. Power of God's nearness, of forgiveness, and of faith."[12]

As was true for both St. Paul and Luther, Bonhoeffer connected Christ's cross with the cross that Christians must bear. As disciples of Jesus, as he will say it later in prison, "is not a religious act that makes someone a Christian, but rather sharing in God's suffering in the worldly life."[13] His *theologia crucis*, therefore, is not a means of escaping the suffering of the world, but rather becomes a means

10. DBWE 14:345ff.
11. This, too, reflects Luther's language. For him it was not just the human Jesus who died on the cross, but because of the *communicatio idiomatum*, he would insist that it is God who suffers and dies.
12. DBWE 14:351.
13. *LPP*, DBWE 8:480.

of connecting the believer to the world, in the same manner that Jesus identified with the world. For those, however, who are anxious about the world and the future, quoting Luther's lectures on Genesis, he concluded, "If predestination frightens you, then flee to the cross (Luther)."[14] It is there that believers have the assurance of God's grace. It is on the cross that Christians have the assurance of God's mercy, which is the foundation of hope for the world.

Again, in preparation for a sermon on 2 Cor. 5:19–21, talking about the gift of God's grace, Bonhoeffer stated that "in Christ's death God's righteousness triumphs for our bene[fit] Luther calls this the 'happy exchange.'"[15] Similarly, in notes for a sermon on Gal. 3:10–13, he said that Christ on the cross becomes the cursed one, taking our place. "Because Christ [is] cursed, we are redeemed. Because everything [has been done by] Christ, hence we [are] free." That, he said, "is the path of God along which God grants human beings life through faith without the curse of the law. Being obedient to this path of God is called faith." Because of Christ's obedience on the cross, humankind has life.[16]

The central character of his theology is brought out again in 1935 in another sermon outline prepared for the Finkenwalde community. Making preparations to preach on Gal. 6:14, he said, "For [a person should boast] only of the cross of Christ. Here is the only place where God can be found in this glory-addicted world."[17] It is only in the "crucified God himself" that the world will find glory. It is not the case that the man Jesus dies and somehow balances the scales of justice, satisfying the demands of God. No, on the cross God himself suffers and dies. "There on the cross hangs my glory. There hangs sin and shame. Christ has become the shame of the world. It falls upon

14. DBWE 14:351. See also Luther's lectures on Romans.
15. Ibid., 352ff.
16. Ibid., 355–58.
17. Ibid., 361–64.

him and he bears it on the cross." And there the old world of sin and death is crucified.

In contrast to the world's search for glory, the Christian's place of glory is found in the cross. Christ's cross is the Christian's cross. "The cross on which I am crucified is the cross of Christ. . . . And because I have genuinely been crucified with Christ by God, by God's judgment, I can suffer that suffering with Christ. . . . Because *we* are crucified with Christ we also bear the sins and suffering of the world. Through our faith and our cross bearing, Christ swallows the sins and the death of the world." The glory, therefore, is that the world is redeemed. "Christ through the cross, which is the cross of the church-community, pardons the world and makes peace."[18]

In highly concentrated language, Bonhoeffer's primary focus, his central concern, is the cross of Christ. The act of God bearing the sins the world, creates the world anew. At the same time, a community shaped by the cross emerges; its faith, its discipleship begins at the foot of the cross and lives in its shadow. The life of Christians in the world bears the marks of the crucified and therefore is cruciform in shape.

In one final example, this one coming in April 1936, in notes on a Trinity Sunday sermon on Exod. 20:2–3, Bonhoeffer focused on God's declaration, "I am the Lord." Throughout the centuries, he admitted, there have been many lords and masters, each of whom eventually disappears, only to be replaced by another, each of whom "would enslave us." It is God who is Lord over them all; God has conquered them and lives. The biblical God speaks:

> "I am the Lord your God!" For the third time, God speaks. What good does a God do us who is in eternity and is stronger than the majesty of the world, stronger than sin and death? This God does not concern us. *How can such a God help us*? Does this God inquire after me? Is this God

18. Ibid., 363–64.

> not instead a reason for me to be fearful, a reason for me to be resigned because even after this present life there is no end, and that instead I will ultimately plunge into a terrible eternity? God says: "I am the Lord your God!" The God who was from the beginning and who will abide, this God belongs to me, is my God, for after all this does mean: this God is with me, next to me, for me, in me. Indeed, someone who says to me: "I am yours!" we belong together. Everything I have is yours. Everything you have is mine! God and human being enter into a bond. God's majesty belongs to me. God is not distant but rather close at hand. What a splendid gospel this is: "I am your God!" Thus does God, the Holy Spirit, speak![19]

The communal life at Finkenwalde was molded by these central ideas. His work *Discipleship*, which is a commentary on the practices and beliefs emanating from there, exhibits that. The same themes will dominate Bonhoeffer's *Ethics* and come to the fore in *Letters and Papers from Prison.* Christ's cross and the Christian life merge. Given the conditions of life in Nazi Germany, discipleship does not mean escaping from the world, but rather involves taking on responsibility for the world. The church, which emerges from the cross and continues to find its life in the cross, therefore has a crucial role to play.

In all these cases, Bonhoeffer's focus in consistently on Jesus Christ and the cross. Clearly, at a time such as this, and in offering a clearly differentiated alternative to the German Christians, reaffirmation of Luther's *theologia crucis* was seen by Bonhoeffer as necessary. Not

19. DBWE 14:636. Italics added. Bonhoeffer's language here mirrors that of Martin Luther, who in his debate over the Lord's Supper with Zwingli, after refuting Zwingli's position, goes on to reaffirm the two natures of Christ: "Our faith maintains that Christ is God and man, and the two natures are one person, so that this person may not be divided in two; therefore, he can surely show himself in a corporeal. . . . Wherever this person is, it is the single, indivisible person, and if you can say, 'Here is God,' then you must also say, 'Christ the man is present too.'"And if you could show me one place where God is and not the man, then the person is already divided and I could at once say truthfully, 'Here is God who is not man and has never become man.' But no God like that for me! . . . No, comrade, wherever you place God for me, you must also place the humanity for me." ("Confession concerning Christ's Supper (1528)," *LW* 37:218–19).

only was it the heart of the gospel, it was a means of restoring the church.

As was demonstrated earlier in both his attempt at writing a catechism and with the Bethel Confession, the one thing Bonhoeffer was convinced of was that the church needed to be clear about was its confession of faith. If the church had that right, it would endure whatever hardship or suffering it faced; however, if it was not clear in its confession, nothing else mattered for it had already ceased to be the church. If the church was the body of Christ and Christ was present in its proclamation, the true test was its clear confession. This concern was lifted up in Bonhoeffer's efforts at preaching or in exegeting a biblical text. As if adopting Luther's belief that Scripture is the "cradle of Christ," all biblical interpretation has a christological center around which all proclamation revolves.

Another consistent theme that emerged in his sermons is the christocentric orientation to his message, even when preaching on the Old Testament. An example is a June 2, 1935 sermon on Psalm 42,[20] one of the first sermons preached after the seminary community was organized at Zingst. Bonhoeffer, in answering the question posed in verse 2, "My soul thirsts for God, for the living God. When shall I come and behold the face of God?" responds with words that sound similar to Luther's: "A God who is merely a thought or an ideal can never quench this thirst. Our soul thirsts for the living God, for the God and origin of all true life. When will God quench our thirst? When we come to the point that we behold the face of God. The goal of all life, indeed, eternal life itself is to behold God's face. We see it in Jesus Christ, the Crucified."[21] Then, he responded to the question in verse 3, "Where is your God?" with a completely christocentric answer that included his oft-repeated quote from Luther: "Where is

20. DBWE 14:845–51.
21. Ibid., 847.

your God? How else can we respond except to point to the man who in life, death, and resurrection proved to be God's true Son, Jesus Christ. In death, he is our life; in sin, our forgiveness; in distress, our helper; in war, our peace. 'To this man you should point and say: that is God' (Luther)."[22]

In a sermon from July 11, 1937, which was one of the last sermons preached at Finkenwalde before its closure, he again provided a christological framework for interpreting Psalm 58.[23] Identifying this as a psalm of vengeance, he asked, "Is this terrible psalm of vengeance really our prayer?" and answered, "No . . . after all, we ourselves bear much of the guilt for the hostility that we encounter and that brings us trouble."[24] Because we are sinful, how can we expect that God must bring wrath upon our enemies? "Only those who are themselves completely without guilt can pray thus." Even though it is David who prays this psalm, it is only in preparation for "the one who will be called the Son of David, Jesus Christ." Therefore, ultimately, it is Christ who prays these words. "He experienced the unjust judgment; he fell into human hands. Here innocence accuses the unjust world."[25] These comments can be compared to his book on the Psalms[26] where a christological interpretation of the Psalms is freely offered. Perhaps in this regard, since Bonhoeffer deviated from the historical-critical method of his teachers in his approach to scriptural interpretation, the direct influence of Luther is apparent. Luther, too, saw Christ in the Psalms, as well as in many parts of the Old Testament.

22. Ibid., 848.
23. Ibid., 963–70.
24. Ibid., 964.
25. Ibid., 964–66. Cf. Geffrey B. Kelly, "Freedom and Discipline: Rhythms of a Christocentric Spirituality," in *Ethical Responsibility: Bonhoeffer's Legacy to the Churches*, ed. John D. Godsey and Geffrey B. Kelly (Lewiston, NY: The Edwin Mellen Press, 1981), 327–28.
26. *Prayerbook of the Bible*, DBWE 5.

But more than praying for justice to be meted out to those who deserve God's vengeance, the justice of God has been fulfilled in the cross of Jesus Christ.

> Jesus Christ died the death of the wicked, struck by God's wrath and vengeance. His blood is the blood demanded by God's righteousness for transgressions against his commandments. . . . Jesus Christ, the innocent one, prays in the hour in which God's vengeance is visited upon the wicked on earth, in which our psalm here is fulfilled: Father, forgive them; for they do not know what they are doing. [Luke 23:24] He who bore this vengeance, he alone is permitted to ask that the wicked be forgiven, for he alone freed us from God's wrath and vengeance, bringing forgiveness to his enemies, and no one prior to him was permitted to pray this way. He alone is permitted. When we look at him, the Crucified, we recognize God's true, living wrath on us, the wicked, and in that very same moment we also recognize our liberation from this wrath, and we hear: Father, forgive them; for they do not know what they are doing.[27]

God's justice is fulfilled on the cross of Jesus Christ. Outside of Christ and his death on the cross one will only encounter God's wrath. Until the day of judgment all of this will remain hidden from us, something accepted only in faith. In the meantime, the reward for the righteous "is not the happiness, power, or glory of this world…, but the community of the cross of Jesus Christ, redemption from God's wrath." If ever we doubt that God's justice is taking shape in this world, "let us look to the cross of Christ: for there is judgment, there reprieve."[28]

## Lectures

When Bonhoeffer turned to his lectures, the same emphasis can be found. His focus was not turned to other matters, but remained

27. DBWE 14:969.
28. Ibid., 970.

narrowly defined by the presence of Christ, the theme that had its foundations and origins in *Sanctorum Communio.* Whatever the subject, it is viewed through the lens of Jesus Christ. In both his approach to homiletics and pastoral care, for example, there is a christological focus,[29] providing both the orientation for and content of his remarks.

In his lectures on homiletics, which were presented as a regular part of the curriculum throughout the duration of Finkenwalde's existence, Christology is identified as the origin and primary basis for preaching. In materials presented during the summer of 1936, reconstructed from student notes, Bonhoeffer began, "*The sermon derives from the incarnation of Jesus Christ.* . . . The incarnate Christ is God. Hence the sermon is actually Christ."[30]

A similar theme was emphasized in his lectures on catechesis from December 11, 1935. He began with a discussion of religion, which in general terms avoids the scandal of the cross. Since this is the case, "Christ is something entirely different from what we by nature have in our hearts. . . . Human yearning, one must note, is by nature not yearning for Christ as long as a person does not yet know Christ but is instead carnal yearning!" Therefore, Christ must be preached.

> The goal of the sermon is the good news. Yet wherever Christ, the crucified, poor Christ is preached as the one who brings joy, it is precisely the proclamation of forgiveness that will inevitably prompt

29. Han Jürgen Abromeit, *Das Geheimnis Christi: Dietrich Bonhoeffers erfahrungsbezognene Christologie* (Neukirchen-Vluyn: Neukirchener, 1991), 17, sees the christological emphasis that had given shape to Bonhoeffer's theology intensified during the Finkenwalde period; this is demonstrated in lectures such as these.

30. DBWE 14:509–10. According to Bethge, "Bonhoeffer's understanding of the sermon was based on his Lutheran Christology." Beginning with the second Finkenwalde course from which these notes come, he says Bonhoeffer's approach to preaching was "grounded in the incarnation: The word of the sermon is Christ accepting and bearing human nature. It is not a new incarnation, but the Incarnate One who bears the sins of the world. The word of the sermon seeks nothing more than to accept human beings. The word of the Bible assumes form as a sermon; thus it goes out to the congregation in order to bear it" (*DB-ER*, 443).

> offense, the offense of the old human being who says, I am, too, religious. No, with all your religiosity, even with all your Christian orientation, you are nothing and live only from forgiveness.—But it would be nonsensical to preach the offense as such. Yet wherever the gospel really is preached as the alien element, the natural human being must take offense, and this offense bears the promise that the natural human being will die from it. The offense is that the old human being dies in Christ. And if we foster the old human being, the new one cannot come into being.[31]

This was a theme reiterated by Bonhoeffer over the years. From *Sanctorum Communio*, where he emphasized the presence of Christ in the proclaimed word, to the 1932 Gland, Switzerland speech where he stressed, "Christ must again become present among us in preaching and sacrament, just as Christ as the crucified one made peace with God and humanity," at Finkenwalde it is once again reformulated to make the point that the church's proclamation is centered on the crucified and risen Christ, through whom God forgives sin and creates a new humanity. In stressing this approach to the church's task, Bonhoeffer shared in Luther's *theologia crucis* that, with its emphasis on the *finitum capax infiniti*, locates God in the world; of this the church must bear witness. Not only is the church founded on Christ, but its proclamation and testimony bear witness to Christ *pro nobis*.

In conjunction with the homiletics lectures offered during the summer semester 1935, he prepared a series of theses to be discussed by his students. Here again Bonhoeffer placed the emphasis on a concrete Christology, claiming that when it comes to the preached word, "God and God alone is what is and remains concrete in a sermon."[32] While it would seem reasonable that emphasis be placed

31. DBWE 14:544.
32. DBWE 14:493. The context for these theses is described by Bethge in the following terms: "Bonhoeffer had difficulty persuading his ordinands that there was more to preaching than the reasonable but useless pattern of an explication followed by an application. In the very first class

on the "concrete historical situation" in order to make preaching relevant, Bonhoeffer claimed that this would make it the criterion for the Bible. Such an ordering becomes problematic because "*the concrete historical* [geschichtlich] *situation is ambiguous* to the extent that *God and the devil are always at work* within it." If the concrete situation were to be given priority, that would reduce God to an object rather than the subject, all of which would mean dismissing God's prior claim on us. Instead, rather than being the "source of the proclamation," the concrete situation is that to which the word of God speaks. In this ambiguous situation, the word of God is spoken, and in the particularity of the situation, God is present for us. The presence of God's word makes the concrete situation real. Because that is the case, "*The true concrete situation* is never the more apparent historical [geschichtlich] situation but rather that of human beings, *of sinners before God*. In their flight, in their attempts to secure themselves against God. That the crucified Christ lives today is proof that the concrete situation of human beings is merely the situation to which Christ is the answer."[33]

His lectures on pastoral care,[34] prepared for use during the second course 1935–1936 and used thereafter, like those on homiletics, are based on the premise of the present Christ, who is made real in the lives of individuals when the gospel is proclaimed to them in their individual situation of need. Here he addressed the central issue for the church in any age: faithful proclamation of God's word, so that individuals might encounter the living God in and through

discussion arose after an ordinand who had been taught by Karl Heim passionately advocated the need for concrete 'application.' Bonhoeffer allowed two of the students to address the topic and then, as was his method, posed his own theses for discussion: God alone is concrete. . .the concrete situation is the substance within which the Word of God speaks; it is the object, not the subject, of concretion" (*DB-ER*, 442–43).

33. DBWE 14:494.

34. Ibid., 559–94. An earlier translation of these lectures appeared as as *Spiritual Care*, trans. and with an introduction by Jay C. Rochelle (Philadelphia: Fortress Press, 1985).

their daily lives. Bonhoeffer saw pastoral care as central and integral to the church's ministry of proclamation. It is proclamation in a personalized and individualized form, allowing persons to hear the good news as personal address, spoken "for you." "The task of pastoral care is given to the pastor along with the task of proclamation (ordination vow). Only to the extent that Christ's word is also spoken through pastoral care are pastoral care and proclamation identical, or does the pastoral conversation bear the promise. Pastoral care is proclamation to the individual."[35] The aim of pastoral care is to speak the living word of God, so that it has the power to expose sin and create new life. Pastoral care's goal is "not the shaping of a person's character or the education of that person into a certain type, but the act of revealing a person as a sinner and of teaching that person how to hear the world."[36] From that stance, Bonhoeffer discussed the theological issues of spiritual care along classical Lutheran lines, focusing on the place of law and gospel, and the central role of confession and forgiveness. Because spiritual care is personalized care, Bonhoeffer gave advice for those situations in which the pastor should be present to speak of word of grace: in home visitation; to the sick, the dying, the indifferent and the tempted; at funerals, weddings, and baptisms.

Based on Luther's Christ *pro me*, which was at the heart of his 1933 Christology lectures, Bonhoeffer believed that as Christ bore the sins of the world, the Christian community is called to bear one another's burdens. The pastor, as the representative of Christ in the congregation, therefore, is called upon to bring the healing and reconciling word of God to bear upon individuals. In a manner consistent with his thinking about the church and its ministry, here Bonhoeffer again asserted that as with the proclamation of the gospel,

35. DBWE 14:560.
36. Ibid., 563–64.

so, too, spiritual care is not a human work but is the work of God. "God alone can provide comfort and strength and help."[37] Therefore, it is not the pastor's role (nor the goal of proclamation and pastoral care) to "produce a certain type of Christian individual," to bring "about a certain spiritual disposition," remove "false comfort," or to "make sad people cheerful or anxious people courageous." Rather, in these circumstances, "pastoral care means proclaiming God as the sole comfort, help, and so on to the individual;" that "Christ and his victory over sickness, birth, death, sinners is proclaimed."[38]

The cross of Christ, therefore, is central for any Christian understanding of pastoral care. Rather than enabling individuals to flee from God and themselves, at the foot of the cross they see themselves as they really are. From Bonhoeffer's perspective, "The task of pastoral ministry is, above all, to arrange the contingencies for an encounter with the Divine."[39] In that context, "The aim of spiritual care is the integration of the person with the human community, beginning with one's relationship to God in the community of faith."[40] The thrust of Bonhoeffer's argument, therefore, is one that "demands us to consider how the gospel message is brought to people in the midst of their personal lives, and his message and counsel use the tools given within the traditional life of the church. Baptism, wedding, funeral, and pastoral visitation are the spokes radiating from a center rooted in confession and forgiveness."[41] In addition to placing Christ at the center of pastoral care, he adopted a classic Lutheran approach to this personal form of proclamation.

37. Ibid., 560.
38. Ibid., 560. See n5.
39. Rochelle, "Introduction," *Spiritual Care*, 23.
40. Ibid., 24.
41. Ibid., 13.

His 1936 lectures on "The Visible Church in the New Testament,"[42] which reflect the same concerns and commitments as *Discipleship* and *Life Together*, show the continual unfolding of Bonhoeffer's theology from its central core. Bonhoeffer linked worship and caring for one another to the cross event of Christ. Worship and service have become one and the same thing because of the cross. Therefore, the cross of Christ has become the foundation for service. Following Luther, Bonhoeffer's concept of discipleship is not that of an *imitatio*, but rather a suffering with that is a part of the theology of the cross. "The law of the church-community is the cross of Christ. The life of the church-community means participating in the cross by bearing the cross, which is the visible form of love for one another. Whoever does not genuinely bear the cross is not worthy of it."[43] In language that links these lectures not only to *Discipleship* but to *Letters and Papers from Prison* as well, Bonhoeffer concluded by saying that on the cross the fellowship between fellow members is created. That is the

> σῶμα Χριστοῦ on the cross and now as well. Bearing the cross indissolubly connected with the cross of Christ. Participation brings about justification, the cessation of sin, transferal into the new kingdom. The law *of the cross* thereby becomes *the law of the church-community*, not as the fullness of statutes and legal ordinances but as the crucified Christ himself.[44]

## Essay on the Question of Church Communion

These themes betray the larger context in which these lectures took place. The Church Struggle and the larger political context always

42. DBWE 14:434–76.
43. Ibid., 475.
44. Ibid., 475–76. Cf. Walter von Loewenich, *Luther's Theology of the Cross* (Minneapolis: Augsburg, 1976), for a description of Luther's theology in which the cross of Christ and the Christian's cross are equated.

formed the backdrop for Bonhoeffer's message. Ultimately, however, he had his eye on the future, a future in which pastors would be called upon to preach the gospel and live out Christian discipleship in a world where the church and its confession were under attack. These concerns were addressed directly in other lectures he presented. In his essay "On the Question of Church Communion," presented in April 1936 at a retreat at Finkenwalde and later published in the journal *Evangelische Theologie* in June 1936,[45] Bonhoeffer argued that the Confessing Church take the claims of the Barmen and Dahlem Synods seriously.[46] After outlining how the church had been defined in the early church and Reformation periods, Bonhoeffer moved into discussing the question about the "true church," which, in turn, was used to explicate the meaning of the church's actions at Barmen and Dahlem. He stated,

> The Confessing Synod in Barmen rejected the key points of the doctrine of the German Christians as false teaching. This rejection means that this false teaching has no place in the church of Jesus Christ. The Confessing Synod in Dahlem assumed responsibility by declaring that through word and deed the Reich Church government [Reichskirchenregierung] has separated itself from the Christian church. Rather than excluding someone from the church, this synod instead

45. DBWE 14:656–97. In their introduction to this text, Kelly and Nelson describe the context as follows: "Though this paper was presented in the milder atmosphere of Finkenwalde, its setting was the turmoil with which the Confessing Church had been convulsed at the time. The leadership of the church seemed willing to backtrack on the pivotal decisions of the Barmen and Dahlem synods, particularly through compromises on its standing rejection of interference in its affairs by the official national church government. Pressure was increased on it to conform to Nazi policies and thus acquire legality and political 'respectability.' . . . Bonhoeffer wished to set his seminarians, and, indeed, the churches themselves straight on the question of membership in the true church of Jesus Christ, now that so many were being tempted to compromise and some church leaders were, in his opinion, avoiding the real issue of what constituted the truth" (*TF*, 158). See DBWE 14:656n1, for information on the publication details of these lectures.

46. Two synods of the Confessing Church, held May 29–31, 1934, and October 19–20, 1934, respectively. Barmen produced the Barmen Declaration and Dahlem formulated the structure for the newly formed church's administration. See Ferdinand Schlingensiepen, *Dietrich Bonhoeffer 1906–1945: Martyr, Thinker, Man of Resistance* (New York: T & T Clark, 2010), 161–67, and *DB-ER*, chapter 8.

> merely confirmed an action that had already taken place. At the same time, it formed its own church administration and made the claim that it represented the true church of Jesus Christ in Germany. Thereafter the Confessing Church accepted the responsibility and commission of being the one, true church of Jesus Christ in Germany. That is a fact of church history.[47]

With this as background, he attempted to define the true church in his time. If the above-stated conclusions were true, then the question was, could the German Christians be considered a part of the church? Or has the Reich Church cut itself off from the church? Such questions indicated "that a definitive boundary has been recognized and confirmed between the Reich Church government and the true church of Christ. The Reich Church government is heretical."[48]

Aside from the political ramifications, this was a pertinent issue for Bonhoeffer because it went to the heart of the question about the church and its mission. Therefore he concluded,

> *Extra ecclesiam nulla salus.* The question of church communion is the question of the community of salvation. The boundaries of the church are the boundaries of salvation. Whoever knowingly separates himself from the Confessing Church in Germany separates himself from salvation. This is the insight that has always forced itself on the true church. This is its humble confession. Those who separate the question of the Confessing Church from the question of their own salvation have not comprehended that the struggle of the Confessing Church is the struggle for their salvation.[49]

His statement, "Whoever knowingly separates himself from the Confessing Church in Germany separates himself from salvation," received a great deal of attention both inside the Confessing Church

47. DBWE 14:667.
48. Ibid., 668.
49. Ibid., 675. Bonhoeffer's reference is to Cyprian, but it also reflects Luther's stance. While in hindsight we might see the truth of Bonhoeffer's claims given the context, at the time his claim was open to other interpretations, both within the Confessing Church as well as among the German Christians.

as well as outside of it, because Bonhoeffer's position was deemed "too radical."[50] While he stopped short of placing judgment on individuals who remained members of the Reich Church, he was clear in his denunciation of the leaders of the Reich Church who had accommodated themselves to the political pressures of the day.

Nevertheless, as he went on to discuss the matter in more detail, his position can be seen as reflecting the historical position articulated by the church throughout the centuries. In addition, it was not as an aberration of his own theological position. From *Sanctorum Communio* onward he defined the church in terms of Luther's conception of the present Christ. Through the church's proclamation the presence of Christ is made a reality for the believers and for the world. Any expression of the church that deviated from that identifying mark could no longer be considered the church. For Bonhoeffer, this "is in the strict sense a statement of faith." Articulating a position reflective of Luther's, he went on to explain,

> Faith is tied to God's salvific revelation, from the perspective of which it perceives absolutely no other salvation than salvation in the visible church. From this perspective, faith is in fact not free to seek God's salvation anywhere other than where the promise is given in the first place. Because salvation beyond the church is fundamentally inconceivable for faith, such a notion can also never constitute a doctrinal point. It is in the promise alone that salvation is recognized. In its own turn, however, the promise includes the proclamation of the pure gospel.[51]

Later in his argument, he returned to the same point, now relating it directly to the responsibilities and work of the Confessing Church as the true church.

50. See Helmut Gollwitzer's article, DBWE 14:678–89, for the nature of the debate Bonhoeffer's comments generated.
51. Ibid., 676.

> One cannot repeat often enough that the church is not performing any sort of compassionate act by denying its own boundaries. The true church will always come up against boundaries. By acknowledging these boundaries, it is performing the work of love toward human beings insofar as it gives priority to the truth. *Extra ecclesiam nulla salus.* If this statement is certain, then the other, which finds its analogy in the doctrine of God, must be added as well. Although God is indeed omnipresent, God does not intend that we perceive God just anywhere. Just because God is present does not mean that God can also be recognized; there is a difference between the two. As assuredly as the God we are able to recognize is alone our God, and as assuredly as the God we are unable to recognize can never be our God, just as assuredly must this distinction remain precisely as a statement of faith, which abides with the revealed God and therein extols the singularity and miraculous nature of revelation itself. Hence one can now also say that the church can be recognized only where God's promise abides, namely, in the visible church.[52]

In this instance, he referenced the same statement of Luther that he had used in his argument about God's freedom in *Act and Being*: "It is one thing if God is present, and another if he is present for you."[53] When compared to other statements from Luther, Bonhoeffer's position with regard to the Confessing Church becomes an even more clearly stated variation of Luther's belief itself. Compare, for example, the following statements from Luther. In the first instance, Luther says, "Outside this Christian church there is no salvation or

52. Ibid., 677.
53. In this case, we can turn to Luther to see the influence of his statement on shaping Bonhoeffer's own thinking. Beyond the words Bonhoeffer quoted, Luther goes on to say, "He [God] is there for you when he adds his Word and binds himself, saying, 'Here you are to find me.' Now when you have the Word, you can grasp and have him with certainty and say, 'Here I have thee, according to thy Word.' Just as I say of the right hand of God: although this is everywhere, as we may not deny, still because it is also nowhere, as has been said, you can actually grasp it nowhere, unless for your benefit it binds itself to you and summons you to a definite place. This God's right hand does, however, when it enters into the humanity of Christ and dwells there. There you surely find it, otherwise you will run back and forth throughout all creation, groping here and groping there yet never finding, even though it is actually there; for it is not there for you" ("That These Words of Christ, 'This is My Body,' etc. Still Stand Firm Against the Fanatics," *LW* 37:68–69).

forgiveness of sins, but everlasting death and damnation." In another, he says, "For outside the Christian church there is not truth, no Christ, and no salvation."[54] When seen from the perspective of Bonhoeffer's own argument, he was not engaged merely in a fight for genuine Lutheranism in the 1930s, but a battle for the heart and soul of the church itself.

### Involvement in the Larger Church

Neither Bonhoeffer's interest nor attention was limited to the Finkenwalde community. As Bethge clearly points out,[55] Bonhoeffer remained an integral part of the Confessing Church's leadership, making regular trips back and forth to Berlin. He also continued his involvement in the work of the larger church. One such example was his contribution on behalf of the Confessing Church at the 1936 Berlin Olympic games. Delivered to an overflowing crowd at the Church of the 12 Apostles in Berlin on August 5, 1936, Bonhoeffer spoke on the subject, "The Inner Life of the German Evangelical Church."[56] While he makes reference to historical figures from the past, his purpose was not simply limited to historical review. Given the context, this was a public declaration meant to separate the true church from the false church.

Historically, he said, when Christians were confronted with persecution and possible martyrdom, they turned to singing as a means of confessing their faith. That was what the early Christians did, for example, as they were thrown to the lions. Likewise, St. Francis of Assisi sang loudly at his time of death. And in 1542 when the Turks stood threateningly at the door of Europe ready to invade, Luther wrote the hymn, "Lord, Keep Us Steadfast in Thy Word,"

54. Cited in Paul Althaus, *The Theology of Martin Luther* (Philadelphia: Fortress Press, 1966), 291.
55. See *DB-ER*, chapter 10.
56. DBWE 14:710–17.

which he described as an expression of childlike prayer. The mystery of the Reformation, Bonhoeffer claimed, is embodied in such acts. Quoting from Luther's *Table Talk*, he provided an answer as to why they turned to such acts: "Pray," said Luther, "for there is no hope in weapons but only in prayer."[57] He continued, "God is not with the stronger battalions but with the small host of the praying, watchful congregation. God's strength is powerful in the weak." Quoting the second verse of Luther's hymn ("Lord Jesus Christ, your pow'r make known, for you are Lord of lords alone; defend you holy church, that we may sing your praise eternally"),[58] he said Christ's power is "the hidden, secret power of the cross and of suffering" and "the church stands under the word and under the cross, called and gathered by the Holy Spirit."[59]

This same pattern of responding to crises with prayerful song was practiced, in turn, by Paul Gerhardt and Nicolas Zinzendorf. But in contrast to such faithful expression, with the Enlightenment, Luther's hymns had been recast. "The human being, not scripture, had become the measure of all piety. Here Christ is no longer mentioned. Is the wisdom, is the Almighty about whom Gellert speaks, really the triune God?"[60] Instead of a childlike faith, which is what marked the hymns of those who represented the Reformation faith, what has been practiced in modern Christianity is an adult religion, a religion that takes place alongside of the church; this religion offers peace, but it is not a peace that comes from the cross of Christ, which offers forgiveness of sins. "It is pious poetry but not the preached word." But now, Bonhoeffer said, "After four hundred

57. Ibid., 711.
58. Luther, "Lord, Keep Us Steadfast in Thy Word," *Evangelical Lutheran Worship* (Minneapolis: Augsburg Fortress, 2006), no. 517. See also "Lord, Keep Us Steadfast in Thy Word," *LW* 53:304–5.
59. DBWE 14:711. The latter phrase is a reference to Luther's explanation of the third article of the Apostles' Creed in his *Small Catechism* (BC) and in the *Evangelical Lutheran Worship*, no. 517.
60. DBWE 14:715.

years of Protestantism, the spirit of the Reformation is emerging again. The forces threatening the church are enormous. Here we must learn again: It is prayer that accomplishes things, including the prayer of children. That is why the Confessing Church has learned to pray again."[61] Not knowing what the future holds for the Confessing Church, "we are not allowed to look back except to the cross of Christ," which frees us "to praise and sing!"[62]

At critical moments and at important venues such as this, Bonhoeffer turned to Luther for both his authority and as a model for the church. But even more, following Luther's lead, it is in the childlike faith in Christ that there is hope for the church.

Giving hope to the church was the goal of Finkenwalde. Through this community, Bonhoeffer hoped to develop an alternative church to national church controlled by the German Christians. According to Wolf Krötke,

> For Bonhoeffer, keeping and actualizing the foundations of the church was identical with keeping and actualizing Luther's genuine understanding of the word of God in law and gospel, faith, the church and Christian action. He dedicated himself uncompromisingly to this task and demanded from the Confessing Church that she speak the clear, decisive 'language of Luther and not Melanchthon.' Because Bonhoffer was keen to reach his own conclusions on Luther's theology on the basis of Luther's writings, his path in the 1930s often collided—both within and outside the Confessing Church—with what was called Lutheranism or Lutheran.[63]

61. Ibid., 716. In commenting on this text, Bethge, *DB-ER*, 539, says that Bonhoeffer "concluded by showing how the spirit of the Reformation was again manifesting itself in prayer in the Confessing Church."
62. DBWE 14:717.
63. Wolf Krötke, "Dietrich Bonhoeffer and Martin Luther," in *Bonhoeffer's Intellectual Formation: Theology and Philosophy in His Thought*, ed Peter Frick (Tübingen: Mohr Siebeck, 2008), 54–55. Compare this to Bonhoeffer's own response to the criticism of his essay on Church communion. In an October 26, 1936, letter to Erwin Sutz, he admitted to being "the most reviled man of our type." But at the same time, he warned, "It will not be long before the beast before whom these idolaters bow will be bearing a distorted Lutheran visage" (DBWE 14:273).

In the face of mounting criticism against his radical position, Bonhoeffer turned to Luther to preserve the *solus Christus*. "For him, the question was how God—who turned toward the world in Jesus Christ, who emptied himself—is relevant to the world and every person in a concrete, life-changing way, even when the world no longer believes in him."[64]

In each instance, from sermons to lectures and public presentations Bonhoeffer, without compromise, maintained that Jesus Christ is the center of the Christian faith. In his understanding of the church, preaching, pastoral care, and theology are all conceived of in terms of the person Jesus Christ, who is a living presence in the world. It is that encounter with the Christ *pro nobis* that brings about discipleship, which is the subject of one of Bonhoeffer's best-known books, *Discipliship.*

See also Bethge, *DB-ER*, 571, where he indicates that Bonhoeffer "was not prepared to leave the Lutheran interpretation of the Gospel to his Lutheran contemporaries."

64. Krötke, "Dietrich Bonhoeffer and Martin Luther," 57.

# 8

# Post-Finkenwalde Writings

The book *Discipleship*, which had its origins during Finkenwalde in the form of lectures offered during the various sessions, was not completed until 1937, after the Gestapo had already shut down Finkenwalde. While Finkenwalde is important for understanding the context that gave rise to Bonhoeffer's subject, it was only as it was coming to an end that Bonhoeffer was compelled to publish the work that would become the most influential of his writings that appeared during his lifetime. Therefore, it, along with *Life Together*, will be examined as part of the post-Finkenwalde period.

## Discipleship

The manuscript that was to become *Discipleship*[1] emerged in several stages and grew out of Bonhoeffer's own passionate interest in the

1. Bonhoeffer's book, entitled *Nachfolge* (following after) in German, was called *The Cost of Discipleship* in early English translations. The editors of the new DBWE titled it *Discipleship* (DBWE 4). The title reveals Bonhoeffer's intent. At a time when der Führer, the leader, was on everyone's mind in Germany, Bonhoeffer offered Jesus Christ as the *one* to be followed. "Whenever Christ calls us, his call leads us to death" (DBWE 4:87). In earlier English versions

subject. The completed manuscript was delivered to the publishers on August 26, 1937, shortly before the Gestapo closed down Finkenwalde, and appeared in print in Advent 1937. The ideas that became the heart of the text, however, were originally presented as lectures at the seminary. He had been fascinated with the subject for several years, and the routine and responsibilities of Finkenwalde gave him the time and the freedom to develop it. By his own admission, being able to give this subject his full attention made this Finkenwalde experience "the most fulfilling period" of his life.[2] But, in addition, it was this subject that gave Finkenwalde its "own badge of distinction." According to Bethge, "For the newcomers the first classes in Zingst[3] were a breathtaking surprise. They suddenly realized that they were not there simply to learn new techniques of preaching and instruction, but would be initiated into something that would radically change the prerequisites for those activities."[4]

Because these were lectures Bonhoeffer gave throughout the course of Finkenwalde's existence, the text we have was not conceived as a whole, but developed and evolved into the form that Bonhoeffer finally had published. Bethge spells out the developing nature of this material: "Bonhoeffer did not appear at the preacher's seminary with a manuscript ready for publication; but entire sections of his lectures went straight into the book. He continued to make alterations and deletions and to insert whole new chapters until the last page of the manuscript was delivered."[5]

this sentence was translated as, "When Christ calls a man, he bids him come and die." The current translation more closely reflects the tone of the German original; see DBWE 4:87n11.

2. DBWE 14:119, see also in *DB-ER*, 450.
3. The first, temporary location of the seminary, before settling at Finkenwalde.
4. *DB-ER*, 450.
5. Ibid., 451. See also Geffrey B. Kelly and John D. Godsey, "Editors' Introduction to the English Edition," *Discipleship*, DBWE 4:24ff, for a discussion of the writing of *Discipleship*, and H. Gaylon Barker, "Editor's Introduction to the English Edition," DBWE 14, for the relationship of *Discipleship* to the rest of Finkenwalde's curriculum.

Early in his discourse on discipleship, Bonhoeffer posed the question that both revealed his overriding concern and laid out the theme for the text. "What does Jesus Christ want of us?" he asked.[6] This is the question about Christian discipleship, and it was a question that had become particularly troubling to Bonhoeffer, because even though people come to church with high expectations to hear God's word, "there are so many dissonant sounds, which still obscure the pure word of Jesus and make a genuine decision more difficult. We surely intend our preaching to be preaching Christ alone."[7] This development created a situation in which Bonhoeffer's question became important, even urgent; while the church had been good at defining itself in terms of a doctrine of grace, or living according to grace as a concept, "the word of grace has become frightfully empty" and the church was void of discipleship.

> Because we cannot deny that we no longer stand in true discipleship to Christ, while being members of a true-believing church with a pure doctrine of grace, but no longer members of a church which follows Christ, we therefore simply have to try to understand grace and discipleship again in correct relationship to each other. We can no longer avoid this. Our church's predicament is proving more and more clearly to be a question of how we are to live as Christians today.[8]

"What does Jesus Christ want of us?" How are we to live as Christians today? Bearing the tone of his more famous question from prison, what these questions and concerns share with that later one is that they all find their focus on the person of Jesus Christ and the demands of discipleship. Ultimately, for Bonhoeffer, the question about discipleship was not about morality but a personal response to Jesus

6. DBWE 4:37.
7. Ibid.
8. Ibid., 55.

Christ. Given the context, it was also a challenge: Whom do you serve—Jesus Christ or der Führer?

This conviction was based on Bonhoeffer's reading of Luther's doctrine of justification by faith alone with its demands of "costly grace." This stood in contradiction to what Bonhoeffer saw in the church of his day, which according to him was a misreading of Luther. As Day explains,

> Luther's teaching on justification by faith alone had been perverted into a legitimation for preaching only the comfortable side of the Word of God, the forgiveness without the imperative. Jesus' address was made to soothe, but not to demand. The church's teaching had become an ideology of political quietism or worse. God's grace was made a real bargain. The doctrine of salvation by faith had led not simply to accepting the sinner in the world, but to accepting the sin and the blasphemous world of the Third Reich. It served to rationalize the secularization of the church and to legitimate the respectable bourgeois existence of professed Christians. But Jesus' call is not soft. It upsets the world of Middle Christianity.[9]

Seeing these developments as a legitimate threat to the church's existence, "what Bonhoeffer was seeking to do in this book was to reaffirm the elusive concept of 'faith' in all its implications."[10] Bonhoeffer's main purpose in writing *Discipleship*, therefore, according to Sorum,

> is to recover grace, the grace that it confesses in the Reformation affirmation that justification is by faith in Jesus Christ alone. Cheap grace is *not* grace and costly grace is *simply* grace. Cheap grace is the most merciless legalism and costly grace is the free gift of Jesus Christ, received by faith alone. Cheap grace is a betrayal of grace in the name

9. Thomas Day, *Dietrich Bonhoeffer on Christian Community and Common Sense* (New York: Edwin Mellen, 1982), 104–5. Cf. Kelly and Godsey, "Editors' Introduction," DBWE 4:7, who, in commenting on the main argument of *Discipleship*, state, "It is clear that here, as throughout his theology, Bonhoeffer's framework is Luther's doctrine of justification by faith alone."
10. *DB-ER*, 454.

> of grace. Costly grace is just plan grace, grace without qualifications, without conditions, without price.[11]

What Bonhoeffer saw was both the need for a new reformation as well as a new vision of the church and Christian life. Certainly the signs exhibited by the German Christians pointed out the real problem that had to be confronted, which was precisely what Bonhoeffer set out to do with *Discipleship.* And the way to do that was to reclaim Luther's understanding of justification by faith.[12]

It is with this specific concern in mind that Martin Kuske and Ilse Tödt caution us in our approach to this text, reminding us that this "is a book that needs to be seen within a specific context," namely the Finkenwalde community and the German Church Struggle. "Bonhoeffer did not intend it to be a piece of 'timeless truth;' rather, he sought to uncover the specific truth for 'today.'"[13]

We cannot approach this text, therefore, without being aware of the basic outline of both Bonhoeffer's life and the conditions in the church and world to which he was responding. Noting Bonhoeffer's

11. Jonathan D. Sorum, "Cheap Grace, Costly Grace, and Just Plain Grace: Bonhoeffer's Defense of Justification by Faith Alone," *Lutheran Forum* 27, no. 3 (August 1993): 20.
12. It should be noted that Bonhoeffer found Søren Kierkegaard an important ally in this task. According to Kelly and Godsey, "Editors' Introduction," DBWE 4:10, "In his retrieval of Luther, Bonhoeffer found an unexpected ally in the Danish philosopher Søren Kierkegaard. Despite their differences over what Bonhoeffer believed to be an exaggerated individualism in Kierkegaard, he believed that Kierkegaard alone of nineteenth-century thinkers had correctly perceived the true dialectic of faith and obedience in Luther's interpretation of the Gospel." In particular, it was Kierkegaard's study of Luther, *Der Einzelne und die Kirche: Über Luther und den Protestantismus* (Berlin: E. Wolff, 1934), where he used the concepts of "the cheapness and costliness of faith in Luther's historical context" and addressed the outcome of Luther's theology, in which grace had been turned into "an abstract principle," that served as a primary source influencing Bonhoeffer's thinking (see DBWE 4:11). See also Martin Kuske and Ilse Tödt, "Editors' Afterword to the German Edition," *Discipleship*, DBWE 4:301, where they point out that Bonhoeffer hoped that Kierkegaard's criticism of the Danish state church of the nineteenth- century would inspire a similar response in the German Lutheran church of his day. Matthew D. Kirkpatrick, *Attacks on Christendom in a World Come of Age: Kierkegaard, Bonhoeffer, and the Question of a Religionless Christianity* (Eugene, OR: Pickwick, 2011), also discusses the extent of Kierkegaard's influence on Bonhoeffer's writing, and argues that Bonhoeffer was also a keen interpreter of Kierkegaard.
13. Kuske and Tödt, "Editors' Afterword," DBWE 4:289.

leading role in the Confessing Church's conflict with the German Christians, which by the mid-1930s had come to be defined legally as well as ecclesiastically, Kelly and Godsey describe the context in which Bonhoeffer was working and in which he was lifting up an alternative vision of the church and the Christian life:

> Bonhoeffer was a leading figure in the Confessing Church, which stood in open conflict with the German Reich Church. The leaders of this Reich Church supported the Nazi government and accused the opposition churches of being disloyal citizens. The Barmen and Dahlem Synods of the Confessing Church has already issued declarations of faith and church policy that set Bonhoeffer's Confessing Church in open hostility to the regnant Nazi ideology. Subsequent state regulations had squeezed this opposition church into narrow enclaves tarred with ecclesiastical illegality. Acts of brutality and psychological coercion followed, as well as imprisonment of dissident pastors, as the Nazi government tightened its control over the ecclesiastical sphere and thus impeded any putative church opposition. Beatings, arrests, police terror, and rampant injustice were commonplace in the years in which the Nazi government reinforced its grip on every aspect of life in Germany. It was not lost on Bonhoeffer that these developments and the sluggish reaction of many church leaders were in sharp contrast to those daring, even shocking, sayings of Jesus, the Beatitudes. For Bonhoeffer, Jesus' words seemed to be addressed as much to persecuted Jews and Christians in Germany as to Jesus' closest followers during his public life.
>
> In the midst of the turmoil of those years, Bonhoeffer delivered his lectures on the Sermon on the Mount that later became a principal theme of *Discipleship.* He was determined to break the church out of its standard mode of compromise with, and accommodation to, political powers for the sake of its own survival as church. That self-serving, ecclesiastical tactic—while eminently practical if the church's sole purpose was to be a sacramental system and an easygoing provider of grace—had convinced Bonhoeffer that the churches of Germany had, in effect, cheapened themselves. He believed that, by not resisting an evil government's temptation, they had misled ordinary citizens in their understanding of salvation. The Protestant principle of "faith alone" appeared to be retooled to justify inaction and indifference. The church seemed awash in pietistic evasions that softened the force of the

> Reformation's insistence on "God's word alone." Patriotic Germans gave glory to Adolf Hitler and thus unwittingly denied the glory due to God alone.[14]

Given that context and Bonhoeffer's own theological stance, this text should be read, therefore,

> as a daring attempt to retrieve Luther from the shambles of his irrelevance in the Hitler era. For Bonhoeffer, Luther seemed to have been eclipsed by the reductionism of Protestant liberalism in which Jesus became a mere teacher of moral truths and the Protestant doctrine of faith alone was tamed by humanistic acculturation. For Luther, though, faith and ethical convictions were one reality; the world of Jesus Christ and the world of human struggles were a single world.[15]

In the opening section Bonhoeffer himself described the problem in the following manner:

> Like ravens we have gathered around the carcass of cheap grace. From it we have imbibed the poison which has killed the following of Jesus among us. The doctrine of pure grace experienced an unprecedented deification. The pure doctrine of grace became its own God, grace itself. Luther's teachings are quoted everywhere, but twisted from their truth into self-delusion. They say if only our church is in possession of a doctrine of justification, then it is surely a justified church! They say Luther's true legacy should be recognizable in make grace as cheap as possible. Being Lutheran should mean that discipleship is left to the legalists, the Reformed, or the enthusiasts, all for the sake of grace. They say that the world is justified and Christians in discipleship are made out to be heretics. A people became Christian, became Lutheran, but at the cost of discipleship, at an all-too-cheap price. Cheap grace had won.[16]

14. Kelly and Godsey, "Editors' Introduction," DBWE 4:2–3. While this is true, Bonhoeffer and the Confessing Church were primarily concentrated on their church, not on the issues related to Jews, Catholics, etc.
15. Ibid., 8. Here, too, the contrast between Bonhoeffer's position and that of the German Christians should be noted. The Nazis used Luther as well, holding him up as an example of "Germanness" and using his views of the Jews in support of their anti-Semitic policies. From this perspective they could see the role of Hitler as that of completing the Reformation. See also Doris L. Bergen, *Twisted Cross: The German Christian Movement in the Third Reich* (Chapel Hill, NC: University of North Carolina Press, 1996).

By turning grace into a principle and, in a sense, replacing the real presence of God in Christ with an abstraction, the church that bore Luther's name had forfeited Luther's heritage. It had held onto grace as a concept, faith as a doctrine, but it had become hollow because it was not attached to Jesus Christ. Unlike some of his contemporaries, Bonhoeffer's understanding of Luther was that of one who did not dismiss obedience, but linked faith and obedience inextricably together. Luther's understanding of justification was not one that led to complacency, in which grace could be used to soothe the guilty conscience without making any demands on the believer. Grace, rather than being distributed freely with no strings attached, was to result in complete obedience to the call to follow Jesus Christ.

Bonhoeffer's presentation of justification was one that had its foundations in his early reading of Luther's theology. Consistent from his student days onward, Bonhoeffer interpreted justification as central to Luther's theology, giving shape to Luther's entire vision of the Christian life. Justification, for Luther and for Bonhoeffer, grew out of the faith relationship with Jesus Christ. Believing that God acts to justify the believer, the believer, in turn, responds in faith. That relationship of faith creates a new person whose life bears witness to the justifying act of God. Because justification brings life out of death, nothing in one's own life remains unchanged.

However, with the church's emphasis on cheap grace, Bonhoeffer did not see this being proclaimed in his day. The distinction he drew between cheap grace and costly grace was his way of reemphasizing the nature of Luther's understanding of justification.[17] Luther, for

16. DBWE 4:53.

17. See Jonathan D. Sorum, "The Eschatological Boundary in Dietrich Bonhoeffer's 'Nachfolge'" (ThD diss., Luther Northwestern Theological Seminary, 1994)," 217 n93. Together with the editors of the new critical edition of this text, he insists that Bonhoeffer maintains Luther's position on justification being the sole act of God on the cross and, therefore, does not represent any attempt to reinsert the law or any role for human action that might contribute to one's justification.

example, in his discussion of the law and Christian freedom in his lectures on Galatians from 1535, addressed a basic problem in Christian living. On the one hand, there is the temptation to see justification by faith as a freeing from the law to such an extent that we use our freedom as a license to do whatever we want. On the other hand, there is the attempt to become righteous by living according to the law, only to become enslaved by it. His response describes a situation not unlike that which Bonhoeffer is addressing with his distinction between "cheap" and "costly" grace. According to Luther,

> Thus there is danger on both sides, although the one is more tolerable than the other. If grace or faith is not preached, no one is saved; for faith alone justifies and saves. On the other hand, if faith is preached, as it must be preached, the majority of men understand the teaching about faith in a fleshly way and transform the freedom of the spirit into the freedom of the flesh. This can be discerned today in all classes of society, both high and low. They all boast of being evangelicals and boast of Christian freedom. Meanwhile, however, they give in to their desires and turn to greed, sexual desire, pride, envy, etc. No one performs his duty faithfully; no one serves another by love. This misbehavior often makes me so impatient that I would want such "swine that trample pearls underfoot" (Matthew 7:6) still to be under the tyranny of the pope. For it is impossible for this people of Gomorrah to be ruled by the Gospel of Peace.

This situation, however, is not the fault of the hearers alone. The problem begins with the preachers and teachers of the gospel. Luther continues,

> What is more, we ourselves, who teach the Word, do not perform our own duty with as much care and zeal here in the light of truth as we used to in the darkness of ignorance. The more certain we are about the freedom granted to us by Christ, the more unresponsive and slothful we are in presenting the Word, praying, doing good works, enduring evil, and the like. And if Satan were not troubling us inwardly with

> spiritual trials and outwardly with persecution by our enemies and with the contempt and ingratitude of our own followers, we would become utterly smug, lazy, and useless for anything good; thus in time we would lose the knowledge of Christ and faith in Him, would forsake the ministry of the Word, and would look for some more comfortable way of life, more suitable to our flesh. This is what many of our followers are beginning to do, motivated by the fact that those who labor in the Word not only do not get their support from this but are even treated shamefully by those whom their preaching of the Gospel has set free from the miserable slavery of the pope. Forsaking the poor and offensive figure of Christ, they involve themselves in the business of this present life; and they serve, not Christ but their own appetites (Rom. 16:18), with results that they will experience in due time.[18]

The task Bonhoeffer set out to accomplish, to reclaim justification by faith alone and to free the churches in bondage to secular powers, was conceived christologically. The question before the church was, "What does Jesus want of us?" That was a question about discipleship or following Jesus Christ. According to Kelly and Godsey, Bonhoeffer

> crafted a Christ-centered spirituality that took the insights developed in his doctoral dissertation, *Sanctorum Communio*, and his *Habilitationsschrift, Act and Being*, into the practical level of church life in the midst of inimical, heathen forces, which in his opinion were corrupting an entire nation. He was convinced that a new way of being church had to come about to counteract the corroding attraction of

18. Martin Luther, "Lectures on Galatians (1535)," chapters 5 and 6, *LW* 27:48–49. Cf. Klemens von Klemperer, "Beyond Luther? Dietrich Bonhoeffer and Resistance against National Socialism" *Pro Ecclesia* 6, no. 2 (Spring 1997): 189, who argues that Bonhoeffer used a Lutheran argument to distinguish between cheap and costly grace: "Cheap grace belongs to the order of works. It encourages the sinner to rely entirely on grace, and therefore, as Bonhoeffer put it poignantly, to 'cling' to his 'bourgeois secular existence' with the expectation of being 'covered' (as by an insurance policy). Costly grace, by contrast, is obtained, as it is according to Luther, by self-negation, by surrender to God and Christ, in short by discipleship. But alas, as Bonhoeffer lamented, the outcome of the Reformation was 'the victory, not of Luther's prescription of grace in all its purity and costliness,' but of grace 'at the cheapest price, grace without discipleship' It was Bonhoeffer's emphasis on the otherness of God and man's need for grace, that is costly grace, that epitomized his rediscovery of Luther."

> a popular ideology that appealed to the baser elements in the human psyche by which people can be manipulated to evil ends.[19]

The center of the book and the core of Bonhoeffer's argument is chapter 4, "Discipleship and the Cross."[20] Here Jesus is clearly the suffering and rejected Christ on the cross and discipleship is the call to suffer with Christ. Bonhoeffer's reflections in this chapter are framed by Jesus' own passion prediction as recorded in Mark 8:31–38. It is after Jesus announces his own suffering, rejection, and death that "he called the crowd with his disciples, and said to them, 'If any want to become my followers, let them deny themselves and take up their cross and follow me'" (Mark 8:34). "The call to discipleship," therefore, according to Bonhoeffer,

> is connected here with the proclamation of Jesus' suffering. Jesus Christ has to suffer and be rejected. . . . So Jesus has to make it clear and unmistakable to his disciples that the need to suffer now applies to them, too. Just as Christ is only Christ as one who suffers and is rejected, so a disciple is a disciple only in suffering and being rejected, thereby participating in crucifixion. Discipleship as allegiance to the person of Jesus Christ places the follower under the law of Christ, that is, under the cross.[21]

To be a follower of Jesus means to be tied to his cross. The cross of Christ and the Christian's are one and the same. To avoid the cross, either Christ's or the Christian's, is to deny Christ. Yet the church has always "taken offense at the suffering Christ," as was evidenced by Peter, the rock upon whom the church is founded, when he rebukes Jesus for talking about his suffering and death. The same avoidance was evident, according to Bonhoeffer, in his church; misplaced or

19. Kelly and Godsey, "Editors' Introduction," DBWE 4:2.
20. *DB-ER*, 450, where Bethge calls it the "cornerstone of the work from the beginning."
21. DBWE 4:84–85.

competing loyalties meant the church had accepted cheap grace and was unwilling to bear the cross.

Jesus, however, cannot be prevented from going to Jerusalem. Clearly, the Christ who calls believers to discipleship is none other than the crucified Christ. He is a suffering and rejected Christ. Bonhoeffer emphasized Christ's rejection, because, as he insisted, suffering alone could have been celebrated. "Indeed, the entire compassion and admiration of the world could focus on the suffering. Looked upon as something tragic, the suffering could in itself convey its own value, its own honor and dignity."[22] Being rejected, however, takes away any dignity and honor from his suffering. "It had to be dishonorable suffering. Suffering and rejection express in summary form the cross of Jesus. Death on the cross means to suffer and die as one rejected and cast out."[23]

God is a God who bears the sins of the world, and the Christian is one who bears suffering in the world for the sake of Christ. Discipleship is "Christ-suffering" and this leads to death. In the first instance, it is death of the old self. Entering into the death of Jesus, the disciple is "summoned away from our attachments to this world" and reoriented toward God. But, secondly, discipleship spells death because the disciple continues Christ's suffering in the world: The good works of Christians are none other than the works that "Jesus himself created in the disciples when he called them, when he made them the light of the world under his cross—poverty, being strangers, meekness, peacemaking, and finally being persecuted and rejected, and in all of them the one work: bearing the cross of Jesus Christ."[24]

Similar language is used elsewhere. In chapter 10, "The Body of Christ," for example, Bonhoeffer described how the baptized people

22. Ibid., 85.
23. Ibid.
24. Ibid., 114. Cf. Sorum, "Cheap Grace, Costly Grace," 22, where he draws a similar conclusion.

of God continue to live "in the bodily presence of and community with Jesus."[25] Since the time of Adam, God has been giving "the divine *word* to sinful humanity, in order to seek and *accept* us."[26] But humanity, in turn, kept "refusing to be accepted by God" until "the Son of God becomes a human being" and comes to earth.

> Now it is no longer only through the word of preaching that God accepts humanity, but also in the body of Christ. God's mercy sends the Son in the flesh, so that in his flesh he may shoulder and carry all of humanity. The Son of God accepts all of humanity in bodily form, the same humanity which in hate of God and pride of flesh had rejected the incorporeal, invisible word of God. In the body of Jesus Christ humanity is now truly and bodily accepted; it is accepted as it is, out of God's mercy.[27]

Clearly, salvation is an act of God alone by which God accepts those who reject divine love and mercy. In language that remains consistent with that of *Sanctorum Communio*, Bonhoeffer continued,

> The earthly body of Jesus is crucified and dies. In his death the new humanity is also crucified and dies with him. Since Christ had not taken on an individual human being, but rather human "form," sinful flesh, human "nature," all that he bore, therefore, suffers and dies with him. All our infirmities and all our sin he bears to the cross. It is we who are crucified with him and who die with him. True, Christ's earthly body dies, but only to rise again from death as an incorruptible, transfigured body. It is the same body—the tomb was, indeed, empty!—and yet it is a new body. Jesus thus brings humanity not only into death with him, but also into the resurrection. Thus even in his glorified body he still bears the humanity which he had taken on during his days on earth.[28]

Similar imagery is used in the final chapter, "The Image of Christ," where Bonhoeffer placed the emphasis on God's mercy, because

25. DBWE 4:213.
26. Ibid.
27. Ibid., 214.
28. Ibid., 215–16.

humanity had been created in God's image. From the beginning, humanity bore the image of God; however, Adam, not content with being a creature and God-like at the same time, chose to become like God in his own way. "Adam became 'like God'—sicut deus—in his own way. Having made himself into a god, he now no longer had a God. . . . Since then, the proud children of Adam have sought to restore this lost image of God in themselves by means of their own efforts."[29] But always to no avail.

God, however, does not give up. "God seeks the divine image in us, in order to love it. But God cannot find it except by assuming, out of sheer mercy, the image and form of the lost human being. God must conform to the human image, since we are no longer able to conform to the image of God."[30] And there is only one way for this to happen.

> Since fallen human beings cannot recover and assume the form of God, there is only *one* way to find help. It is not other than God, who assumes human form and comes to us. The Son of God who, in the form of God, lived with the Father, empties himself of this divine form and comes to human beings in the form of a servant (Phil. 2:5ff). Changing one's form, something which was not possible for human beings, now takes place within God. God's own image, which had remained with God through eternity, now assumes the image of the fallen, sinful human being. God sends the divine Son in the likeness of sinful flesh (Rom. 8:2f). God sends God's Son—that is the only way to find help. Neither a new idea nor a better religion would suffice to accomplish this goal.[31]

In this instance, Bonhoeffer compared and contrasted human beings and God: humans want to become like God, which is the source of all our woe. God, on the other hand, becomes like us, refashioning and transforming us. The only way is for God to "take human form

29. Ibid., 281–82.
30. Ibid., 282.
31. Ibid., 283.

and come to us." In Jesus Christ the image of God becomes real in the world. "The incarnation, Jesus' word and deed, and his death of the cross are integral elements in this image." The form that God takes in the world is very different from the image of God that human beings wanted to assume for themselves. "The one born in poverty, who befriended and sat at table to eat with tax collectors and sinners, and who, on the cross, was rejected and abandoned by God and human beings—this is God in human form, this is the human being who is the new image of God."[32]

Followers of Jesus in the world, followers of the image of God in the world, must be conformed

> to the image of the obedient, suffering servant of God on the cross. Whoever seeks to bear the transfigured image of Jesus must first have borne the image of the crucified one, defiled in the world. No one is able to recover the lost image of God unless they come to participate in the image of the incarnate and crucified Jesus Christ. It is with this image alone that God is well-pleased.[33]

To be conformed to the crucified Christ is not based on some human ideal nor is it some kind of work done on the part of human believers; even this remains the work of God in Christ.

> To be conformed to the image of Jesus Christ is not an ideal of realizing some kind of similarity with Christ which we are asked to attain. It is not we who change ourselves into the image of God. Rather, it is the very image of God, the form of Christ, which seeks to take shape with us. . . . Our goal is to be shaped into the entire *form* of the *incarnate*, the *crucified*, and the *risen one*."[34]

32. Ibid., 284.
33. Ibid.
34. Ibid., 284–85.

And because God is known only in and through Christ, those who are his disciples take on the same cruciform shape in the world as does God. Bonhoeffer continued,

> The form of Christ on earth is the *form of death* [*Todesgestalt*] of the crucified one. The image of God is the image of Jesus Christ on the cross. It is into this image that the disciple's life must be transformed. It is a life in the image and likeness of Christ's death (Phil. 3:10; Rom. 6:4f). It is a crucified life (Gal. 2:19). . . . Those who live out of their baptism live out of their death. Christ marks the life of his own with their daily dying in the struggle of the spirit against the flesh, and with their daily suffering the pains of death which the devil inflicts on Christians. It is the suffering of none other than Jesus Christ that all of his disciples on earth have to endure.[35]

Ultimately, Christ is alive in the world and is present in and through the church, where the work of God continues:

> The life of Jesus Christ here on earth has not yet concluded. Christ continues to live it in the lives of his followers. . . . The incarnate, crucified, and transfigured one has entered into me and lives my life. . . . The incarnate, the crucified, and the transfigured Christ takes on form in individuals because they are members of his body, the church. The church bears the incarnate, crucified, and risen form of Jesus Christ. The church is, first of all, Christ's image. . . . The followers look only to the one whom they follow. But now the final word about those who as disciples bear the image of the incarnate, crucified, and risen Jesus Christ, and who have been transformed into the image of God, is that they are called to be "imitators of God." The follower [Nachfolger] of Jesus is the imitator [Nachnahmer] of God.[36]

35. Ibid., 285.

36. Ibid., 286–88. Sorum, "Eschatological Boundary," 388–89, offers the following explanation about how Luther and Bonhoeffer understand this term: "Because he [Christ] truly carries on his own life in Christians, they can live and act as he did. . . . The life of following is not what is usually thought of in the English word 'imitation.' Rather, Christians are only a mirror for the image of Christ as they themselves look only to the present Jesus Christ himself, the one whom they follow. But of such it can finally be said that they are indeed 'imitators of God.'"

Bonhoeffer's discussion about cheap grace and costly grace, those phrases that have entered the theological lexicon and are used by theologians of all stripes, are conceived of christologically as well. "Costly grace" is the very "incarnation of God," he says, whereas "cheap grace," by contrast, is "grace without discipleship, grace without the cross, grace without the living, incarnate Jesus Christ."[37] Grace, as defined by Bonhoeffer, only makes sense and is real where it is understood from the perspective of God's act in Christ. Grace, by definition, according to Bonhoeffer, is costly because of what it cost God:

> Above all, grace is costly, because it was costly to God, because it costs God the life of God's Son—"you were bought with a price"—and because nothing can be cheap to us which is costly to God. Above all, it is grace because the life of God's Son was not too costly for God to give in order to make us live. God did, indeed, give him up for us. Costly grace is the incarnation of God.[38]

If God in Christ pays that kind of price, how is it possible that followers of Christ should expect grace to be cheaply dispensed? Therefore, true faith results in obedience, which is nothing other than being conformed to the image of the crucified Christ in the world. Accordingly, "*Only the believers obey*, and *only the obedient believe*."[39] Both faith and obedience must be maintained or else neither can be. To state the first without the second proves unfaithful to the Bible.

> Only the believer obeys—we think we can understand that. Of course, obedience follows faith, the way good fruit comes from a good tree, we say. First there is faith, then obedience. If this meant only that faith alone justifies us and not deeds of obedience, then it is a firm and necessary precondition for everything else. But if it meant a chronological

37. DBWE 4:44.
38. Ibid., 45.
39. Ibid., 63.

> sequence, that faith would have to come first, to be later followed by obedience, then faith and obedience are torn apart, and the very practical question remains open: when does obedience start? Obedience remains separated from faith. Because we are justified by faith, faith and obedience have to be distinguished. But their division must never destroy their unity, which lies in the reality that faith exists only in obedience, is never without obedience. Faith is only faith in deeds of obedience.[40]

It is under this rubric of faith and obedience that Bonhoeffer's discussion of Luther's understanding of justification is to be understood. Obedience is an act of faith by which a person loses oneself in Jesus Christ.

Obedience to the call of Jesus is an act of faith whereby the believer sees all of life in terms of the cross of Christ. It is there that one for the first times sees oneself as one is and can acknowledge the justifying act of Jesus Christ to create new life. "Therefore, obedience is *already* faith, trust in Jesus Christ alone." At the same time, "The moment of obedience, then, is the decisive break with the world of enmeshed unbounded selves, the sinful world, the old age,"[41] and is the first step into the new life in Christ.

This, by no means, should be taken as a turning away from the world. New life in Christ is not meant to take the Christian out of the world, but places them back in the world, which is the place that God is to be found. Bonhoeffer explained it in the following manner:

> Christians are to remain in the world, not because of the God-given goodness of the world, nor even because of their responsibility for the course the world takes. They are to remain in the world solely for the

40. Ibid., 63–64. James Burtness, *Shaping the Future: The Ethics of Dietrich Bonhoeffer* (Philadelphia: Fortress Press, 1985), 112, compares this statement of Bonhoeffer to Luther's statement from his treatise on *Freedom of the Christian* (*LW* 31:344), where he says, "A Christian is perfectly free, Lord of all, subject to none. A Christian is a perfectly dutiful servant of all, subject to all." This comparison is significant, because *Discipleship* was for Bonhoeffer what *Freedom of the Christian* was for Luther.
41. DBWE 4:218 and 220.

> sake of the body of the Christ who became incarnate—for the sake of the church-community. They are to remain in the world in order to engage the world in a frontal attack. . . . The world must be contradicted within the world. That is why Christ became a human being and died in the midst of his enemies.[42]

For Bonhoeffer, Luther's return to the world from the monastery is a prime example of the meaning of discipleship in the world.

> Luther did not return to the world based on a "more positive assessment" of this world, or even by abandoning the expectation of the earliest church that Christ's return was imminent. His return rather was meant as a protest and criticism of the secularization of Christianity within the monastic life. By calling Christians back into the world, Luther in fact calls them to become unworldly in the true sense. This actually proved to be his own experience. Luther's call to return into the world always was a call to become a part of the visible church-community of the incarnate Lord. And the same is also true of Paul.[43]

He had made a similar point at the beginning of his work on the discussion of cheap grace and costly grace. Cheap grace, he insisted, would have allowed Luther to remain in the monastery; but that was grace without obedience, grace without discipleship. Costly grace, on the other hand, is grace combined with obedience and is marked by following Christ back into the world, rather than being a retreat from the world. Discipleship, marked by costly grace, rather than stressing "the meritorious achievement of individuals" and the "self-denial of the disciple," both of which were part of Luther's constant struggle that, first, led him into the monastery and then shaped his life in the monastery, shattered Luther's attempts "to achieve a pious life" and threw him back into the arms of God's mercy.

42. Ibid., 244. This has overtones of Luther's teaching on vocation, in which the shoemaker, the housewife and the hangman serve God in their daily lives as much as the priests do.

43. Ibid., 245.

> It shattered his whole existence. Once again, he had to leave his nets and follow. The first time, when he entered the monastery, he left everything behind except himself, his pious self. This time even that was taken from him. He followed, not by his own merit, but by God's grace. He was not told, yes, you have sinned, but now all that is forgiven. Continue on where you were and comfort yourself with forgiveness! Luther had to leave the monastery and reenter the world, not because the world itself was good and holy, but because even the monastery was nothing else but world. . . . Following Jesus now had to be lived out in the midst of the world. What had been practiced in the special, easier circumstances of monastic life as a special accomplishment now had become what was necessary and commanded for every Christian in the world. Complete obedience to Jesus' commandments had to be carried out in the daily world of work. This deepened the conflict between the life of Christians and the life of the world in an unforeseeable way. The Christian had closed in on the world. It was hand-to-hand combat.[44]

From this perspective, the call of obedience to Christ is a call that is profoundly this-worldly. It is this-worldly, not for the sake of the world, but for the sake of Christ. This same emphasis will be repeated clearly in his *Ethics*; there Bonhoeffer will insist that because of Christ, God and the world must be understood together as a whole.

This emphasis on the part of Bonhoeffer that unites faith and obedience into the concept of costly grace is one that has parallels in Luther's theology.[45] A similar conclusion was made earlier by Regin

44. Ibid., 48–49.

45. Cf. Sorum, "Cheap Grace, Costly Grace," 22. Kelly and Godsey, "Editors' Introduction," DBWE 4:5, offer a similar evaluation: "The connection made between obedience and faith . . . was not, as some critics contended, a dangerous swing away from the Pauline/Protestant doctrine of justification by faith alone toward a more Catholic emphasis on good works. On the contrary, Bonhoeffer saw himself engaged in a struggle for the very soul of the Reformation, namely, personal faith lived in obedience to the call of Jesus Christ in correlation and simultaneity with the commands of Christ inspirited by the gift of faith. Such discipleship does not derive from abstract theologies or neatly packaged doctrinal systems. Nor is it expressed in punctilious obedience to approved laws or ritual correctness. The idea of Christ is not the force behind the call to discipleship, but the living Christ, to whom the Christian must be exclusively attached."

Prenter who, in his study comparing the theology of Bonhoeffer to the young Luther, points out that Luther linked faith and humility, insisting that only the one who is humble has faith. Citing passages from Luther's lectures on the Psalms and *Bondage of the Will*, he sees humility as that aspect of faith that recognizes one's sinfulness and acknowledges the justifying act of Christ.[46]

It should be emphasized, however, that for both Luther and Bonhoeffer, justification remains the sole act of Jesus Christ alone. By assuming the life of the sinner, Jesus himself through his own obedience to death on the cross accomplishes that which sinful humanity on its own could not. Even obedience is the act of Jesus on behalf of sinful humanity. The relationship of Christ and discipleship inherently places Christ (not an idea about him) at the center of the Christian life and the Christian squarely in the world; Bonhoeffer's comments are particularly poignant when seen in terms of the following perspective he provided on the German Church Struggle:

> Discipleship is commitment to Christ. Because Christ exists, he must be followed. An idea about Christ, a doctrinal system, a general religious recognition of grace or forgiveness of sins does not require discipleship. In truth, it even excludes discipleship; it is inimical to it. One enters into a relationship with an idea by way of knowledge, enthusiasm, perhaps even by carrying it out, but never by personal obedient discipleship. *Christianity without the living Jesus Christ remains necessarily a Christianity without discipleship; and Christianity without discipleship is always a*

46. Regin Prenter, "Bonhoeffer and the Young Luther," in *World Come of Age*, ed. Ronald Gregor Smith (Philadelphia: Fortress Press, 1970), 166; the psalm citation, which is taken from Luther's first lectures on the Psalms, reads, "No one is justified by faith unless he has already confessed himself through humility to be unjust. This is humility" (*WA* 4:345, 29). In *The Bondage of the Will*, Luther states, "It is thus for the sake of the elect that these things are published, in order that being humbled and brought back to nothingness by this means they may be saved" (*LW* 33:62). Cf. Christian Gremmels, "Rechtfertigung und Nachfolge: Martin Luther in Dietrich Bonhoeffers Buch 'Nachfolge,'" in *Dietrich Bonhoeffer heute: Die Aktualität seines Lebens und Werkes*, ed. Rainer Mayer and Peter Zimmerling (Giessen/Basel: Brunnen, 1992), 90–98, where he also draws upon the theme of faith and obedience in relationship to Bonhoeffer's understanding of Luther's article of justification.

> *Christianity without Jesus Christ.* It is an idea, a myth. A Christianity in which there is only God the Father, but not Christ as a living Son actually cancels discipleship. In that case there will be trust in God, but not discipleship. God's Son became human, he is the *mediator*—that is why discipleship is the right relation to him. Discipleship is bound to the mediator, and wherever discipleship is rightly spoken of, there the mediator, Jesus Christ, the Son of God is intended. Only the mediator, the God-human, can call to discipleship.[47]

*Discipleship* is a clear statement by Bonhoeffer that indicates that justification and Christology are inextricably linked.

As these examples show, Bonhoeffer's *Discipleship* is a work that is firmly rooted in Luther's *theologia crucis.*[48] As was true for his previous writings, here in *Discipleship,* Bonhoeffer's *theologia crucis* is a method for doing theology that has justification by faith as its content—and justification is conceived christologically. By linking justification and discipleship, Bonhoeffer provided the orientation that refuses to allow God to be separated from the world. Since God and the world are linked together, justification has an ethical component. Both are themes that will be expressed in Bonhoeffer's next major project, his *Ethics.*

As for Bonhoeffer's understanding of Jesus in *Discipleship,* it reflects the earlier christological orientation of the 1933 Christology lectures, going so far as to cite the same Luther quotation he had relied upon repeatedly. In this instance, he linked it to a series of statements that

47. DBWE 4:59 (emphasis added).

48. Cf. Kelly and Godsey, "Editors' Introduction," DBWE 4:6: "Here [*Discipleship*] as elsewhere, Bonhoeffer's writings are infused with a theology of the cross. The cross of Christ gives the lie to human claims that the world of cravings for domination is not the world of Christ. Bonhoeffer makes it clear that followers of Jesus Christ live immersed in the world, only to be called forth by their Lord to live in genuine worldliness. The Sermon on the Mount for Bonhoeffer is, after all, a worldly document. Paul's understanding of baptism and his directives for practical living in community entail dying to a world that, without Christ, is itself dying and in decay. Bonhoeffer is on solid theological ground when he delivers Christ's mandate for his followers to break with any world and culture that, in denying the dignity of people whom Christians are to affirm in faith as their brothers and sisters, denies Jesus Christ himself."

show the nature of faith: "Our human eyes see the body of Jesus; faith knows him as the Son of God. Our human eyes see the body of Jesus; faith knows him as the body of God incarnate. Our human eyes see Jesus in the flesh; faith knows him as bearing our flesh. 'To this human being you shall point and say: "Here is God"' (Luther)."[49]

Bethge supports such a conclusion with his own observation about the nature of *Discipleship* and its christological orientation. Drawing the conclusion that Bonhoeffer's theological development is marked by continuity, he says,

> Bonhoeffer's theological development showed an intrinsic consistency and continuity. Its tendency to concentrate on the issues and narrow them down was determined by a deep inner need, not by the requirement of methodology. In 1927 Bonhoeffer had sought the concrete entity of the body of Christ in the church in the form of a sociological structure (*Sanctorum Communio*). In 1929 he reformulated the question, asking whether the earthly continuity of revelation, in its free contingency, could be conceived in terms of the concrete church (*Act and Being*). In 1932 he examined the relationship of the body of Christ to the world by inquiring into the actual obedience to God's commandments. In 1933 his exposé of the structure of Christology was based upon the implications of all his previous thinking. And now, by interpreting belief in Christ as discipleship, he raised this Christology from its academic deathbed.[50]

But not only is *Discipleship* a continuation of the christological emphasis that came before it, it is clearly linked to what comes after as well. For example, the closing chapter, "The Image of Christ," sounds like the earliest manuscript, "Ethics as Formation," written for *Ethics*; there Bonhoeffer declared that discipleship is not a matter of imitating Jesus, but rather it means "being drawn into the form of Jesus Christ, by *being conformed to the unique form of the one who became*

49. DBWE 4:225.
50. *DB-ER*, 460.

*human, was crucified, and is risen.*" It has nothing to do with us striving "to be like Jesus," but rather happens when "the form of Jesus Christ himself so works on us that it molds us, conforming our form to Christ's own."[51] Noting the parallels in language, Kelly and Godsey conclude,

> Because the wording of the two texts is so very close, we can surmise that Bonhoeffer took elements from the last chapter of *Discipleship* in order to incorporate "Ethics as Formation" into the first part of his *Ethics*. Neither text suffers from pious spiritualizing. For Bonhoeffer, the primary challenge of ethical thinking is how to conform one's life to the teachings of Jesus and the patterns of his life lived in obedience to his Father's will.[52]

But it does not stop there. There are echoes of *Discipleship* in *Letters and Papers from Prison* as well. "One can hardly miss the close relationship between the theology of the cross throughout the pages of *Discipleship* and Bonhoeffer's theology of a suffering God whose power lies in God's paradoxical weakness that animated several sections of the prison letters."[53]

It is possible, if one reads Bonhoeffer's theology backward, namely, from the perspective of *Letters and Papers from Prison*, to conclude that *Discipleship* represents a break in the continuous development of worldly engagement. However, when viewed from within its context and in the ongoing development of Bonhoeffer's theology, it is not "a detour from his path"; instead, "it was an act of both preservation and preparation. Finkenwalde was envisioned as an alternative community prepared to withstand the temptations of Nazi ideology."[54]

51. *Ethics*, DBWE 6:93.
52. Kelly and Godsey, "Editors' Introduction," DBWE 4:21.
53. Ibid. See DBWE 14:37n8 for other examples of language from Finkenwalde finding its way into *LPP*.
54. Barker, "Editor's Introduction to the English Edition," DBWE 14:34.

> The ghetto of *Discipleship* is not the peaceful backwater of the pietists, nor is it the otherworldliness of the visionaries, neither of whom are particularly loyal to the world. *Discipleship* is a call to battle, it is concentration and hence restriction, so that the entire earth may be reconquered by the infinite message. To use Bonhoeffer's later terminology, when the penultimate, in its lust for glory and its thirst for adulation and sacrifice, thrust itself forward—and even in the church those who bowed before it are legion—Bonhoeffer turned toward the ultimate, for the sake of the penultimate.[55]

Seen in this manner, "instead of being a detour, Finkenwalde existed for the purpose of construction, because of the need to build a firm foundation to preserve the church's future";[56] in that light, *Discipleship* and Finkenwalde are integral parts of Bonhoeffer's theological legacy. Therefore,

> far from being a detour along the path to the worldliness of the prison letters, *Discipleship* stands, instead, as a pivotal text that explains the steps that led Bonhoeffer from the academic podium to his imprisonment and, despite the "dangers" he conceded (LPP 369), serves to illuminate some of the more moving passages of the prison letters that address the problem of human suffering.[57]

When seen in the context of Bonhoeffer's previous writings, the emphasis Bonhoeffer brings to *Discipleship* remains unchanged. When the Finkenwalde period is understood within the Lutheran parameters of Bonhoeffer's theology, then *Discipleship* is not a narrowing or retreat from the world. It was a means to nurture the people of God for life in the world.[58] In a world in which choices made all the difference, Bonhoeffer follows Luther and goes the way

55. *DB-ER*, 459.
56. Barker, "Editor's Introduction," DBWE 14:35.
57. Kelly and Godsey, "Editors' Introduction," DBWE 4:21.
58. This is supported by the conclusion drawn by Kelly and Godsey, ibid., 16: "While Bonhoeffer presents a countercultural picture of the church, "this countercultural perspective was not a flight *from* the world, but a struggle to establish a critical church presence *in* the world. Hence *Discipleship* contains ample exhortations for Christians to engage positively with the world."

of the cross, rather than sounding the note of triumphant German nationalism.

### *Life Together*

*Life Together*[59] was not a book Bonhoeffer planned to write. In fact, "in an ironical way we are indebted to the Gestapo for this remarkable book."[60] It was because of the action by the Gestapo in the summer of 1937 to close down the illegal seminaries of the Confessing Church that Bonhoeffer was motivated to put his thoughts down on paper; before that he was hesitant to provide a written description of life at Finkenwalde. Even though it was a clearly formulated idea, up to this time Bonhoeffer had produced only a rough draft of reflections on morning prayer and a brief introduction to meditation that had been included in one of the many circular letters distributed to former members of the seminary. Bonhoeffer was reluctant to write down these reflections because he realized that what they were doing was not for everyone. He was also concerned that his ideas for a spiritual discipline, once written down, would be interpreted as being a "law," as something that had to be done in a prescribed way.[61] Only with the closing of the seminary and the dispersal of the seminarians did he see the need to record for posterity not only their daily regimen and its rationale, but also to voice his conviction that the church needs to promote a sense of community like this if it is to have new life breathed into it.

59. Dietrich Bonhoeffer, *Life Together* and *Prayerbook of the Bible,* DBWE 5.
60. Kelly, "Editor's Introduction to the English Edition," DBWE 5:3.
61. Bonhoeffer's preface, which was not included in earlier English translations, makes it clear that his intention was not for *Life Together* to be seen as prescriptive. Instead, it is a description of one model to be commended to a church that is concerned about its faithfulness to God and worried about its future: "The variety of new ecclesial forms of community makes it necessary to enlist the vigilant cooperation of every responsible party. The following remarks are intended to provide only one individual contribution toward answering the extensive questions that have been raised thereby. As much as possible, may these comments help to clarify this experience and put it into practice" (DBWE 5:25).

So it was that over the course of four weeks in September/October of 1938, while staying at the home of his twin sister Sabine in Göttingen, that Bonhoeffer wrote *Life Together.* At the same time, the world outside his study was filled with turmoil. It was a world on the verge of war. It was "in this politically, ecclesiastically, and personally strained situation that Dietrich Bonhoeffer worked with the highest concentration." He was convinced that "if the Confessing Church claimed to be *the* church of Jesus Christ at that time in Germany," it had to be a community that lived according to the Word of God. "It is as a contribution to such that *Life Together* is to be understood."[62]

This little book is also significant because it was the last work of Bonhoeffer to be published while he was alive. If it were not for Eberhard Bethge, whose life-long friendship with Bonhoeffer grew out of that Finkenwalde experience, *Life Together* may well have been the final word from Bonhoeffer. It is possible that *Letters and Papers from Prison* would never have been known to the world. Without those prison reflections, our theological thinking would be poorer, for sure. Nevertheless, it is *Life Together* that stands as a living testimony of the power of Bonhoeffer's faith, which surely was not limited to the time and location of Finkenwalde. Without it, *Letters and Papers from Prison* could not have been written.

Ideas that were foundational for *Sanctorum Communio* and *Act and Being*, and later given expression in his Berlin lectures, were at the heart of *Life Together* and were lived out at Finkenwalde. The reality of the present Christ that was the dynamic that gives life to the church, which was Bonhoeffer's understanding in *Sanctorum Communio* onward, was lived out in *Life Together.* This text and the

62. See Gerhard L. Müller and Albrecht Schönherr, "Vorwort," in Dietrich Bonhoeffer, *Gemeinsames Leben. Das Gebetbuch der Bibel*, DBW 5 (Munich: Chr. Kaiser, 1987), 8-9.

experiment at community living that was Finkenwalde were literally a translation of Bonhoeffer's theology into reality.

The nature of this community as described by Bonhoeffer is infused with language of the *theologia crucis.* Jesus and his cross are the definition and measurement of community. It is by this means that God enters into the world and restores human community broken by sin. It is on the cross the God bears the pain and suffering of such brokenness. It is that same cross that both judges and justifies the world.

Like Finkenwalde, *Life Together* neither advocates a monastic escape from the world nor some form of legalism, but is a call to consider the serious demands of justification. This is seen in Bonhoeffer's own definition of Christian community, which is God's grace lived out in the world—not escape from the world, but preparation for life in the world.

Sounding the same theme as he did in *Sanctorum Communio*, but now addressing a community of believers who by their confession of faith could be persecuted, Bonhoeffer added another dimension to his discussion of Christian community. Christianity, by definition, equals community in Jesus Christ, nothing more and nothing less. "We belong to one another only through and in Jesus Christ."[63] He said, "The physical presence of other Christians is a source of incomparable joy and strength to the believer."[64] And yet such community should not be taken for granted, because Christians, as the body of Christ in the world, follow the way of Christ; therefore, they will find their life not in the safety and security of a closed community but in the midst of the world.

> Jesus Christ lived in the midst of his enemies. In the end all his disciples abandoned him. On the cross he was all alone, surrounded by criminals

63. DBWE 5:31.
64. Ibid., 29.

> and the jeering crowds. He had come for the express purpose of bringing peace to the enemies of God. So Christians, too, belong not in the seclusion of a cloistered life but in the midst of enemies. There they find their mission, their work. "To rule is to be in the midst of your enemies. And whoever will not suffer this does not want to be part of the rule of Christ; such a person wants to be among friends and sit among the roses and lilies, not with the bad people but the religious people. O you blasphemers and betrayers of Christ! If Christ had done what you are doing, who would ever have been saved?" (Luther).[65]

Three things are essential for understanding what it is he means when he talks about Christian community. First, "the Christian community is not a spiritual sanatorium,"[66] and those who seek refuge in to the Christian community as a means of escape both misunderstand and misuse community. Second, that is because the community is not an escape from the world. It is not a place to run away from the world's problems, but rather pushes the believer back into the world.[67] To seek escape in the church is only a distraction. Finally, Christian community is a divine reality and not a human ideal toward which one is to strive.[68] God's grace does not allow Christians to live in a dream world—nor an idealistic one, for that matter—to which people bring their aspirations. That is still a human community, and as such, is shaped by *human* dreams and hopes—and injected with *human* emotions and egos. While that might work for a utopian

65. Ibid., 27–28. The Luther citation is an abridgement of a passage from Luther's *Auslegung des 109. Psalms* (An interpretation of Psalm 109 [110], 1518), in *WA*, 1:696–97. The quotation as cited here is taken from Karl Witte, *Nun fruet euch lieben Christen gmein*, 226. See DBWE 5:28n3.
66. DBWE 5:82.
67. This corresponds to the stated purpose of the Finkenwalde community. In a letter of application to establish the "House of Brethren," which was conceived of as a means for some of the students who had completed their studies to remain a part of the Finkenwalde community, that was submitted to the Old Prussian Provincial Councils of the Brethren, the group responsible for the seminaries, Bonhoeffer defined the goal and purpose as follows: "The goal is not monastic isolation, but rather the most intensive concentration for ministry to the world" (DBWE 14:96). See Müller and Schönherr, "Editors' Afterword to the German Edition," DBWE 5:120.
68. DBWE 5:35.

vision, it stands opposed to God's community. In God's community, rather than coming with our demands or visionary ideals, "we enter into that life with other Christians, not as those who make demands, but as those who thankfully receive, . . . because God has already laid the only foundation" in Jesus Christ.[69] That is the true nature of community. Therefore, "Christian community is not an ideal we have to realize, but rather a reality created by God in which we may participate."[70]

When Bonhoeffer moves to discuss the centrality of community for the Christian life, the direct link to his understanding of the church presented first in *Sanctorum Communio* can be seen. Community is central to a definition of Christianity for three reasons:

First, because of Christ, Christians need others. The Christian's life, according to Bonhoeffer, has been taken up into the life of God. Therefore it is no longer characterized by self-centered needs, desires, or concerns. Because of the "alien righteousness" that comes from God, it is not something that comes from within the person (but is always *extra nos*); for that reason, the Christian needs others. Since God's word always comes to us from without, it must be spoken by others.

> Christians need other Christians who speak God's Word to them. They need them again and again when they become uncertain and disheartened because, living by their own resources, they cannot help themselves without cheating themselves out of the truth. They need other Christians as bearers and proclaimers of the divine word of salvation. They need them solely for the sake of Jesus Christ.[71]

Therefore, each member of the church-community serves as a messenger of salvation for another. This is determined by grace alone.

69. Ibid., 36.
70. Ibid., 38.
71. Ibid., 32.

Second, "a Christian comes to others only through Jesus Christ." Without Christ, human relationships are characterized by conflict. In fact, there is no relationship with God or one another without Christ. But because of Jesus Christ, "now Christians can live with each other in peace; they can love and serve one another; they can become one."[72]

Third, Jesus Christ, who has taken on human nature, unites humanity with God. "Now we are in him. Wherever he is, he bears our flesh, he bears us. And, where he is, there we are too—in the incarnation, on the cross, and in his resurrection."[73] That is the meaning of the body of Christ. And that unites us for all eternity.

This is the definition of community that formed the foundation for the communal life at Finkenwalde. The implications of Bonhoeffer's vision of community are very decisive:

> The other who comes face to face with me earnestly and devoutly seeking community is not the brother or sister with whom I am to relate in the community. My brother or sister is instead that other person who has been redeemed by Christ, absolved from sin, and called to faith and eternal life. What persons are in themselves as Christians, in their inwardness and piety, cannot constitute the basis of our community, which is determined by what those persons are in terms of Christ. Our community consists solely in what Christ has done to both of us.[74]

If people, especially our enemies, were to be judged from a human point of view, the focus would most likely be on the differences and the dislikes. Likewise, the response to them would be one of tension, anger, fear, and hatred. But in God's eyes, all people are equal. In Christ, all people share a common bond. According to Bonhoeffer, all are brothers and sisters by virtue of what Christ has done for us.[75] In the truest sense, Christian community is based on justification of

72. Ibid., 33.
73. Ibid.
74. Ibid., 34.

sinners through grace alone. For that reason, it is not a human but a spiritual reality.

Because the church is a community based in God's reality rather than any human ideal, it will not be limited by any "principle of selection" or characterized by "divisions" that are the result of self-love. It will not be an exclusionary community, but will be marked by its inclusivity. The very nature of exclusivity denies the reality of the church, Jesus Christ himself. "The exclusion of the weak and insignificant, the seemingly useless people, from everyday Christian life in community may actually mean the exclusion of Christ; for in the poor sister or brother, Christ is knocking at the door."[76]

As a community of faith called together in the name of Jesus, it is nourished and strengthened by God's word—for it is there, in God's word, that we know of God's love and will for us. Whether in public worship or in individual private meditation on God's word, Bonhoeffer was concerned about the importance that Scripture has for Christian life and faith.

75. This same idea is expressed in similar terms when Bonhoeffer turns to the subject of intercessory prayer: "Offering intercessory prayer means nothing other than Christians bringing one another into the presence of God, seeing each other under the cross of Jesus as poor human beings and sinners in need of grace. Then everything about other people that repels me falls away. Then I see them in all their need, hardship, and distress. Their need and their sin become so heavy and oppressive to me that I feel as if they were my own, and I can do nothing else but bid: Lord, you yourself, you alone, deal with them according to your firmness and your goodness. Offering intercessory prayer means granting other Christians the same right we have received, namely, the right to stand before Christ and to share in Christ's mercy" (ibid., 90–91). This is language similar to that which he used in *Sanctorum Communio*, where he described the church along the lines of Luther.

76. DBWE 5:45–46. In Nazi Germany this was more than a theoretical discussion. This statement could, in fact, be viewed as a political statement meant to contradict the ideology of Hitler's Germany. But, in addition, this statement is a concrete expression of Bonhoeffer's Christology that portrays Jesus consistently as one who identifies with the poor, the weak, and the outcast. See ibid., 46n23, where the editor connects this statement to two previous statements by Bonhoeffer in which Jesus is portrayed as a beggar: first, in his 1928 Advent sermon in Barcelona, where Bonhoeffer uses of the image of Jesus knocking at the door asking for help "in the form of a beggar, in the form of a ruined human being in torn clothing," and, secondly, in his Christology lectures where Jesus is presented as one who hides himself in weakness, "as a beggar among beggars, as an outcast among outcasts." See chapter 5 above.

For Bonhoeffer, then, it is not a question about whether or not one reads the Bible, but rather *how* one reads it. In approaching the Bible, it is God's word that is important. Not pious feelings. Not emotions. Not even experience. More than "aphoristic worldly wisdom," the Bible is "God's Word of revelation in Jesus Christ."[77] It is the word of God alone that is the source of our salvation; therefore concentrated attention to that word is the necessary corollary to what it means to be a Christian. After all, when it comes to salvation, our lives are not the measure; Christ's death on the cross is what counts. In a rather lengthy but vivid manner, he described what reading the Bible means, namely, entering into God's world and identifying with the incarnate, crucified, and risen Christ. Reading the Bible puts

> the listening congregation in the midst of the wonderful revelatory world of the people of Israel with their prophets, judges, kings, and priests, with their wars, festivals, sacrifices, and sufferings. The community of believers is drawn into the Christmas story, the baptism, the miracles and discourses, the suffering, dying, and rising of Jesus Christ. It participates in the events that once occurred on this earth for the salvation of the whole world. In so doing, it receives salvation in Jesus Christ here and in all these events. For those who want to hear, reading the biblical books in a sequential order forces them to go, and to allow themselves to be found, where God has acted once and for all for the salvation of human beings. The historical books of the Holy Scriptures come alive for us in a whole new way precisely when they are read during worship services. We receive a part of that which once took place for our salvation. Forgetting and losing ourselves, we too pass through the Red Sea, through the desert, across the Jordan into the promised land. With Israel we fall into doubt and unbelief and through punishment and repentance experience again God's help and faithfulness. All this is not mere reverie, but holy, divine reality. We are uprooted from our own existence and are taken back to the holy history of God on earth. There God has dealt with us, and there God still deals with us today, with our needs and our sins, by means of the divine wrath and grace. What is important is not that god is

77. DBWE 5:61.

> a spectator and participant in our life today, but that we are attentive listeners and participants in God's action in the sacred story, the story of Christ on earth. God is with us today only as long as we are there. A complete reversal occurs here. It is not that God's help and presence must still be proved in our life; rather God's presence and help have been demonstrated for us in the life of Jesus Christ. It is in fact more important for us to know what God did to Israel, in God's son Jesus Christ, than to discover what God intends for us today. The fact that Jesus Christ died is more important than the fact that I will die. And the fact that Jesus Christ was raised from the dead is the sole ground of my hope that I, too, will be raised on the day of judgment. Our salvation is "from outside ourselves" (*extra nos*). I find salvation not in my life story, but only in the story of Jesus Christ. Only those who allow themselves to be found in Jesus Christ—in the incarnation, cross, and resurrection—are with God and God with them.[78]

It is here in the world of the Bible that God acts. It is here that we know God not as a vague idea, but as the one who out of love acts decisively for the world. For that reason Scripture is the norm for the Christian life; as Luther stated, God is present everywhere, but it is only in word and sacrament that we know that God is present for us. Like Luther, Bonhoeffer saw God's word as being more than providing guidelines for the moral life; it has the power to create and transform. The Bible is not just a little proverb, a piece of wisdom; it declares salvation, thus creating a new reality.[79] Our salvation takes place in the events recorded in Scripture. And this is not discovered in little bits and pieces here and there, taken out of their context. This

78. Ibid., 61–62.

79. Bonhoeffer shares this perspective with Luther who, in distinction from other sixteenth-century reformers, insisted that the Bible was the good news of God's salvific act in Jesus Christ and not a guidebook from which to glean insights for moral living. See Alister McGrath, *Reformation Thought: An Introduction*, 3rd ed. (Oxford: Blackwell Publishing, 1999), chap. 7 and 8. This, in turn, leads to the conclusion that the Bible is not a moral guidebook, but rather contains the word of God, which doesn't simply inform the life of faith, but creates faith. As a result, faith—or discipleship—is not a question of imitating Jesus but rather means being conformed to Christ. Cf. Eberhard Jüngel, *The Freedom of a Christian: Luther's Significance for Contemporary Theology* (Minneapolis: Augsburg, 1988), 21.

is God's story, the story where God has acted once and for all for our salvation. Through the presence of God's Spirit in the community, we become a part of that story, which is important because it leads to what is the key: "God is with us today only as long as we are there."

Central to this approach to Scripture is the emphasis that is placed on God's work, God's story into which we are drawn, thereby making Christ's crucifixion our crucifixion. This fits with and reflects Bonhoeffer's basic orientation articulated in his earlier writings, where he made the distinction between Christianity and religion. Whereas religion leads from humanity to God, Christianity leads from God to the world. When expressed as the *theologia crucis*, this distinction reaffirms the posture that acknowledges that the initiative belongs to God and that God is committed to this world.[80]

If the purpose of reading Scripture is to draw us into God's story, we might conclude, as does Luther in describing his theology of the cross, that this enables us to see things the way they really are.[81] When everything is viewed through the lens of "suffering and the cross," we see ourselves and world for what they are—a broken, sinful world, yet at the same time loved by God. We "see in the death of Jesus on the cross our rebellion against that life, and we note that there is absolutely no way out now except one. God vindicated the crucified Jesus by raising him from the dead." Therein is our hope. As a result, rather than turning our back on the world looking for a better life elsewhere, we turn "to face the problems, joys, and sorrows of everyday life."[82]

80. Cf. Luther, "A Meditation on Christ's Passion," *LW* 42:7–14, and Gerhard Forde's commentary, *On Being a Theologian of the Cross: Reflections on Luther's Heidelberg Disputation* (Grand Rapids: Eerdmans, 1997), 7–8.
81. See Luther, "Heidelberg Disputation," (*LW* 31), theses 19–21.
82. Forde, *On Being a Theologian of the Cross*, 10.

In other places Luther draws on similar imagery to show how Scripture points us to God and helps us to recognize God in Christ. For example, in a sermon on John 3:1–15, he says,

> We can, therefore, establish no firmer foundation for the divinity of Christ than that we wrap and seal our hearts in the promises of scripture. Scripture lifts us up with supreme gentleness and leads us to Christ—first, to Christ as a human being; thereafter, to Christ as the lord of all creation, and finally, to Christ as God. In that way I am brought carefully along and learn to recognize God [in Christ]. But the philosophers and those who are worldly wise want to begin at the top—which is where they become fools. We must begin from the bottom and only then move upward [in our knowledge], that Solomon's proverb not be fulfilled in us: "It is not good to eat much honey, or to seek honor on top of honor" (Prov 25:27).[83]

This same approach to Scripture as demonstrated by Bonhoeffer is a further example of the influence of Luther's *theologia crucis*. This emphasis is applied to other aspects of community life as well. Let two examples, the service of helping others and the service of bearing with others, suffice in demonstrating how they both find their origin and orientation in the cross of Christ. When it comes to helping others, Bonhoeffer maintained that this is the manner in which we encounter God. Rather than seeing the demands placed upon us by the needs of others as an intrusion into or disruption of our daily routine, we should view them as a means that points us to the way

83. Sermon on John 3:1–15 (Gospel for Trinity Sunday), *WA* 10:1/2:297. Translated by Frederick Gaiser; cited in Frederick Gaiser, "The Quest for Jesus and the Christian Faith: Introduction," in *The Quest for Jesus and the Christian Faith*, Word and World Supplement Series 3, ed. Frederick J. Gaiser (Sept. 1997): 11. In his "Corollary to the Heidelberg Disputation," Luther makes a similar point regarding Scripture and what it reveals: "God wants to be known by us, here on earth by faith, yonder by sight, that He is one God and yet three Persons. . . . To this end He gave us His Word and Holy Scripture, attested with great miracles and signs. We must learn from it. To attain that knowledge of God, it is surely necessary that He Himself instruct us, that he reveal Himself and appear to us. By ourselves we could not ascend into heaven and discover what God is or how His divine essence is constituted. Well, for this purpose He employs visible elements in His creation, as Scripture teaches us, so that we may comprehend this; for invisible creatures do not make an impression on our senses" (*LW* 37:306–7).

of God in the world. In language similar to that which he used in Barcelona, Bonhoeffer said that God uses such occasions to cross our path.

> Those who worry about the loss of time entailed by such small, external acts of helpfulness are usually taking their own work too seriously. We must be ready to allow ourselves to be interrupted by God, who will thwart our plans and frustrate our ways time and again, even daily, by sending people across our path with their demands and requests. We can, then, pass them by, preoccupied with our more important daily tasks, just as the priest—perhaps reading the Bible—passed by the man who had fallen among robbers. When we do that, *we pass by the visible sign of the cross raised in our lives to show us that God's way, and not our own, is what counts.* It is a strange fact that, of all people, Christians and theologians often consider their work so important and urgent that they do not want to let anything interrupt it. They think they are doing God a favor, but actually they are despising God's "crooked yet straight path" (Gottfried Arnold).[84]

Clearly, the way of God is not the way of humanity in the world. The way of God is that of bearing the burdens of the world, which is also the way of the Christian in the world. This is but the expression of God's own bearing of human sin and weakness on the cross. The Christian community is to bear the suffering of the world, for that is nothing other than the work of Christ himself. Unlike "pagans" who are not burdened by anyone, "bearing the burden of another" is the mark of Christian living.

> They must suffer and endure one another. Only as a burden is the other really a brother or sister and not just an object to be controlled. The burden of human beings was even for God so heavy that God had to go to the cross suffering under it. God truly suffered and endured human beings in the body of Jesus Christ. But in so doing, God bore them as a mother carries her child, as a shepherd the lost lamb. God took on human nature. Then, human beings crushed God to the ground. But

84. DBWE 5:99–100; emphasis added.

> God stayed with them and they with God. In suffering and enduring human beings, God maintained community with them. It is the law of Christ that was fulfilled in the cross. Christians share in this law. They are obliged to bear with and suffer one another; but what is more important, now by virtue of the law of Christ having been fulfilled, they are also able to bear one another.[85]

It is significant that Bonhoeffer used the language here that he did. God as a mother and as a shepherd are images that indicates that God really suffers with and because of humanity. God does not remain a distant, dispassionate God, but filled with compassion, God enters into the suffering of the world and transforms it. That work continues in the world through the Christian community, the body of Christ, that bears the suffering of others.

For Bonhoeffer, the foundation of real community is the cross of Christ. When he turned to the subject of confession at the end of *Life Together*, the distinctions between a *theologia gloriae* and a *theologia crucis* are clearly drawn, as are the implications. Confession of sin becomes a way for Bonhoeffer to summarize his theology as it is lived out in the Christian community.

By exposing us as sinners, the cross enables us to see ourselves in our true light. Far too often, however, Christians never find real community, because they remain isolated in their sin.[86] Their piety (in actuality, a *theologia gloriae*), which does not permit anyone to be a sinner, stands in the way. "Hence, all have to conceal their sins from themselves and from the community." Deceiving themselves as to their own true nature, "many Christians would be unimaginably horrified if a real sinner were suddenly to turn up among the pious.

85. Ibid., 100–1.

86. Ibid., 108ff. In this discussion, the same emphasis on sin as the barrier to true community that characterizes life in Adam, a theme Bonhoeffer first developed in his dissertations, remains a critical barrier to community, overcome only through God's act in Christ. In this instance, Bonhoeffer is applying the same basic insight to the practical reality of community life.

So we remain alone with our sin, trapped in lies and hypocrisy, for we are in fact sinners."[87]

Confessing one's sins, seeing oneself as a sinner (or seeing oneself as one really is, in the words of the *theologia crucis*), on the other hand, breaks through the isolation sin creates and leads to community. According to Bonhoeffer,

> The grace of the gospel, which is so hard for the pious to comprehend, confronts us with the truth. It says to us, you are a sinner, a great, unholy sinner. Now come, as the sinner that you are, to your God who loves you. For God wants you as you are, not desiring anything from you—a sacrifice, a good deed—but rather desiring you alone. . . . This message is liberation through truth. You cannot hide from God. The mask you wear in the presence of other people won't get you anywhere in the presence of God. God wants to see you as you are, wants to be gracious to you. You do not have to go on lying to yourself and to other Christians as if you were without sin. You are allowed to be a sinner.[88]

Confession of sin has its justification in this gracious act of God. Confession, therefore, is a call to the congregation to claim the grace of God. When the congregation does, confession leads to a "breakthrough to community, a "breakthrough to the cross," a "breakthrough to new life," and a "breakthrough to assurance." With regard to the first, a "breakthrough to community," sin is what isolates people; sin causes people to keep secrets, to hide behind facades, to remain in the dark. Confession brings it all out into the light; all attempts at self-justification are abandoned and the community both forgives the sinner and bears the sin. No longer left alone to wrestle with sin in isolation, "the sinner stands in the community of sinners who live by the grace of God in the cross of Jesus Christ. Now one is allowed to be a sinner and still enjoy the grace of God."[89]

87. Ibid., 108.
88. Ibid.

But this is not simply a matter that stops with the community. Claiming that confession leads to a "breakthrough to the cross," Bonhoeffer continued:

> The root of all sin is pride, *superbia*. I want to be for myself; I have a right to be myself, a right to my hatred and my desires, my life and my death. The spirit and flesh of human beings are inflamed by pride, for it is precisely in their wickedness that human beings want to be like God. Confession in the presence of another believer is the most profound kind of humiliation. It hurts, makes one feel small; it deals a terrible blow to one's pride. To stand there before another Christian as a sinner is an almost unbearable disgrace. By confessing actual sins the old self dies a painful, humiliating death before the eyes of another Christian. Because this humiliation is so difficult, we keep thinking we can avoid confessing to one another. Our eyes are so blinded that they no longer see the promise and the glory of such humiliation. It is none other than Jesus Christ who openly suffered the shameful death of a sinner in our place, who was not ashamed to be crucified for us as an evildoer. And it is nothing else but our community with Jesus Christ that leads us to the disgraceful dying that comes in confession, so that we may truly share in this cross. The cross of Jesus Christ shatters all pride. We cannot find the cross of Jesus if we are afraid of going to *the place where Jesus can be found*, to the public death of the sinner. And we refuse to carry the cross when we are ashamed to take upon ourselves the shameful death of the sinner in confession. In confession we break through to the genuine community of the cross of Jesus Christ;[90] in confession we affirm our cross. In the profound spiritual and physical pain of humiliation before another believer, which means before God, we experience the cross of Jesus as our deliverance and salvation. The old humanity dies, but God has triumphed over it. Now we share in the resurrection of Christ and eternal life.[91]

This, in turn, leads to a "breakthrough to new life." When sin is confessed, "there is a break with sin, there is conversion. Confession

89. Ibid., 111.
90. This is the same emphasis that Bonhoeffer presented in his understanding of the church as community in *Sanctorum Communio*.
91. DBWE 5:111–12; emphasis added.

is conversion." It puts us on a path in fellowship with God and humanity. With the power of sin broken, new life emerges. "What happened to us in baptism is given to us anew in confession. We are delivered from darkness into the rule of Jesus Christ. That is joyful news."[92]

With this, the Christian arrives at a "breakthrough to assurance." No longer needing to hide our sin and, hence, delude ourselves, we are freed from all attempts at "self-forgiveness" that "can never lead to the break with sin. This can only be accomplished by God's own judging and pardoning Word." Christians experience this when they confess their sins to one another. In that act, they "know that they are no longer alone with themselves; they experience the presence of God in the reality of the other." Through the other, God works to assure believers of divine forgiveness. "As the acknowledgment of my sins to another believer frees me from the grip of self-deception, so, too, the promise of forgiveness becomes fully certain to me only when it is spoken by another believer as God's command and in God's name."[93]

Here again, rather than being a "detour," *Life Together* fits into the core of Bonhoeffer's life and thought, recalling the central themes of his theology. Commitment to Jesus Christ keeps it from falling victim to some romantic notion of community or spirituality. It is not a self-centered mystical experience that is being advocated, but rather a church prepared to follow Jesus into the world. This idea in *Life Together* is carried over into *Letters and Papers from Prison* via the term *arcane discipline.*[94] The core of Bonhoeffer's thought and faith remain;

92. Ibid., 112.
93. Ibid., 113.
94. The term arcane discipline (*disciplina arcana*) is one that Bonhoeffer borrows from the ancient church. In a context when the church was a persecuted minority, it was necessary to develop practices that maintained the integrity of the church's faith in distinction from heretical alternatives. In the context of Nazi Germany, Bonhoeffer drew on this ancient term and practice in his prison correspondence to protect the mysteries of the Gospel. According

the only difference is the changes in the world; therefore, no longer are the practices of the faithful displayed clearly for the world to see, but instead they are hidden, in order that they be preserved and the church thereby strengthened for life in the world.

## Post-Finkenwalde Correspondence

The themes of *Life Together* are given expression and carried forward in a letter Bonhoeffer wrote to his brother-in-law Rudiger Schleicher in April 1936,[95] while Finkenwalde was still in existence. In much the same way that he talked about the purpose and manner of reading the Bible in *Life Together*, he explained to Schleicher why the Bible is important. As if addressing the question from the opposite side of his description in *Life Together*, here, instead of talking about our need to enter into God's story in order to know and experience God's grace, he pointed out the deficiency of human attempts to locate God outside of Scripture. Again, conscious of the pull between the values of the world and the Christian faith, he wrestled with the question, "Where do I find God?" and located the truth about God and the world in God's revelation in the Bible. Expressing his thoughts in the language of the *theologia crucis*, Bonhoeffer wrote,

> Now, I know about the God for whom I am searching either out of my own experiences and understanding, from my own interpretation of history or nature, that is, from within myself—or I know about that God

to John Matthews, his "intent was to reinstate a careful discipline for authentic discipleship in every realm of life, private and public, personal and communal, inward and outward, spiritual and physical." Bonhoeffer employed this idea because he "thought that the church then as in the first centuries, was at risk of losing sight of the love and life of God for all people—in Christ—through Nazi pagan hostility, Aryan theological distortion, and German cultural domestication" (*Anxious Souls will Ask . . . the Christ-Centered Spirituality of Dietrich Bonhoeffer* [Grand Rapids, MI: Eerdmans, 2005), 59. See also DB-R, 80-84, where Bethge describes the use of the arcane discipline in LPP in terms of "the actual relationship to Christ as present, which can never be separated from the question: Who is Christ for us today?" (881).

95. DBWE 14:166–70.

> on the basis of his revelation of his own word. Either I determine the place where I want to find God, or I let him determine the place where he wants to be found.[96]

This corresponds to what Luther says about true knowledge of God coming through faith, as opposed to reason's attempt to know God. Gerhard Ebeling, in his discussion of the hidden and revealed God in Luther, describes Luther's understanding of the limits of reason:

> Reason cannot rightly accord him his deity nor attribute it to him as his own, though it rightly belongs to him alone. It knows that God exists. But who or what person it may be who is properly called God, it does not know. . . . Thus reason plays blindman's-buff with God and makes vain errors and always misses the mark, calling God what is not God, and not calling god what is god, which it would not do if it did not know that god existed, or if it did know what thing was God, or what God was. Thus it rushes in and accords the name and the divine honour, and the title, God, to what it thinks God is, and so never hits on the true God, but always finds the Devil or its own darkness, which the Devil rules. Thus there is a great difference between knowing that a god exists, and knowing what or who God is. The first is known to nature, and is written in every heart. The second is taught only by the Holy Spirit.[97]

After making the distinction about the proper way of knowing God, Bonhoeffer continued,

> If it is I who says where God is to be found, then I will always find a God there who in some manner corresponds to me, is pleasing to me, who is commensurate with my own nature. But if it is God who says where he is to be found, then it will probably be a place that is not at all commensurate with my own nature and that does not please me at all. This place, however, is the cross of Jesus. And those who want to find God there must live beneath that cross just as the Sermon on the Mount demands. Doing so, however, is wholly incommensurate with our nature, indeed, is wholly contrary to it. Precisely this, however,

96. Ibid., 168.
97. Gerhard Ebeling, *Luther: An Introduction to His Thought* (Philadelphia: Fortress Press, 1970), 229–30.

> is the message of the Bible, not only in the New but also in the Old Testament (Isa. 53!). In any event, both Jesus and Paul intended it thus: the cross of Jesus fulfills Scripture, that is, the Old Testament. Hence the entire Bible claims to be this word in which God wants us to find him. It is not at all a place that we find pleasant or that might be clear a priori, but a place alien to us in every way, a place utterly repugnant to us. But that is the very place where God chose to encounter us.[98]

Christ on the cross is the full expression of God's reality in and for the world. There the reality of God intersects with the reality of the world. There we find a God not of our own making, but God as God actually exists for us. It is this self-revelation of God that stands over against every attempt we make to imagine God. Theologically, this is significant, because Bonhoeffer's questions were always focused on the intersection of faith and life. Instead of steering Bonhoeffer away from worldly concerns, faith in God drove him back into the midst of the world. Bonhoeffer's life demanded a cross of reality, it demanded a faith that takes this world seriously, a faith that allows us to call evil evil, while at the same time empowering us to take responsible action on behalf of the world. Because of God's act on the cross, justification of sinners and justice in the world go hand in hand. They are two sides of one reality.

Shortly after he had finished writing *Life Together*, with the seminary having been closed down, it was becoming increasingly more certain that Bonhoeffer would not be able to avoid the political net closing in on him; therefore, he was faced with a decision: either face the certainty of being drafted into the military or go to America, where friends like Reinhold Niebuhr and Paul Lehmann had made arrangements for him to live out the war in safety. So it was in the summer of 1939 that he set sail for New York.

98. DBWE 14:168.

During his very brief stay in America, he worshiped at Riverside Church in New York City. What he experienced there was far from the Christ-centered church-community he had created at Finkenwalde; he left the service wanting more from worship, while at the same time becoming more convinced that the challenges facing the church were not limited to the German context alone. He recorded his reactions in his diary, June 18, 1939, where he described the worship experience as

> a discreet, opulent, self-satisfied celebration of religion. With such an idolization of religion, the flesh, which was accustomed to being held in check by the word of God, revives. Such preaching renders people libertine, egoistic, indifferent. Do the people really not know that one can do as well or better without "religion"—if only it weren't for God himself and his word? Perhaps the Anglo-Saxons really are more religious than we, but they may not be more Christian, if they tolerate such sermons. For me there is no doubt that someday a storm will blow forcefully into this religious hand-out, if God himself is still in the plan at all.[99]

Couched in these observations is what he missed in worship—"the biblical focus on Christ's word and his judgment against the 'rubbish' which posed as genuine religion."[100] What he witnessed had ceased being God's work.

This experience reflects the very concern he had in writing *Life Together*. Coming almost simultaneously with the publication of that book, this experience only reconfirmed his belief that the church (not only in Germany, but in America as well) was in need of reforming. It was a renewal that could only come when God's word took root and affected change in people's lives. That is what *Life Together* was

99. DBWE 15:224–25.
100. Geffrey B. Kelly, "Freedom and Discipline: Rhythms of a Christocentric Spirituality," in *Ethical Responsibility: Bonhoeffer's Legacy to the Churches*, ed. John D. Godsey and Geffrey B. Kelly (New York: The Edwin Mellen Press, 1981), 320.

meant to accomplish. It was a call to people of God to live as if they take seriously the promises of God's word.

Two other pieces of correspondence belong to this time. The first was to Reinhold Niebuhr, explaining his decision to return to Germany. He concluded that going to America had been a mistake, saying that "I must life through this difficult period of our national history with the Christian people of Germany. I will have no right to participate in the reconstruction of Christian life in Germany after the war if I do not share the trials of this time with my people."[101] His sense of community and responsibility were more important than his own safety. The second was his report, "Protestantism without Reformation,"[102] submitted to his superiors; in it he shared his observations on American church life. Among other things, he painted a rather negative picture of American theology, judging it in terms of its lack of Christology and serious theological reflection. In part, he acknowledged his failure to understand American theology, which held to a different orientation than what he was accustomed to; his problem with American Christianity was obviously theological in nature:

> The failure in Christology is characteristic of all current American theology. . . . Christendom in American theology is essentially still religion and ethics. Hence, the person and work of Jesus Christ recedes into the background for theology and remains ultimately not understood, because the sole foundation for God's radical judgment and radical grace is at this point not recognized.[103]

On the one hand, this can be seen to fit in with his disappointment over American theology that he had experienced in 1930–1931 while in New York. In that regard, it can be viewed as a European

101. DBWE 15:210.
102. Ibid., 438–62.
103. Ibid., 460–62.

observation that, while pointing out the differences between America and Europe, may or may not be an accurate portrayal of American church life. On the other hand, while Bonhoeffer's "Protestantism without Reformation" can indeed be read as a European perspective on the American context, it could also be read as a Lutheran commentary on the pronounced influences of Reformed thought on the development of American Christianity. Rather than dealing in the categories of doctrine, which is a Lutheran tendency, American Christianity has been shaped by those traditions that tend to place more emphasis on the moral aspect of life. As a result, a European Lutheran would find his experience in America to be quite different. This difference posed a basic challenge, with which he ended his essay: "The decisive task today is the conversation between the Protestantism without Reformation and the churches of the Reformation."[104] The distinctions he maintained throughout his life are at play here and so what was being called for might be a dose of Luther's christologically-centered *theologia crucis.*

Victoria Barnett describes the period after the closure of Finkenwalde as a "bleak period" for the Confessing Church that "exposed both the church's lack of internal unity and its utter failure to oppose National Socialism."[105] With Finkenwalde's closure in the fall of 1937, Bonhoeffer's work with his Finkenwalde students continued, albeit in different form. In a sense, Bonhoeffer and his students went further underground, dividing up and finding shelter in the various churches and communities open to their work. They created "collective pastorates," where the students lived together "almost as they had lived in Finkenwalde, only in smaller numbers and under more primitive conditions," and served as "apprentice vicars." Through this system, they built a network of supportive

104. Ibid., 462.
105. Victoria Barnett, "Editor's Introduction to the English Edition," DBWE 15:1.

congregations; Bonhoeffer worked through them to continue his work of training the future pastors of the Confessing Church. This lasted until March 1940 when the police closed down these sites as well.[106]

One of the ways that Bonhoeffer showed ongoing support to the ordinands under his care and extended the Finkenwalde community was through regular circular letters sent to all of them. Not only was this a means of sharing news about events in the Confessing Church and fellow members of their circle, many of whom had been called up for military service; it also became an avenue for Bonhoeffer to share his theological reflections with them and demonstrated "Bohoeffer's dogged and eloquent attempts to keep his seminarians on the Confessing side."[107] Several of these letters survived the war and what they reveal are not only the struggles of this small community but Bonhoeffer's theological concerns as well. In content, they provide a means of seeing the continuity between the Finkenwalde period and Bonhoeffer's resistance activity that followed.

In one such letter, written in September 1939,[108] the first after returning from his short-lived American stay, he asked, as was his custom, about the meaning of the Christian faith today. He said, and here his Lutheran concern comes through, "We are preachers of justification through grace alone. What [does] this mean today?"[109] This is but a variation on the question he had been asking since Barcelona and would ask again to the very end in his prison correspondence. It is a question about the concrete reality of God in the world. Asked now from the perspective of justification as shaped by Luther's theology, it becomes a question about how God works

106. *DB-ER*, 589.
107. Barnett, "Editor's Introduction," DBWE 15:7.
108. DBWE 15:273–78.
109. Ibid., 275.

in the world. His answer, which came from his certainty of faith, can serve as a summary of his theology:

> Very simply it means that we no longer equate human ways and goals with divine ways and goals. God is beyond all human plans and deeds. Everything must be judged by God. Whoever evades this judgment of God must die, but whoever submits to it will live; for to be judged by God is grace for life. God judges for the sake of mercy; God humbles in order to lift up. Only the humble will succeed. God does not confirm human action, but thwarts it and with that tugs our gaze upward to God's grace. By thwarting our paths, God comes to us and speaks his merciful Yes to us, but precisely only through the cross of Jesus Christ. He has placed this cross on the earth; if under the cross he gives us back to the earth and its work and toil, so he commits us anew to the earth and the human beings who live, act, struggle, and suffer on it.[110]

In language similar to that which he used earlier, Bonhoeffer made a distinction between God and humankind and insisted that they not be confused. To confuse the two is to lose sight of God's grace, to refuse God's justifying action to work in the lives of believers. It means denying the way that God has chosen to work in the world to bring about reconciliation and new life, and substituting in its place another gospel. As it is, God works through the cross, which is God's way of keeping us tied to the earth rather than permitting us to escape from it. Bonhoeffer's cross of reality, which is an earth-bound theology, makes the obvious connection between God's act in the world and the Christian's task as God's body in that same world. Under the cross, "Christians participate in God's suffering" in the world.

He continued in the same letter to address another obvious question or concern on the part of those who were suffering: Where is God in all of this? Drawing on the text of Psalm 42, he asked, "'Where is your God?' Is it true that God is silent?" While that is a

110. Ibid.

natural human question arising out of the circumstances of war and devastation, it is at the same time a question that emerges from a false concept of God. "It is only true for those whose God is the God of their own ideals and thoughts."[111] The God of the Bible, on the other hand, is the Creator of all that exists, without whom nothing in all the world happens. In and through Jesus Christ "God speaks the silent language of his fearful power and glory, so that we become small and humble and worship God alone." Because of this assurance, he says,

> Therefore, our hearts and our gaze are not trapped and captivated by the daily events, as attentively as we follow them. We seek and find through them God the Lord and see his works in awe. We seek and find our Lord Jesus Christ and believe firmly in his victory and in the glory of his church-community. We seek and find God, the Holy Spirit, who makes his word win power over us, greater power than the world can ever win over us. And we pray that the work of the Trinitarian God may soon be fulfilled.[112]

Here Bonhoeffer continued to rely on the cross of Christ for his understanding of God and for his understanding of and approach to the world. Even at a time of war, or perhaps especially at such a time, hope is possible because of God in Christ.[113]

In another of the circular letters sent to the members of the Finkenwalde community after the start of the war at Christmas 1939, reflecting on the Christmas story, Bonhoeffer provided a miniature study on Christology, centered on the incarnation.[114] He provided an outline of the major points of Christology and their significance for those who were struggling with the issues of their day. He began,

111. Ibid., 275. Cf. an earlier sermon on Psalm 42 prepared at the beginning of Finkenwalde's first sesson, DBWE 14:847ff.

112. DBWE 15:276.

113. Cf. Ernst Feil, *TDB*, 83.

114. DBWE 15:528–33.

> No priest, no theologian stood at the cradle of Bethlehem. And yet all Christian theology finds its origin in the miracle of miracles, that God became human. . . . Without that holy night, there is no theology. "God revealed in the flesh," the God-human Jesus Christ, that is the holy mystery, which theology was instituted to preserve and protect. What foolishness, as if it were the task of theology to decode God's mystery, pulling it down to the commonplace, miracle-less words of wisdom based on human experience and reason! Whereas this alone is its charge—to keep the miracle of God a miracle, to comprehend, defend, and exalt the mystery of God, precisely as mystery. The early church meant the very same thing when it concerned itself with the mystery of the Trinity and the person of Jesus Christ with tireless fervor. What superficiality and thoughtlessness, particularly among theologians, when theology is disparaged, when they boast about not being and not wanting to be theologians, ridicule their own office and ordination, and nonetheless at the end of it all, they have and advocate a bad theology instead of a correct theology! But then, where among the theological professorships has the mystery of God in the flesh, of the birth of Jesus Christ, as God-human and Savior, been depicted and taught to us as the unfathomable mystery of God? Where do we hear it preached?
>
> If Christmastide does not succeed in kindling in us anew something like a love toward holy theology, so that we, captured and overcome by the miracle of the cradle of the Son of God, must devoutly ponder the mysteries of God—then it might be the case that the fire of the divine mysteries is already extinguished and dead, even for our hearts.[115]

The *theologia crucis* is a theology of revelation that stands in sharp contrast to speculation or ideas about God. God has revealed himself, and it is the task of theology to concern itself with God as God has chosen to be revealed, instead of constructing preconceived notions of God that ultimately must be destroyed. According to Bonhoeffer, it is not the task of theology, therefore, to provide a rational framework for the incarnation and mysterious workings of God in the world, to explain it all away. As he had noted in his Trinity Sunday sermon in 1934, mystery is at the heart of the Christian

115. Ibid., 528–29.

gospel; theology's task, therefore, is to preserve the mystery. The lack of mystery is part of the problem, and any theological attempt to do away with the mystery of God is bad theology. According to a *theologia crucis* the mystery of God is God's presence in Jesus Christ; that mystery should be the focus of theological investigation. Challenging the conclusions of modern Protestant theology, he concluded that what must be recaptured is a *theologia crucis* that seeks God in the human Jesus.

> The early church pondered the Christ question over several centuries. In so doing, it made reason captive to obedience to Jesus Christ and vividly testified, in stern and contradictory statements, to the mystery of the person of Jesus Christ. It did not yield to the modern illusion that this mystery could only be felt and experienced, because it knew about the corruption and egocentricity of all human feeling and experience. The church did not mean, of course, that this mystery could be logically conceived, but in that it did not shy away from uttering the ultimate conceptual paradoxes, it declared and glorified the mystery as mystery for all natural thinking. The early church Christology really originated at the cradle of Bethlehem, and the splendor of Christmas lies on its eroded countenance. Even today, this Christology wins the hearts of those who come to know it. So during the time of Christmas, let us take a lesson once again from the early church and try to understand devoutly what it thought and taught about the glorification and defense of the faith in Christ. The stern concepts from that age are like the flints from which one makes a spark of fire.[116]

After laying out the contours of the Christmas story, in this circular letter he summarized the main points of christological reflection contained in the Lutheran Confessions;[117] he believed the ideas contained therein capture the mystery and wonder of the ancient church's Christology and, therefore, serve "to place our thinking and

116. Ibid., 529–30.

117. Cf. Formula of Concord, Epitome, article 8 and Solid Declaration, article 8 (in *Book of Concord*, 508–14 and 616–34), which deal with "the Person of Christ."

our recognition as preachers of the word in the light of the holy night."[118] He identified three points as particularly relevant for his current context:

First, Jesus Christ takes on *human nature:* the birth of Christ is not simply about God becoming one man, but taking on human nature and all that represents.[119] Using language that shows the continuity of his thought on this point, he said,

> The body of Jesus Christ—that is our flesh. He bears our flesh. Therefore, where Jesus Christ is, we are, whether we know it or not. This is so by virtue of God's becoming human; what happens to Jesus Christ, happens to us. It is truly the "poor flesh and blood" of all of us that lies there in the manger. It is our flesh that he sanctifies and cleanses in obedience and suffering. It is our flesh that dies with him on the cross and is buried with him. He took on human nature so that we can be with him in eternity. Wherever the body of Jesus Christ is, there we are. Indeed, we are his body. Therefore, the testimony of Christmas for all human beings is you have been accepted; God has not despised you but bodily bears the flesh and blood of you all. Look to the manger! In the body of the little child, in the incarnate Son of God is your flesh, all your misery, fear, temptation, even all your sin, borne, forgiven, and sanctified. If you lament: my nature, my entire being is without salvation, and I must be lost forever, then the message of Christmas answers: your nature, your entire being has been accepted; Jesus bears it, so he has become your Savior. Because Christmas is the bodily assumption of all human flesh by the God of grace, therefore it must be said: God's Son took on human nature.[120]

Second, he addressed the question about the "Two Natures and One Person" of Jesus Christ. In a paradoxical manner, God is fully present in the human baby in the manger. It is important to affirm both the presence of God and human nature of Jesus in the incarnation,

118. DBWE 15:530.
119. See Rasmussen, "Editor's Introduction to the English Edition," DBWE 12, for a discussion of humiliation.
120. DBWE 15:530–31.

because it is a question of salvation. "If Jesus Christ is not true God, how could he *help* us? If Christ is not true human, how can he help *us*?" And yet it remains a mystery. God is "hidden in the manger; only here and there in the life of Jesus does it shine through the beggar's garment of human nature. But although mysteriously hidden, it is nonetheless present; it is hidden for our sake, it is present for our sake." It is only there in Jesus Christ that God and humanity are united. That which was "separated from each other before Christ came, united with each other alone in the becoming human of the Son of God."[121]

Third, he concluded with a discussion of the contribution the Lutheran church made to the early church's Christology with its doctrine of *genus majestaticum*, which sought to explain how "the mediation of the properties of the divine nature to the human nature took place in the incarnation." Because of this doctrine, the church can confess Jesus is God. While it does not break through the mystery of the incarnation, it affirms the unity between God and humankind. He made his point by drawing on the words of Luther cited by the confessors: in the first, a variation on his oft-repeated citation from Luther, he quoted, "Wherever you can say, Here is God, there you must also say, Then Christ the man is also there. And if you could point a place out where God is, and not the man, the person would already be divided. . . . No, my friend, wherever you place God for me, there you must also place the humanity for me." And second, he quoted, "It is the honor of our God, however, that, in giving the divine self for our sake in deepest condescension, entering into the flesh."[122]

121. Ibid., 532.

122. Ibid., 533. The Luther citations are "Confession Concerning Christ's Supper, 1528," *LW* 37:218–19 and "That These Words of Christ, 'This is My Body," etc., Still Stand Firm Against the Fanatics," 1527, *LW* 37:72. Here Bonhoeffer follows the writers of the Formula of Concord,

It is this same understanding of the unity of God and humanity in Christ affirmed in the incarnation that informs our understanding of Christ's words, "This is my body," in the Eucharist. "The same God who came in the flesh for our salvation gives himself to us with his body and blood in the sacrament. 'The end of the way of God is bodiliness' [Leiblichkeit] (Oetinger)."[123] Bonhoeffer told his seminarians that the point of these reflections was "that through one or another of these thoughts we will be led to read and contemplate the biblical testimony to the mystery of God's becoming human with more reverence and adoration, and perhaps even to sing Luther's Christmas hymns more thoughtfully and joyously."[124]

In another circular letter written in January 1940 for the Epiphany season,[125] Bonhoeffer focused on the meaning and significance of Epiphany as it relates to Christmas and the cross. Here the emphasis was placed on Jesus' baptism, not for his own sake, but for our sake, and through Bonhoeffer's discussion, the same ideas are emphasized once again. Jesus, he explained, as the Son of God does not need to be baptized; he does not need forgiveness. Therefore, Jesus' baptism is not something he needs for himself, but is something he undergoes "for the sake of those who need it, for the sake of sinners. . . . Jesus goes to baptism not out of penitence but out of love, and in this way takes the side of sinners." This is Jesus' identification with sinners. He is not baptized in order to make him more holy or God-like; this act "does not add anything new to his being, but it brings something decisively new in his doing; for from now on Jesus acts before all the world as the one he is from eternity." The baptism of Jesus, therefore, commemorates his "appearance in

who drew heavily on Luther's writings, using large segments of work almost verbatim, in these articles on Christology.

123. DBWE 15:533.

124. Ibid.

125. Ibid: 534–37.

lowliness, ranking equally with sinners." Even in baptism and as remained true throughout his life, "the divine power remains hidden. . . . The glory of Jesus is hidden in his humility, and is perceived only in faith."[126] Rather than manifesting a *theologia gloriae* that demonstrates God's power, the baptism of Jesus remains a hidden presence of God, revealed only through the eyes of faith.

In another piece of correspondence from roughly the same time, a letter written to Ruth Roberta Stahlberg,[127] a cousin of Bonhoeffer's fiancée Maria von Wedemeyer, on March 23, 1940, Bonhoeffer revealed what, according to him, was a possible danger at times of such great uncertainty as those in which they were living. The letter is a response elicited by a previous letter and conversation with her.[128] After having been attracted to National Socialism in its early days—even having joined the Nazi party and served as a leader in a Nazi student organization—she eventually became disillusioned, resigned from the Party and "was at sea when it came to a spiritual anchor." Looking for some sense of security in the midst of the chaos of 1930s Germany, she turned to the writings of the nineteenth-century writer Adalbert Stifter, whose works evoked an idealized world of peace and harmony. She wrote and published an essay on one of his novellas, in which she described "her longing for such a utopia, rather than the helter skelter existences that she observed in Germany before and during the early Nazi years." In her earlier letter to Bonhoeffer she indicated that she believed that a similar culture of "good taste" could be a source of renewal in the church, which had grown suspect in the eyes of intellectuals. By infusing the

126. Ibid., 536–37.
127. DBWE 16:36-41.
128. For background on this letter, see Jane Pejsa, "Dietrich Bonhoeffer's Letter to an Unknown Woman," *International Bonhoeffer Society—English Language Section Newsletter* 52 (1993): 3–5. Originally published without the identity of its recipient, Pejsa uncovered her identity and has provided details on the exchange that resulted in this response from Bonhoeffer.

church with some human creativity, she believed "the church should be revitalized and reformed by substituting the fruits of modern creativity and good taste for the kitsch with which the German Church was heavily burdened."[129]

Bonhoeffer's response, which was long overlooked because the identity of the recipient was originally unknown, could not disagree more. The letter is brief, a mere five and one-half pages, but is revealing in its brevity and, therefore, could serve as a summary of his thinking at this critical time in his life. He argued that creativity could not be used to revitalize the church, stating that "we cannot simply approach the matter with whatever preconceived standards we may have, however creative or widely accepted, nor cherish the hope that everything would fall into place if we would only put these standards to use." Reformation comes about not because of human ideas, but is the work of God alone: "We are not the ones who reform the church, but we are indeed very capable of blocking the way if God has decided to renew it." He argued for what is essential, claiming that one cannot have anything "beyond and besides Christ himself," because "there is no room in the church for Christ *and* human creativity but, strictly speaking, only for Jesus Christ." [130]

He went on to outline his position, stating that even though the language and imagery used by the church to communicate the essentials of the faith might have lost their impact because of overuse or familiarity, they nevertheless remain the means by which the church proclaims its faith; therefore, the language of the church is not something to be altered because it might suit our tastes. According to him, Stahlberg's concerns dealt only with surface issues. Far more important than seeking alternate words is God's word itself and its

129. Ibid., 4.
130. DBWE 16:37–38.

relationship of faith, "the depth from which they come and the context in which they stand." Church renewal will not depend on

> some semantic reflection or observation but quite simply from daily personal intimacy with the crucified Jesus Christ. This is the depth from which a word must come if it is to carry weight. One could also say that what matters is that we daily orient ourselves to the image of the crucified Christ and allow ourselves to be called to conversion. When our words come directly, as it were, from the cross of Jesus Christ himself, when Christ is so present to us that it is he who is speaking our words, only then can we be released from the terrible danger of empty spiritual verbosity.[131]

In fact, "a radical measure like excising the words 'cross,' 'sin,' 'grace, etc. from our vocabulary does not help."[132] It is not the language that is important. In the end, the measure of authentic talk about God has nothing to do with the language we speak but is dependent upon the relationship one has to the crucified Christ. That means that we are not simply talking about Christ, but that this is God's word, Christ himself, present for us, speaking to us.

In all of Bonhoeffer's correspondence, one of the central themes was the conscious need to retain a relationship with God. Never forsaking God for the world, God becomes the key to understanding the world. It seems the closer Bonhoeffer comes to God, the more deeply involved in the world he becomes. God as revealed in the incarnation and on the cross is so deeply identified with the world that he cannot think of God as a means of escaping the problems of the world, but finds in God's hidden revelation the answer to the world's hope and future.

With the closing of Finkenwalde on September 29, 1937, Bonhoeffer continued teaching and guiding his seminarians

131. Ibid., 16:41.
132. Ibid.

underground in "collective pastorates" scattered around the Pomeranian countryside. At the same time, it was a period in which his own personal well-being was at stake as Gestapo surveillance of his activities increased, restrictions on his travel enforced, and the fear of being drafted into the military became more real. These latter conditions are what had led him to consider living out the war in America as an option.[133]

133. See Barnett, "Editor's Introduction," DBWE 15 for additional information.

# 9

## Resistance and *Ethics*

Upon his return to Germany in the summer of 1939, Bonhoeffer resumed his responsibilities to his students.[1] But the war changed everything and when the "collective pastorates" were eventually closed in March 1940, Bonhoeffer, who had been hoping to avoid military service, with the help of his brother-in-law Hans von Dohnyani was able to join the resistance under the guise of working for the Abwehr, the intelligence arm of the German military. From the fall of 1940 until his arrest in April 1943, Bonhoeffer's efforts to secure peace and build a foundation for future generations was carried out as he led a double life as an undercover agent.[2]

1. See *DB-ER*, chapter 12, for information on Bonhoeffer's activities during the time he was working on his ethics. The different approaches to ethics Bonhoeffer pursued during this period of time represent the struggles he was living through as a member of the resistance. For that reason, the editors of DBW 6 suggest that the individual texts should be read with what was taking place in Bonhoeffer's life and in the life of the church and society as background. See Ilse Tödt, Heinz Eduard Tödt, Ernst Feil, and Clifford Green, "Editors' Afterword to the German Edition," DBWE 6:409ff.
2. See Victoria Barnett, "Editor's Introduction to the English Edition," DBWE 15:13–14. See also Sabine Dramm, *Dietrich Bonhoeffer and the Resistance* (Minneapolis: Fortress Press, 2009) for insights into this aspect of his life.

As a point of entrée, let the words found in a letter written on January 22, 1939, to Theodore Litt, guide us:

> Solely because God became a poor, wretched, unknown, unsuccessful human being, and because God wants to be found from now on solely in this poverty, in the cross, it is for this reason that we cannot get away from the human being and from the world, for this reason that we love our neighbors. Because the Christian faith is such that indeed the "unconditional is included in the conditional," the "hereafter" has entered the "this-worldliness" out of a sovereign freedom of grace, for that reason the believer is not torn apart, but rather finds in this single place in this world God and human being in one, and from now on the love of God and love for one's human neighbor are indissolubly united.[3]

Because God became human, Christians cannot escape from the world. Faith in the God revealed in the incarnate, crucified, and risen Christ[4] ties Christians to the world. Both of these emphases are worked out in greater detail in his *Ethics*,[5] where "the point of

3. DBWE 15:111–12. See John Godsey, "The Legacy of Dietrich Bonhoeffer," in *A Bonhoeffer Legacy: Essays in Understanding*, ed. A. J. Klassen (Grand Rapids: Eerdmans, 1981), 162, and Ernst Feil, *TDB*, 83.
4. This threefold christological formula, which Bonhoeffer began using with greater frequency with his 1933 Christology lectures, is used with even more frequency throughout his *Ethics*. Hans-Jürgen Abromeit, *Das Geheimnis Christi: Dietrich Bonhoeffers erfahrungsbezognene Christologie* (Neukirch-Vluyn: Neukirchen, 1991), 230, calls it "the structural principle of his entire ethical outline."
5. Bonhoeffer approached the subject of ethics as his "actual life work." The text we have, however, "is not the Ethics which Dietrich Bonhoeffer intended to have published. It is a compilation of the sections which have been preserved, some of them complete and others not, some already partly rewritten and some which had been committed to writing only as preliminary studies for the work which was planned. These are the parts of the work which it was possible to conceal in a place of safety before they could be seized by the police. . . . The manuscripts which are now before us were written between 1940 and 1943 in Berlin, at the monastery of Ettal and at Kieckow. The work was interrupted by various tasks undertaken on behalf of the Brotherhood Council of the Confessing Church, by various journeys in connection with political activities, and finally by Bonhoeffer's arrest" (Eberhard Bethge, "Editor's Preface," to Dietrich Bonhoeffer, *Ethics*, ed. Eberhard Bethge, trans. Neville Horton Smith, rearranged ed. (New York: Macmillan, 1965), 7–8. Since the text that we have entitled *Ethics* is not a unified manuscript but rather represents several different attempts by Bonhoeffer to do ethics, each section will be discussed separately. In addition, recent research concludes that the ordering followed in previous editions does not necessarily follow the order in which Bonhoeffer wrote the various approaches to ethics. In an effort to follow the development

departure for Dietrich Bonhoeffer's concrete ethics is the theological question of how the reality of God revealed in Jesus can take form in human life in the world."[6] The significance of these words stand out when compared to words Bonhoeffer penned a couple of years later. In an essay written for his fellow conspirators in the resistance and friends at the turn of the year 1942–1943, entitled "After Ten Years,"[7] Bonhoeffer reflected back on the ten years since Hitler had come to power and concluded that "the great masquerade of evil has played havoc with all our ethical concepts," leaving "reasonable people" with little "ground under their feet" by which they could make sense of good and evil. In fact, Bonhoeffer believed that his generation had reached a unique time in history; having lived through ten years of upheaval, which had turned the traditional upside down, the traditions that people of previous generations had relied on as guides had now failed them.

> Have there ever been people in history who in their time, like us, had so little ground under their feet, people to whom every possible alternative open to them at the time appeared equally unbearable, senseless, and contrary to life? Have there been those who like us looked for the source of their strength beyond all those available alternatives? Were they looking entirely in what has passed away and in what is yet to come? And nevertheless, without being dreamers, did they await with calm and confidence the successful outcome of their endeavor?[8]

in Bonhoeffer's thinking, this discussion will follow the new ordering. See Clifford Green, "The Text of Bonhoeffer's *Ethics*," in *New Studies in Bonhoeffer's* Ethics, ed. William J. Peck (Lewiston, NY: Edwin Mellen, 1987), 3–66, and Ilse Tödt, "Vorwort der Herausgeber," *Ethik*, DBW 6:7–28. See also appendices 1–3, DBWE 6.

6. Green, "Editor's Afterword to the English Edition," DBWE 6:409.
7. DBWE 8:37–52. By this time Bonhoeffer was directly involved in the resistance against Hitler. He believed that as a Christian he must oppose Hitler, even through direct political action, if need be. Cf. John Godsey, *Theology of Dietrich Bonhoeffer* (Philadelphia: Westminster, 1960), 197ff.
8. DBWE 8:38.

Given such circumstances, where were conscientious people to turn? Was there any possibility of retrieving anything from the traditions of western culture? What Bonhoeffer offered in terms of an answer provides a framework around which we can seek to understand Bonhoeffer's approach to ethics. He said,

> Who stands firm? Only the one whose ultimate standard is not his reason, his principles, conscience, freedom, or virtue; only the one who is prepared to sacrifice all of these when, in faith and in relationship to God alone, he is called to obedient and responsible action. Such a person is the responsible one, whose life is to be nothing but a response to God's question and call.[9]

Together these words from 1939 and 1942–1943 bracket Bonhoeffer's life in the resistance and, at the same time, provide an outline of the sum and substance of his theology. Finding their center in Jesus Christ, the only anchor in the midst of a sea of change, because God is found "solely in his poverty, in his cross," there is both stability and hope. But, as his words indicate, the security and surety of answers given in Christ do not remove thoughtful people of faith from the rough and tumble of making real-life decisions. They find that because of their faith, they are forced back into the world confronted with hard decisions. From these words, what can be seen is that Bonhoeffer's radical "this-worldly" orientation that comes to full expression in his late theology has its foundations firmly rooted in the cross of Christ. There on the cross we know that God has not abandoned the world. On the contrary, God has taken the human situation seriously, indeed, has taken the world so seriously as to have identified with its pain. The cross is the place, the only place, where God is to be found in the world.

9. Ibid., 40.

This cross is a cross of reality. It is at this point that God as God really is, meets the world as it really is. Only in Jesus Christ do we come to know God in and for the world. This orientation guides the development of Bonhoeffer's ethics.

Ethics, as conceived by Bonhoeffer, was not really a matter of living according to certain principles, arriving at clear-cut distinctions of right and wrong, or any of the traditional means of defining ethics. In fact, the first act of ethical reflection on the part of a Christian "is to supersede that knowledge," for it is precisely such knowledge that separates us from God.[10] Instead of asking, "How can I be good?" or "How can I do something good?," which are the classical expressions of ethics, Christian ethics seeks to take its cues from the reality of God as revealed in Jesus Christ. Therefore, conceived christologically, the question now becomes, "What is the will of God?" and, since God is the ultimate reality revealed in Jesus Christ, "the question of the good becomes the question of participating in God's reality revealed in Christ."[11]

For Bonhoeffer, for any Christian ethic to be Christian, it must begin with Christology. The problem of Christian ethics, he insisted, "is the realization among God's creatures of the revelational reality of God in Christ, just as the problem of dogmatics is the truth of the revelational reality of God in Christ."[12] This means that even though the world and reality cannot be ignored, Christian theology does not take these as its orientation, but rather the living presence of the incarnate, crucified, and risen Christ.

Christ is the starting point for ethics, according to Bonhoeffer, because God's presence in Christ is reality. In the well-known passage from *Ethics*, from the section entitled, "Christ, Reality and

10. DBWE 6:299.
11. Ibid., 47.
12. Ibid., 49. Cf. Tödt et al., "Editor's Afterword," DBWE 6:435.

Good," which was the first segment to be written in the late summer and fall 1940, he said,

> *In Jesus Christ the reality of God entered into the reality of this world.* The place where the questions about the reality of God and about the reality of the world are answered at the same time is characterized solely by the name: Jesus Christ. God and the world are enclosed in this name. In Christ all things exist (Col. 1:17). From now on we cannot speak rightly of either God or the world without speaking of Jesus Christ. All concepts of reality that ignore Jesus Christ are abstractions.[13]

Reality, as Bonhoeffer saw it, is conceived of properly only in Jesus Christ. Only in him are God and the world known, not as separate entities, but as two poles of one reality. To know this means the rejection of "two realms thinking," which allows for God and the world to be considered as separate and independent entities, each bumping up against the other. Ethics, so conceived, ends up splitting reality "into two parts, and the concern of ethics becomes the right relation of both parts to each other";[14] in the end, such distinctions were illusory and do not lead to God.

Christ on the cross is the full expression of God's reality in and for the world. There the reality of God intersects with the reality of the world. Because of God's act on the cross, justification of sinners and justice in the world go hand in-hand. They are two sides of one reality; therefore, the ethical problem is not about relating two separate entities to one another, but about "the reality of God show[ing] itself everywhere to be the ultimate reality."[15] Ethics, so conceived, means "to participate in the indivisible whole of God's reality."[16]

13. DBWE 6:54.
14. Ibid., 56.
15. Ibid., 48.
16. Ibid., 53.

By his own admission, Bonhoeffer wanted to deal with the real world and not simply with the world of ideas and imagination. Several studies of his theology have stressed that his theological works were attempts to make God concrete and to avoid abstraction. The difference between imagination and reality were important distinctions in Bonhoeffer's mind. It was impossible for abstract imagining to correspond with something as it really was. This came out of his own experience, as early as 1924, when he accompanied his brother Klaus on a trip to Italy. Beginning to see the country with his own eyes led him to write, "Imagination is beginning to turn into reality." We gain a better understanding of what he meant by this phrase from another passage, written sometime later on the trip: "One can read anything one wants about a country, and yet every image remains a picture painted on one's own native canvas in the most magnificent colors."[17]

It is this same understanding that is the basis for Bonhoeffer's understanding of reality in his ethics. According to Ernst Feil, Bonhoeffer's concept of reality is "understandable only in relation to his christology."[18] The reality of God in Jesus Christ stands in sharp contrast to and overcomes "our illusionary reality." True reality is quite different:

> It means thereby the reality of God as the ultimate reality beyond and in all that exists. It means also the reality of the existing world that is real only through the reality of God. The reality of God is not just another idea. Christian faith perceives this in the fact that the reality of God has revealed itself and witnessed to itself in the middle of the real world. *In Jesus Christ the reality of God has entered into the reality of this world.*[19]

17. DBWE 9:95.
18. Feil, *TDB*, 30.
19. DBWE 6:54.

From such a definition of reality, Bonhoeffer concluded that Christian ethics is participation in this reality.[20] But even more, because of Jesus Christ it is impossible to seek God without the world or the world without God; they are not separate entities, but one. In a passage that may be the key to his *Ethics*,[21] he continued,

> In Christ we are invited to participate in the reality of God and the reality of the world at the same time, the one not without the other. The reality of God is disclosed only as it places me completely into the reality of the world. But I find the reality of the world always already borne, accepted, and reconciled in the reality of God. That is the mystery of the revelation of God in the human being Jesus Christ. The Christian ethic asks, then, how this reality of God and of the world that is given in Christ becomes real in our world. It is not as if "our world" were something outside this God-world reality that is in Christ, as if it did not already belong to the world borne, accepted, and reconciled in Christ; it is not, therefore, as if some "principle" must first be applied to our circumstances and our time. Rather, the question is how the reality in Christ—which has long embraced us and our world within itself—works here and now or, in other words, how life is to be lived in it. What matters is *participating in the reality of God and the world in Jesus Christ today*, and doing so in such a way that I never experience the reality of God without the reality of the world, nor the reality of the world without the reality of God.[22]

It is such a definition of the relationship between God and the world that leads Bonhoeffer to reject what he calls "thinking in two realms," a manner of defining reality that had characterized traditional Christian thought, including the "pseudo-Lutheranism's"[23] proclamation of the "autonomy of the orders of this

20. Cf. to his earlier statement in DBWE 5:38: "Christian community is not an ideal we have to realize, but rather a reality created by God in Christ in which we may participate."

21. Cf. Wolfgang Huber, "Bonhoeffer and Modernity," in *Theory and Practice of Responsibility*, ed. Wayne Whitson Floyd Jr. and Charles Marsh (Valley Forge, PA: Trinity Press International, 1994), 11; Heinz Eduard Tödt, "Glauben in einen religionslosen Welt: Muß man zwischen Barth und Bonhoeffer wählen?" In *Genf '76: Ein Bonhoeffer-Symposium*, ed. Hans Pfeifer (Munich: Chr. Kaiser, 1976), 99; and Abromeit, *Geheimnis Christi*, 122.

22. DBWE 6:55.

world." Such a scheme conceives of the world as two realms that "bump against one each other: one divine, holy, supernatural, and Christian; the other worldly, profane, natural, and unchristian." This approach was problematic because it was able to carve out a small piece of the world reserved for God, with the result that any claim on the part of God is only partial, but never complete, "a provincial affair within the whole of reality." It assumes that there are "realities outside the reality of Christ," thereby reducing God to a "partial reality amid alongside others."[24]

The problem with such an approach to the world, according to Bonhoeffer, is that this division of the whole of reality into sacred and profane, or Christian and worldly, sectors creates the possibility of existence in only one of these sectors: for instance, a spiritual

23. Ibid., 56. The *Pseudo-Lutherans* is Bonhoeffer's "term to describe a teaching that called itself Lutheran but was not authentically so" (see ibid., 56n36). In general, while this position bore the name Lutheran, it was not an authentic representation of Luther's teaching. Bonhoeffer's criticism stemmed, in part, to the debates he had with Werner Elert, Paul Althaus, and Emmanuel Hirsch that had begun in the early 1930s in what Bonhoeffer perceived as an overdue emphasis they placed on natural orders of creation and their Nazi connections. In this this particular context, it is likely a reference to Althaus and Elert, two leading Lutheran voices, who were the authors of the June 11, 1934, Ansbach Memorandum, a document in which they laid out the "authentic voice of Lutheranism" in opposition to the Barmen Declaration. The purpose of the memorandum was to "stake out an orthodox Lutheran tradition that was pro-Nazi, although distinct from that of the German Christians and their Luther Renaissance advisors." (James M. Stayer, *Martin Luther: German Saviour; German Evangelical Theological Factions and the Interpretation of Luther* [Montreal, ON: McGill-Queens University Press, 2000], 132). See also Paul R. Hinlicky, *Before Auschwitz: What Christian Theology Must Learn from the Rise of Nazism* (Eugene, OR: Cascade, 2013).

24. Ibid., 56–57. From this discussion we can see that in spite of his rejection of "two realms thinking," he remained committed to Luther's ethical orientation laid out in his teaching on the "two kingdoms." By separating the realms, Luther maintained a dynamic understanding of God's rule that acknowledged God as the Lord of the whole created order. Luther's intent with his separation of the two kingdoms was to differentiate the ways in which God is present in and rules the world: in the "kingdom on the left," God rules through power, in which the state can be the arm of God for justice; in the "kingdom on the right," God rules through the gospel. Given Luther's basic orientation, it is Bonhoeffer's contention that if the kingdoms are separated in such a way as to limit God's activity to the "kingdom on the right," this could only lead to disaster; yet this is what happened in Nazi Germany and was sanctioned by Lutheran theologians. Cf. his earlier statement on the relationship between church and state in his "Lectures on Christology," DBWE 12:326–27.

existence that takes no part in worldly existence, and a worldly existence that can make good its claim to autonomy over against the sacred sector.

For Bonhoeffer, this was problematic for two reasons. First, it made it possible to talk about the separation of the church from politics, with the implication the church had nothing to do with the secular world. The result would be to limit the church's role in the world. Second, one could be led to view the church as a refuge from the world. This would allow the church to wrap itself in matters spiritual while ignoring the pressing issues in the world. The result of such a division was one in which the sacred and secular realms occupied separate, independent spheres. But at a time when the church's theologians, including the Lutherans, were giving voice to such a stance and while Hitler was welcoming the silence of the church in matters political, it was an issue that could not go unchallenged.[25]

But even more, this was a denial of reality. By laying claims to the Christian confession of the centrality of the incarnate, crucified, and risen Christ, it was no longer possible to see the world in terms of such stark contrasts that existed in opposition to one other. To do so meant to deny God's reconciling work on the cross. To conceive of

25. Already in 1935 laws meant to bring the church into compliance with the state had been passed. The Nazi goal of *Gleichschaltung*, of bringing everything in line with Nazi ideology, posed a particular challenge to the churches, since it meant that Hitler was not merely setting out to rule Germany politically, but wanted to rule the hearts and souls of its people as well. Ultimately, this meant that at its most fundamental level, Nazism was as much a religious battle as a political one. As Victoria Barnett describes it, "The *Gleichschaltung* of the German nation encompassed every level of society. Each citizen was affected, step by step, by a series of laws regulating everything from mandatory party membership for the practice of many professions to the requirement that civil servants replace the traditional German greeting, *Guten Tag*, with *Heil Hitler*. . . . The ultimate goal of *Gleichschaltung* was to capture the souls and minds of the German people. Hitler demanded not only obedience but a kind of faith" (Victoria Barnett, *For the Soul of the People: Protestant Protest Against Hitler* (New York: Oxford University Press, 1992), 30, 32). See also H. Gaylon Barker, "Editor's Introduction to the English Edition," DBWE 14:3ff.

the world as an autonomous realm was to deny "the community that God has formed with it in Christ."[26] Because of Christ, the church exists for the world. Therefore, any premise that would separate the church and the world was a faulty one. Bonhoeffer goes on to explain it in the following manner:

> As long as Christ and the world are conceived as two realms [Räume] bumping against and repelling each other, we are left with only the following options. Giving up on reality as a whole, either we place ourselves in one of the two realms, wanting Christ without the world or the world without Christ—and in both cases we deceive ourselves. Or we try to stand in the two realms at the same time, thereby becoming people in eternal conflict.[27]

The problem is this manner of approaching the world contradicts both the Bible and the thinking of the Reformation. For, in actuality,

> there are not two realities, but *only one reality*, and that is God's reality revealed in Christ in the reality of the world. Partaking in Christ, we stand at the same time in the reality of God and in the reality of the world. The reality of Christ embraces the reality of the world in itself. The world has no reality of its own independent of God's revelation in Christ. It is a denial of God's revelation in Jesus Christ to wish to be "Christian" without being "worldly," or [to] wish to be worldly without seeing and recognizing the world in Christ. Hence there are not two realms, but only *the one realm of the Christ-reality [Christuswirklichkeit]*, in which the reality of God and the reality of the world are united.[28]

26. DBWE 6:60.
27. Ibid., 57–58.
28. Ibid., 58. This conception of reality that rejects two realms thinking is the logical conclusion of a Christology shaped by the *communicatio idiomatum*. Reality is understood christologically in such a way that Christ is the embodiment of God. As Luther insisted, one cannot have God without the person of Christ or Christ without God. This reflects the same thinking conveyed in his December 1939 meditation, where Bonhoeffer drew heavily on the Formula of Concord, 7, where the contours of Lutheran Christology were spelled out. In that place he stated, "The Christological formula of two natures, one person, therefore, at the same time contains the highest soteriological significance: Godhead and humankind separated from each other before Christ came, united with a other alone in the becoming human of the Son of God. Only through the person are the natures in communion with each other. That means: only through

With reality so conceived, it follows that Christian ethics is defined similarly. Maintaining the continuity of his previous thought, wherein the vicarious suffering of Christ for the sake of the world becomes the manner of the church's existence in the world, now in Bonhoeffer's definition of a singular reality, there is no room for segregating Christian life off from secular life; in this he follows Luther.[29]

> Just as the reality of God has entered the reality of the world in Christ, what is Christian cannot be had otherwise than in what is worldly, the "supernatural" only in the natural, the holy only in the profane, the revelational only in the rational. The unity of the reality of God and the reality of the world established in Christ (repeats itself, or, more exactly) realizes itself again and again in human beings. Still, that which is Christian is not identical with the worldly, the natural with the supernatural, the revelational with the rational. Rather, the unity that exists between them is given only in the Christ-reality, and that means only as accepted by faith in this ultimate reality.[30]

The rejection of "two realms thinking" finds its foundation in such an affirmation. In order to affirm Jesus Christ as the center of all reality, one cannot divide the world into separate spheres. According to James Burtness, this rejection lies at the heart of Bonhoeffer's ethical theology. "[It] is a direct result of the affirmation of Jesus Christ as radical center of space and time. The rejection is for the sake of and because of the affirmation. Being clear about what one rejects can give greater freedom in the elaboration of what one affirms."[31] Because Bonhoeffer did not want to limit the role of God in the world, he could not conceive of two separate, autonomous spheres,

Jesus Christ are Godhead and humankind united" (DBWE 15:532). Here the soteriological significance bears an ethical significance.

29. Cf. Luther, "Temporal Authority: To What Extent it Should be Obeyed," *LW* 45:81–129.

30. DBWE 6:59.

31. James Burtness, *Shaping the Future: The Ethics of Dietrich Bonhoeffer* (Philadelphia: Fortress Press, 1985), 39.

where it might be possible to exclude God altogether. That would only serve to deny the central conviction of the Christian faith.

In his rejection of "two realms thinking," it is reasonable to say that Bonhoeffer was attempting to restore Luther's dialectic that had been lost in the practice of two kingdoms thinking. He believed the way in which Luther's two kingdoms teaching had come to be understood and applied in 1930s—'40s Germany made church leaders hesitant to criticize Hitler. It had come to be used in absolutistic terms, in which the sphere of the church had oversight in matters of spiritual issues, on the one side, and the political sphere dealt with the ordering of society on the other. It was not Luther's intent, however, as Bonhoeffer saw it, to create such a division. In fact, in arguing against such a move, he stated,

> In the name of a better Christianity Luther used the worldly to protest against a type of Christianity that was making itself independent by separating itself from the reality in Christ. Similarly, Christianity must be used polemically today against the worldly in the name of a better worldliness; this polemical use of Christianity must not end up again in a static and self-serving sacred realm. Only in this sense of a polemical unity may Luther's doctrine of the two kingdoms [Zwei Reiche] be used. That was probably its original meaning.[32]

Therefore, in rejecting "two realms thinking," Bonhoeffer was summarizing what for him was the central message of the New Testament. This rejection thus serves to provide an understanding of his theological perspective:

> The dark, evil world may not be surrendered to the devil, but [must] be claimed for the one who won it by coming in the flesh, by the death and resurrection of Christ. Christ gives up nothing that has been won, but holds it fast in his hands. Because of Christ it will not do to partition the world into a demonized and a Christian world. . . . The central message of the New Testament is that in Christ God has loved

32. DBWE 6:60.

> the world and reconciled it with himself. This message presupposes that the world needs reconciliation with God, but cannot achieve it by itself. Acceptance of the world is a miracle of divine mercy. Therefore the church-community's relation to the world is completely determined by God's relation to the world. There is a love of the world that is enmity toward God (James 4[:4]; [1] John 2[:15]), because it arises from the essence of the world in itself and not from God's love for the world. The world "in itself," as [it] understands itself and as it defends itself against—yes, even repudiates—the reality of God's love in Jesus Christ that is valid for it, is subject to God's judgment upon all enmity to Christ. This world is engaged in a life-and-death struggle with the church-community. Still, it is the task and the essence of the church-community to proclaim precisely to this world its reconciliation with God, and to disclose to it the reality of the love of God, against which the world so blindly rages. Thus, even the lost and condemned world is being drawn ceaselessly into the event of Christ.[33]

As these reflections display, Bonhoeffer was not an advocate of accepting the world without any critique of worldly ways. The world must be judged and affirmed in its relation to God. It is only from this perspective that Bonhoeffer can speak positively about the world. He continued,

> It is hard to give up an image that we have customarily used to integrate our thoughts and concepts. Yet we must get beyond this two-realms image. The question is now whether we can replace it with another image that is just as simple and plausible.
>
> Above all we must turn our eyes to the image of Jesus Christ's own body—the one who became human, was crucified, and is risen. In the body of Jesus Christ, God is united with humankind, all humanity is accepted by God, and the world is reconciled to God. In the body of Jesus Christ, God took on the sin of all the world and bore it. There is no part of the world, no matter how lost, no matter how godless, that has not been accepted by God in Jesus Christ and reconciled to God. Whoever perceives the body of Jesus Christ in faith can no longer speak of the world as if it were lost, as if it were separated from God; they can no longer separate themselves in clerical pride from the world. The

33. Ibid., 65–66.

> world belongs to Christ, and only in Christ is the world what it is. It needs, therefore, nothing less than Christ himself. Everything would be spoiled if we were to reserve Christ for the church while granting the world only some law, Christian though it may be. Christ has died for the world, and Christ is Christ only in the midst of the world. It is nothing but unbelief to give the world—for well-intended pedagogical reasons to be sure, which nonetheless leave an aftertaste of clericalism—less than Christ. It means not taking seriously the incarnation, the crucifixion, and the bodily resurrection. It means denying the body of Christ.[34]

This is a perspective on the world shaped by Bonhoeffer's theological view. First, it is centered on the cross, the bodily incarnation and suffering of God in Christ. Second, it ties God to the world and the world to God. The incarnation, crucifixion, and resurrection are the basis for his understanding of God and the world.

In turn, it is Christ crucified who defines God and God's mission in the world. The marks of God that become evident in Jesus Christ are not self-serving love, but a self-giving, other-directed love; not indifference and distance, but involvement and intimacy, compassion and love; not dominating arrogance, but humble servanthood; not power and invincibility, but vulnerability. It is a costly love and the marks are there to prove it—nail-pierced hands and a wounded side are the signs of God's enduring love. In contrast to the expectations of how and where God should be found among us, the gospel of Jesus Christ is cruciform in shape.

It is in this context that Bonhoeffer clearly spelled out the church's role and responsibility for the sake of the world; again, this role is defined christologically. As Bonhoeffer had repeatedly insisted, the church as the body of Christ exists for the purpose of proclaiming the present Christ to the world. Even in these extreme circumstances, the church's role had not changed.

34. Ibid., 66–67.

> The space of the church is not there in order to fight with the world for a piece of its territory, but precisely to testify to the world that it is still the world, namely, the world that is loved and reconciled by God. It is not true that the church intends to or must spread its space out over the space of the world. It desires no more space than it needs to serve the world with its witness to Jesus Christ and to the world's reconciliation to God through Jesus Christ. The church can only defend its own space by fighting, not for space, but for the salvation of the world. Otherwise the church becomes a "religious society" that fights in its own interest and thus has ceased to be the church of God in the world.[35]

Because of Christ, the church does not exist to fight against the world; rather, the church is only the church when it exists for the world. This conception of the church's responsibility in and for the world has its foundation in Bonhoeffer's original claims that Christ was present in the church. In his early thinking, where he drew on Luther's Christ *pro me* language, Bonhoeffer defined the church as the presence of Christ for the sake of the world. Here in *Ethics*, all of reality is defined in terms of Christ; while this does not represent a change in orientation, a new emphasis emerges. Now Christ is clearly identified with the world, which he presents as a challenge to the church. This new emphasis, however, says more about the church in Bonhoeffer's day in its failure to be the body of Christ than about the world.

In the section of *Ethics* on "History and Good," written during the summer 1942, Bonhoeffer described ethics as "accordance with reality," using language that even more clearly connects reality to Christology. God in Christ is the ultimate reality, and "trying to understand reality without the Real One means living in an abstraction, which those who live responsibly must always avoid; it means living detached from reality and vacillating endlessly between

35. Ibid., 63–64. This was one of the criticisms he leveled against the Confessing Church when it became apparent that its responses to Hitler did not go far enough.

the extremes of a servile attitude toward the status quo and rebellion against it. . . . The reason for this," according to Bonhoeffer,

> is that *reality [die Wirklichkeit]* is first and last not something impersonal [Neutrum], but *the Real One [der Wirkliche]*, namely, the God who became human. Everything that actually exists receives from *the* Real One, whose name is Jesus Christ, both its ultimate foundation and its ultimate negation, its justification and its ultimate contradiction, its ultimate Yes and its ultimate No.[36]

It is for that very reason that "it is only in and from Christ that it is possible to act in a way that is in accord with reality."[37]

In language consistent with his desire to locate God in the world, Bonhoeffer refused to base ethics on general principles or ideas. Reality, as defined by the real God, God in Christ, can be the only basis for ethics. Not the invisible God of ideas, but the visible God in the life, death, and resurrection of Jesus Christ: only the real God, God present in history, can help us grasp the reality of life in this world. For Bonhoeffer, God is always a concrete reality and, if we are to deal with God, we must do so within the confines of this concrete world, which is both our reality and God's reality.[38]

36. Ibid., 261–62. Everything has to do with Christ. As Bonhoeffer explained, "God became human, taking on human being in bodily form, thus reconciling humanity's world with God. The affirmation of human beings and their reality was based on God's taking on humanity, not vice versa. God did not take on humanity because human beings and human reality were worthy of divine affirmation. Instead, it is because human beings and human reality deserved the divine No that God took on humanity and affirmed it; God became human in the body, thus bearing and suffering, as God, the curse of the divine No upon human nature. Because of what God has done, because of the Real One, because of Jesus Christ, reality now receives its Yes and its No, its legitimacy and its limitation. Affirmation and protest now unite in the concrete action of those who have come to know the Real One. Neither affirmation nor contradiction now comes from an unreal world, nor from a programmatic understanding of the expedient or the ideal. Instead, they come from the reality of the world's reconciliation with God as it has taken place in Christ. In Jesus Christ, the Real One, all reality is taken on and summed up; Christ is its origin, essence, and goal" (262–63).
37. Ibid., 263.
38. Cf. Ernst Feil, *TDB*, 36ff.

As a logical conclusion to his thinking about God in terms of a *theologia crucis*, Bonhoeffer claimed Christ over the whole of social reality. And because one finds God in this world, "in the midst of horror," the church cannot avoid addressing the concrete problems of the day. In the face of an assault on basic human values, such as truth, justice, and freedom, the church is forced to become the protectors of such values, which is part and parcel of its proclamation of Christ. The church does this, because Jesus Christ is the origin of such values.[39] Rather than being viewed as an attempt by the church to expand its influence into the worldly or secular realm, defending such values is part of its confession of Christ. Therefore, Bonhoeffer declared,

> It is not Christ who has to justify himself before the world by acknowledging the values of justice, truth, and freedom. Instead, it is these values that find themselves in need of justification, and their justification is Jesus Christ alone. It is not a "Christian culture" that still has to make the name of Jesus Christ acceptable to the world; instead, the crucified Christ has become the refuge, justification, protection, and claim for these higher values and their defenders who have been made to suffer. It is with the Christ, persecuted and suffering together with his church-community, that justice, truth, humanity, and freedom seek refuge. It is the Christ who is unable to find shelter in the world, the Christ of the manger and the cross who is cast out of the world, who is the shelter to whom one flees for protection; only thus is the full breadth of Christ's power revealed. The cross of Christ makes both sayings true: "whoever is not for me is against me" and "whoever is not against us is for us."[40]

39. DBWE 6:341. In this context, Bonhoeffer's knowledge of the Holocaust and attitude toward the Jews must be acknowledged. See Eberhard Bethge, "Bonhoeffer and the Jews," in *Ethical Responsibility: Bonhoeffer's Legacy to the Churches*, ed. John D. Godsey and Geffrey B. Kelly (New York & Toronto: Edwin Mellen, 1981), 43–96, and Barnett, "Editor's Introduction," DBWE 15.
40. DBWE 6:345–46.

For Bonhoeffer, the church's role to defend and affirm the values "that liberate from oppression rather than dehumanize is christologically grounded, indeed, grounded in the theology of the cross. For 'it is with the Christ who is persecuted and who suffers in his church that justice, truth, humanity and freedom now seek refuge.'"[41] It is in that way that the church fulfills its public responsibility.

Bonhoeffer's concern in dealing with reality rather than ideas or speculation is an expression of Luther's *theologia crucis.* In fact, Bonhoeffer gave his own definition of the theology of the cross that parallels Luther's. In the section entitled, "The Concrete Commandment and the Divine Mandates," which was the final section produced, written between January and April 1943, he wrote,

> Seeking to understand God's will with creation apart from Christ is futile. *Jesus Christ, the God who became human*—this means that God has bodily taken on human nature in its entirety, that from now on divine being can be found nowhere else but in human form, that in Jesus Christ human beings are set free to be truly human before God. Now the "Christian" is not something beyond the human, but it wants to be in the midst of the human. What is "Christian" is not an end in itself, but means that human beings may and should live as human beings before God. In becoming human, God is revealed as the one who seeks to be there not for God's own sake but "for us." To live as a human being before God, in the light of God's becoming human, can only mean to be there not for oneself, but for God and for other human beings.[42]

Coming as they do shortly before his arrest for his involvement in the resistance, these reflections articulate Bonhoeffer's understanding the church's role in the world, which follows "from God's revelation itself." That revelation, contained in Scripture, provides the basis

41. John de Gruchy, "*Sanctorum Communio* and the Ethics of Free Responsibility," in *For All the Peoples: Global Theologies in Context*, ed. Else Marie Wiberg Pedersen, Holger Lam, and Peter Lodberg (Grand Rapids: Eerdmans, 2002), 105. Included here is a quote from an earlier translation of Bonhoeffer's *Ethics*; the new translation is in DBWE 6:346.

42. DBWE 6:400.

for the church's call to proclaim "Christ as the Lord and Savior of the world. There can be no legitimate proclamation by the Church which is not a proclamation of Christ."[43] Even in such extraordinary times as 1930s Germany, the church and its mission in the world could not be separated from this essential calling. Even then, the church was not called to proclaim a different message, nor could it seek to offer a message based on some universal human principal. Likewise, unless the church willingly fulfilled its mission, it could not insist that the government or others fulfill theirs.

In an explication of this point, Bonhoeffer offered a summary of his christological thinking, which remained anchored in the *theologia crucis*. Maintaining the threefold designation for Christ, he laid out the meaning of the incarnation, crucifixion, and resurrection for the world. First, identifying Jesus as the "God who became human," he said, "This means that God has bodily taken on human nature in its entirety, that from now on divine being can be found nowhere else but in human form, that in Jesus Christ human beings are set free to be truly human before God." In the incarnation, God becoming human, "God is revealed as the one who seeks to be there not for God's own sake but 'for us.'" Therefore, to be a Christian, to live before God, "is not an end in itself"; it means "to be there not for oneself, but for God and for other human beings." Consequently, "seeking to understand God's will with creation apart from Christ is futile."[44]

Second, Jesus is also the "crucified Reconciler." This means that the cross of Christ stands as the judgment over all humanity, but at the same time it is the place of reconciliation for the world.

> The cross of reconciliation sets us free to live before God in the midst of the godless world, sets us free to live in genuine worldliness

43. Ibid., 398–99.
44. Ibid., 400.

> [Weltlichkeit]. The proclamation of the cross of reconciliation frees us to abandon futile attempts to deify the world, because it has overcome the divisions, tensions, and conflicts between the "Christian" and the "worldly," and calls us to single-minded action and life in faith in the already accomplished reconciliation of the world with God. A life of genuine worldliness is possible only through the proclamation of the crucified Christ. Thus it is not possible in contradiction to the proclamation, and also not beside it in some kind of autonomy of the worldly; but it is precisely "in, with, and under" the proclamation of Christ that a genuinely worldly life is possible and real.[45]

The church and the world are one in Christ; this means that if one is to live a life of faith, it will be in the world. Because of the cross of Christ, any attempt to think of the world in terms of "two realms thinking" is rejected.

Finally, he affirmed Jesus as the "risen and exalted Lord," which means he is Lord over the whole world. "All worldly powers are subject to and bound to serve Christ, each in its own way." Rather than being a mandate for the church to exercise dominion over the government, or vice versa, all of creation is set free in Christ to fulfill its purpose. Claiming lordship over the entire creation means that Christ rules over all: "Church, family, culture and government. But it does so by simultaneously setting each of these mandates free to exercise their respective functions." Within these various mandates, the church is "to proclaim God's revelation in Jesus Christ." When the church fulfills this mandate, it is a deputy; "the Christian community stands in the place in which the whole world should stand. In this respect it serves the world as vicarious representative; it is there for the world's sake."[46]

What Bonhoeffer's thought reveals at this point is that not only is reality understood christologically, but that Christians, having been

45. Ibid., 400–1.

46. Ibid., 401–4. With such language, Bonhoeffer draws on Luther's understanding of vocation and underscores the dynamic nature of Luther's teaching on the "two kingdoms."

freed to live as persons before God, are free to live not for themselves, but for others. The "theology of the cross" that Bonhoeffer had used to define reality is also the basis for his understanding of Christian life in the world. The cross, according to Bonhoeffer, sets Christians free to live in a godless world "in genuine worldliness." No longer do God and the world live in opposition to one another, as was the case when the world was gripped in sinfulness, but they are now marked by reconciliation. Therefore, because of the cross, there is no need to either "deify the world" or define it according to "Christian" and "worldly" elements in tension with one another. All such distinctions have been done away through God's reconciling act on the cross. Now, Christians are "called to single-minded action and life in faith in the already accomplished reconciliation of the world with God." That is what it means to live in genuine worldliness.[47]

Based on these texts, Ernst Feil's conclusion regarding Bonhoeffer's understanding of reality having its roots in Christology can be supplemented by identifying the nature of that Christology as having been shaped by Luther's *theologia crucis*. Taken together, what is presented is the passion and single-mindedness with which Bonhoeffer drives home his conviction of a cross of reality. Like Luther, his *theologia crucis* is not something that can be narrowly defined as having only to do with church. God's love is for the entire world and it is there in that world that Christians must live out their faith.

In fact, it is probably this aspect of his theology that gives Bonhoeffer his strongest voice. He will not allow the gospel or the church to be shoved into a corner, nor will he allow it to be relativized by voices clamoring to set the agenda. This God who enters into our world and dies on the cross for us has to do with every

47. Ibid., 400.

facet of life. God cannot be confined within the walls of the church; because this is the case, the church must be orientated toward the world. God has created a new reality. The cross that Christians and the world have turned into a religious icon is in actually the "cross of reality." The forgiveness of sins that comes with Jesus' death on the cross is not just a religious feeling—it is something that restructures the world. Enemies of God have become friends; that which was separated by sin has now been reunited. And the result is that his is not a pietistic privatized faith in Jesus. In fact, it is something much bigger than his experience. It has to do with the reality of the world—a reality that encompasses all.

# 10

# Imprisonment 1943–1945

Bonhoeffer was arrested on April 5, 1943, along with his sister and brother-in-law, Christine and Hans von Dohnanyi. He spent the last two years of his life in prison, first in Berlin, then when Berlin was threatened to be overtaken by allied troops, he was transferred to Buchenwald concentration camp, where he remained from February 24, 1944 until his transfer first to Schönberg on April 3, then on to Flossenbürg, where he arrived on the evening of April 8.[1] It is from his prison cell, primarily while at Tegel, that his final, often revolutionary ideas come to expression. In letters written primarily to Eberhard Bethge, who saved them and later edited them for publication, we find Bonhoeffer's final thoughts, whose rich phrases become a shaping influence on later twentieth-century Christian thought and faith.

1. See DB-ER, 780-87 and chapter 13, and Ferdinand Schlinginsiepen, *Dietrich Bonhoeffr 1906-1945: Martyr, Thinker, Man of Resistance* (New York: T & T Clark, 2010), chapter 12, for details of Bonhoeffer's arrest and imprisonment.

### Letters and Papers from Prison

Finally, in *Letters and Papers from Prison,* in which the pages are littered with references to the centrality of Jesus Christ, Bonhoeffer is led to confess his faith in the only way he knows. In his well-known words contained in the July 16, 1944, letter to Eberhard Bethge, his theology comes to full expression. Telling Bethge there was a need for honesty, he said,

> we have to live in the world—"etsi deus non daretur."[2] And this is precisely what we do recognize—before God! God himself compels us to recognize it. Thus our coming of age leads us to a truer recognition of our situation before God. God would have us know that we must live as those who manage their lives without God. The same God who is with us is the God who forsakes us (Mark 15:34!). The same God who makes us to live in the world without the working hypothesis of God is the God before whom we stand continually. Before God, and with God, we live without God. God consents to be pushed out of the world and onto the cross;[3] God is weak and powerless in the world and in precisely this way, and only so, is at our side and helps us. Matt. 8:17 makes it quite clear that Christ helps us not by virtue of his omnipotence but rather by virtue of his weakness and suffering![4]

2. "As though God were not given."
3. This sounds very much like Luther's exposition of the Magnificat: "But it is different when God Himself works, with His own aim. Then a thing is destroyed or raised up before one knows it, and no one sees it done. Such works as these He does only among the two divisions of mankind, the godly and the wicked. He lets the godly become powerless and to be brought low, until everyone supposes their end is near, whereas in these very things He is present to them with all His power, yet so hidden and in secret that even those who suffer the oppression do not feel it but only believe. There is the fullness of God's power and His outstretched arm. For where man's strength ends, God's strength begins, provided faith is present and waits on Him. And when the oppression comes to an end, it becomes manifest what great strength was hidden underneath the weakness. Even so, *Christ was powerless on the cross; and yet there He performed His mightiest work and conquered sin, death, world, hell, devil, and all evil.* Thus all the martyrs were strong and overcame. Thus, too, all who suffer and are oppressed overcome" (*LW* 21:340) [emphasis added]).
4. *LPP*, DBWE 8:478–79. Commenting on these central ideas found in *LPP*, John de Gruchy, "Editor's Introduction to the English Edition," DBWE 8:25, concludes, "If we start with such ideas as God's omnipotence, omniscience, and omnipresence, we will never arrive at a true knowledge of God. However, if we participate by faith in Jesus Christ as the one who 'is there

"Before God"—this is how we are to live. The declaration is one that comes as a result of God's own presence in the world. The emphasis is on *before* God, not on *without* God. This is a confession based not on doubt, but one profoundly shaped by a concrete "this-worldly" understanding of Christ *pro nobis*. This was not a rejection of everything that he had said previously, but stands as the culmination of the dynamic center of his faith. In fact, all of *Letters and Papers from Prison* can be read as a commentary on Bonhoeffer's own theology, for rather than representing a break from his previous thinking, what was expressed fragmentarily in letters was the logical conclusion to a this-worldly *theologia crucis*, a "cross of reality." Here is a faith that takes both God and the world seriously—because of God.[5]

It is quite specifically God in Jesus Christ who makes it possible—and necessary—for us to live in this world as though God were not given.[6] In that same letter he continued,

> This is the crucial distinction between Christianity and all religions. Human religiosity directs people in need to the power of God in the world, God as deus ex machina. The Bible directs people toward the powerlessness and the suffering of God; only the suffering God can help. To this extent, one may say that the previously described development toward the world's coming of age, which has cleared the way by eliminating a false notion of God, frees us to see the God of the Bible,

for others,' we are liberated from self and experience the transcendence that is truly the God of the Bible. Only then does the reality of God become meaningful."

5. James Burtness, "As Though God Were Not Given: Barth, Bonhoeffer and the *Finitum Capax Infiniti*," *Dialog* 19 (Fall 1980): 249, states "that there is a direct line from Luther's insistence that the finite is capable of bearing the infinite to Bonhoeffer's insistence that God is teaching us to live in the world as though he were not given, that is, from the *finitum capax infiniti* to the *etsi deus non daretur*."
6. Bonhoeffer's statement that we must live in the world as if God does not exist represents a radical departure from that of his teacher Adolf von Harnack. In his discussion of religion, Harnack says, "Humanity labors in history 'as if God exists.'" Cited in Carl Jürgen Kaltenborn, "Adolf von Harnack and Dietrich Bonoheffer," in *A Bonhoeffer Legacy: Essays in Understanding*, ed. A. J. Klassen (Grand Rapids: Eerdmans, 1981), 52.

> who gains ground and power in the world by being powerless. This will probably be the starting point for our "worldly interpretation."[7]

In contrast to those who understood Bonhoeffer's "nonreligious" or "worldly interpretation" to mean that he had abandoned the church and theology,[8] when viewed in light of the *theologia crucis,* what Bonhoeffer is doing is simply restating the fundamental view of the Bible. In Bonhoeffer's mind, what we must live without is not God per se, but our caricatures or versions of God—be they liberal, pietistic, or fundamentalistic. Such views of God, he believed, separate God from humanity, serving to cut God off from the world (the result of which is "two realms thinking"); in addition, such views of God only serve to cut humanity off from the world as well (for in order to be holy, human beings must strive to ascend to God; or in the words from *Ethics*, humanity cannot be whole—it is split, either focusing on God or on things of this world). Such a view of God only serves to "devalue God's transcendence into an unreal beyond."[9]

According to Bonhoeffer, this was a false conceptuality. By focusing on the biblical witness, it is not possible to limit God or to separate God for the world, for the God of the Bible enters into the created world, taking on human form and dwelling with us. God is not removed from the world of daily life, but becomes a part of it. This is a God who exists for others, who enters into personal relationships with humanity.

7. DBWE 8:479–80. For a fuller understanding of the framework from which Bonhoeffer was analyzing the relationship between Christianity and other religions, see Christiane Tietz, "Bonhoeffer's Strong Christology in the Context of Religious Pluralism," in *Interpreting Bonhoeffer: Historical Perspectives, Emerging Issues*, ed. Clifford J. Green and Guy C. Carter (Minneapolis: Fortress Press, 2013), 181–96.
8. Hanfried Müller, *Von der Kirche zur Welt: Ein Beitrag zu der Beziehung des Wortes Gottes auf die societas in Dietrich Bonhoffers theologischer Entwicklung* (Hamburg-Bergstedt: Herbert Recin Evangelisch, 1961), for example.
9. Gerffrey B. Kelly, "Revelation in Christ: A Study of Bonhoeffer's Theology of Revelation," *Ephemerides Theologica Lovanienses* 50, no. 1 (May, 1974): 60.

Likewise, his words *etsi deus non daretur* make it quite clear that his emphasis on the cross is not weakened. Rather, it is quite the opposite. The weakness of God displayed on the cross is intensified.[10] In addition to God being hidden in weakness, God seems to be absent altogether. It is this very weakness that is the starting point and the key to understanding God's presence in the world. While humanity seeks God in his power, Bonhoeffer insists that the Christian witness stands as a counter to such efforts, pointing us to where God is to be found. "The Bible directs people toward the powerlessness and the suffering of God; only the suffering God can help." Only a suffering God can help overcome all false conceptions of God that stand in the way of true faith that sees "the God of the Bible, who gains ground

10. Wolfgang Huber, "Bonhoeffer and Modernity," in *Theology and the Practice of Responsibility*, ed. Wayne Whitson Floyd Jr. and Charles Marsh (Valley Forge, PA: Trinity Press Internationsl, 1994), 13, draws a similar conclusion. With regard to Bonhoeffer's phrase *etsi deus non daretur*, he says, "Bonhoeffer's interpretation of the world without God as a working hypothesis is not a withdrawal from the theological argument, but its intensification. In christological terms, this intensification takes the form of Bonhoeffer's unfolding his theology of incarnation as a radical theology of the cross. The key for that theological decision can be found in the letter of July 16, 1944."

and power in the world by being powerless."[11] Hence, the "suffering God" is the real God.

And it is God with whom we are dealing on the cross. Again, Huber:

> The basis for the *theologia crucis* of this letter is the conviction that it is really God himself who is suffering on the cross. It is not only the human person Jesus with whom, as the crucified, God identifies himself in the resurrection—a way of speaking often used in theology. No, it is God, in the human person Jesus, who is suffering and dying on the cross. So it is God himself who is crying on the cross, "My God, my God, why hast thou forsaken me?". . . It is extremely strange to imagine that God himself complains that he abandoned himself. But it symbolizes that God himself experiences being abandoned by God. God himself participates in a world without God. So the cross is the place with respect to which it is not a self-contradiction to say: "Before God and with God we live without God."[12]

11. The term *suffering God* is not new for Bonhoeffer at this point, but reflects a continuity in his thinking. See, for example, his London sermon from 1934 in which he says, "Our God is a suffering God." When we take this to be a confession of faith, a suffering God is the only God available to Christians. The context for its use here is important. In Germany, with the emphasis on the superiority of the Aryan race and their power to transform or restore Germany, Bonhoeffer's emphasis on salvation residing in the weakness and suffering of God cannot be overlooked. If Hitler used religious language and symbols and identified "power" with godliness, then it becomes necessary to say the opposite. The new age comes through the cross and suffering, it does not go around it. The language Bonhoeffer uses here has parallels in Luther. Based on the *communicatio idiomatum*, Luther's language is striking and rather radical. In his "Disputation on the Humanity and Divinity of Christ" (1540), thesis 4, he says, "It is true to say: This man created the world, and this God suffered, died, was buried, etc." (www.projectwittenberg.org/pub/resources/text/wittenberg/luther/luther-divinity.txt.). In his "Confession Concerning Christ's Supper" (1528), Luther argued against Zwingli, who insisted that only the human Jesus suffered. For Luther this is not enough: "Rather, (the man) is one person with God, so that whatever God is, there also the man is: God is also said the suffer." (*LW* 37:210). Equally radical is his language in a sermon on the Gospel of John: "Now we can say: 'God became man, God suffered, and God died.'. . . Since God and man are one Person, the properties characteristic of humanity alone are attributed to the deity; for the properties of the two natures are also united" (*LW* 22:492).
12. Huber, "Bonhoeffer and Modernity," 13.

Bonhoeffer had so clearly stated his belief that God in Christ took on human form throughout this theological writings that not even God is unaffected by bearing the sins of the world.

It is such an affirmation of God that forms the foundation for Bonhoeffer's critique of religion, on the one hand, and affirmation of the world, on the other.[13] There is little doubt that the critique of religion is one of the major themes that emerges in *LPP*.[14] There is reference upon reference from Bonhoeffer about the negative implications of religion. Viewed from a variety of perspectives, there are two aspects in particular that become the foundation for his other reflections: metaphysics and inwardness or individualism. Having examined earlier usages Bonhoeffer had made of these terms, Ralf Wüstenberg captures the tone of Bonhoeffer's critique by saying that metaphysics is interpreted "under the aspects of 'deus ex machina,' 'stopgap,' and working hypothesis 'God;' 'inwardness/individualism' under the aspects of 'something partial,' 'religiously privileged, and guardianship of 'God.'"[15]

13. We have seen that Bonhoeffer made a distinction between religion and Christianity from his earlier writings. It is that same impulse that is operative now in his declaration that in a "world come of age" religion is a thing of the past. Drawing a similar conclusion, he says the problem with religion is that it is based on a philosophical or metaphysical premise that is no longer valid. Eberhard Bethge, *Bonhoeffer: Exile and Martyr* (New York: Seabury, 1976), 144–45, explains Bonhoeffer's differentiation in the following manner: "That which in fact organizes the world today, plans it, runs it, explains it, that which answers for what is real and sustains it politically, economically, scientifically is not religion. In this sense, its time has irrevocably gone. But for Bonhoeffer that never meant that the time of Christ has gone. . . . It becomes immediately evident from these themes that Bonhoeffer's religionless never meant the end of faith in God, but only the end of a certain prevailing kind of faith in God; and what he was really concerned with during his imprisonment was the fresh authenticity of the Gospel in changed circumstances, of which the Church so far had not taken account. Long-cherished ideas had to be given up; but only in order to liberate man to know the Gospel more truly, and at the same time help him to become aware of his own epoch."

14. See Ralf Wüstenberg, *A Theology of Life: Dietrich Bonhoeffer's Religionless Christianity* (Grand Rapids: Eerdmans, 1998), for a detailed analysis of this concept in Bonhoeffer's theology, both in terms of its origins and expressions in his earlier theology and as it is developed in his Tegel theology. Clifford Green, *Bonhoeffer: A Theology of Sociality* (Grand Rapids: Eerdmans, 1999), 258ff, also offers a framework for understanding Bonhoeffer's concern with religion, as does Bethge, *DB-ER*, 871ff.

One problem this concept of religion produces, from Bonhoeffer's perspective, is that it plays on human weakness.[16] In the world in which people live out their lives, however, this means a disjuncture or contradiction. Daily people rely on their strengths, in which case they don't need God. In practical terms, therefore, God is pushed to the margins, turned to only as a "stop-gap" when other sources have given out.[17] Then God, perceived as a *deus ex machina*, is brought in to rescue people.[18] This, in turn, leads to the religious conception of God and religion in general as being only partially necessary; they are not essential, but peripheral. All of this leads to intellectual dishonesty,[19] which is not so unlike Luther's description of the theology of glory. The strength of the theology of the cross, on the other hand, is that it calls a thing what it is. It is honest about both God and the world, thereby enabling one to live in the world without seeking recourse in heavenly or escapist religious practices. Additionally, such religious thinking leads to the creation of a God to suit human needs, which again has a parallel in Luther's *theologia crucis*. For Bonhoeffer and Luther, however, the real God is one who doesn't appear only in the form that we might expect, one whom we can incorporate into our worldview or lifestyle. God is one who is always beyond our grasp, but at the same time is a hidden presence in the world.

15. Wüstenberg, *Theology of Life*, 22.
16. Cf. Green, *Bonhoeffer: A Theology of Sociality*, 261: "The essential components of 'religion' are always human weakness which turns in dependence to a power God."
17. See his May 29, 1944 letter, DBWE 8:404–6.
18. Green, *Bonhoeffer: A Theology of Sociality*, 263, refers to this phenomenon as "episodic." "It is a crisis phenomenon, an emergency device. People live most of their lives and manage their concerns by reason, knowledge, technology, organizing ability, and other secular methods. Only when a crisis appears, when they are reduced to a state of weakness which cannot yet be managed by such methods, do some people revert to the religious posture. This episodic character is consistently indicated in religious 'theology' by the role of 'God' as stop-gap, *deus ex machina*, and working-hypothesis."
19. Cf. ibid., 264–65.

While these are the negative aspects of religion, Bonhoeffer also offered a positive affirmation, which has its basis in his earlier theology as well. Scattered throughout his letters from prison, one dominating theme remains at the center. Restating his opening concerns from *Discipleship*, Bonhoeffer's point of departure had to do with the question of relating faith in Jesus Christ to the world. This is the beginning point for Bonhoeffer's "new" theological reflections from prison. Yet when examined from the perspective of his earlier theology and through the lens of the cross, they are not really new at all, but rather the culmination and the bringing together of the thoughts that guided his theology from the beginning.

Bonhoeffer's critique of religion had its basis in Christology and found its answer in a nonreligious interpretation. According to Bethge, among others, what is important in this new formulation is not nonreligious interpretation itself, but the christological motivation that gives shape to these reflections.[20] Again, Bethge:

> His quest is part of a journey, as it were, from past engagement to new engagement. Bonhoeffer's theme entails setting out in order to discover the presence of Christ in the world of today: it is not a discovery of the modern world, nor a discovery of Christ from this modern world, but discovering *him* in this world. Bonhoeffer asks the simplest of questions, from which it is impossible to emerge unchanged: "Who are *you*?" . . . Hence this question governs Bonhoeffer's dialogue and must preserve, in the correct relation and proportion the explosive formulas of the world come of age, nonreligious interpretation, and arcane discipline. Without the overriding theme of this question these concepts would fall apart and become stunted or superficial. As isolated intellectual

20. *DB-ER*, 856. In addition, Bethge concludes that the Christology found in LPP is continuous with Bonhoeffer's early Christology. See also his essay, "Bonhoeffer's Assertion of Religionless Christianity—Was He Mistaken?" in Klassen, *Bonhoeffer Legacy*, 4–5., where he points out that the question about "Who is Christ actually for us today?" was Bonhoeffer's primary concern. "Non-religious interpretation" was the "tool . . . [that] helped to bring Bonhoeffer to a better knowledge of Christ and a more concrete relationship with him. This was its function." In other words, it was simply a hermeneutical framework that Bonhoeffer used to reflect on the core christological question.

> phenomena, they have little to do with Bonhoeffer's thought; but within the christological perspective of his central theme they achieve their full and independent justification.[21]

An additional voice of support for this christological interpretation comes from Gerhard Ebeling, who had been a student of Bonhoeffer at Finkenwalde. He asserts,

> It is surely incomprehensible how anyone could overlook the fact that the letters show not even the slightest trace of any doubt of Jesus Christ, that on the contrary Bonhoeffer is chiefly concerned in ever more elementary ways with personal faith in Christ and that to his mind speaking about God, which has certainly become problematical to a degree, can find its proper foundation solely in Jesus Christ. . . . The problem of non-religious interpretation arises for Bonhoeffer not from any doubt of Jesus Christ, but precisely from faith in Jesus Christ. It is not Jesus Christ, but the word God, indeed all religious concepts as such, that he finds problematical. The question of non-religious interpretation derives directly from the foundation and heart of his theology, from his Christology. Non-religious interpretation is for Bonhoeffer nothing other than Christological interpretation.[22]

Along those lines, the purpose of Bonhoeffer's "worldly interpretation" can be identified as a means of reclaiming the core of his *theologia crucis.* The language about nonreligious or worldly interpretation emerges for the first time in the April 30, 1944 letter; Bonhoeffer stated his chief concern as follows: "What keeps gnawing at me is the question, what is Christianity, or who is Christ actually for us today."[23] His reflections continued along the line of trying

21. *DB-ER*, 866.
22. Gerhard Ebeling, "The Non-religious Interpretation of Biblical Concepts," in *Word and Faith* (Philadelphia: Fortress Press, 1963), 107–8.
23. DBWE 8:362. According to Bethge, *Bonhoeffer: Exile and Martyr*, 138–39, this is a reformulation of Bonhoeffer's basic question. "He did not ask this question anxiously . . . nor did he ask: 'How may faith survive today?' This very question would have been for him an admission of defeat, which he never considered. Neither did he ask: 'What does modern man need?' His faith in the majesty of Christ did not allow such a question. He asked positively,

to answer that question if people are no longer religious. If religion had been the primary means of expressing faith, even in the church, then how is it possible to talk about Christ now in a world come of age, a world that no longer needed religion? In nonreligious ways, of course. So, too, he wanted to talk about Christ not as "an object of religion," but as the "Lord of the world."[24] In order to get at that question, Bonhoeffer attempted to clear away all that which keeps people from encountering God in Jesus Christ; "he felt that here he had to 'break through the knots.'"[25]

This primary concern was stated repeatedly in the letters that follow. Questioning the validity of "individualistic doctrine of salvation," using language that reflects Luther, in a May 5, 1944 letter, he said,

> What matters is not the beyond but this world, how it is created and preserved, is given laws, reconciled, and renewed. What is beyond this world is meant, in the gospel, to be there *for* this world—not in the anthropocentric sense of liberal, mystical, pietistic, ethical theology, but in the biblical sense of the creation and the incarnation, crucifixion, and resurrection of Jesus Christ.[26]

In contrast to a theology of glory that turns to speculation, locating God apart from the world, Bonhoeffer's theology is tied to the world. This concern was stated similarly in his June 8, 1944 letter as "Christ and the world that has come of age,"[27] where he holds Christ and the world together. It is because of this world that we need to be

presupposing Christ as present. He did not start a discussion on the necessity and usefulness of this presence, but he discussed the fact of this presence, and who Christ is for us today."

24. As Bethge indicates, *DB-ER*, 864, this is a continuation of what Bonhoeffer had said as early as 1932: "It is not a question of how we ought to proclaim the Gospel today but, in view of the historical development of the western world, of who is its content. Given the presupposition of the presence of Christ, Bonhoeffer sought to understand his presence today."
25. Ibid., 856.
26. DBWE 8:373.
27. Ibid., 428.

concerned about Christ and it is because of Christ that we come to understand the world. In this regard, one of the weaknesses of liberal theology "was that it allowed the world the right to assign to Christ his place within it; that it accepted, in the dispute between church and world, the—relatively mild—peace terms dictated by the world."[28] But at the same time, liberal theology's strength, according to Bonhoeffer, was its affirmation of the world; its error lay in the foundation of that affirmation.

In one of his final surviving letters, from July 21, 1944, written the day after the failed assassination plot on Hitler's life, Bonhoeffer both summed up his theology and, indirectly, points to his understanding and appreciation of Luther. Even at this late stage, assuming that the worst was yet to come and no longer in a position to hold out much hope for a positive outcome, Bonhoeffer did not renounce the worldly orientation of his faith. In fact, he did quite the opposite. In light of his circumstances, he acknowledged that he has come to understand the "profound this-worldliness" of Christianity. He then went on to explain what this means:

> The Christian is not a *homo religiosus* but simply a human being, in the same way that Jesus was a human being—in contrast, perhaps, to John the Baptist. I do not mean the shallow and banal this-worldliness of the enlightened, the bustling, the comfortable, or the lascivious, but the profound this-worldliness that shows discipline and includes the ever-present knowledge of death and resurrection. I think Luther lived in this kind of this-worldliness.[29]

Even though Bonhoeffer comes to the point of rejecting religion, he does not reject Jesus Christ. His prison reflections make clear that for him the two are not to be equated.

28. Ibid.
29. Ibid., 485.

Finally, in his "Outline for a Book,"[30] written in August 1944, he offers some of his last theological reflections. Rather than looking to the past, he looks to the future, trying to envision what this "worldly" Christianity might look like.[31] In words that replicate his earlier thinking, in the second chapter, which forms the centerpiece of the text and is the section developed the most, he offered us a clear statement of the *theologia crucis*; it is one that focuses on the question of God:

> Who is God? Not primarily a general belief in God's omnipotence, and so on. That is not a genuine experience of God but just a prolongation of a piece of the world. Encounter with Jesus Christ. Experience that here there is a reversal of all human existence, in the very fact that Jesus only "is there for others." Jesus's "being-for-others" is the experience of transcendence! Only through this liberation from self, through this "being-for-others" unto death, do omnipotence, omniscience, and omnipresence come into being. Faith is participating in this being of Jesus. (Becoming human [Menschwerdung], cross, resurrection.) Our relationship to God is no "religious" relationship to some highest, most powerful, and best being imaginable—that is no genuine transcendence. Instead, our relationship to God is a new life in "being there for others," through participation in the being of Jesus. The transcendent is not the infinite, unattainable tasks, but the neighbor within reach in any given situation. God in human form! Not as in oriental religions in animal forms as the monstrous, the chaotic, the remote, the terrifying, but also not in the conceptual forms of the absolute, the metaphysical, the infinite, and so on, either, nor again the Greek god—human form of the "God-human form [Gott-Menschgestalt] of the human being in itself." But rather "the human being for others"! therefore the Crucified One. The human being living out of the transcendent.[32]

30. Ibid., 499–504.

31. Here again it is important to note the context in which Bonhoeffer is writing. "What he was writing then did not involve a struggle against Hitler. Hitler was no longer worthy to be dealt with theologically. It was the future task of the Church which entirely engaged Bonhoeffer's attention" (Bethge, *Bonhoeffer: Exile and Martyr*, 141.)

32. DBWE 8:501. De Gruchy, "Editor's Introduction," DBWE 8:25, provides the following commentary: "As Bonhoeffer writes in the 'Outline': 'Our relationship to God is no "religious" relationship to some highest, most powerful, and best being imaginable—that is no genuine

Here, in these final words, he does not deviate from his earlier thought. In the life, death, and resurrection of Jesus, God is rearranging the landscape, creating a new reality. This is not the God of our own making, the God of religion; rather, it is God *pro nobis*, but yet *extra nos*. In this way, Jesus was there for others and, in faith, Christians share in his suffering in the world. Along the same line, when he turned his attention to the church in the third and final chapter, it is with the same understanding of the present Christ that gave expression to the church in and for the world. "The church is the church only when it is there for others." If Christ is the one who exists for others, then the church, the body of Christ, is the church only when it assumes the same posture. For that reason, Bonhoeffer envisioned a church that does not seek to find a place for itself, but begins by giving "away all its property to those in need" and will "participate in the worldly tasks of life in the community—not dominating but helping and serving," existing not at the center of power but on the margins. Bereft of any external security, the church will take risks for others.[33]

transcendence. Instead, our relationship to God is a new life in "being there for others," through participation in the being of Jesus.' This is the meaning of Christ becoming fully human and dying on the cross. In other words, by 'nonreligious interpretation,' Bonhoeffer proposed not a return to the anthropocentric approach of liberal, mystical, pietistic, or ethical theology but a recovery of 'the biblical sense of the creation and the incarnation, crucifixion and resurrection of Jesus Christ.' Only from this perspective is it possible to interpret key biblical concepts and the creed and engage in liturgical renewal in a nonreligious way. Bonhoeffer did not see his task as popular 'apologetic' in the sense of adapting the gospel to the modern mind, that is, a 'secular gospel.'"

33. De Gruchy, "Editor's Introduction," DBWE 8:26, explains the implications of Bonhoeffer's thought this way: "The consequences of this for the church and for Christian life in the world were, as Bonhoeffer recognized, far reaching. For what is at stake in Bonhoeffer's 'nonreligious' interpretation is not apologetics or even hermeneutics—that is, simply interpreting Christianity in a new historical context in a new linguistic and conceptual key—but a fundamental reorientation, or metanoia, that leads to an identification with Christ in his sufferings, and therefore to a different way of being the church-community in the world. If Jesus exists only for others, then the church must not seek its own self-preservation but be 'open to the world' and in solidarity with others, especially those who are oppressed and suffering. Undoubtedly Bonhoeffer had in mind here the persecution, incarceration, and death of the Jews and other

Bonhoeffer's statement, "The church is the church only when it is there for others," is a succinct reformulation of the understanding of the church he had held since *Sanctorum Communio*. As the body of Christ, the church is the presence of God in the world. Christ's vicarious representative act on the cross is lived out in the church's presence in the world. In the same way that Christ suffered for us, the church suffers for the sake of the world. In the same way that Christ is only Christ *pro me*, the church as the body of Christ is only the church when it exists for others. The church is never an end in and of itself, but always a means of God's presence in the world. To be otherwise would be a contradiction, or worse, a denial of the gospel.

Following up on these reflections, in a letter written to Bethge on August 21, 1944, in what is probably the last letter containing theological reflections, he provided an even more succinct answer to his question, "Who is God?"

> Everything we may with some good reason expect or beg of God is to be found in Jesus Christ. What we imagine a God could and should do—the God of Jesus Christ has nothing to do with all that. We must immerse ourselves again and again, for a long time and quite calmly, in Jesus's life, his sayings, actions, suffering, and dying in order to recognize what God promises and fulfills.[34]

"Everything we may with some good reason expect or beg of God is to be found in Jesus Christ": here again, this is not the God of our own making. In fact, we do not find God where we think God should be located. If we want to know God and receive the promises of God, "we must immerse ourselves again and again, for a long time and quite calmly, in Jesus's life, his sayings, actions, suffering, and dying." This is the basis for faith, the norm for life in the world, and

'undesirables' in Nazi Germany, though for obvious reasons he could not mention this in his letters."

34. DBWE 8:514–15.

"the solid ground upon which we stand." It is what gives meaning to life and is the ultimate ground of hope. Refusing to take his cues from the world around him, he pointed to the human Jesus:

> Again and again in these turbulent times, we lose sight of why life is really worth living. We think that our own life has meaning because this or that other person exists. In truth, however, it is like this: If the earth was deemed worthy to bear the human being Jesus Christ, if a human being like Jesus lived, then and only then does our life as human beings have meaning. Had Jesus not lived, then our life would be meaningless, despite all the other people we know, respect, and love.[35]

This is indeed a statement of the *theologia crucis* that contains all the elements important to both Bonhoeffer and Luther.

As his own words demonstrate, the emphasis on suffering did not lead Bonhoeffer to become pessimistic or hopeless. He continued to affirm God's creation, even suggesting, as he did in a June 27, 1944 letter, that Christ's crucifixion and resurrection prevent us from "abolishing" this-worldliness "ahead of its time." On the contrary, resurrection does not provide the Christian an escape from this world of suffering, deceit, and death. To suggest that Christian redemption means "being redeemed out of sorrows, hardships, anxieties, and longings, out of sin and death, in a better life beyond," is to misinterpret the New Testament's proclamation of Christ.

> The Christian hope of resurrection is different from the mythological in that it refers people to their life on earth in a wholly new way. . . . Unlike believers in the redemption myths, Christians do not have an ultimate escape route out of their earthly tasks and difficulties into eternity. Like Christ ("My God . . . why have you forsaken me?"), they have to drink the cup of earthly life to the last drop, and only when they do this is the Crucified and Risen One with them, and they are crucified and resurrected with Christ.[36]

35. Ibid., 515.
36. Ibid., 447–48.

Christian faith, by its very definition, keeps us tied to this world. But even more, as he stated in a July 18, 1944, letter, "The human being is called upon to share in God's suffering at the hands of a godless world."[37] The same sentiment is echoed in his poem, "Christians and Heathens," that he had included in a July 8, 1944 to Bethge, where in the second verse he said, "People go to God when God's in need, find God poor, reviled, without shelter or bread, see God devoured by sin, weakness, and death. Christians stand by God in God's own pain."[38]

## Other Letters from Prison

In the "other" letters from prison, written to his fiancée, Maria von Wedemeyer, while perhaps not intended to be theological reflections, Bonhoeffer's thoughts present themselves as genuine expressions of faith, again expressed in the language of the *theologia crucis*. In Advent and Christmas letters to Maria in December 1943, for example, he wrote in language very similar to that which he used in his other letters from prison. Reflecting on Christmases past in which he delighted in gift giving, in a letter on December 1, he noted the contrast his present circumstances created for himself and others. But rather than detracting from Christmas, he found himself "content with what is truly essential" and having "nothing to give." He told her,

> The gift God gave us in the birth of Christ will seem all the more glorious; the emptier our hands, the better we understand what Luther meant by his dying words: "We're beggars, it's true." The poorer our quarters, the more clearly we perceive that our hearts should be Christ's home on earth. So let us approach this Christmas-tide not only undaunted but with complete confidence.[39]

37. Ibid., 480.
38. Ibid., 461.

The language used to describe Christmas for the first time in Barcelona, and again in the circular letters to the House of Brethren, emerged again in a December 13, 1943 letter. Recognizing and accepting the separation that they would experience at Christmas, which was contrary to his earlier expectations, and coming to terms with the experience of "a few dark hours," he found hope in the message of Christmas.

> We shall ponder the incomprehensibility of our lot and be assailed by the question of why, over and above the darkness already enshrouding humanity, we should be subjected to the bitter anguish of a separation whose purpose we fail to understand. How hard it is, inwardly to accept what defies our understanding; how great is the temptation to feel ourselves at the mercy of blind chance; how sinister the way in which mistrust and resentment steal into our hearts at such times; and how readily we fall prey to the childish notion that the course of our lives reposes in human hands! And then, just when everything is bearing down on us to such an extent that we can scarcely withstand it, the Christmas message comes to tell us that all our ideas are wrong, and that what we take to be evil and dark is really good and light because it comes from God. Our eyes are at fault, that is all. God is in the manger, wealth in poverty, light in darkness, succor in abandonment. No evil can befall us; whatever others may do to us, they cannot but serve God who is secretly revealed as love and rules the world and our lives. We must learn to say: "I know how to be abased, and I know how to abound; in any and all circumstances I have learned the secret of facing plenty and hunger, abundance and want. I can do all things in him who strengthens me" (Philippians 4:12 and 13)—and this Christmas, in particular, can help us to do so. What is meant here is not stoical resistance to all extraneous occurrences, but true endurance and true rejoicing in the knowledge that Christ is with us. . . . Let us celebrate Christmas in that way. Be as happy with the others as a person can only be at Christmastime.[40]

39. Ruth-Alice von Bismarck and Ulrich Kabitz, eds., *Love Letters from Cell 92: The Correspondence between Dietrich Bonhoeffer and Maria von Wedemeyer 1943–45*, trans. John Brownjohn (Nashville: Abingdon Press, 1995), 128.
40. Ibid., 133–34.

Finally, offering Maria a sense of comfort, he drew on the image of Matthew 25, telling her, "Don't entertain any awful imaginings of me in my cell, but remember that Christ, too, frequents prisons, and that he will not pass me by."[41] This, too, recalls his strong faith in the present Christ that does not waver. Christmas is not just a matter of our celebrations, the remembering of a past event, but rather is God's coming to us anew, visiting us in our present circumstances, and offering hope and the gift of new life in the here and now.

Clearly, Bonhoeffer found hope not in any message that comes from culture or that reflects the realities of life as understood by the political or social forces at work. Where he finds hope is in the very contradiction that is the Christian message, one that comes to us in ways we don't expect and in forms that remain hidden or strange to the world at large. Nevertheless, that is where God is present. Therein is our only hope.[42]

Bonhoeffer's affirmation of the world is evident as he rejected any "spiritualization" of their relationship. In his response to the insistence on the part of Maria's mother that her visits to Bonhoeffer in prison have some spiritual content or focus, Bonhoeffer wrote in March 1944, "God subsists not only in fundamentals but in everyday life as well."[43] This is expressed similarly when he wrote to Maria the previous summer about their wedding. Pointing to the state of the world and the confusion it had created, he saw their relationship as a "token of God's grace and goodness." Much in the same way

41. Ibid., 134.
42. See Jan Willem Schulte Nordholt, "Bonhoeffers Liebesbriefe," in *Bonhoeffer Jahrbuch 2003* (Gütershoh: Chr. Kaiser/Gütersloher Verlagshaus, 2003), 47, where he describes the tone of the *theologia crucis* presented in these letters as a paradox. Recognizing the paradox of the hidden but present God, he says, "If everything is impossible, there is total grace." Bonhoeffer does not find his hope in this world but in God, yet God and God's rule become real only in this world. Cf. Feil, *TDB*, for an extended discussion of paradox in Bonhoeffer's theology.
43. March 11, 1944 letter, *Love Letters*, 202. Cf. Fritz de Lange, *Waiting for the Word: Dietrich Bonhoeffer on Speaking about God* (Grand Rapids: Eerdmans, 2000), 43.

that the prophet Jeremiah was able to offer hope for Israel's future because new life was springing forth from the earth in the midst of devastation, Bonhoeffer claimed faith in God's working through such natural means gave him "confidence in the future." It takes faith to see it, but, as he said, it

> don't mean faith that flees the world, but the faith that endures *in* the world and loves and remains true to that world in spite of all the hardships it brings us. Our marriage must be a "yes" to God's earth. It must strengthen our resolve to do and accomplish something on earth. I fear that Christians who venture to stand on earth on only one leg will stand in heaven on only one leg too.[44]

"A 'yes' to God's earth."[45] This is not the faith of someone who is prematurely writing off the world. This is not someone seeking refuge elsewhere. This is the same person who had said that one learns to have faith by living unreservedly in life's duties. This is the faith of one who knows and finds God in the world.

### "Only a Suffering God Can Help"

In *Letters and Papers from Prison* that concern came to be expressed as "only a suffering God can help." Why? It is only a God who comes to us, a God who enters fully into the human condition, who can save us. Only by suffering the full effects of sin and suffering death can God overcome the power of sin. For that reason, the cross stands at the center of Christian theology and proclamation. While the incarnation and resurrection are important and necessary pieces, without the cross God could have remained untouched by the pain and struggles of humanity. Without the cross the incarnation could be viewed simply as an envoy who brings a message, negotiates a

44. August 12, 1943 letter, in von Bismarck and Kabitz, *Love Letters*, 64.
45. Larry Rasmussen, *Ethic Community, Earth Ethics* (Maryknoll, NY: Orbis Books, 1996), 295, identifies this as "Bonhoeffer's theme from beginning to end."

deal, but who is personally unaffected by the local conditions. And the resurrection could be, as it has been, viewed as a rescue operation that spared Jesus the agony of suffering. It stands as the supreme escape mechanism.

An insistence on a suffering God, however, is not motivated by a passive enduring in the face of unrelenting pain; rather it is the way that God displays power in the world. Being the very opposite of what we would expect from God, it remains hidden except for the eyes of faith.

Coming full circle, which is appropriate if we consider Christ the center around which everything in Bonhoeffer's thought revolves, we conclude with Ronald Thiemann's observations about Bonhoeffer's prison theology:

> Religionless or secular interpretation is an implication of Bonhoeffer's radical *theologia crucis.* If God has been "pushed out of the world on to the cross," then those who seek to follow a crucified God must identify with "God's powerlessness and suffering." In order to be disciples of *this* God we must "share in God's sufferings at the hands of a godless world . . . It is not the religious act that makes the Christian, but participation in the suffering of God in the secular life." Genuine faith involves commitment to those with whom Christ identified: sinners, the unclean, shepherds, the centurion, Joseph of Arimathea, and the women at the tomb. "Jesus calls [us], not to a new religion, but to life." Religionless interpretation is thus grounded in a cruciform faith. Discipleship is itself the act of identification with those who suffer; theology, then, becomes the reflective act whereby disciples view the world "from the perspective of those who suffer." Bonhoeffer's rejection of forms of theology that rely upon a correlation between "the religious" and "the Christian" or upon a metaphysical analysis of *homo religiosis,* or upon an appeal to human inwardness as a "point of contact" with God stems directly from his cruciform understanding of Christian faith and discipleship. . . . "Non-religious interpretation" flows directly from Bonhoeffer's radical understanding of the theology of the cross and that Dilthey's thesis is merely a useful tool in support of his argument. The fundamental logic of Bonhoeffer's position is not finally dependent upon any philosophical,

> historical, or metaphysical analysis; it is, rather, an implication of his Christology.[46]

It was a cold, rainy spring morning. A band of people, uncertain of their whereabouts and even more uncertain of their future, except to know that they were headed for disaster, asked a pastor among them to lead them in a worship service. Using the text of Isa. 53:5, the pastor focused his thoughts on "by his stripes we are healed." The next morning, after bowing for prayer, he followed the guard, mounted the platform and was hanged. Focused on God is how Bonhoeffer died; but even more importantly, this is how he lived. That is the enduring witness he left us—a life that shows where such close attention to God's word leads: hope and confidence in the future. It was such a faith and attitude toward the world that enabled him to enter selflessly into the resistance, into the troubles of his tormented world. He was freed to live for others.

The God whom we confess is a hidden God, visible only to the eyes of faith. The world, as Bonhoeffer says, lives as if God did not exist. But faith, if it is genuine, moves us beyond that level to discern the presence of God in the world.

## Summary

Far more than a pedantic refrain, the *theologia crucis* is the heartbeat of Bonhoeffer's theology. The repeated focus on Christ on the cross is the very lifeblood of his life and thought. Through his concentrated attention on Christ alone, he sought to reclaim the Reformation tradition of Luther for the modern world. Drawing on the insights of Luther's Reformation theology, Bonhoeffer's theology revolved around a christoncentric core. The crucified Christ, who is present in

46. Ronald Thiemann, "Waiting for God's Own Time: Dietrich Bonhoeffer as Public Intellectual," in *Religion im Erbe: Dietrich Bonhoeffer und die Zukunftsfähigkeit des Christentums,* ed. by Christian Gremmels and Wolfgang Huber (Gütersloh: Chr. Kaiser/Gütersloher, 2002), 101–3.

the church, is present for the world. Christ alone, asked in a variety of ways, is Bonhoeffer's key refrain.

The nature of that christological core is expressed in the oft-used phrase Bonhoeffer borrowed from Luther. "To this man you should point and say, There is God." Not only is this an important aspect of Luther's theology with which Bonhoeffer identified, it also becomes the core of his theological reflections. For Bonhoeffer the man Jesus is God. In Jesus God is present for the world.

Along with Luther, by insisting that God is wholly present in Christ's suffering and death on the cross, Bonhoeffer portrayed a God who doesn't remain far off and distant, removed from the suffering of the world. But at the same time, God is not merely one who suffers with us in our suffering, in a misery loves company sort of way—so that we don't have to suffer alone; God's suffering is a redemptive suffering. God suffers on our behalf, so that we do not have to suffer and die. God suffers so that instead of our needing to stand guilty before God, we stand as forgiven and free.

Only a suffering God can help. Only the God who goes to the cross and dies for us is God. All other gods are of our own making. Therefore, not just any God, but the God who suffers and dies on the cross is the only source of hope and life.

What these selections from his theology have sought to show is the single-minded focus on this subject. Through them we see how the center, which is Jesus Christ shapes everything. Because God is present in Christ, the church is to be present in the world. Because God suffers on the cross, the church suffers in the world. There is a clear connection between this focus and Bonhoeffer's own life and responsible action in the world.

For Bonhoeffer, how we portray Jesus has everything to do with what we think of God and the world. In addition, who we confess

Jesus to be affects how we live in the world. In other words, what we believe matters—and Bonhoeffer challenges us to live as if it does.

When viewed in its entirety and seen from within its historical development, continuity becomes an overwhelming characteristic of Bonhoeffer's theology. What is dynamic about Bonhoeffer's thought is the way in which he applies the same ideas to new contexts. Yet even though his theology was characterized by a marked continuity, there was a gradual progression or development in Bonhoeffer's theology, determined not by changing theological concerns but as a result of changing contextual settings. Whereas the crucified Christ remains at the center of Bonhoeffer's thought, the emphasis on the cross is intensified. The more narrowly focused Bonhoeffer becomes on God in Christ, the more deeply he is driven back into the world. While he maintains a continuous emphasis on knowing God only in Christ, who suffers and dies on the cross, from *Ethics* onward it is impossible to think of God apart from the world or the world without God. God has entered so deeply into the world that they become one reality. Yet this is but an intensification of God's creation of a new humanity, reconciled both to God and the world, that was a central concern since the time of *Sanctorum Communio*. The early Bonhoeffer talked about Christ present in the church; by the end Christ is the center of all reality.

The *theologia crucis*, therefore, rather than appearing in the later writings of Bonhoeffer and marking a new departure in his thinking, is something that has its foundations in the earliest of Bonhoeffer's writings and finds expression throughout his theological corpus. It is given different emphases and the language is nuanced to address specific contexts, but there remains a continuous thread. It is the *cantus firmus* giving structure to his entire theological vision as well as serving as the dynamic that moves his thought, keeping it contextual rather than falling into a neat systematic edifice. It is Christ on the cross, God himself who suffers for the sake of the world. It is Christ on the cross—that is where we find God.

As he moved from the academic podium to the church's pulpit during turbulent times, what had been formulated in an academic setting became the foundation for life in the world. What we witness in his writings, therefore, is a man who was never merely an academic theologian, but was first and foremost a man of faith who struggled with the life of faith in the real world. As a result, there is always a dialectic to his thought and life—God and the world, Jesus and today. He offers no abstract reflections on Jesus, limiting his discussion to the historical questions, but seeks always to discover how the present Christ encounters us in the world now.

To find a way to summarize Bonhoeffer's theology, we can do no better than to let Bonhoeffer speak for himself. In the section of *Ethics* entitled "Ethics as Formation," we find not only a mature statement of Bonhoeffer's theology, but also the culmination of his entire theological orientation. He says,

> One can look at God and at the reality of the world with undivided gaze as long as God and the world are torn apart. Despite all efforts to prevent it, the eyes still wander from one to the other. Only because there is one place where God and the reality of the world are reconciled with each other, at which God and humanity have become one, is it possible there and there alone to fix one's eyes on God and the world together at the same time. This place does not lie somewhere beyond reality in the realm of ideas. It lies in the midst of history as a divine miracle. It lies in Jesus Christ the reconciler of the world. As an ideal, the unity of simplicity and wisdom is as much doomed to failure as are all other efforts to face reality; it is an impossible, highly contradictory ideal. Grounded, however, in the reality of the world reconciled with God in Jesus Christ, the command of Jesus gains meaning and reality. Whoever looks at Jesus Christ sees in fact God and the world in one. From then on they can no longer see God without the world, or the world without God.[47]

God revealed in Jesus Christ: that is the heart of the *theologia crucis.* When Bonhoeffer's theology is understood in this light, his "non-religious interpretation of biblical concepts," which he sets out to describe in his *Letters and Papers from Prison,* are the logical working out of this "theology of the cross." It was his Lutheran roots that would not allow him to turn his back on the problems and tragedies of the world. Because God had turned toward the world, in fact, had entered into the world, identifying with suffering individuals, the only proper sphere for theological reflection was this world. Theology, properly conceived, is very this-worldly. It is this aspect of Bonhoeffer's theology that continues to give it the power to speak in our world.

After reviewing Bonhoeffer's theology, we can draw the following conclusions: 1) Both his theology and faith find their center in God in human flesh, God on the cross; it is there that we find and know God. "To this man you should point and say, 'There is God.'" 2) God and the world are constant themes, neither in abstraction nor in isolation, but always together—in Christ. 3) God is never located in transcendent abstraction, but in concrete reality—in Christ. 4) God is buried deep in the flesh. Taking on human form, God bears the sin of the world—through Christ. 5) Christianity is never a religion that provides sanctuary from the world, but exists for the world—because of Christ. 6) The Christian faith is not a world-renouncing, but a world-embracing faith—in Christ. 7) The Christian faith is earthbound, but never without God—in Christ. 8) God appears absent but in actuality is the hidden reality of all—in Christ. 9) The Christian faith is not an individualized, privatized faith, but a community of believers—in Christ. 10) Having been reconciled to God, Christians stand by God—in Christ. 11) Humankind is not

47. DBWE 6:82.

left to its own resources to find God, but God has already found humanity—in and through Christ. And finally, 12) in his theology and in his life we see a posture that is both world-affirming and at the same time critical—because of Christ.

Everything hinges on "in Christ." Who is God? God is always God in Christ Jesus. God in Christ reconciles humankind to God's own self. No longer divided by sin, but reunited in Christ, God and the world no longer are separate entities. God found enfleshed in the world, and living at its center, creates a new reality. That's Bonhoeffer's message.

PART V

# Conclusion

# 11

# Bonhoeffer's Cross of Reality

A line from the Greek poet Archilochus reads, "The fox knows many things, but the hedgehog knows one big thing." With such a distinction comes the acknowledgment that there are different ways of looking at the world. In the case of the latter, everything is organized around one central idea, a core theme that gives shape to everything else. In that sense, Bonhoeffer is the hedgehog and for him he knows God only in Jesus Christ, God clothed in human weakness, God who through suffering and death creates new life. If we are to talk about God, we must do so in the way God is revealed in the world, namely, through Jesus Christ. In other words, we are to think as "theologians of the cross," that is, as those "who speak of the crucified and hidden God."[1]

Throughout the course of his theological career, Bonhoeffer revealed what was most important to him by the questions he asked. As he sought to give concrete expression to the presence of God

1. Martin Luther, "Explanations of the Ninety-Five Theses," *LW* 31:225.

in the world, he asked questions, and through those questions we can track the developments in his thinking. They are variations on a single theme: from "Who is Jesus?" in the 1930s to "Who is God?" in his final theological reflections in 1944, the cross of Christ stands at the center, providing both the focus and the driving dynamic of his thinking and witness. The questions are simple and straightforward; they are questions of faith:

1. In 1928 Barcelona, the question was, "What does the cross have to say to *us, today*?"
2. A few years later in *Discipleship*, the question was stated in terms of responsibility: "What does Jesus Christ want of us?"
3. When writing to his seminarians in 1939, it became a question of the proclamation of the gospel to a troubled world: "We are preachers of justification through grace alone. What [does] that mean today?"
4. Finally, in *Letters and Papers from Prison*, it became, "What is Christianity, or who is Christ actually for us today?"

Each question is an attempt to answer the same basic question from different perspectives. And always, the answer points to the cross. And what is revealed there is God not in transcendent eternity, but God for us.

Because of what was at stake, Bonhoeffer could not get over the all-important question: Who is Christ actually for us today? That is the same question asked of all believers. Beginning with Jesus' disciples, every generation of Christian believers must come to terms with Jesus; because Jesus is the crucified and risen Lord, he is a living presence. Therefore, the Christian life is always more than reflection on and adherence to a set of principles or doctrines. The confession of faith leads to a life of discipleship. And because the way Christ is identified in the mind and heart of the believer affects their view of the world and approach to the world, that question is particularly important.

Bonhoeffer's answer, not only to the identity of God, but to Jesus as well, comes through the cross. Taking its orientation from the cross of Christ, Bonhoeffer's theology, from beginning to end, is shaped by and is an explication of that one thing; in that regard, it is a consistent unfolding of one theme. Responding to the changing contexts and circumstances taking place in the world, the tone of his language changes, but the person Jesus Christ remains the *cantus firmus*, the driving force standing behind his thought and life.

In an early summary of Bonhoeffer's theology, John Godsey sees significance in Bonhoeffer's theology precisely because "he discerns the universal meaning of Jesus Christ."[2] Insisting that Bonhoeffer's attention to our knowledge of God in Christ the crucified one prevents human religiosity from misusing or misappropriating God for their own purposes, he concludes,

> If we really want to be "honest to God," then our question must be: Who is Jesus Christ for us today? This is the question Bonhoeffer has put to the church. Only ultimate honesty in answering this question will save the church from irrelevance; Bonhoeffer's insistence that Jesus, the man for others, does not separate us from reality precisely because all reality is christologically structured seems to us to lead in the right direction.[3]

The voice of one like Bonhoeffer is significant because one problem facing theology today is the lack of attention to Christology. But even more of a problem than Christology itself is the type of

2. John Godsey, "Bonhoeffer the Man," in his *Preface to Bonhoeffer: The Man and Two of His Shorter Writings* (Philadelphia: Fortress Press, 1965), 11.
3. Ibid., 15.

Christology. Bonhoeffer's answer comes in the form of a *theologia crucis*.

Bonhoeffer's theology is an expression of the *theologia crucis* in that everything we know about God we know in and through Jesus Christ. And the key to understanding Jesus Christ for us lies in the cross. At the cross all human schemes and plans are brought to naught. No longer can it be assumed that we can work our way to God. The cross is a clear indictment that we can no longer even try. What is quite clear in the cross is that this is God's way to us. If we want to find God, we must go to where God has chosen to place himself. As we move through Bonhoeffer's theology, which becomes increasingly concentrated on the present Christ for us, we see that the cross is his hermeneutic for understanding the Christ event.

Taken together and viewed through the lens of the *theologia crucis*, we gain a clear sense of Bonhoeffer's theological commitments, development, and expression. This can be expressed under the rubric of a cross of reality. From the beginning Bonhoeffer's theology was governed by a concern for the concrete expression of the Christian faith in the world. For Bonhoeffer the cross of Christ is a cross of reality because, first, in the cross we are dealing with God as revealed in Scripture, as opposed to any abstract conception of God. What Scripture points to is God in Jesus Christ, God for us. It is for that reason that Bonhoeffer asserts that only a suffering God can help—that is, the only true God; all others are of our making. Second, because God is in the world in Christ, the cross of reality deals with the real world and not an ideological construct. Third, this, in turn, means that this theological orientation takes real life struggles seriously and does not overlook the here and now of lived life; as a result, it is a contextual theology.

As a contextual theology, the cross of reality draws us deeper and deeper into the world, the real world as it is. That means we are confronted with the need to be honest in our judgment and evaluation of who we are and what we are doing to our world. It forces us to be engaged in critical analysis with our culture and its assumptions. This is what Bonhoeffer did.

What Bonhoeffer had come to experience, for example, was a church that had grown comfortable with its position in the world, and hence had become ineffective. It was either unwilling or unable to speak out against Hitler and the German Christians; it had fallen into the trap of seeking self-preservation. The church is the church, however, only when it exists for others. That was Bonhoeffer's analysis seventy-plus years ago, and is one that remains valid today. The church as church exists to engage and intersect with the world. If it becomes preoccupied with its own existence or internal issues, it ceases to be the church because it no longer represents the present Christ in and for the world. The church is "Christ existing as church-community," no more but most assuredly no less.

Fourth, because it takes its orientation from God in Christ, the cross of reality rejects two-realms thinking, because such a conception allows us to view God and world as independent entities, without any relationship to one another. If God is pushed so far to the margins, it is easier to assume there is no God than it is to find any evidence of God's presence. In a *theologia crucis*, however, God is where we fail to look: that to which we turn our backs, the corners into which we do not want to look—there is God. As a result, a theological orientation influenced by the *theologia crucis* does not have to deny the world in order to affirm God or deny God in order to affirm the world. From its perspective, the paradoxical nature of God's relationship to the world is one that allows both to be taken seriously.

If God is not to be found in otherworldly places, then Christians are prevented from fleeing the earth. But instead, by defining reality as God and world together in Jesus Christ, this theology keeps us earthbound, oriented to the real issues of real people in the real world, and not focused on otherworldly concerns. Therefore, this is a very this-worldly theology, because it takes the world as seriously as does God. In a real sense, it is a practical theology, the gospel engaged with the world, at the intersection of faith and life. That is precisely where Bonhoeffer wanted it.

Finally, it impels us back into this world with a sense of responsibility for the world's future. In light of God's presence in the world, Christian discipleship is understood as the Christian going the way of God in the world. At the same time, by emphasizing the Christian's connection to the world, discipleship has consequences; discipleship under the aegis of the cross will result in suffering. However, if we are to talk about suffering in this context, it is not suffering for suffering's sake,

> but the indelible connectedness of this faith with responsibility in and for the city of Earth—*civitas terrena*—God's world. The risen Christ, in his eternal reign as in his historical sojourn, is always going toward this world, the world's rejection notwithstanding, and discipleship, when it is authentically so, is always a matter of being taken up into this world-directedness, despite one's own preference for security and peace.[4]

Because God's way moves toward the world, Bonhoeffer's cross of reality places the emphasis on a this-worldly faith, which is conformation to the crucified Jesus. As a result, in Bonhoeffer we see one that will not provide "an escape from the terrors of finite existence," according to Hall, "but will instead beckon us toward an immersion in creation the like of which we should never have chosen on our own." Christian faith, rather than seeking flight from the world, "is a journey toward the world; if it is said that such a

4. Douglas John Hall, *The Cross in Our Context: Jesus and the Suffering World* (Minneapolis: Fortress Press, 2003), 54.

definition confuses God with God's creation, confuses theocentrism with geocentrism, one must answer, as a Christian, that *that* confusion seems to have been introduced by God himself, who will be loved only as one who loves the world (John 3:16)."[5]

What we witness in Bonhoeffer's theology, therefore, is not a posture turned away from the world. His goal, in fact, was quite the opposite. It was to place his inherited theological tradition into dialogue with the real issues facing people in this world. In Christ, God entered into the world; therefore, the world is not to be abandoned for a better one elsewhere, but rather it is in the midst of the real world that we meet God. God has chosen to be revealed in the weakness and suffering of Jesus Christ on the cross; *by this very fact*, only by grasping this, can we relate to the world and its problems. The world cannot be avoided and neither can God; in fact, we must seek God here in this place.

If we want to appropriate Bonhoeffer for our context, we must know and understand not only his context but the foundations and sources of his insights as well. By tracing Bonhoeffer's use of Luther's writings and developing his thinking along the lines of Luther's *theologia crucis*, not only do we see the dominant influence on Bonhoeffer's thinking but the dynamic core of his explosive theology as well. This work relies upon the conclusions of others, and while affirming those conclusions, it has attempted to fill in the details of an important link in our understanding the Bonhoeffer corpus. To the degree it does that, it contributes to a fuller understanding of Bonhoeffer's position, helps to point out the differences between him and others, and exposes the foundation for his involvement in the resistance. The enduring nature of his witness is served by this understanding of his thinking.

5. Ibid., 55.

This points us to the enduring significance of Bonhoeffer's legacy. The oeuvre of Douglas John Hall's theological writing, assembled over the past thirty years, has addressed one overriding issue: Christianity in North America has been dominated by triumphalism to such an extent that the Christian gospel has been silenced. Equating the dominant Christian tradition in North America with the *theologia gloriae*, he turns to Luther's *theologia crucis*, where he find an alternative Christian voice, one that is able to address the reality of people in this context. Unlike Christian triumphalism that either dominates and identifies with culture or seeks refuge in world-denying activities, Hall sees the *theologia crucis* as world affirming, on the one hand, but through its identification with suffering and weakness, it has no false or misplaced ideas about the sinful nature of humankind, on the other. Not content with talk of retreating from the world, his theology encourages (demands) engagement with the world.

If Hall is correct in his analysis of North American religious life, and particularly with regard to the influential role religion plays in shaping attitudes toward the world, then the *theologia crucis* is a valuable resource for the church in the twenty-first century.

This coincides with Bonhoeffer's assessment seventy-five years ago in his report, "Protestantism without Reformation." While we might grant that Bonhoeffer's analysis is limited inasmuch as it was based on his "narrow" perceptions of American theology and religion at the time, the concerns he raised then have not disappeared over time; if anything, there is a growing chorus of voices joining him.

Carl Braaten, for example, is an American Lutheran theologian who has also been critical of American religion and theology. He uses Bonhoeffer's 1939 reflections on America as a means of discussing today's context, which he sees as being similar to the one at the end of the nineteenth century, and observes:

> Bonhoeffer knew that Lutheranism in America has been relatively isolated from the religious mainstream. Its confessional theology has been kept alive in ethnic ghettos remote from the chief centers of theological learning: the divinity schools of Harvard, Yale, and Chicago universities. Only in this generation have Lutheran theologians joined the pluralistic faculties of theology, but they are mostly specialists in some field of religious studies and not systematic theologians; therefore, the heart of the theology of the Reformation—its witness to the God of the gospel—remains marginal in the variety of schools of theology on the American scene. If Bonhoeffer would return to America today, he would have to say déjà vu! He would probably observe that there has still been no reformation of the church and theology in America and the Protestantism still lacks a reformation. . . . We are engulfed in a culture of theological pluralism whose common denominator is exactly what Bonhoeffer observed—a rejection of Christology, a failure to work within a theological paradigm whose flaming center is the definitive revelation of the gospel of God in the person and work of Jesus Christ.[6]

6. Carl Braaten, *No Other Gospel! Christianity among the World's Religions* (Minneapolis: Fortress Press, 1992), 16–17. Other theologians, in drawing similar conclusions, lend support to Bonhoeffer's response. Richard Cimino, "Introduction," *Lutherans Today: American Lutheran Identity in the 21st Century*, ed. Richard Cimino (Grand Rapids: Eerdmans, 2003), ix, begins with the 1958 *Time* magazine report that stated that Lutherans stood out in American Christianity because they were different. "They stood out in an era when American churches of different denominations were beginning to look and act alike as they moved to suburbia and assimilated to mainstream America. Lutherans were influenced by the same forces, but their strong confessional nature, with a stress on theology rather than practical Christian living, as well as their liturgy and ethnicity, set this tradition apart form other Protestants. . . . They were Protestants with a difference at a time when differences were supposed to be dissolving in the American melting pot." See also Mark Noll, *The Old Religion in a New World: The History of North American Christianity* (Grand Rapids: Eerdmans, 2003) and "American Lutherans Yesterday and Today," in Cimino, *Lutherans Today*, who has noted the "Lutheran difference" in many of his writings on American church history. Like others, he insists that Lutheran theology has not been a vibrant presence in shaping American theology or church practice. From a different perspective and context, Eberhard Jüngel provides the following criticism of contemporary theology: "No doubt, one of the most striking characteristics of contemporary theology is its lack of orientation. This is indicated in the capriciousness of its themes. Contemporary theology speaks to everything and everyone. But by doing so, it has less and less specifically theological to say. It has no *thema probandum* (theme needing testing) of its own. If it had such a theme, then on the basis of it *everything* could in fact be theologically relevant" (*The Freedom of a Christian: Luther's Significance for Contemporary Theology* [Minneapolis: Augsburg, 1988], 22).

These combined voices indicate that far from being the misunderstood observations of a young German theologian, Bonhoeffer's reflections are still relevant. In that regard, his answers, too, rather than being limited to the context of 1930s and '40s Europe, are ones that are still needed today.

In the North American context, where faith is often reduced to morality or equated with positive thinking, the cross is offensive. Given such a mindset, Americans are ill-prepared to deal with the negative aspects of life, unable to accept that life may have limits, not likely to recognize that not everything can be fixed by a "can-do" attitude. A theology forged in the midst of conflict, which strips faith down to the basics, is a resource that can speak with credibility.[7]

At the same time, the beginning of the twenty-first century has brought a change; the optimism and sense of progress that marked much of the last century have given way to a less optimistic perspective on our future. Confronted daily with human degradation, rather than being encouraged by technology's power to alleviate suffering, we have become aware that no advances in human achievement can alter the fact that we cannot change the human condition through efforts of our own. Given this reality, Douglas John Hall makes the case for a theology of the cross today:

> As the art and literature of the past hundred years testify, post-Enlightenment humanity has acquired an exceptional awareness of its own vulnerability, degradation, and potential annihilation. The metaphor of crucifixion is not as inaccessible to us as it was to our Enlightenment forebears. There is a "cross of reality" visible in every honest news broadcast. It is in fact this everyday human cross that makes it both possible and necessary for us, as Christians, to develop a contextually sensitive *theology* of the cross. As Moltmann writes, "The

7. See Douglas John Hall, *Lighten Our Darkness: Toward an Indigenous Theology of the Cross* (Philadelphia: Westminster, 1976).

> more the 'cross of reality' is taken seriously, the more the crucified Christ becomes the general criterion of theology."[8]

Bonhoeffer's theological voice, focused on the crucified Christ and growing out of a lived discipleship, can serve as a witness and model for the church's proclamation in this changed and changing world.

Based on an overview of Bonhoeffer's writings, we have seen how Luther's *theologia crucis* provides continuity to Bonhoeffer's thought, weaving all his concerns together. The question is, how was that theological tradition appropriated by Bonhoeffer and was it faithful to Luther?

To help answer that question, a review of Robert Kolb's discussion on the role of the "hidden God" in Luther provides a helpful orientation. On the distinction between the hidden and revealed God in Luther, Kolb makes the following observation, which is one that fits with Bonhoeffer's stance toward National Socialism and the way it was distorting the gospel in his day. According to Kolb, the term *hidden God* has two points of reference in Luther's thought. First, it refers to "the essence of God which lies beyond the grasp of creatures—particularly when their rebellion has blinded and deafened them." But in the second place, the term refers to "the pictures of God that fallen human beings construct as they try to identify and domesticate Him." It is this latter reference, in particular, that highlights Bonhoeffer's concern. According to Kolb, these gods are important because they hold society together, providing meaning to its members. But, at the same time, the system they create has little room for Christ, who appears "impotent and foolish," coming as he does as a "crucified convict." Therefore, "Jesus had come as a kid in a crib, no way for God to make His entrance in any culture. He had taken His throne as a criminal on a cross. He made His exit,

8. Hall, *Cross in Our Context*, 71.

people thought, as a corpse in a crypt. And there is no other way to explain who Jesus is in any culture because that is who God really is." Because that is who he is, he must come "from outside their way of imagining God" and, therefore remains outside the boundaries of culture, confounding "cultural values constructed in opposition to His will."[9]

Two things emerge from these observations that relate to Bonhoeffer's cross of reality. First, it is a critique of culture—any culture that seeks to equate its values with God must be questioned and challenged. In this regard, it is easy to recall Luther's explanation to the first commandment in the *Large Catechism*, in which he points out that anything in which we place our faith is our god;[10] likewise, any ideology, not just those limited to religion, can become idolatrous.[11] These remarks reveal that for Luther theology was not just something of concern for the church, but involved all of life. It plays a role in shaping our "reality." Second, our knowledge of God always comes from outside and cannot be identified with the culture; therefore, theology offers a clearly defined alternative to the dominant voice of culture. As Bonhoeffer stated repeatedly, God's

9. Robert A. Kolb, "Nothing but Christ Crucified," in *The Theology of the Cross for the 21st Century*, ed. Alberto L. García and A. R. Victor Raj (St. Louis: Concordia Publishing House, 2002), 41–42.

10. "A 'god' is the term for that to which we are to look for all good and in which we are to find refuge in all need. Therefore, to have a god is nothing else than to trust and believe in that one with your whole heart. As I have often said, it is the trust and faith of the heart alone that make both God and an idol. . . . For these two belong together, faith and God. Anything on which your heart relies and depends, I say, that is really your God." Martin Luther, "The Large Catechism," in *The Book of Concord*, 386:3.

11. Hall equates ideology with the theology of glory, to the extent that ideology is "a theoretical statement or system of interpretation that functions for its adherents as a full and sufficient credo, a source of personal authority, and an intellectually and psychologically comforting insulation from the frightening and chaotic mishmash of daily life. For the ideologue, whether religious or political, it is not necessary to expose oneself constantly to the ongoingness of life; one knows in advance what one is going to find in the world. . . . The ideological personality . . . is constantly on guard against the intrusion of reality, of the unallowable question, of that data that does not 'fit' the system" (Hall, *Cross in Our Context*, 25).

way to humanity in Christ can never be equated with human religiosity.[12]

Guided by such an orientation, Bonhoeffer was able to offer a clearly articulated critique of National Socialism and the church from his christocentric perspective. But in addition, his words stand as a corrective to any Lutheran theologian or theological position that found a point of contact between the Church's proclamation of the gospel and the pseudo-religious nationalistic claims of the Nazis.

However, there is one real danger when talking about the theology of cross, be it Luther, Bonhoeffer, or any other theologian. The danger is to turn it into a principle or another ideology, much in the same way that Bonhoeffer accused the church in Germany of turning grace into a principle. If we limit our vision to the theology of the cross as a principle, it will not help us to see reality more clearly, but will only further cloud our vision. If we reach the stage where we think we have it all figured out, we are no longer operating from the perspective of a theology of the cross. A true theology of the cross

12. It is worth repeating another of Kolb's observations regarding Luther's theology, for it bears on the significance of Bonhoeffer's own attempts. While Luther's *theologia crucis* "created a paradigm shift within Western Christian thought in the understanding of God's revelation" and provided a "new constellation of perspectives on the biblical description of God and of human reality," unfortunately Luther's followers "did not find Luther's theology of the cross particularly helpful" and did not maintain his orientation; as a result, the cross came to represent something different entirely. In Melanchthon's use, for example, the "'cross' treated treated human suffering, not God's suffering on the cross," with the result that "the cross served a very different, and less all-encompassing, purpose than providing the point of view from which to assess God's revelation of himself, humanity—defining trust in that revelation, the atonement accomplished through Christ's death and resurrection, or the Christian life. In subsequent Lutheran dogmatic textbooks, this topic consistently treated only one aspect of the Christian life, persecution and afflictions of other kinds" (Robert Kolb, "Luther on the Theology of the Cross," *Lutheran Quarterly* 16 (2002): 443–44. Cf. Hall's assessment of Luther's heritage, whom he says is "the least known of the sixteenth-century Reformers in anglo-Protestant settings." In addition, those who have been more influential "have emphases significantly different from, if not inimical to, Luther's theology of the cross. Nevertheless, what has kept the churches from exploring this tradition lies in another direction entirely—a fact that is demonstrated, if by nothing else, by the reluctance also of many Lutheran Protestants themselves to give this tradition much more than a theoretical or reverential nod" (*Cross in Our Context,* 14.) In this context, he identifies Bonhoeffer's "critical theology" as "perhaps the greatest exponent of the theology of the cross in the modern church" (232n5).

means discipleship, following after the one who has gone through the horrors of human life ahead of us. It demands that we constantly seek to uncover the hidden presence of God, but even then to make modest claims. For we never truly see God face to face, as God is in the reality of God's own being. We see only that portion of God that God has chosen to reveal to us. Hopefully, that will be enough, however, as we seek to lead faithful lives.

This brings us to Bonhoeffer's appropriation of Luther's *theologia crucis*. Is his cross of reality an adequate restatement of that tradition, giving it new power to address the modern situation?

When one seeks to locate Bonhoeffer's position on the theological map, one cannot help but refer to his own description of himself in prison. As his own words indicate, Bonhoeffer saw himself as one who owed a debt to liberal theology: "As a 'modern' theologian who has nevertheless inherited the legacy of liberal theology, I feel responsible to address these questions."[13] With this perception of his own social location, Bonhoeffer acknowledged the divide separating his context from that of the Reformation. Modern theology, with its assumptions and conclusions, forever changed the theological landscape, making it impossible to return to Luther's time. So by his own acknowledgment he admitted it is impossible to simply repeat the words of Luther as a defense. Turning Luther into the German savior, however, is precisely what the German Christians had done.

In addition, Bonhoeffer's theological position was more complicated, eliminating the possibility of returning to Luther. He stated it clearly in a segment of his *Ethics*. In the section entitled "Ultimate and Penultimate Things," written in November 1940, we find words that describe Bonhoeffer's intentions and desires with regard to Luther:

13. DBWE 8:498–99.

> From the beginning, the qualitatively ultimate word of God forbids us from looking at the way of Paul or the way of Luther as if we had to go that way again. . . . Strictly speaking, we should not repeat Luther's way any more than the way of the woman caught in adultery, the thief on the cross, Peter's denial, or Paul's zealous persecution of Christ. The qualitatively ultimate word excludes every method once and for all. It is the word of forgiveness, and only in forgiving does it justify.[14]

His goal cannot be and was not intended to be a return to Luther. Rather, Bonhoeffer found in Luther a way of doing theology that enabled him to bear witness to the modern era. He was conscious of his reality. At the same time, he was convinced that the church of his day was ill-prepared to speak credibly to the world because it had forfeited the gospel message by confusing it with human ideologies and aspirations.

In addressing that confused state, Bonhoeffer therefore insisted on rejecting two-realms thinking, which he believed was a distortion of Luther. In that regard, he sought to challenge and correct the misinterpretation of Luther that led to a false application of Luther's two-kingdoms doctrine. Seen in that light—and from within the broader confines of the German Church Struggle, which for Bonhoeffer was a theological battle first and foremost—he was engaged in a fight for genuine Lutheranism; but more, it was a battle between the true and false church, and he turned to Luther as his ally.

Since Bonhoeffer was reading Luther through the lens of the realities of modern life, his position was not merely a repeat of Luther's, but one that moved beyond him. Bonhoeffer's cross of reality, having its foundation in Luther's *theologia crucis*, therefore, was not limited to Luther's concerns. Luther's attention in the *Heidelberg Disputation*, for example, was focused on how we know God. While that is Bonhoeffer's question as well, Bonhoeffer's

14. DBWE 6:150.

concern is broadened, so that Christ's cross not only tells us about the nature of God, but becomes the definition of the world.

For the same reasons that Bonhoeffer did not seek a return to Luther, we cannot seek to return to Bonhoeffer, simply repeating his words without noting the changed context in which we live. Our time is not his time, and not every place provides the same setting for theological reflection. We are anchored to the particulars of our context, and if we are to properly receive and understand the word of God for us and for our world, we must seek to uncover "what is" today. Therefore, if we are to attempt to appropriate Bonhoeffer's theology for our time, it cannot be without noting the time in which we live.

In *Ethics*, for example, when Bonhoeffer stated that we cannot return to Luther, he was giving voice to the premise of the theology of the cross, namely, the contextual nature of theology. To seek to return to or attempt to replicate Luther's theology would have amounted to creating a system or working from a particular ideology, both of which are impossible if one seeks reality. Because it is the nature of the world to be marked by change, it is impossible to freeze one particular answer that will be good for all time. That was the reason Bonhoeffer was opposed to principles in ethics. It is for the same reason that he would oppose such a systematic approach to theology.

Even though we do not inhabit Bonhoeffer's world, his attempt to relate the Christian faith to the world nevertheless can serve as a guide. While willing to enter into debate with culture and the modern thinking that informs it, Bonhoeffer did not allow them to become the norm to which the church or faith provided answers. In every circumstance, God in Christ is the norm and authority standing over against all human thought or ideology. But at the same time, God is not wholly other, so different and distanced from the world as to be removed from it. Drawing on the *theologia crucis*, Bonhoeffer draws God into the world while, at the same time, maintaining the distinction between God and the world.

If there is anything we have learned from Bonhoeffer, it is that genuine theology must take the context of its world seriously. It was the changing context of his own life that provides the basis for any nuanced change in emphasis in Bonhoeffer's thinking from 1920s to the 1940s. For us that means going beyond Bonhoeffer—taking our context seriously, defining our reality, and articulating the meaning of faith in Jesus Christ for the world.

Let the comments of Charles Taylor set the stage for understanding the significance of Bonhoeffer's theology and witness in the twenty-first century. Taylor's study titled *A Secular Age*[15] in one sense traces the trajectory of Bonhoeffer's thinking about a "world come of age," even paralleling some of Bonhoeffer's own conclusions. Taylor's comments, rather than rejecting the early modern claims about the disappearance of religion, acknowledge that secularism has created a new context for belief. The effects of secularism, in his words, mean an end of "the era of naive religious faith." What he means is that we have moved from "a condition in which belief was the default option . . . to a condition in which for more and more people unbelieving construals seem at first blush the only plausible ones." This has created an "index of doubt" and, therefore, we cannot assume that everyone believes or, if they do, that everyone believes the same thing. He says, "We live in a condition where we cannot help but be aware that there are a number of different construals, views which intelligent, reasonably undecided people, of good will, can and do disagree on." In practical terms all this means that we have witnessed a massive shift. He asks, "Why was it virtually impossible not to believe in God

15. Charles Taylor, *A Secular Age* (Cambridge, MA: Belknap, 2007).

in, say, 1500 in our Western society, while in 2000 many of us find this not only easy, but even inescapable?"[16] This is the new context in which religious faith is lived.

While the language is slightly different from what we find in Bonhoeffer's prison reflections, much of what Taylor describes matches what Bonhoeffer was saying. In a world where one cannot take faith for granted, the church finds itself in uncharted waters. In a world such as Bonhoeffer and Taylor describe, the church's role cannot be to force people to believe. However, such circumstances can force the church to be clear about its beliefs.

What Taylor describes reflects the context Bonhoeffer was envisioning when he talked about the "world has come of age." As we read his varied reflections on this subject, what stands out is his conclusion about the world in which belief is no longer necessary and could no longer be assumed. The time for a taken-for-granted approach to religious faith is no longer possible. As a result, there is no common religious understanding, even within the Christian community, all of which has produced a plurality of faith options—everything from no belief to some form of blended belief that has borrowed elements from various religious traditions. Taken together, this change in culture has led to a great deal of confusion. There are atheists, for example, who admit to a believe in some kind of god, while Christians in mainline traditions no longer believe in a personal God or doubt the existence of God altogether. This confused state has produced a rather "fuzzy" understanding of God.

This is a world in which faith cannot be assumed or taken for granted, either in terms of people believing in anything at all or the specific character of that belief. All too often, when there are many choices, the tendency is to view them as equal, while not making any distinction between them. The danger in this, of course, is that any

16. Ibid., 11, 12, 24.

religious voice is reduced to the preferential option of the believer and the voice of the church is threatened to be drowned out.

At a time and in a world where confusion reigns when it comes to religion, the clarity of Bonhoeffer's witness is a welcome conversation partner. This, however, does not mean that we can read Bonhoeffer as if he was anticipating our context. Nevertheless, we can take cues from him based on the way he responded to the changes he witnessed in the 1930s–'40s. At a time when the church's teachings were blended with Nazi ideology and when the church and religious faith were used for political ends, people were left to wonder what to believe, and Bonhoeffer, sifting through the myriad voices, maintained a singular, unwavering focus on the core confession of the church. At a time when one could no longer assume that faith meant the same thing to everyone, Bonhoeffer sought to make the church's voice credible in a public of competing and conflicting voices and loyalties. At a time when there was a great deal of confusion about what might pass for the Christian faith, he returned to the essentials, to the biblical witness and Luther's interpretation of that witness. In a world in which there is no agreement on the role of the church, or religion more generally, Bonhoeffer's insistence on the clear proclamation of the gospel is still very worthy of our attention.

His conclusion that the world has come of age is a recognition that secularization has had an effect. It is no longer a question of returning to a pre-modern mindset, for that is an impossibility. Rather, given this new reality, Bonhoeffer lays out a credible witness for the church in this changed world. And unlike many who either reject God or reject the world, Bonhoeffer's answer is to affirm both God and the world.

It is for that reason that while distancing himself from the theological stance of liberal theology, he acknowledged a debt to them inasmuch they "did not try to put the clock back, . . . but genuinely accepted the battle." Likewise, given the nature of the changed world, he challenged the church to "get out of its stagnation. We must also get back out into the fresh air of intellectual discourse with the world. We also have to risk saying controversial things, if that will stir up discussion of the important issue in life."[17]

Accepting the fact that the world can get along without God, rather than taking an apologetic stance of defending space for God, he asked a different question. His question was always, "Who is Christ? For us?" It is not a matter of imposing God on the world, but rather confessing who God is for us. From beginning to end, his concern was not to attack the world; rather, he wanted to be clear about what the church believes. He was concerned about the church's confession and the integrity of its witness. That this is so can be seen in one of his notes from July 1944: "A confession of faith expresses not what someone else '*must*' believe, but what one *believes* himself."[18] This insight alone from Bonhoeffer's prison theology provides a helpful perspective when the church or Christians engage a pluralistic world.

Leading with this confessional stance, while being willing to enter into dialogue with culture, Bonhoeffer did not cede power to the world to set the agenda; he did not allow the world to be the norm (which had been the mistake of liberal theology) to which the church or faith provided answers. Instead, God in Christ was the norm and authority standing over against all human thought or ideology. This God, however, is not wholly other, so different and distanced from the world as to be removed from the world. Rather, relying on Luther's *theologia crucis*, Bonhoeffer draws God into the world while maintaining the distinction between the two. Such language does not

17. DBWE 8:498.
18. Ibid., 453.

speak against God, but is wholeheartedly for God—because of God. At the same time, it does not speak out against the world, but is for the world—again, because of God.

In a world shaped and influenced as it is by a global media community, people have access to the world and all its diversity with the click of a button. Given that reality in which we live, where people can receive information from such a wide variety of sources, it is likely they will be influenced by what they hear and experience in the world as much as they might take from church. The church is no longer the only source for things religious; it may not even be the primary source for our understanding of God. That means that even for those who hold unto Christian faith, what they ultimately believe is as likely to be filtered through values perpetuated by a culture at odds with the church. If this is true, then for the sake of the integrity of the church's witness, Bonhoeffer's voice makes a significant contribution. For when anything passes as faith, then nothing does. And when so many elements foreign to the Christian gospel are infused into the Christian message, there is a danger that the truth of the church's message is altered. That was a danger Bonhoeffer did not take lightly.

But such a concern was not Bonhoeffer's alone. Today's church finds itself in a similar place. When the church finds itself in situations in which the gospel is in competition with other voices, there is always the danger of creating a new, different gospel, one that is not centered on Jesus Christ. Being clear on the gospel gives the church new life and the freedom to move about freely in the world.

In a world where there are competing and conflicting claims about the truth, it is easy to end up arguing over God. The question, however, is, "Which god?" In response, Bonhoeffer encourages us to live without God. Again, "Which god?" Not the God of the Bible, but the god of our own making, the god of human ideology. Yet at the same time, Bonhoeffer proclaimed that we are to live with God. "Which one?" The one who reveals himself in the Jesus Christ. And this God is a suffering God. "Only a suffering God can help."

By declaring God as the beyond in our midst, Bonhoeffer was indeed saying that the real God, rather than our images of God, is incarnate and therefore present in Christ. God is always beyond our imagining, therefore just beyond our grasp. If we think we have identified God, therefore, we are sadly mistaken, for to do so would imply that we can somehow or other control God. But God always wiggles away, is always beyond our grasp. No matter how hard we might try to tame him or domesticate him, God eludes us. So in the end, we must admit that our attempts are all partial, at best. Therefore, if we wish to know God, our only recourse is to show up where God is present—on the cross.

Even though Bonhoeffer's view was limited by his own context, his vision remains helpful as we seek to negotiate the new landscape of twenty-first-century America. While we cannot say religion and its influence is a thing of the past, we can say that the prominent role the churches played in shaping the public life of America has changed. This means that while the public square is not naked, it is not necessarily Christian either. There is an unlimited palette of religious choices available to any discerning believer, so that one is bound to find a religion or God of one's own liking. As Christianity competes with other religions for people's faith, many of these beliefs are filtering into the Christian worldview; if this continues, the face of Christianity will be changed. In such a context, Bonhoeffer's argument proves helpful. Be it by Nazi ideology or secular religiosity, new elements can be inserted into the church's message that will eventually change the gospel. By drawing a clear distinction between Christianity and religion, Bonhoeffer notes that real differences exist between religious claims and, therefore, we cannot simply pick and choose the elements we want. To do so creates a religion of our own liking, and one that is no longer Christian. In a context where nearly one quarter of American Christians believe in reincarnation, the Christian message is threatened today as much as it was by Nazi ideology yesterday.

In the end, if we are genuinely concerned about the church, its witness, and its future, what we believe matters—and our ability to articulate that to a world growing both weary and suspicious of religion and its role in society depends on it.

Therefore, to be the church, we must ask, "Who is Christ actually for us today?" It is a question that must be asked and answered anew in every generation. Is Jesus Christ who we make him out to be? Or is he the revelation of God? As we seek to proclaim the good news of Christ today, how we answer that question makes all the difference in the world.

# Bibliography

## Luther's Theology

### Primary Sources


Luther, Martin. "Auslegung des 109. Psalms." *Luthers Werke* 1:696–97.

———. "The Babylonian Captivity of the Church (1520)." In *Luther's Works*, edited by Abdel Ross Wentz, 36:3–126. Philadelphia: Fortress Press, 1959.

———. "The Blessed Sacrament of the Holy and True Body of Christ, and the Brotherhoods (1519)." In *Luther's Works,* edited by E. Theodore Bachman, 35:45–73. Philadelphia: Fortress Press, 1960.

———. *The Bondage of the Will* (1525). In *Luther's Works*, edited by Philip S. Watson, vol. 33. Philadelphia: Fortress Press, 1972.

———. "Confession concerning Christ's Supper (1528)." In *Luther's Works*, edited by Robert H. Fischer, 37:161–372. Philadelphia: Fortress Press, 1961.

———. "Disputation on the Divinity and Humanity of Christ (1540)." Translated by Christopher. B. Brown. http://www.project wittenberg.org/pub/resources/text/wittenberg/luther/luther-divinity.txt.

———. "Early Sermons." In *Luther's Works*, edited by John W. Doberstein, 51:5–31. Philadelphia: Fortress Press, 1959.

———. "Explanations of the Ninety-Five Theses." In *Luther's Works*, edited by Harold J. Grimm, 31:77–252. Philadelphia: Fortress Press, 1957.

———. "The Freedom of A Christian." In *Luther's Works*, edited by Harold J. Grimm, 31:327–77. Philadelphia: Fortress Press, 1957.

———. "Heidelberg Disputation." In *Luther's Works*, edited by Harold J. Grimm, 31:35–69. Philadelphia: Fortress Press, 1957.

———. "The Large Catechism." In *The Book of Concord: The Confessions of the Evangelical Lutheran Church*, edited by Robert Kolb and Timothy J. Wengert. Minneapolis: Fortress Press, 2000.

———. *Lectures on Galatians* (1535). In *Luther's Works*, edited by Jaroslav Pelikan and Walter A. Hanson, vols. 26–27. St. Louis: Concordia, 1963 & 1964.

———. "Lectures on Hebrews." In *Luther's Works*, edited by Jaroslav Pelikan and Walter A. Hanson, 29:109–242. St. Louis: Concordia, 1968.

———. *Lectures on Romans*. Translated and edited by Wilhelm Pauck. Library of Christian Classics, vol 15. Philadelphia: Westminster, 1961.

———. "Lord, Keep Us Steadfast in Thy Word." In *Luther's Works*, edited by Ulrich S. Leupold, 53:304–5. Philadelphia: Fortress Press, 1965.

———. "Luther's Last Observation Left in a Note, February 16, 1546." In *Luther's Works*, edited by Theodore G. Tappert, 54:476. Philadelphia: Fortress Press, 1967.

———. *Luthers Werke. Kritische Gesamtausgabe* (*Weimarer Ausgabe*). 57 vols. Edited by J. F. K Knaake et al. Weimar: Böhlau, 1883ff.

———. "The Magnificat." In *Luther's Works*, edited by Jaroslav Pelikan, 21:295–355. St. Louis: Concordia, 1956.

———. "A Meditation on Christ's Passion." In *Luther's Works*, edited by Martin O. Dietrich, 42:7–14. Philadelphia: Fortress Press, 1969.

———. "Operationes in Psalmos." *Kritische Gesamtausgabe*, vol. 5.

———. "Sermons on the Gospel of John, Chapters 1–4." In *Luther's Works*, edited by Jaroslav Pelikan, vol. 22. St. Louis: Concordia, 1957.

———. "Sermon on John 3:1–15," *WA* 10/1/2:297.

———. "A Sermon on Preparing to Die (1519)." In *Luther's Works*, edited by Martin O. Dietrich, 42:95–115. Philadelphia: Fortress Press, 1969.

———. "The Small Catechism." In *The Book of Concord: The Confessions of the Evangelical Lutheran Church*, edited by Robert Kolb and Timothy J. Wengert. Minneapolis: Fortress Press, 2000.

———. "Temporal Authority: To What Extent It Should be Obeyed." In *Luther's Works*, edited by Walther I. Brandt, 45:81–129. Philadelphia: Fortress Press, 1962.

———. "Ten Sermons on the Catechism (1528)." In *Luther's Works*, edited by John W. Doberstein, 51:133–93. Philadelphia: Fortress Press, 1959.

———. "That These Words of Christ, 'This is my Body,' etc., Still Stand Firm against the Fanatics (1527)." In *Luther's Works*, edited by Robert H. Fischer, 37:13–150. Philadelphia: Fortress Press, 1961.

## Secondary Sources

Althaus, Paul. "Die Bedeutung des Kreuzes im Denken Luthers." *Evangelium und Leben, Gesammelte Vorträge,* 51-62. Gütersloh: C. Bertelsmann, 1927.

———. *The Theology of Martin Luther.* Translated by Robert C. Schultz. Philadelphia: Fortress Press, 1966.

Altmann, Walter. *Luther and Liberation: A Latin American Perspective.* Minneapolis: Fortress Press, 1992.

Anthony, Neal J. *Cross Narratives: Martin Luther's Christology and the Location of Redemption.* Princeton Theological Monograph Series. Eugene, OR: Pickwick, 2010.

Bainton, Roland. *Here I Stand: A Life of Martin Luther.* Nashville: Abingdon, 1950.

Barth, Karl. "An Introductory Essay." In *The Essence of Christianity*, by Ludwig Feuerbach, translated by George Eliot, x–xxxii. New York: Harper & Row, 1957.

Bayer, Oswald. *Martin Luther's Theology: A Contemporary Interpretation.* Translated by Thomas H. Trapp. Grand Rapids: Eerdmans, 2008.

Bense, Walter F. "Editor's Introduction." In *The Reconstruction of Morality.* Edited by James Luther Adams and Walter F. Bense. Translated by Fred W. Meuser and Walter R. Wietzke. Minneapolis: Augsburg, 1979.

———. "Editor's Introduction." In *What Did Luther Understand by Religion?* Edited by James Luther Adams and Walter F. Bense. Translated by Fred W. Meuser and Walter R. Wietzke. Philadelphia: Fortress Press, 1977.

Brecht, Martin. *Martin Luther: His Road to Reformation, 1483–1521.* Translated by James L. Schaaf. Philadelphia: Fortress Press, 1985.

Bodenstein, Walter. *Die Theologie Karl Holls im Spiegel des Antiken und Reformatorischen Christentums.* Berlin: Walter De Gruyter, 1968.

Bühler, Pierre. *Kreuz und Eschatologie: Eine Auseinandersetzung mit der politischen Theologie, im Anschluß an Luthers theologia crucis.* Tübingen: J. C. B. Mohr (Paul Siebeck), 1981.

Carter, Guy C. "Martin Luther in the Third Reich: Recent Research on Luther as Iconic Force in Hitler's Germany." *Seminary Ridge Review* (Lutheran Theological Seminary at Gettysburg) 12, no. 1 (Autumn 2009): 42–62.

Dillenberger, John. *God Hidden and Revealed: The Interpretation of Luther's* Deus Absconditus *and Its Significance for Religious Thought.* Philadelphia: Muhlenberg Press, 1953.

Ebeling, Gerhard. *Luther: An Introduction to His Thought.* Translated by R. A. Wilson. Philadelphia: Fortress Press, 1970.

Forde, Gerhard. *The Captivation of the Will: Luther vs. Erasmus on Freedom and Bondage.* Edited by Steven Paulson. Grand Rapids: Eerdmans, 2005.

———. "The Exodus from Virtue to Grace: Justification by Faith Today." *Interpretation* 34, no. 1 (January 1980): 32–44.

——. "Forensic Justification and the Christian Life: Triumph or Tragedy?" In *A More Radical Gospel*, edited by Mark C. Mattes and Steven D. Paulson. Grand Rapids: Eerdmans, 2004.

——. "Justification by Faith Alone," *Dialog* 27 (Fall 1988): 260–67.

——. *Justification by Faith—A Matter of Death and Life*. Philadelphia: Fortress Press, 1983.

——. *The Law–Gospel Debate*. Minneapolis: Augsburg, 1969.

——. *On Being a Theologian of the Cross: Reflections on Luther's Heidelberg Disputation*. Grand Rapids: Eerdmans, 1997.

——. *Theology Is for Proclamation*. Minneapolis: Fortress Press, 1990.

——. "The Work of Christ," and "The Christian Life." In *Christian Dogmatics*, edited by Carl Braaten and Robert Jenson, vol. 2. Philadelphia: Fortress Press, 1984.

Gassmann, Günther, ed. *Historical Dictionary of Lutheranism*. In cooperation with Duane H. Larson and Mark W. Oldenburg. Lanham, MD: Scarecrow, 2001.

Gritsch, Eric W. *Martin—God's Court Jester: Luther in Retrospect*. Philadelphia: Fortress Press, 1983.

——. "The Origins of the Lutheran Teaching on Justification." In *Justification by Faith*, Lutherans and Catholics in Dialogue VII, ed. H. George Anderson, T. Austin Murphy, and Joseph A. Burgess, 162–71. Minneapolis: Augsburg, 1985.

Hall, Douglas John. "Luther's Theology of the Cross." *Consensus* 15, no. 2 (1989): 7–19.

Hamm, Berndt. *The Early Luther Stages in a Reformation Reorientation*. Translated by Martin J. Lohrmann. Grand Rapids: Eerdmans, 2014.

Helmers, Christine. "The American Luther." *Dialog: A Journal of Theology* 47, no. 2 (Summer 2008): 114–24.

Hendel, Kurt. "Theology of the Cross." *Currents in Theology and Mission* 39, no. 5 (October 2012): 223–31.

Hildebrandt, Franz. *EST. Das Lutherische Prinzip*. Studien zur systematischen Theologie 7. Göttingen: Wissenschaftliche Buchgesellschaft, 1931.

Hinlicky, Paul R. *Luther and the Beloved Community: A Path for Christian Theology after Christendom*. Grand Rapids: Eerdmans, 2010.

Holl, Karl. *Distinctive Elements in Christianity*. Translated by Norman V. Hope. Edinburgh: T & T Clark , 1937.

——. *Gesammelte Aufsätze zur Kirchengeschichte*, vol. 1, *Luther*. Tübingen: J. C. B. Mohr (Paul Siebeck), 1921.

——. *Gesammelte Aufsätze zur Kirchengeschichte*, vol. 3, *Der Westen*. Darmstadt: Wissenschaftliche Buchgesellschaft, 1965.

——. "Martin Luther on Luther." In *Interpreters of Luther: Essays in Honor of Wilhelm Pauck*, edited by Jarslav Pelikan. Philadelphia: Fortress Press, 1968.

——. *The Reconstruction of Morality*. Edited by James Luther Adams and Walter F. Bense. Translated by Fred W. Meuser and Walter R. Wietzke. Minneapolis: Augsburg, 1979.

——. "Was hat die Rechtfertigungslehre dem modernen Menschen zu sagen?" in GA 3, 558–567.

——. *What Did Luther Understand by Religion?* Edited by James Luther Adams and Walter F. Bense. Translated by Fred W. Meuser and Walter R. Wietzke. Philadelphia: Fortress Press, 1977.

Huber, Wolfgang. *Konflict und Konsensus: Studien zur Ethik der Verantwortung*. Munich: Chr. Kaiser, 1990.

Iwand, Hans J. *The Righteousness of Faith according to Luther*. Edited by Virgil F. Thompson. Translated by Randi H. Lundell. Eugene, OR: Wipf & Stock, 2008.

Jüngel, Eberhard. *The Freedom of a Christian: Luther's Significance for Contemporary Theology*. Translated by Roy A. Harrisville. Minneapolis: Augsburg, 1988

Kern, Udo. "*Theologia crucis* als Fundamentalkritik." *Theologische Zeitschrift* 50 (1994): 63–70.

Kierkegaard, Søren. *Der Einzlne und die Kirche: Über Luther und den Protestantismus.* Translated with a foreword by W. Kütemeyer. Berlin: E. Wolff, 1934.

Kolb, Robert. "Luther's Theology of the Cross 15 Years after Heidelberg: Lectures on the Psalms of Ascent." *Journal of Ecclesiastical History* 61, no. 1 (January 2010): 69–85.

———. "Luther on the Theology of the Cross." *Lutheran Quarterly* 16 (2002): 443–66.

———. "Nothing but Christ Crucified." In *The Theology of the Cross for the 21st Century,* edited by Alberto L. García and A. R. Victor Raj, 37–53. St. Louis: Concordia, 2002.

Lazareth, William H. *Christians in Society: Luther, the Bible, and Social Ethics.* Minneapolis: Fortress Press, 2001.

Lienhard, Marc. *Luther: Witness to Jesus Christ.* Translated by Edwin H. Robertson. Minneapolis: Augsburg, 1982.

Lietzmann, Hans."Ansprache bei der Beerdigung am 26 Mai 1926," In *Karl Holl: Zwei Gedächtnisreden von Adolf von Harnack und Hans Lietzmann* (AKG 7), Bonn 1926.

Lohse, Bernhard. *Martin Luther: An Introduction to His Life and Work.* Translated by Robert Schultz. Philadelphia: Fortress Press, 1986.

———. *Martin Luther's Theology: Its Historical and Systematic Development.* Edited and translated by Roy A. Harrisville. Minneapolis: Fortress Press, 1999.

Lotz, David W. *Ritschl and Luther: A Fresh Perspective on Albrecht Ritschl's Theology in the Light of His Luther Study*. Nashville: Abingdon, 1974.

Madsen, Anna M. *The Theology of the Cross in Historical Perspective.* Distingushed Dissertations in Christian Theology Series. Eugene, OR: Pickwick, 2007.

Maurer, Wilhelm. "Die Anfänge von Luthers Theologie." *Theologische Literaturzeitung* 75 (1952): 1–12.

McGrath, Alister E. *Luther's Theology of the Cross: Martin Luther's Theological Breakthrough.* Oxford: Basil Blackwell, 1985.

———. *Reformation Thought: An Introduction.* 3d edition. Oxford: Blackwell, 1999.

Nestingen, James Arne. "Luther's Heidelberg Disputation: An Analysis of the Argument." *Word and World, Supplement Series* 1 (1992): 147–54.

Ngien, Dennis. "Chalcedonian Christology and Beyond: Luther's Understanding of the Communicatio Idiomatum." *Heythrop Journal* 45 (2004): 54–68.

———. *The Suffering of God according to Martin Luther's* "Theologia Crucis." Eugene, OR: Wipf and Stock, 2001.

Pauck, Wilhelm. "The Historiography of the German Reformation during the Past Twenty Years." *Church History* (Dec. 1940): 311.

Prenter, Regin. *Luther's Theology of the Cross.* Facet Books. Philadelphia: Fortress Press, 1971.

———. *Spiritus Creator: Luther's Concept of the Holy Spirit.* Translated by John M. Jensen. Philadelphia: Muhlenberg Press, 1953.

Ruge-Jones, Philip. *Cross in Tensions: Luther's Theology of the Cross as Theologico-Social Critique.* Princeton Theological Monograph Series. Eugene, OR: Pickwick, 2008.

Rupp, E. Gordon. "Luther's Ninety-Five Theses and the Theology of the Cross." In *Luther for an Ecumenical Age*, edited by Carl Meyer, 67–80. St. Louis: Concordia, 1967.

———. *The Righteousness of God: Luther Studies.* London: Hodder and Stoughton, 1953.

Seeberg, Reinhold. *Text-Book of the History of Doctrines.* Translated by Charles E. Hay. Grand Rapids: Baker, 1977.

Siemon-Netto, Uwe. *The Fabricated Luther: The Rise and Fall of the Shirer Myth.* St. Louis: Concordia, 1995.

Simmons, Ernest L. "Creation in Luther's Theology of the Cross." *Dialog* 30, no. 1 (Winter 1991): 50–58.

Stayer, John M. *Martin Luther, German Saviour: German Evangelical Theological Factions and the Interpretation of Luther, 1917–1933.* Montreal: McGill-Queens University Press, 2000.

Steiger, Johann Anselm. "The *Communicatio Idiomatum* as the Axle and Motor of Luther's Theology." *Lutheran Quarterly* 14, no. 2 (2000): 125–58.

Thompson, Deanna A. *Crossing the Divide: Luther, Feminism, and the Cross.* Minneapolis: Fortress Press, 2004.

Vogelsang, Erich. *Der Angefochtene Christus.* Berlin: Walter de Gruyter, 1932.

Von Loewenich, Walter. *Luther's Theology of the Cross.* 5th ed. Translated by H. J. A. Bouman. Minneapolis: Augsburg, 1976.

Walter, Gregory A. "Historical Introduction." In *The Righteousness of Faith according to Luther*, by Hans J. Iwand, edited by Virgil F. Thompson, translated by Randi H. Lundell. Eugene, OR: Wipf & Stock, 2008.

———. "Karl Holl (1866–1926) and the Recovery of Promise in Luther." *Lutheran Quarterly* 25 (2011): 398–414.

Witte, Karl. *Nun fruet euch lieben Christen gmein: Luthers Word in täglichen Andachten.* Berlin: Im Wichern Verlag, 1934.

## Bonhoeffer's Theology

### Primary Sources

Bonhoeffer, Dietrich. *Dietrich Bonhoeffer Werke.* Edited by Eberhard Bethge et. al. 17 vols. Munich: Chr. Kaiser Gütersloh: Gütersloher Verlagshaus, 1986–99. English translation: *Dietrich Bonhoeffer Works.* Edited by Wayne

Whitson Floyd Jr. Victoria J. Barnett, and Barabara Wojhoski. 17 vols. Minneapolis: Fortress Press, 1996–2014.

Vol. 1. *Sanctorum Communio: Eine dogmatische Untersuchung zur Soziologie der Kirche.* Edited by Joachim von Soosten. Munich: Chr. Kaiser, 1986. English translation: *Sanctorum Communio: A Theological Study of the Sociology of the Church.* Edited by Clifford J. Green. Translated by Reinhard Krauss and Nancy Lukens. Minneapolis: Fortress Press, 1998.

Vol. 2. *Akt und Sein: Transzendentalphilosophie und Ontologie in der systematischen Theologie.* Edited by Hans-Richard Reuter. Munich: Chr. Kaiser, 1988. English translation: *Act and Being: Transcendental Philosophy and Ontology in Systematic Theology.* Edited by Wayne Whitson Floyd Jr. Translated by H. Martin Rumscheidt. Minneapolis: Fortress Press, 1996.

Vol. 3. *Schöpfung und Fall.* Edited by Martin Rüter and Ilse Tödt. Munich: Chr. Kaiser, 1989. English translation: *Creation and Fall: A Theological Exposition of Genesis 1–3.* Edited by John. W. de Grucy. Translated by Douglas Stephen Bax. Minneapolis: Fortress Press, 1997.

Vol. 4. *Nachfolge.* Edited by Martin Kuske and Ilse Tödt. Munich: Chr. Kaiser, 1989. English translation: *Discipleship.* Edited by Geffrey B. Kelly and John D. Godsey. Translated by Barbara Green and Reinhard Krauss. Minneapolis: Fortress Press, 2001.

Vol. 5. *Gemeinsames Leben. Das Gebetbuch der Bibel.* Edited by Gerhard L. Müller and Albrecht Schönherr. Munich: Chr. Kaiser, 1987. English translation: *Life Together and Prayerbook of the Bible.* Edited by Geffrey B. Kelly. Translated by Daniel W. Bloesch and James H. Burtness. Minneapolis: Fortress Press, 1996.

Vol. 6. *Ethik* 2d edition. Edited by Ilse Tödt, Heinze Eduard Tödt, Ernst Feil, and Clifford Green. Gütersloh: Chr. Kaiser Gütersloher Verlagshaus, 1998. English translation: *Ethics.* Edited by Clifford J. Green. Translated by Reinhard Krauss and Charles West. Minneapolis: Fortress Press, 2005.

Vol. 7. *Fragmente aus Tegel.* Edited by Renate Bethge and Ilse Tödt. Munich: Chr. Kaiser Verlag, 1994. English translation: *Fiction from Tegel.* Edited by Clifford J. Green. Translated by Nancy Lukens. Minneapolis: Fortress Press, 2000.

Vol. 8. *Widerstand und Ergebung.* Edited by Christian Gremmels, Eberhard Bethge, and Renate Bethge. Gütersloh: Chr. Kaiser Gütersloher Verlagshaus, 1998. English translation: *Letters and Papers from Prison.* Edited by John W. de Gruchy. Translated by Isabel Best, Lisa Dahill, Reinhard Krauss, and Nancy Lukens, with Barbara and Martin Rumscheidt and Douglas W. Stott. Minneapolis: Fortress Press, 2010.

Vol. 9. *Jugend und Studium, 1918–1927.* Edited by Hans Pfeifer in cooperation with Clifford J. Green and Carl-Jürgen Kaltenborn. Munich: Chr. Kaiser, 1986. English translation: *The Young Bonhoeffer: 1918–1927.* Edited by Paul Duane Matheny, Clifford J. Green, and Marshall D. Johnson. Translated by Mary C. Nebelsick with the assistance of Douglas W. Stott. Minneapolis: Fortress Press, 2003.

Vol. 10. *Barcelona, Berlin, Amerika, 1928–1931.* Edited by Reinhart Staats and Hans Christoph von Hase in cooperation with Holger Roggelin and Matthias Wünsche. Munich: Chr. Kaiser, 1992. English translation: *Barcelona, Berlin, New York: 1928–1931.* Edited by Clifford J. Green. Translated by Douglas W. Stott. Minneapolis: Fortress Press, 2008.

Vol. 11. *Ökumene, Universität, Pfarramt, 1931–1932.* Edited by Eberhard Amelung and Christoph Strohm. Gütersloh: Chr. Kaiser Verlag, 1994. English translation: *Ecumenical, Academic, and Pastoral Work: 1931–1932.* Edited by Victoria J. Barnett, Mark S. Brocker, and Michael B. Lukens. Translated by Anne Schmidt-Lange, with Isabel Best, Nicolas Humphrey, and Marion Pauck, with Douglas W. Stott. Minneapolis: Fortress Press, 2012.

Vol. 12. *Berlin, 1932–1933.* Edited by Carsten Nicolaisen and Ernst-Albert Scharffenorth. Gütersloh: Chr. Kaiser Gütersloher Verlagshaus, 1997. English translation: *Berlin: 1932–1933.* Edited by Larry L. Rasmussen.

Translated by Isabel Best and David Higgins, with Douglas W. Stott. Minneapolis: Fortress Press, 2009.

Vol. 13. *London, 1933–1935.* Edited by Hans Goedeking, Martin Heimbucher, and Hans-Walter Schleicher. Gütersloh: Chr. Kaiser Gütersloher Verlagshaus, 1994. English translation: *London: 1933–1935.* Edited by Keith Clements. Translated by Isabel Best, with Douglas W. Stott. Minneapolis: Fortress Press, 2007.

Vol. 14. *Illegale Theologan-Ausbildung: Finkenwalde 1935–1937.* Edited by Otto Dudzus and Jürgen Henkys, assisted by Sabine Bobert-Stützel, Dirk Schulz, and Ilse Tödt. Gütersloh: Chr. Kaiser Gütersloher Verlagshaus, 1996. English translation: *Theological Education at Finkenwalde: 1935–1937.* Edited by H. Gaylon Barker and Mark. S. Brocker. Translated by Douglas W. Stott. Minneapolis: Fortress Press, 2013.

Vol. 15. *Illegale Theologian-Ausbidlung: Sammelvikariate 1937–1940.* Edited by Dirk Schulz. Gütersloh: Chr. Kaiser Gütersloher Verlagshaus, 1998. English translation: *Theological Education Underground: 1937–1940.* Edited by Victoria J. Barnett. Translated by Victoria J. Barnett, Claudia Bergmann, Peter Frick, and Scott Moore, with Douglas W. Stott. Minneapolis: Fortress Press, 2011.

Vol. 16. *Konspiration und Haft, 1940–1945.* Edited by Jørgen Glenthøj, Ulrich Kabitz, and Wolf Krötke. Gütersloh: Chr. Kaiser Gütersloher Verlagshaus, 1996. English translation: *Conspiracy and Imprisonment: 1940–1945.* Edited by Mark S. Brocker. Translated by Lisa E. Dahill, with Douglas W. Stott. Minneapolis: Fortress Press, 2006.

Vol. 17. *Register und Ergänzungen.* Edited by Herbert Anzinger and Hans Pfeifer, assisted by Waltraud Anzinger and Ilse Tödt. Gütersloh: Chr. Kaiser Gütersloher Verlagshaus, 1999. English translation: *Indexes and Supplementary Materials.* Edited by Victoria J. Barnett and Barbara Wojhoski, with Mark S. Brocker. Minneapolis: Fortress Press, 2014.

——. *Gesammelte Schriften* (collected writings). Edited by Eberhard Bethge. 6 vols. Munich: Chr. Kaiser, 1958–1974. English selections edited by Edwin H. Roberson, translated by Edwin H. Robertson and John Bowden in *No Rusty Swords* (New York: Harper & Row, 1965), *The Way to Freedom* (New York: Harper & Row, 1966), and *True Patriotism* (New York: Harper & Row, 1973).

——. *Spiritual Care.* Translated and with an introduction by Jay C. Rochelle. Philadelphia: Fortress Press, 1985.

——. *A Testament to Freedom: The Essential Writings of Dietrich Bonhoeffer.* Edited by Geffrey B. Kelly and F. Burton Nelson. Revised and expanded edition. San Francisco: Harper Collins, 1995.

Bonhoeffer, Dietrich, and Maria von Wedemeyer. *Love Letters from Cell 92: The Correspondence between Dietrich Bonhoeffer and Maria von Wedemeyer, 1943–45.* Edited by Ruth-Alice von Bismarck and Ulrich Kabitz. Translated by John Brownjohn. Postscript by Eberhard Bethge. Nashville: Abingdon, 1995.

## Secondary Sources

Abromeit, Hans-Jürgen. "Die Einzigartigkeit Jesu Christi: Die Frage nach dem Absolutheitsanspruch des Christentums bei Dietrich Bonhoeffer." *Pastoraltheologie* 80 (1991): 584–602.

——. *Das Geheimnis Christi: Dietrich Bonhoeffers erfahrungsbezognene Christologie.* Neukirchen-Vluyn: Neukirchener, 1991.

Barker, H. Gaylon. "Bonhoeffer, Luther, and *Theologia Crucis.*" *Dialog* 34, no. 1 (Winter 1995): 10–17.

——. "Editor's Introduction to the English Edition." In *Theological Education at Finkenwalde: 1935–1937.* Dietrich Bonhoeffer Works, vol. 14. Edited by H. Gaylon Barker and Mark S. Brocker. Minneapolis: Fortress Press, 2013.

———. "Without God, We Live with God: Listening to Bonhoeffer's Witness in Today's Public Square," in *Dietrich Bonhoeffers Theologie heute: ein Weg zwischen Fundamentalismus und Säkularismus?/ Dietrich Bonhhoeffer's Theology Today: A Way between Fundamentalism and Secularism?*, ed. John de Gruchy, Christiane Tietz, and Stephen Plant. Gütersloh: Gütersloher, 2009.

Barnett, Victoria. "Editor's Introduction to the English Edition." In *Theological Education Underground: 1937–1940.* Dietrich Bonhoeffer Works, vol. 15. Edited by Victoria J. Barnett. Minneapolis: Fortress Press, 2011.

———. *For the Soul of the People: Protestant Protest Against Hitler.* New York: Oxford University Press, 1992.

Benktson, Benkt-Erik. *Christus und die Religion. Der Religionsbegriff bei Barth, Bonhoeffer und Tillich.* Stuttgart: Calwer, 1967.

Bethge, Eberhard. "Bonhoeffer and the Jews." In *Ethical Responsibility: Bonhoeffer's Legacy to the Churches*, edited by John D. Godsey and Geffrey B. Kelly, 43–96. Toronto Studies in Theology, 6. New York and Toronto: Edwin Mellen, 1981.

———. *Bonhoeffer: Exile and Martyr.* Edited and with an essay by John W. de Gruchy. New York: Seabury, 1976.

———. "Bonhoeffer's Assertion of Religionless Christianity—Was He Mistaken?" In *A Bonhoeffer Legacy: Essays in Understanding*, ed. A. J. Klassen, 3–13. Grand Rapids: Eerdmans, 1981

———. "Bonhoeffer's Christology and His 'Religionless Christianity." In *Bonhoeffer in a World Come of Age*, ed. Peter Vorkink, II, 46–72. Philadelphia: Fortress Press, 1968.

———. "The Challenge of Dietrich Bonhoeffer's Life and Theology." *The Chicago Theological Seminary Register* 51, no. 2 (February 1961): 1–38.

———. *Dietrich Bonhoeffer: A Biography.* Edited and revised by Victoria Barnett. Rev. ed. Minneapolis: Fortress Press, 2000.

———. "Editor's Preface." In Dietrich Bonhoeffer, *Ethics*. Edited by Eberhard Bethge, translated by Neville Horton Smith. Rearranged ed. New York: Macmillan, 1965.

Bethge, Renate. "Bonhoeffer's Family and Its Significance for His Theology." In *Dietrich Bonhoeffer—His Significance for North Americans,* edited by Larry Rasmussen, 1–30. Minneapolis: Fortress Press, 1990.

Burtness, James. "As Though God Were Not Given: Barth, Bonhoeffer and the *Finitum Capax Infiniti*." *Dialog* 19 (Fall 1980): 249–55.

———. *Shaping the Future: The Ethics of Dietrich Bonhoeffer*. Philadelphia: Fortress Press, 1985.

Carter, Guy. "Confession at Bethel, August 1933—Enduring Witness: The Formation, Revision and Significance of the First Full Theological Confession of the Evangelical Church Struggle in Nazi Germany." PhD diss., Marquette University, 1987.

Clements, Keith. "Editor's Introduction to the English Edition." In *London: 1933–1935*. Dietrich Bonhoeffer Works, vol. 13. Edited by Keith Clements. Minneapolis: Fortress Press, 2007.

Day, Thomas. *Dietrich Bonhoeffer on Christian Community and Common Sense*. Toronto Studies in Theology, vol. 11, Bonhoeffer Series, no. 2. New York: Edwin Mellen, 1982.

De Gruchy, John, ed. *The Cambridge Companion to Dietrich Bonhoeffer*. Cambridge: Cambridge University Press, 1999.

———. *Daring, Trusting Spirit: Bonhoeffer's Friend Eberhard Bethge*. Minneapolis: Fortress Press, 2005.

———, ed. *Dietrich Bonhoeffer: Witness to Jesus Christ*. The Making of Modern Theology. San Francisco: Collins, 1988.

———. "Editor's Introduction to the English Edition." In *Letters and Papers from Prison*. Dietrich Bonhoeffer Works, vol. 8. Edited by John W. de Gruchy. Minneapolis: Fortress Press, 2010.

———. "*Sanctorum Communio* and the Ethics of Free Responsibility: Reflections on Bonhoeffer's Ecclesiology and Ethics." In *For All People:*

*Global Theologies in Contexts*, edited by Else Marie Wilberg Pedersen, Holger Lam, and Peter Lodberg, 86–108. Grand Rapids: Eerdmans, 2002.

DeJonge, Michael P. *Bonhoeffer's Theological Formation: Berlin, Barth, and Protestant Theology*. Oxford: Oxford University Press, 2012.

———. "The Presence of Christ in Karl Barth, Franz Hildebrandt and Dietrich Bonhoeffer." In *Dietrich Bonhoeffer Jahrbuch/Yearbook 4 2009/2010*, edited by Kristen Busch Nielson, Hans Pfeifer, Christianne Tietz, and Clifford Green. Gütersloh: Gütersloher, 2010.

De Lange, Frits. *Waiting for the Word: Dietrich Bonhoeffer on Speaking about God*. Translated by Martin N. Walton. Grand Rapids: Eerdmans, 2000.

Dramm, Sabine. *Dietrich Bonhoeffer and the Resistance*. Translated by Margaret Kohl. Minneapolis: Fortress Press, 2009.

Ebeling, Gerhard. "The 'Non-Religious Interpretation of Biblical Concepts.'" In *Word and Faith*. Translated by James W. Leitch. Philadelphia: Fortress Press, 1963.

Feil, Ernst. "Dietrich Bonhoeffer's Understanding of the World." In *A Bonhoeffer Legacy: Essays in Understanding*, ed. by Abram John Klassen, 237–55. Grand Rapids: Eerdmans, 1981.

———. *Die Theologie Dietrich Bonhoeffers: Hermeneutik, Christologie, Weltverständnis*. 3rd ed. Munich: Chr. Kaiser, 1979.

———. *The Theology of Dietrich Bonhoeffer*. Translated by Martin Rumscheidt. Philadelphia: Fortress Press, 1985.

Feil, Ernst, and Ilse Tödt, eds. *Konzequenzen. Dietrich Bonhoeffers Kirchenverständnis heute*. Internationales Bonhoeffer–Forum. Munich: Chr. Kaiser, 1980.

Floyd, Wayne Whitson, Jr. "Editor's Introduction to the English Edition." *Act and Being*. Dietrich Bonhoeffer Works, vol. 2. Edited by Wayne Whitson Floyd Jr. Minneapolis: Fortress Press, 1996.

Floyd, Wayne Whitson Jr., and Charles Marsh, eds. *Theology and the Practice of Responsibility: Essays on Dietrich Bonhoeffer.* Valley Forge, PA: Trinity Press International, 1994.

Ford, Charles. "Dietrich Bonhoeffer, the Resistance, and the Two Kingdoms." *Lutheran Forum* 27, no. 3 (August 1993): 28–34.

Frick, Peter, ed. *Bonhoeffer's Intellectual Formation: Theology and Philosophy in His Thought.* Tübingen: Mohr Siebeck, 2008.

Godsey, John. "Barth and Bonhoeffer: The Basic Difference," *Quarterly Review: A Scholarly Journal for Reflection on Ministry* 7, no. 1 (Spring 1987): 9–27.

———. "Bonhoeffer the Man." In *Preface to Bonhoeffer: The Man and Two of His Shorter Writings.* Philadelphia: Fortress Press, 1965.

———. "The Legacy of Dietrich Bonhoeffer." In *A Bonhoeffer Legacy: Essays in Understanding*, ed. by A. J. Klassen, 160–66. Grand Rapids: Eerdmans, 1981.

———. *The Theology of Dietrich Bonhoeffer.* Philadelphia: Westminster, 1960.

Green, Clifford J. "Editor's Introduction to the English Edition." In *Sanctorum Communio.* Dietrich Bonhoeffer Works, vol. 1. Edited by Clifford J. Green. Minneapolis: Fortress Press, 1998.

———. "Editor's Introduction to the English Edition." In *Ethics.* Dietrich Bonhoeffer Works, vol. 6. Edited by Clifford J. Green. Minneapolis: Fortress Press, 2005.

———. "Editor's Introduction to the English Edition." In *Barcelona, Berlin, New York: 1928–1931.* Dietrich Bonhoeffer Works, vol. 10. Edited by Clifford J. Green. Minneapolis: Fortress Press, 2008.

———. *Bonhoeffer: A Theology of Sociality.* Rev. ed. Grand Rapids: Eerdmans, 1999.

———. "The Text of Bonhoeffer's *Ethics.*" In *New Studies in Bonhoeffer's Ethics*, edited by William J. Peck, 3–66. Lewiston, NY: Edwin Mellen, 1987.

Gremmels, Christian, ed. *Bonhoeffer und Luther: Zur Sozialgestalt des Luthertums in der Moderne*. Internationales Bonhoeffer Forum 6. Munich: Chr. Kaiser, 1983.

———. "Rechtfertigung und Nachfolge. Martin Luther in Dietrich Bonhoeffers Buch 'Nachfolge.'" In *Dietrich Bonhoeffer heute: Die Aktualität seines Lebens und Werkes*, edited by Rainer Mayer and Peter Zimmerling, 81–99. Giessen/Basel: Brunnen, 1992.

Gremmels, Christian and Hans Pfeifer. *Theologie und Biographie. Zum Beispiel Dietrich Bonhoeffer*. Munich: Chr. Kaiser, 1983.

Grünwaldt, Klaus, Christiane Tietz, and Udo Hahn, ed. *Bonhoeffer und Luther: Zentrale Themen ihrer Theologie.* Hanover: VELKD, 2007.

Hall, Douglas John. "Ecclesia Crucis: The Disciple Community and the Future of the Church in North America," in *Theology and the Practice of Responsibility*, edited by Wayne Whitson Floyd and Charles Marsh, 59–76. Valley Forge, PA: Trinity Press International, 1994.

Haynes, Stephen R. *The Bonhoeffer Legacy: Post-Holocaust Perspectives.* Minneapolis: Fortress Press, 2006.

———. *The Bonhoeffer Phenomonon: Portaits of a Protestant Saint.* Minneapolis: Fortress Press, 2004.

Hinlicky, Paul. "Verbum Externum—Dietrich Bonhoeffer's Bethel Confession," in *God Speaks to Us: Dietrich Bonhoeffer's Biblical Hermeneutics*, edited by Ralf K. Wüstenberg and Jens Zimmermann, 189–216. Frankfurt am Main: Peter Lang, 2013. (International Bonhoeffer Interpretations 5).

Huber, Wolfgang. "Bonhoeffer and Modernity." In *Theology and the Practice of Responsibility*, ed. by Wayne Whitson Floyd Jr. and Charles Marsh, 5–20. Valley Forge, PA: Trinity Press International, 1994.

———. "Wahrheit und Existenzform: Anregungen zu einer Theorie der Kirche bei Dietrich Bonhoeffer." In *Konsequenzen: Dietrich Bonhoeffers*

*Kirchenverständnis heute*, edited by Ernst Feil and Ilse Tödt, 87–139. IBF 3. Munich: Chr. Kaiser, 1980.

———. "Wer ist Christus für uns? Bonhoeffers Bedeutung für die Zukunft der Christenheit." *Evangelische Kommentare* 19 (April 1986): 191–94.

Kaltenborn, Carl-Jürgen. "Adolf von Harnack and Bonhoeffer." In *A Bonhoeffer Legacy: Essays in Understanding*, ed. by A. J. Klassen, 48–57. Grand Rapids: Eerdmans, 1981.

Kelly, Geffrey B. "Editor's Introduction to the English Edition." In *Life Together* and *Prayerbook of the Bible*. Dietrich Bonhoeffer Works, vol. 5. Edited by Geffrey B. Kelly. Minneapolis: Fortress Press, 1996.

———. "Freedom and Discipline: Rhythms of a Christocentric Spirituality." In *Ethical Responsibility: Bonhoeffer's Legacy to the Churches*, edited by John D. Godsey and Geffrey B. Kelly, 307–32. Toronto Studies in Theology, 6. New York: Edwin Mellen, 1981.

———. *Liberating Faith. Bonhoeffer's Message for Today*. With an introduction by Eberhard Bethge. Minneapolis: Augsburg, 1984.

———. "Revelation in Christ: A Study of Bonhoeffer's Theology of Revelation." *Ephemerides Theologicae Lovanienses* 50, no. 1 (May, 1974): 39–74.

Kelly, Geffrey B., and Burton Nelson, ed. *The Cost of Moral Leadership: The Spirituality of Dietrich Bonhoeffer*. Grand Rapids: Eerdmans, 2003.

———. *A Testament to Freedom: The Essential Writings of Dietrich Bonhoeffer*. With a forward by Eberhard Bethge. Revised and expanded edition. San Francisco: Harper Collins, 1995.

Kelly, Geffrey B., and John D. Godsey. "Editors' Introduction to the English Edition." In *Discipleship*. Dietrich Bonhoeffer Works, vol. 4. Edited by Geffrey B. Kelly and John D. Godsey. Minneapolis: Fortress Press, 2001.

Kirkpatrick, Matthew D. *Attacks on Christendom in a World Come of Age: Kierkegaard, Bonhoeffer, and the Question of a Religionless Christianity*. Eugene, OR: Pickwick, 2011.

Klassen, A. J., ed. *A Bonhoeffer Legacy: Essays in Understanding*. Grand Rapids: Eerdmans, 1981.

Krumwiede, Hans-Walter. "Dietrich Bonhoeffers Luther-Rezeption und seine Stellung zum Luthertum." In *Die Lutherischen Kirchen und die Bekenntnissynode von Barmen: Referate des Internationalen Symposiums auf der Reisenburg* 1984, edited by Georg Kretschmar and Carsten Nicolaisen. Göttingen: Vandenhoeck & Ruprecht, 1984.

Krötke, Wolf. "Dietrich Bonhoeffer and Martin Luther." In *Bonhoeffer's Intellectual Formation: Theology and Philosophy in His Thought*, edited by Peter Frick. Tübingen: Mohr Siebeck, 2008.

Kuhns, William. *In Pursuit of Dietrich Bonhoeffer*. New York: Doubleday, 1969.

Kuske, Martin, and Ilse Tödt. "Editors' Afterword to the German Edition." In *Discipleship*. Dietrich Bonhoeffer Works, vol. 4. Edited by Geffrey B. Kelly and John D. Godsey. Minneapolis: Fortress Press, 2001.

Lovin, Robin. "Biographical Context." In *New Studies in Bonhoeffer's Ethics*, edited by William J. Peck, 67–101. Toronto Studies in Theology, vol. 30, Bonhoeffer Series, no. 3. Lewiston, NY: Edwin Mellen, 1987.

Marsh, Charles. *Reclaiming Dietrich Bonhoffer: The Promise of His Theology*. New York: Oxford University Press, 1994.

Matthews, John W. *Anxious Souls Will Ask...The Christ-Centered Spirituality of Dietrich Bonhoeffer*. Forward by Martin Rumscheidt. Grand Rapids, MI: Eerdmans, 2005.

Marty, Martin E. "Introduction." In *The Place of Bonhoeffer*, edited by Martin E. Marty. New York: Association Press, 1962.

Matheny, Paul. "Editor's Introduction to the English Edition." In *The Young Bonhoeffer 1918–1927*. Dietrich Bonhoeffer Works, vol. 9. Edited by Paul Duane Matheny, Clifford J. Green, and Marshall D. Johnson. Minneapolis: Fortress Press, 2003.

Mayer, Rainer. *Christuswirklichkeit: Grundlagen, Entwicklung und Konsequenzen der Theologie Dietrich Bonhoeffers*. Stuttgart: Calwer, 1969.

Meyer, Dietrich, with Eberhard Bethge. *Nachlass Dietrich Bonhoeffer. Ein Verzeichnis. Archiv, Sammlung, Bibliothek*. Munich: Chr. Kaiser, 1987.

Moses, John A. *The Relutant Revolutionary: Dietrich Bonhoeffer's Collision with Prusso-German History*. New York, NY: Berghahn, 2009.

Müller, Christine-Ruth. *Bekenntnis und Bekennen: Dietrich Bonhoeffer in Bethel (1933); Ein lutherischer Versuch*. Munich: Chr. Kaiser, 1989.

Müller, Gerhard L. and Albrecht Schönherr. "Editors' Afterword to the German Edition," (abridged). In *Life Together* and *Prayerbook of the Bible*. Dietrich Bonhoeffer Works, vol. 5. Edited by Geffery B. Kelly. Minneapolis: Fortress Press, 1996.

———. "Vorwort." In *Gemeinsames Leben. Das Gebetbuch der Bibel*. Edited by Gerhard L. Müller and Albrecht Schönherr. Munich: Chr. Kaiser, 1987.

Müller, Hanfried. *Von der Kirche zur Welt: Ein Beitrag zu der Beziehung des Wortes Gottes auf die societas in Dietrich Bonhoeffers theologischer Entwicklung*. Hamburg-Bergstedt: Herbert Reich Evangelisch, 1961.

Nessan, Craig L. "Forward." In Dietrich Bonhoeffer, *Who Is Christ for Us?*, edited by Craig L. Nessan and Renate Wind. Translated by Craig L. Nessan. Minneapolis: Fortress Press, 2002.

Nicolaisen, Carsten. "Concerning the History of the Bethel Confession." In *Berlin: 1932–1933*. Dietrich Bonhoeffer Works, 12:509–13. Edited by Larry L. Rasmussen. Minneapolis: Fortress Press, 2009.

Nordholt, Jan Willem Schulte. "Bonhoeffers Liebesbriefe." In *Bonhoeffer Jahrbuch 2003*, 43–48. Gütershoh: Chr. Kaiser/Gütersloher, 2003.

Ott, Heinrich. *Reality and Faith: The Theological Legacy of Dietrich Bonhoeffer*. Translated by Alex A. Morrison. Philadelphia: Fortress Press, 1972.

Pangritz, Andreas. *Karl Barth in the Theology of Dietrich Bonhoeffer*. Translated by Barbara Rumscheidt and Martin Rumscheidt. Grand Rapids: Eerdmans, 2000.

———. "Who Is Jesus Christ, for Us, Today?" In *The Cambridge Companion to Dietrich Bonhoeffer*, edited by John W. de Gruchy, 134–53. New York: Cambridge University Press, 1999.

Pejsa, Jane. "Dietrich Bonhoeffer's Letter to an Unknown Woman." *International Bonhoeffer Society–English Language Section Newsletter* 52 (1993): 3–5.

Peters, Tiemo Rainer. *Die Präsenz des Politischen in der Theologie Dietrich Bonhoeffers.* Munich: Chr. Kaiser Verlag; Matthais–Grünewald, 1976.

Pfeifer, Hans. "Dietrich Bonhoeffers Kirchenverstandnis: Ein Beitrag zur theologischen Prinzipienlehre." PhD diss., Universität Heidelberg, Evang-theol Fak, 1964.

———. "Dietrich Bonhoeffers Studienfreundschaft mit Walter Dreß Briefe aus den Jahren 1920–1927." *Zeitschrift für Neure Theologiegeschichte* 4 (1997): 265–280.

———. "Editor's Afterward to the German Edition." *The Young Bonhoeffer: 1918–1927.* Dietrich Bonhoeffer Works, vol. 9. Edited by Paul Duane Matheny, Clifford J. Green, and Marshall D. Johnson. Minneapolis: Fortress Press, 2003.

———. "Forms of Justification." In *A Bonhoeffer Legacy: Essays in Understanding*, edited by A. J. Klassen, 14–47. Grand Rapids: Eerdmans, 1981.

———. "Vorwort der Herausgeber." In *Jugend und Studium, 1918–1927.* Dietrich Bonhoeffer Werke, vol. 9. Edited by Hans Pfeifer in cooperation with Clifford J. Green and Carl-Jürgen Kaltenborn. Munich: Chr. Kaiser, 1986.

Phillips, John A. *Christ for Us in the Theology of Dietrich Bonhoeffer.* New York: Harper & Row, 1967.

Plathow, Michael. "Die Mannigfaltigkeit der Wege Gottes: zu Dietrich Bonhoeffers kreuztheologischer Vorsehungslehre." *Kerygma und Dogma* 26, no. 2 (April/June 1980): 109–27.

Prenter, Regin. "Bonhoeffer and the Young Luther." In *World Come of Age*, edited by Ronald Gregor Smith. Philadelphia: Fortress Press, 1970.

Rades, Jörg. "The Intellectual Background of Dietrich Bonhoeffer." University of Saint Andrews. Photocopy, unedited manuscript. Bonhoeffer Archive, Union Theological Seminary, New York.

Rasmussen, Larry. "A Community of the Cross." *Dialog* 30, no. 2 (Spring 1991): 150–62.

———. *Dietrich Bonhoeffer: Reality and Resistance*. Nashville: Abingdon, 1972.

———. *Earth Community, Earth Ethics*. Ecology and Justice Series. Maryknoll, NY: Orbis Books, 1996.

———. "Editor's Introduction to the English Edition." In *Berlin: 1932–1933*. Dietrich Bonhoeffer Works, vol. 12. Edited by Larry L. Rasmussen. Minneapolis: Fortress Press, 2009.

Rasmussen, Larry and Renate Bethge. *Dietrich Bonhoeffer—His Significance for North Americans*. Minneapolis: Fortress Press, 1990.

Reuter, Hans-Richard. "Editor's Afterword to the German Edition." In *Act and Being*. Dietrich Bonhoeffer Works, vol. 2. Edited by Wayne Whitson Floyd Jr. Minneapolis: Fortress Press, 1996.

Robinson, John A. T. *Honest to God*. London: SCM, 1963.

Rochelle, Jay. "Introduction." In *Spiritual Care*, by Dietrich Bonhoeffer. Translated and with an introduction by Jay C. Rochelle. Philadelphia: Fortress Press, 1985.

Rumscheidt, Martin. "The Formation of Bonhoeffer's Theology." In *The Cambridge Companion to Dietrich Bonhoeffer*, edited by John W. de Gruchy, 50–70. Cambridge: Cambridge University Press, 1999.

Scharffenorth, Ernst-Albert. "Editor's Afterword to the German Edition." In *Berlin: 1932–1933*. Dietrich Bonhoeffer Works, vol. 12. Edited by Larry L. Rasmussen. Minneapolis: Fortress Press, 2009.

Schild, Maurice. "Hermann Sasse and Dietrich Bonhoeffer: Churchmen on the Brink," *The Bonhoeffer Legacy: Australasian Journal of Bonhoeffer Studies* 2, no. 1 (2014): 45–56.

Schlingensiepen, Ferdinand. *Dietrich Bonhoeffer 1906–1945: Martyr, Thinker, Man of Resistance.* Translated by Isabel Best. New York: T & T Clark, 2010.

Schmidt, Hans. "The Cross of Reality?" In *World Come of Age*, edited by Ronald Gregor Smith, 215–55. Philadelphia: Fortress Press, 1967.

Sorum, Jonathan D. "Bonhoeffer's Early Interpretation of Luther as the Source of His Basic Theological Paradigm." *Fides et Historia* 29, no. 2 (Summer 1997): 35–51.

———. "Cheap Grace, Costly Grace, and Just Plain Grace: Bonhoeffer's Defense of Justification by Faith Alone." *Lutheran Forum* 27, no. 3 (August 1993): 20–23.

———. "The Eschatological Boundary in Dietrich Bonhoeffer's 'Nachfolge.'" ThD diss., Luther Northwestern Theological Seminary, 1994.

Thiemann, Ronald. "Waiting for God's Own Time: Dietrich Bonhoeffer as Public Intellectual." In *Religion im Erbe: Dietrich Bonhoeffer und die Zukunftsfähigkeit des Christentums*, edited by Christian Gremmels and Wolfgang Huber, 92–111. Gütersloh: Chr. Kaiser/Gütersloher, 2002.

Tietz, Christiane. "Bonhoeffer's Strong Christology in the Context of Religious Pluralism." In *Interpreting Bonhoeffer: Historical Perspectives, Emerging Issues*, edited by Clifford J. Green and Guy C. Carter, 181–96. Minneapolis: Fortress Press, 2013.

Tödt, Heinz Eduard. *Authentic Faith: Bonhoeffer's Theological Ethics in Context.* Edited by Ernst-Albert Scharffenorth and Glen Harold Stassen. Translated by David Stassen and Ilse Tödt. Grand Rapids: Eerdmans, 1993.

———. "Dietrich Bonhoeffer's Decisions in the Crisis Years 1929–33," *Studies in Christian Ethics* 18, no. 3 [2005]: 107–23.

———. "Glauben in ein Religionslosen Welt: Muß man zwischen Barth und Bonhoeffer wählen?" In *Genf '76: Ein Bonhoeffer-Symposium.* International

Bonhoeffer Forum Forschung und Praxis, 1:98–107. Edited by Hans Pfeifer. Munich: Chr. Kaiser, 1976.

Tödt, Ilse. "Vorwort der Herausgeber." In *Ethik*, 2nd ed. Dietrich Bonhoeffer Werke, vol. 6. Edited by Ilse Tödt, Heinz Eduard Tödt, Ernst Feil, and Clifford Green. Munich: Chr. Kaiser, 1998.

Tödt, Ilse, Heinz Eduard Tödt, Ernst Feil, and Clifford Green. "Editors' Afterword to the German Edition." In *Ethics*. Dietrich Bonhoeffer Works, vol. 6. Edited by Clifford J. Green. Minneapolis: Fortress Press, 2005.

Von Klemperer, Klemens. "Beyond Luther? Dietrich Bonhoeffer and Resistance against National Socialism." *Pro Ecclesia* 6, no. 2 (Spring 1997): 184–98.

Von Soosten, Joachim. "Editor's Afterword to the German Edition." In *Sanctorum Communio: A Theological Study of the Sociology of the Church.* Dietrich Bonhoeffer Works, vol 1. Edited by Clifford J. Green. C Minneapolis: Fortress Press, 1998.

———. *Die Sozialität der Kirche: Theologie und Theorie der Kirch in Dietrich Bonhoeffers "Sanctorum Communio."* Munich: Chr. Kaiser, 1992.

Williams, Reggie L. *Bonhoeffer's Black Jesus: Harlem Renaissance Theology and an Ethic of Resistance.* Waco, TX: Baylor University Press, 2014.

———. "Developing a *Theologia Crucis:* Dietrich Bonhoeffer in the Harlem Renaissance." *Theology Today* 71, no. 1 (2014): 43–57.

Wind, Renate. "Church Struggle and Contemplation: A Rediscovery of Bonhoeffer's Political Christology." In Dietrich Bonhoeffer, *Who Is Christ for Us?*, edited and introduced by Craig L. Nessan and Renate Wind. Minneapolis: Fortress Press, 2002.

———. *Dietrich Bonhoeffer: A Spoke in the Wheel.* Translated by John Bowden. Grand Rapids: Eerdmans, 1991.

Woelfel, James. *Bonhoeffer's Theology: Classical and Revolutionary.* Nashville: Abingdon, 1970.

Wüstenberg, Ralf K. "'Religionless Christianity:' Dietrich Bonhoeffer's Tegel Theology." In *Bonhoeffer for a New Day: Theology in a Time of Transition*, edited by John de Gruchy. Grand Rapids: Eerdmans, 1997.

———. *A Theology of Life: Dietrich Bonhoeffer's Religionless Christianity*. Forward by Eberhard Bethge. Translated by Douglas W. Stott. Grand Rapids: Eerdmans, 1998.

Young III, Josiah Ulysses. *No Difference in the Fare: Dietrich Bonhoeffer and the Problem of Racism*. Grand Rapids: Eerdmans, 1998.

Zerner, Ruth. "Dietrich Bonhoeffer's American Experiences: People, Letters, and Papers from Union Seminary." *Union Seminary Quarterly Review* 31, no. 4 (Summer 1976): 261–82.

Zimmermann, Wolf-Dieter, and Ronald Gregor Smith, eds. *I Knew Dietrich Bonhoeffer*. Translated by Käthe Gregor Smith. Fontana Books. New York: Harper & Row, 1973.

## Other

Barth, Karl. *Church Dogmatics* II/2. Edinburgh: T & T Clark, 1957.

———. *Church Dogmatics* IV/1. Edinburgh: T & T Clark, 1956.

Bertram, Robert W. *A Time for Confessing*. Edited by Michael Hoy. Grand Rapids: Eerdmans, 2008.

Bergen, Doris L. *Twisted Cross: The German Christian Movement in the Third Reich*. Chapel Hill, NC: University of North Carolina Press, 1996.

Braaten, Carl. E. "Introduction: Revelation, History, and Faith in Martin Kähler," in *The So-Called Historical Jesus and the Historic Biblical Christ*, by Martin Kähler, translated and edited by Carl E. Braaten. Philadelphia: Fortress Press, 1964.

———. *Justification: The Article by Which the Church Stands or Falls*. Minneapolis: Fortress Press, 1990.

———. *No Other Gospel! Christianity among the World's Religions*. Minneapolis: Fortress Press, 1992.

———. "The Person of Jesus Christ," in *Christian Dogmatics*, edited by Carl E. Braaten and Robert W. Jenson, vol. 1. Philadelphia: Fortress Press, 1984.

Cimino, Richard, ed. *Lutherans Today: American Lutheran Identity in the 21st Century*. Grand Rapids: Eerdmans, 2003.

Correll, Mark R. *Shepherds of the Empire: Germany's Conservative Protestant Leadership—1888–1919.* Minneapolis: Fortress Press, 2014.

Cousar, Charles B. *A Theology of the Cross: The Death of Jesus in the Pauline Letters*. Minneapolis: Fortress Press, 1990.

*Evangelical Lutheran Worship.* Evangelical Lutheran Church in America. Minneapolis: Augsburg Fortress, 2006.

Gaiser, Frederick. "The Quest for Jesus and the Christian Faith: Introduction," in *The Quest for Jesus and the Christian Faith*, Word and World Supplement Series 3, edited by Frederick J. Gaiser (Sept. 1997): 11.

Hall, Douglas John. "The Changing North American Context of the Church's Ministry," "A Theological Proposal for the Church's Response to Its Context," and "The Church and Its Ministry: Responding to the Changing Context in Worship, Preaching, Education, Outreach." *Currents in Theology and Mission* 22 (December 1995): 405–433.

———. *Confessing the Faith.* Minneapolis: Fortress Press, 1996.

———. *The Cross in Our Context: Jesus and the Suffering World.* Minneapolis: Fortress Press, 2003.

———. *Lighten Our Darkness: Toward an Indigenous Theology of the Cross.* Philadelphia: Westminster, 1976.

———. *Professing the Faith.* Minneapolis: Fortress Press, 1993.

———. *Thinking the Faith: Christian Theology in a North American Context.* Minneapolis: Augsburg, 1989.

Hinlicky, Paul R. *Before Auschwitz: What Christian Theology Must Learn from the Rise of Nazism.* Eugene, OR: Cascade Books, 2013.

Hockenos, Matthew D. *A Church Divided: German Protestants Confront the Nazi Past.* Bloomington, IN: Indiana University Press, 2004.

Jantzen, Kyle. *Faith and Fatherland: Parish Politics in Hitler's Germany.* Minneapolis: Fortress Press, 2008.

Kähler, Martin. *The So-Called Historical Jesus and the Historic Biblical Christ.* Translated and edited by Carl E. Braaten. Philadelphia: Fortress Press, 1964.

Käsemann, Ernst. "The Saving Significance of the Death of Jesus in Paul." In *Perspectives on Paul.* Translated by Margaret Kohl. Philadelphia: Fortress Press, 1971.

Kolb, Robert, and Timothy J. Wengert, eds. *The Book of Concord: The Confessions of the Evangelical Lutheran Church.* Translated by Charles Arand, Eric Gritsch, Robert Kolb, William Russell, James Schaaf, Jane Strohl, and Timothy J. Wengert. Minneapolis: Fortress Press, 2000.

Luz, Ulrich. "*Theologia crucis* als Mitte der Theologie im Neuen Testament," *Evangelische Theologie* 34 (1974): 116–41.

Moltmann, Jürgen. *The Crucified God: The Cross of Christ as the Foundation and Criticism of Christian Theology.* Translated by R. A. Wilson and John Bowden. New York: Harper & Row, 1974.

Niebuhr, H. Richard. *The Kingdom of God in America.* New York: Harper, 1937.

Noll, Mark. "American Lutherans Yesterday and Today." In *Lutherans Today: American Lutheran Identity in the 21st Century*, edited by Richard Cimino, 3–25. Grand Rapids: Eerdmans, 2003.

———. *The Old Religion in a New World: The History of North American Christianity.* Grand Rapids: Eerdmans, 2003.

Pew Research Center. "'Nones' on the Rise: One in Five Adults Have No Religious Affiliation." October 9, 2012. http://www.pewforum.org/2012/10/09/nones-on-the-rise.

Scholder, Klaus. *The Churches and the Third Reich*, volume 1, *Preliminary History and the Time of Illusions 1918–1934.* Translated by John Bowden. Philadelphia: Fortress Press, 1988.

Schroeder, Edward H. "Forward," in *A Time for Confessing*, by Robert W. Bertram. Edited by Michael Hoy. Grand Rapids: Eerdmans, 2008.

Taylor, Charles. *A Secular Age.* Cambridge, MA: Belknap, 2007.

Tillich, Paul. *The Protestant Era.* Translated by James Luther Adams. Abridged ed. Chicago: The University of Chicago Press, Phoenix Books, 1957.

# Index